ENDORSEMENTS

"*The Miraculous Medal: Pendant of Power* is riveting. It looks into the roots of the Medal and the life of St. Catherine Labouré and the stunning miracles that have taken place over almost two centuries. The book studies the profound providence of God through the Miraculous Medal: the conversions and graces that have touched the lives of so many, from ordinary people to canonized saints. The Medal's effects range from 1830 with Our Lady's request that it be made, up to our modern times, with stories such as how the Medal sparked hope and resilience at Ground Zero immediately following the fall of the World Trade Center Towers on September 11, 2001. I loved this book. It is a must read for devotees of Our Lady!"

—*Very Rev. Daniel J. Reehil, V.F.*
Director of Radio Maria, pastor and exorcist

"In this well-written exploration of one of the greatest devotions given to the Church by Our Lady, Christine Watkins shares many fascinating stories, all with the Miraculous Medal playing a crucial role. What an important devotion for our times, and a great way to honor Our Lady, the Immaculate Conception! Saint Catherine Labouré, pray for us!"

—*Very Rev. Chris Alar, MIC*
Provincial Superior, Blessed Virgin Mary, Mother of Mercy Province of the Congregation of Marian Fathers of the Immaculate Conception
Host of the EWTN show *Living Divine Mercy*
Director of the Association of Marian Helpers

"It is with great joy that I endorse this beautiful book. This work is a masterpiece, well researched, and provides its readers with a profound understanding and appreciation of the power hidden in the Miraculous Medal."

—*Fr. Jose D'Souza OFM*
Capuchin and exorcist

"I joyfully endorse Christine Watkins' book. She brings the stories of people wearing the Miraculous Medal to life. When I traveled to Paris, I explored the convent on the Rue du Bac where St. Catherine Labouré was visited by Our Blessed Mother and told to don this beautiful Medal—and I have been wearing one now for many years. Please obtain and put on the Miraculous Medal and enjoy this excellent book. Our Blessed Mother wants nothing more than for you and me to love her Son Jesus more each day."

—Bishop Joseph Coffey
Archdiocese for the Military Services, U.S.A.

"I have worn a Miraculous Medal for over sixty years, ever since I found one, as a young boy, in the basement of our new home. I was raised nominally Catholic, but there was an instant connection between myself and this wonderful person on the Medal, whom I recognized as "My beautiful Mother." Only later, with some theological training, did I realize that this beautiful Mother happened to also be the Mother of God and the Queen of Heaven and Earth. I had a most powerful intercessor! My life has been truly graced in abundant and undeserved ways, which I attribute to this woman who is "full of grace," I encourage everyone to read this book and to wear a Miraculous Medal, not just for the graces that our Mother promises, but especially out of love for her, and thus for her Divine Son."

—Msgr. Stephen J. Rossetti, Ph.D. D.Min.
President and Founder, Saint Michael Center for Spiritual Renewal
Exorcist of the Archdiocese of Washington
Author of several books, including *Diary of an American Exorcist: Demons, Possession, and the Modern-Day Battle Against Ancient Evil*

"I recommend this book to all who doubt that miracles still happen today. Every Miraculous Medal testimony in this book is powerful, but that of Zachary King, a former high wizard, is the most heavy hitting, as it touches on the many temptations Satan and his minions are using, in particular against our young people. Having known Zachary through the ministry of deliverance and having heard him give talks of his testimony, revealing the satanic agenda in the world, I can attest to his honesty and integrity. This book presents a much-needed wake up call to believers and unbelievers alike."

—Susan Kirtland, Oblate of Saint Benedict
Leader for the Flame of Love of the Immaculate Heart of Mary

"Watkins has done a remarkable job in bringing to life how one small Medal can have huge implications in the lives of those who place their trust in Mary. *The Miraculous Medal: Pendant of Power* is a beautiful testament to the power of prayer and sacramentals in the life of Catholics and unbelievers. The Miraculous Medal itself, bearing the image of the Immaculate Virgin, is indeed a potent weapon against the power of Satan. This great read gives witness to lives which were totally transformed and will draw more people to put greater faith in the power of sacramentals, particularly the Miraculous Medal."

—Fr. Edward Murphy
Holy Faith Catholic Church
Gainesville, Florida

THE MIRACULOUS MEDAL

PENDANT OF POWER

CHRISTINE WATKINS

www.QueenofPeaceMedia.com
Novato, California

Drawings by Charles Jaskiewicz. Used with permission.

Books may be purchased in quantity by contacting the publisher directly at orders@queenofpeacemedia.com.

ISBN: 978-1-947701-21-2

TABLE OF CONTENTS

INTRODUCTION

In 1830, in a beautiful chapel on a Paris street called Rue du Bac, the Blessed Mother gave us an antidote to the darkness, a light that could never be extinguished. Through apparitions to a young novice in Paris, France, she revealed her desire for a tiny, metal, oval object, bearing her image, to be spread throughout the world. Her wish was granted by the Church, and the devotion passed from hand to hand, country to country, with lightning speed. Why? Because the small metal object was truly a Miraculous Medal.

The graces that have followed the Medal, as It rippled through time, have done nothing less than bring the Gospel to life. The blind see, the crippled walk, the dying come to life, and a divine hand of protection does the impossible—but most importantly, lost souls are brought through Mary into the Heart of Jesus Christ.

The Miraculous Medal: Pendant of Power is an unprecedented and captivating compilation of nearly two centuries of iron-clad proof of the Medal's real power: Mary's intercession before the throne of God. It begins with the story of St. Catherine Labouré, the apostle of the

Miraculous Medal, captured in a new light with little-known, intriguing facts. Then it tells how the Medal grew in fame, beguiling into Catholicism a rich, rabidly anti-Catholic Jewish agnostic connected to the Rothschild family. Among many remarkable stories, the book recounts how the Medal inspired a man destined for the electric chair and defeated a high wizard of Satanism, a top title granted in that malevolent world—and the head-to-head battle was no contest. The book journeys through time and nations, telling tales of how the Medal has battled and conquered Freemasonry, atheism, religious indifference, sickness, death, danger, and despondency.

Read on and you will understand why St. Maximilian Kolbe called the Medal his silver bullet, and why St. Mother Teresa of Calcutta called It her Medal of Charity. You will learn of the many ways the Miraculous Medal can be used, why It is a sacramental in the Catholic Church, and discover the accompanying novenas that bring extravagant grace. When faith and confidence in the Medal are enkindled in hearts, miracles spread like wildfire—and the supernatural comes to be expected.

The goal of this book is as grand as the Medal is small. It is to awaken and revive a dormant giant in the Catholic Church. Those who are inspired to become apostles of the Miraculous Medal will bring much needed hope, comfort, and holy awe to a world suffering from spiritual starvation. Our Lady is calling out to her children now. Perhaps one of these apostles is you.

HEAVEN SENT

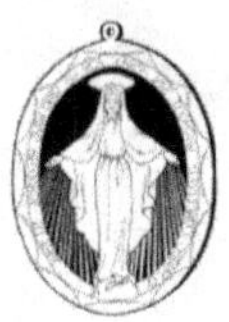

THE STORY OF ST. CATHERINE LABOURÉ (1806-1876)

Nothing powerfully or beautifully good comes into the world without a fight. The incredible story of how the Miraculous Medal came to be is no exception. It all began with the faith of a little country girl, known by her family as Zoé. She would come to be known to the rest of the world by her religious name, Catherine Labouré.

Zoé grew up in the town of Fain-lès-Moutier, located in the region of Burgundy, France. Her home, a high-end farm property, was perched on a shelf among rolling hills, overlooking the countryside below. Her father, Pierre Labouré, was a respected and well-educated farm-owner, a stern and hard-working man. Of the two hundred inhabitants of Fain, he was considered a leader, and even ended up as mayor of the hamlet from 1811 to 1815.[1]

Pierre Labouré & Madeleine Louise Gontard

Around the age of twenty, Pierre had begun his studies to be a priest,[2] but everything fell apart when the French Revolution shut down the seminaries. With his life's plans rerouted, he ended up marrying a warm and saintly woman, Madeleine Gontard.

Entrance to the Labouré farmhouse where Catherine was born and lived

Together, Pierre and Madeleine had seventeen children in less than twenty years. Zoé was the eighth of the ten children who survived.[3] For Madeline, who had been brought up in a genteel environment, the daily workload of the farmland, the animals, the farmworkers, and the children, proved too overwhelming to handle. By the end of her life she was stretched so thin that she was not even able to teach her youngest children how to read,[4] and on October 9, 1815, she passed from this life into the next at the age of forty-two.[5]

The statue that Catherine held

Nine-year-old Zoé was devastated. Her best friend and greatest role model was gone. She loved her dad, but he could be rough and demanding. Her mom had been the warmth in the family, and now she wasn't there anymore.

Shortly after her Madeleine's burial, Zoé was forced to turn to the only other mother she knew. Alone and in tears, she embraced a statue of Our Lady, which stood on a high shelf in the room where her mother had once dwelt.

Sobbing heavily, she whispered, "Now, dear Blessed Mother, you will be my Mother."[6]

Pierre, grieved and overwhelmed by the loss of his wife, sent his two youngest daughters, Zoé and Tonnie, to live with his sister. His five-year-old boy, Augustine, who was crippled from a carriage accident, remained at home.[7] For the next two years, Marie-Louise, his eldest daughter, took over his wife's role on the homestead. Life went on, and the family, though radically changed and grieving, weathered the storm of the loss by clinging to their deep Catholic faith. After two years of this arrangement, Zoé was summoned home by her father. Marie-Louise then left to enter the order of the Daughters of Charity of St. Vincent de Paul. Now, at the young age of twelve, Zoé became the mistress of the household, a role that most women did not reach until their fifties—if ever. Under her father's oversight, she was given authority over the farmyard, the garden, the bakehouse, the orchard, the cowshed, the pigpen, the henhouse, and the dovecote—a freestanding structure with 1,121 pigeonholes for up to 800 birds to nest in. But that was only the outside of their large family property, with its arched entryway and rectangle of buildings resembling a cloister. She also ran the inside of the sprawling home, making and serving meals for her family and snacks for the dozen farmhands,[8] while looking after her younger sister by two years, Tonine, and her little brother, Auguste, whom she treated with tender care.

The dining room in the family farmhouse

The dovecote on the Labouré farm

Zoé had to be the first up at 4 a.m. to brave the long day of work that the family would always close in prayer. From where did she get the fortitude, ingenuity, and skills of organization at age twelve to manage such a life? Perhaps the answer lay in the privacy of what took place between her and God in the small church in Fain, where she would go to pray alone amidst the cold flagstones, every day. It was a church with an empty tabernacle and without a priest, as thousands of clergy had faded away during the French Revolution. On a rare Sunday, a roving priest would come, but on most Sundays the family travelled to the next village of Moutiers to attend services. For daily Mass, Zoé would sometimes walk the five-mile round trip alone.

At age fourteen, Zoé began the habit of fasting every Friday and every Saturday, all year long. Worried for her, Tonine threatened to tattle the news to their father. "Go on then. Tell him!" said Catherine. And Tonine did, but nothing changed. Her father was her father. But God was God. While uncompromising in her religious convictions, Zoé was also tenderhearted. When a young contemporary of Zoé's was interviewed many years later in her eighties, she said of her:

> *Catherine was not pretty, but she was kind and good, always good-natured and gentle with her companions, even when they teased her, as children are wont to do. And if she saw anyone getting cross with somebody else, she would try and make peace between them. If a poor person came up, she would give away all her own delicacies...Catherine Labouré prayed like an angel...never turning her head left or right.*[9]

For these reasons, and many more, Tonine suspected that Zoé had a vocation to religious life. She said her sister had become "all mystic since her First Communion." Her inklings proved correct, for shortly thereafter Zoé secretly shared with her sister, and no one else, her calling to be a nun.[10] Zoé's religious vocation was not born of her desire to follow in the footsteps of her older sister, Marie-Louise, as one might assume. It began in the stirrings of her heart and unfolded mysteriously over the course of her adolescence.

St. Vincent de Paul (1581-1660)

When Zoé was about eighteen, she had a dream she did not understand. She was in the little church of Fain-lès-Moutier, where an elderly priest with a loving gaze was celebrating Mass. He wore a black skull cap and had a white mustache, a small beard and a long nose, rounded at the end. After the closing prayer, he gazed directly at her and motioned for her to draw near. Afraid, she hesitated, though fascinated by the brilliance of his eyes. She then left the church to visit a sick person, but the old priest found her there and said these words: "My daughter, it's good to care for the sick. You may be running from me now, but one day you'll be happy to come to me. God has plans for you. Do not forget this!"[11]

This dream, every detail of it, stayed with Zoé, as she continued to ponder how she might enter religious life. She knew she would not be accepted anywhere if she remained illiterate, so she convinced her father to let her attend a boarding school, run by her first cousin on her mother's side, in Châtillon-sur-Seine. During her stay there, she visited a house of the Sisters of Charity on Rue de la Juiverie—an order also known as the Daughters of Charity. When she stepped in the parlor, she was stunned. In a picture hanging on the wall before her was the priest she had seen in her dream. It was St. Vincent de Paul, the founder of the Daughters of Charity. She then understood part of what the dream meant. The saint was calling her from heaven into his order—to be his spiritual daughter.

Zoé's time of study lasted for a shorter time than expected, her peasant sensibilities clashing with the refined stylings of the boarding-school girls. After returning home, she worked again on the family farm and waited to come of age, then considered to be twenty-one, before provoking an inevitable storm with her father over her holy desire. He had consented to one daughter leaving forever to become a nun, but wasn't going to suffer the loss of another. Later, when reflecting on this time in her life, Zoé wrote of her disappointment regarding the lack of formal religious practices in her area. Normally of a joyful disposition, her sarcasm reveals a soul longing for more and ready for the rules of religious life:

> *What a lot of religion there is in the district! One Mass on a Sunday—and even then, it's only a binating priest from a neighboring district who says it. Vespers are sung by the schoolmaster, and so there is no Benediction. To go to confession, you have to search out a confessor. Go and see if what little religion there is, is still safe.*[12]

Then on May 2, 1827, when she had already turned twenty-one, Zoé told her father of her decision. Pierre immediately became her adversary in the matter. Not only did he forbid her entry into religious life, but he fished for obstacles, such as young suitors. Young men had already proposed to her, so why not get married?

For two more years, Zoé suffered from her father's rejection and stubbornness, and when her brother Charles lost his wife and needed a worker for his restaurant in Paris, her father agreed to have her sent there, instead of allowing her to pursue her vocation. Feeling exiled from her home and stripped of her calling, she once again worked through her grief, this time dutifully serving Parisian customers. She was in a new and worldly atmosphere that stung her spiritual sensibilities and showed her much less respect than did the laborers she had worked with on the family farm, who had honored her place as a twelve-year-old homemaker.

Seeing her distress, Zoé's eldest brother and sister-in-law came to her aid. They pleaded her cause to her father, who capitulated sullenly. They even offered 693 francs for her dowry, required at the time, since her father flatly refused to help. Another godsend was a twenty-seven-year-old Sister of Charity, Victoire Séjole, who immediately took a liking to the twenty-two-year-old farm girl. Both had an older sister in the order, came from peasantry, and had a great love for the poor and the Blessed Mother. Sr. Séjole would say of her: "Never have I known a soul so guileless and so pure."[13] She recommended that Zoé be received into the Daughters of Charity and promised to teach her any reading and writing skills she still lacked.

140 Rue du Bac, Paris: The Motherhouse of the Daughters of Charity

Finally, at twenty-three, Zoé was received as a postulant for the Daughters of St. Vincent de Paul in Châtillon-sur-Seine. The Mistress of Novices welcomed her and prepared her for her new life. She was given her new apparel: a black bodice tied at the waist, with a gathered skirt, and a black bonnet with wide white trim. From that moment on, she would be known as Sister Catherine Labouré. That day her happiness was such that she felt "no longer on the earth." Three months later, Sr. Catherine was transferred as a novice to a house on the Rue du Bac in Paris—a street name that would become world-famous, due to what would happen next.

During the dark days of the French Revolution, and in particular the Reign of Terror in 1793, the relics of St. Vincent de Paul had to be hidden—a wise decision, since priests were being beheaded and churches sacked. In the name of freedom, the desecrators had done such deeds as dance impurely on the altar of Notre Dame. Even the body of the great St. Geneviève, who had graced her beloved Paris with so many miracles, was yanked from its tomb in the church built for her by King Louis XV—and her body then burned in the public Place de Grève.

The French Revolution had scattered the two families of St. Vincent de

The glass and silver reliquary displayed today for veneration at the Paris Shrine of St. Vincent de Paul

Paul—the Vincentian Fathers, and the Sisters of Charity, up and across the length and breadth of France. Their orders, founded on a solid love for the poor, were now persecuted. Priests and sisters had gone underground in secular dress, pressing on in spirit while reaching out to souls on the street corners. In time, the French religious began to emerge again, though scattered and greatly diminished.[14]

But shortly after Sr. Catherine arrived at Rue du Bac, a large and magnificent display of faith graced the streets of Paris. The celebrated occasion was the transfer of St. Vincent de Paul's remains. The saint's body had remained incorrupt for approximately fifty years, and then began to decay, but for his heart, which had been removed immediately after his death because of its status as a relic. On April 25, 1830, a beautifully ornate silver reliquary carrying the saint's bones made to his likeness with wax, was publicly transferred in a sacred procession led by the Archbishop of Paris. King Charles, eight bishops, and a vast array of clergy and the faithful, including over a thousand Daughters of Charity in their distinctive winged hats, walked from Notre Dame Cathedral to the priory chapel of Saint-Lazare.

The Paris procession of St. Vincent de Paul's body in 1830

The physical heart of St. Vincent de Paul, still incorrupt 170 years after his death, was transferred separately from its place of hiding. Entrusted to the Daughters of Charity, it was displayed in the convent at Rue du Bac where Sr. Catherine lived. One could find the heart in a small metal cabinet with glass windows to the left of the main altar in the chapel. During this time of veneration of the saint, Catherine had been asking St. Vincent to teach her what she should pray for. Hidden behind her calm, seemingly unmoved exterior that never betrayed her inner fire, she petitioned him in earnest.[15]

The week following the procession, Catherine was given a vision of St. Vincent's heart. It appeared, as she wrote, "above the shrine where the small relics of St. Vincent de Paul were exposed." "It appeared to me at three different times, three days running: white, color of flesh, announcing peace, calm, innocence, and unity. Then I saw red like fire, which must light the flame of charity in people's hearts. It seemed to me that the whole community should renew itself and spread to the farthest points of the world. And then I saw red-black, which brought sadness into my heart. Waves of sadness came over me, and I suffered much in overcoming them." at the same time, Sr. Labouré was, given interior knowledge that the "red-black" color signified a lamentable change in French leadership, which pierced Catherine's heart with a felt sense of God's profound sorrow. "I did not know why, or how this suffering had to do with the change in government."[16]

The reliquary of St. Vincent de Paul's incorrupt heart in the Chapel on Rue du Bac

Sr. Labouré told her spiritual director, a young and respected priest named Fr. Jean Marie Aladel, of the vision. At twenty-nine years old, Fr. Aladel was the confessor, chaplain, preacher, and retreat master for the sisters on Rue du Bac. While pious, fervent, and capable of carrying his high posts in the Vincentian Congregation and advancing the Sisters of Charity under his hand, he was also stubborn and aloof by temperament. Upset over what he thought was a deception, he chastised Sr. Catherine: "Do not listen to those temptations. A Sister of Charity is made to serve the poor, not to dream."

After entering the novitiate, Sr. Catherine had also begun to see the Lord in the Eucharist. In one of the first of these visions, Jesus appeared to her as a king with a cross on His breast that fell to His heel along with His vestments. "I do not know how to explain it," she said, "but I had the thought that the King of the earth [Charles X] would be lost [i.e.: dethroned] and stripped of his royal garments." She confided this to Fr. Aladel, but he disregarded her completely. The throne of King Charles seemed more secure than ever—until a few short months later, when history would vindicate her forebodings.[17]

Fr. Jean Marie Aladel, Sr. Catherine Labouré's confessor

"God has plans for you," St. Vincent de Paul had said to Catherine in her dream of long ago. Now these plans would be unveiled... It all began on the vigil of the feast of St. Vincent de Paul, July 18, 1830. The sisters' directress, Mother Marthe, spoke that evening of their founder's devotion to the Virgin Mary and gave a feast-day gift to the novices: a small piece of a surplice that St. Vincent de Paul had worn. That night, as if struck by an inspiration, Sr. Catherine tore the tiny piece of cloth into two pieces, and then—"I swallowed it [one of these tiny second-class relics] and fell asleep thinking that St. Vincent would obtain for me the grace of seeing the Blessed Virgin." The saints are known for eccentricities in their zeal, and Catherine was no different.

That night would grace history. Twenty-four-year-old Catherine went to sleep in her curtained bed in the dormitory of the novices in the Motherhouse of the Sisters of Charity. There, she waited in eager hope for her Mother to come. This expectation that she would see the Blessed Mother, and her impatience for it, are expressed in the word, "Finally," which begins her account of what happened next:

> *Finally, at half past eleven in the evening, I heard someone calling my name. "Sister, sister!" Waking up, I looked in the direction that I had heard the voice coming from, which was toward the hallway: I pulled back the curtain and saw a child dressed in white, about four or five years old, who said to me: "Get up promptly and come to the chapel. The Blessed Virgin is there waiting for you."*

I immediately thought, "But someone will hear me." The child replied [to her thought]: "Do not worry, it is half past eleven, and everyone is sound asleep. Come, I shall wait for you."

I hurried to get dressed and went to the side of this child, who had stayed standing without going any farther than the head of my bed. He followed me—or rather, I followed him, all the time on my left, bringing rays of brightness wherever he passed. The lights were lit everywhere that we passed, which I found most astonishing. Much more surprising, when I entered the chapel [...], the door opened on its own when the child had scarcely touched it with his fingertip.

My surprise was even greater when I saw that all the candles and candelabras were lit, which reminded me of Midnight Mass. I still saw nothing of the Blessed Virgin. The child led me to the sanctuary, next to Fr. Director's chair. There, I went on my knees, and the child stayed standing the whole time.

As I found the time passing slowly, I looked around to see if the sisters who kept watch in the house were passing through the gallery. At last, the hour came; the child forewarned me. He said, "Here is the Blessed Virgin. Here she is."

I heard a sort of noise... like the rustle of a silk dress, coming from the direction of the gallery, near the picture of St. Joseph, which came and alighted on the altar steps, on the Gospel side, in a chair like St. Anne's.[18]

The actual chair that was in the Rue du Bac Chapel on which the Blessed Mother sat

As Sr. Catherine stood in the choir loft on the left, in front of the Communion table, she watched Our Lady sit down in a brown wooden chair with a blue covering, which has since become a cherished relic.[19]

The child repeated: "Here is the Blessed Virgin!" But Catherine stayed where she was, thinking the woman was St. Anne, like in the picture hanging on the wall in front of her above St. Vincent's relic, which depicted St. Anne sitting in a matching chair.

It was then that the child spoke to me, no longer as a child, but as if a man, the strongest man, and with the strongest words. Then, looking at the Blessed Virgin, I was at her side in a single bound, on my knees on the altar steps, with my hands resting on the Blessed Virgin's knees.

There, a period of time passed, the sweetest of my life. It would be impossible for me to say what I experienced. She told me how I should behave toward my spiritual director and also several other things that I must not mention; the way in which to comfort myself when suffering."[20]

"Come to the foot of the altar. [The Virgin Mary indicated the spot with her left hand.] *There, graces will be shed upon all, great and little, who ask for them. Graces will be especially shed upon those who ask for them."*[21]

"My child," said the Blessed Mother. "The good Lord wants to entrust you with a mission. You will have plenty of suffering, but you will overcome it through the knowledge that what you do is for the glory of God. You will know what comes from the good Lord. You will be tormented by it until you have told it to him whose task it is to direct you. You will be contradicted. But you will have grace. Do not fear. Tell everything with confidence and simplicity..."[22]

The Blessed Mother's apparition on July 18, 1830, to the novice for the Daughters of Charity, Sr. Catherine Labouré

Our Lady also foretold, among other things, that two other communities would join her order, once its rule was more rigorously observed. (Twenty years later, in 1850, this prophecy came true: the Sisters of Charity founded by St. Elizabeth Ann Seton and those of Austria founded by Sr. Léopolidine de Brandis would enter the Vincentian fold.[23]) The Blessed Mother also spoke of a new Association of Children of Mary that her confessor would found (which he later did). She spoke of a month that would be dedicated in the Church to St. Joseph,[24] moments of great devotion to the Sacred heart and of great attacks against the Church, all of which came to pass. But Our Lady also promised that God, St. Vincent de Paul, and she, herself, would protect the Sisters of Charity and the Vincentian community of men, while other orders would have victims.

Novices on the left, professed sisters on the right, in the chapel of the motherhouse. Paris, 1800s

The Blessed Mother mentioned a period in the future, a time of great dangers, when people would think that all was lost and when there would, again, "be victims among the clergy of Paris: Monsignor the Archbishop (fresh tears filled her as this word was uttered) will die."

Recalling this vision, Catherine later wrote, "At these words, I thought, 'When will [this] be?' I understood forty years very clearly." (And forty years later, in 1871, the Archbishop Monsignor Darboy was killed during the Paris commune.)

There were also prophecies of misfortunes that would not be long in coming: "My child, the cross will be held in contempt. It will be thrown to the ground. Blood will flow. Our Savior's side will be opened anew. The streets will run with blood. Monsignor the Archbishop will be stripped of his vestments." (Here, the Blessed Mother could not continue speaking; her grief, so visible in her expression, prevented it.) "My child, the whole world will be plunged into gloom."

The apparition finally came to a close. Sr. Labouré recalled:

I stayed for I do not know how long. All I know [is that] when she departed, I only perceived that something had been extinguished, then no more than a shadow that went alongside the gallery, by the same

route that she had taken when arriving. I got up from above the altar steps and saw the child where I had left him. He said to me, "She has gone."

We went back the way we had come, everything still lit up and the child still on my left. I believe that child was my guardian angel, who had made himself visible to take me to see the Blessed Virgin, because I had prayed a lot for him to obtain this favor for me. He was dressed in white and a miraculous light went with him—that is to say, he was shining with light. He was about four or five years old.

When I got back to my bed, it was two o'clock in the morning... I heard the clock strike. I did not go back to sleep at all.[25]

Only days later, an insurrection known as the "Three Glorious Days" burst upon France from July 27 to July 29, 1830. King Charles X was deposed in a liberal and bloody revolution. Churches were profaned; religious communities invaded, devastated, and dispersed; and priests hunted down and murdered. The mobs desecrated churches, destroyed statues, and threw down crucifixes and trampled them. Bishops and priests were imprisoned, beaten, and killed. The Archbishop of Paris, Hyacinth de Quélen, had to flee into hiding twice to save his life, and was stripped of his vestments for a time. Yet menacing threats somehow stopped at the very doors of the Vincentians and the Sisters of Charity—all as Our Lady had stated.

Fr. Aladel was informed of the apparition. When these first events came to pass, he acted like he hadn't noticed the prophetic bullseyes.

Four months later, Sr. Catherine was seized, again, with a conviction that she would see the Blessed Mother. "I thought that she would grant me this grace, but this desire was so strong that I was convinced that I would actually see her at her most beautiful."[26] Later that same day, at half past five in the evening, the novices and the professed sisters, wearing their respective black and white bonnets and their white and winged cornetts, gathered in the chapel of the Motherhouse for prayer and a topic of meditation. It was the eve of the first Sunday of Advent, November 27. As she knelt alongside her sisters in prayer, Sr. Labouré heard the familiar, faint rustling of silk, the sound of Our Lady's gown as she walked!

Sr. Catherine looked up excitedly to see before her in the sanctuary, on a white globe, "the Blessed Virgin at the same height as St. Joseph's picture...standing, dressed in white, medium height, her face so beautiful that it would be impossible for me to tell of her beauty. She had a silk dress, white like the dawn." She wore a high-cut neckline and plain sleeves, a bluish-white veil draped down to her feet, and "under the veil, her hair, in coils, was bound with a fillet ornamented with lace, about three centimeters in height or of two fingers' breadth, without pleats, and resting lightly on her hair." Later, St. Catherine would describe the details of a snake underneath her feet: "green with yellow spots."[27]

Our Lady, with her eyes raised heavenward, and holding in her hands a golden ball with a gold cross on top of it, extended her arms at the level of her waist in a gesture of offering the globe to God.[28] Suddenly, her hands were resplendent with three rings on each finger, each adorned with precious stones that flashed brilliant streams of light onto the large white sphere of earth below her, "especially on a spot where *France* was written."[29] Sister Catherine later recorded the words that she heard interiorly in that moment: *"I pour out [these graces] upon those who ask them of me."*

Statue of Our Lady holding the globe in the Rue du Bac Chapel in the Mother House

"She made me understand," said Sr. Catherine, "how pleasing it was to pray to the Blessed Virgin and how generous she was toward those who pray to her, what graces she granted to those who ask them of her, what joy she felt in granting those graces."[30]

The Blessed Mother then lowered her eyes and looked intently at Sr. Labouré. Her lips did not move, but Catherine heard a voice say, *"The ball, which you see, represents the whole world, especially France, and each person in particular."*

"These rays symbolize the graces I shed upon

those who ask for them. The gems from which rays do not fall are the graces for which souls forget to ask."[31]

Then the streams of light from Our Lady's jeweled fingers rushed down with such glory and brilliance upon the white globe at her feet that the golden globe she held and her feet were no longer visible. An oval frame formed around her, and written within its borders were the following words in gold: *"O Mary, conceived without sin, pray for us who have recourse to thee."*[32]

Novices walking single file in the Rue du Bac Mother House convent in the 1800s

Then the image revolved to show a reverse side. An image of a cross above large M appeared, and below it, the two Hearts of Jesus and Mary—the first crowned with thorns and the second pierced with a sword. Twelve stars encircled the entire oval tableau.

The 2nd phase of Our Lady's 2nd apparition to the novice, Sr. Catherine Labouré

With a tone of command, Our Lady stated: *"Have a Medal struck after this model. All who wear it will receive great graces; they should wear it around the neck. The graces will be abundant for those who wear it with confidence."*

And then the vision was gone. Sr. Catherine did not remember her body saying the closing prayers alongside the other sisters in the chapel. She did not remember taking her place in line to walk into the dining hall. Nor did she recall sitting down at the meal table. The first thing that brought her back to earth was hearing the Mistress of Novices say dryly: "Sister Labouré must still be in ecstasy." Startled, embarrassed, and caught between two worlds, Sr. Labouré knew not to say a word.

A few days later in December, Our Lady would visit Sr. Catherine Labouré for a third time in the chapel on Rue du Bac—the exact date was not noted down. Like on November 27, the apparition happened at 5:30 p.m. after the presentation of a topic of meditation. Our Lady's coming was announced in the same way, with the rustle of her silk dress, but with small differences. She came from behind the altar, not from the gallery side. The image of the Medal, which had appeared "at the same height as the picture of St. Joseph" on the right, was now a little behind and "near the Tabernacle." The Blessed Virgin looked just as she had a few days before with her "hair parted down the middle," her robe "the color of dawn," and the same "blue veil." Again, Sister Catherine heard in the depths of her soul: *"These rays of light are the symbol of the graces that the Blessed Virgin obtains for those who ask them of her."*

The apparition vanished with a farewell. *"You will not see me anymore,"* said Our Lady, *"but you will hear my voice during your prayers."*[33]

With this simple promise—so simple that it is easy for the mind to overlook it, a familiar conversation began between Sr. Catherine Labouré and the Blessed Mother that would last for forty-six years. Catherine had only to speak to Our Lady and she would reply through an inner locution, or the Virgin herself would begin the conversation. In various moments throughout Sr. Labouré's life, evidence of this supernatural familiarity with her Mother in heaven would reveal itself.

Third apparition of Our Lady to Sr. Catherine

"Pure illusion!" scoffed Fr. Jean Marie Aladel, when Catherine told him of the second apparition of the Medal. "If you want to honor Our Lady, 'imitate her virtues' and beware of your imagination!"[34] Sr. Labouré was so silenced on the matter that she wasn't able to even mention to him the Blessed Mother's third apparition. But she did succeed in making Fr. Aladel promise never to reveal to anyone her name or identity as the visionary. This he did with no problem, undoubtedly because he didn't believe she was a visionary at all.[35] Sr. Labouré's joy in seeing Our

Lady became the martyrdom of carrying a hidden gift for the entire world, a gift entrusted to her from heaven that only one man could implement. And that one man thought she was ludicrous.

"You will have plenty of suffering," the Blessed Mother had told her.

The novitiate ended for Sr. Catherine on January 30, 1831, and she received her habit in the order of the Sisters of Charity. Secure in her vows, she donned her voluminous blue habit and her new oversized, starched, white headdress: the iconic cornette.[36] With her secret for the world burdening her heart, Sr. Catherine was moved and assigned to Enghien Hospice, a retirement home for the poor, closer to where Fr. Aladel could keep an eye on her. This large and simple house was nestled in a desolate suburb southeast of Paris, three miles from Rue du Bac and only two-and-a-half miles from the restaurant of her brother, Charles Labouré. There she would live out the rest of her long years.

Sr. Catherine Labouré was first assigned to kitchen duties, then to the cleaning and care of the clothes and linens, and the oversight of the henhouse. It was soon apparent that she knew what she was doing. Sr. Catherine's proficient past of running so much of the family farm and household, combined with her previous experience serving clientele in her brother's restaurant, made her an exemplary minister to the poor—though she wrestled with the head cook, Sr. Vincent, whose parsimony clashed with her magnanimity. Sr. Catherine loved to give generously to the poor elderly she served, as they lived out their last days. "Do you have enough?" she would always ask them. But her competence in running the henhouse was her ideal domain. Each year, she increased the production of food for the poor. She added cows—and therefore milk—to the thousands of chickens and pigeons she tended for meat, and she streamlined the workflow with small farm methods from her native Burgundy.[37]

For the remainder of Sr. Catherine's life, up until a short time before her death—a total of forty-six years—she would keep her identity of being the visionary of Our Lady of Rue du Bac a carefully guarded secret. When rumors began to fly that someone in the community, a novice, had seen Our Lady, Sr. Labouré acted just as curious about it as the other sisters did.

Over the course of more than a year after Our Lady's last apparition in the chapel of the Motherhouse, Sr. Catherine tried a couple more times in vain to talk to Fr. Aladel. In both attempts, he rebuked, ridiculed, and resisted her insistence that a Medal be made at the request of Our Lady of the Immaculate Conception. She confessed to him, in a moment of frustration, that she had told Our Lady that she "had better appear to someone else, since no one will believe me." He responded with indignance, calling her a "wicked wasp."[38]

Tormented and frustrated over the matter, Sr. Labouré said to the Blessed Virgin, "He does not want to listen to me!"

Our Lady answered her in an interior locution: "He is my servant, and he should be frightened of displeasing me."

Shortly thereafter, in the fall of 1831, Sr. Catherine made a third attempt. There is sworn testimony that she often approached Fr. Aladel's confessional trembling.[39] Garnering what inner fortitude she could find, she said candidly to her confessor, "The Virgin is angry," and relayed Our Lady's words: "He is my servant, and he should be frightened of displeasing me."

Fr. Aladel responded like slab of marble. But this time, he was interiorly perplexed. One part, at least, of what Catherine said was true: he was frightened to displease the Virgin Mary. That small opening of doubt within Fr. Aladel led him to accompany his superior on a visit to see the Archbishop of Paris, Monsignor Hyacinth de Quélen, in January 1832. Taking advantage of the opportunity, he informed the Archbishop of the apparitions at the chapel of Rue du Bac: the visions of an unnamed seer and the alleged request of Our Lady to imprint a Medal with her image.

The Archbishop listened keenly and questioned Fr. Aladel closely as to the character of the hidden sister and the appearance and words of Our Lady. The significant theological details and imagery of the revealed Medal, which Fr. Aladel shared in great detail, did not escape the Archbishop's notice. They are many:

Our Lady, standing on a white globe, crushing the serpent. This was a sign of her Queenship of Heaven and Earth, and the power that God had given her to destroy Satan's works and protect her children ("I will put enmity between you and the woman, and between your offspring and hers; He will strike at your head, while you strike at his heel"—Gn. 3:15.)

The words adorning the rim of the Medal, "O Mary, conceived without sin, pray for us who have recourse to thee." This signified her Immaculate Conception,[40] the manner in which she was conceived in her mother, Anne's, womb. Being sinless, Mary was "full of grace" and "blessed among women" (Luke 1:28). The circular words also pointed to Mary's role as intercessor before God on behalf of her "offspring," and as words placed in the mouths of her children, they encouraged humankind to say them and turn to the Blessed Mother, requesting her prayers.

The rays of grace streaming from the gems on the rings on Our Lady's fingers onto the world. These demonstrated the power God has given her to dispense graces upon all of humanity.[41] The Medal also showed the relationship between those asking for prayer ("pray for us who have recourse to thee") and Mary's response—inundations of grace.

On the reverse side of the Medal, the twelve stars. These were reminiscent of Apostles, representing the entire Church as it surrounds Mary. They also recalled the vision of St. John, and his words in the Book of Revelation (12:1): "a great sign appeared in heaven, a woman clothed with the sun, and the moon under her feet, and on her head a crown of twelve stars."

The simple cross of Christ. This symbolized the Redeemer. The bar underneath it: a sign of the earth or an altar. **The "M" stood for Mary.** The interweaving of her initial and the cross showed Mary's close involvement with Jesus, the world, and the Holy Mass, and revealed her faithfulness to her Son, especially at the foot of the Cross. **Their two Hearts with flames of fire** represented the burning love of Jesus and Mary for everyone (see also Luke 2:35). The thorns piercing the Lord's Heart and the sword in Mary's pointed to what they suffered and continue to suffer over the sins of the world.

The Archbishop of Paris was satisfied. He saw in the Medal an apt and beautiful expression of the doctrines of the Church. Providentially, Monsignor de Quélen had a special devotion to the Immaculate Conception of Our Lady. He gave his permission for the Medal to be struck at once and asked that some of the first ones be sent to him.

Relieved and encouraged, Fr. Aladel changed his dour attitude. Four months later, he ordered that 20,000 Medals be minted. When the design of the Medal, as we know of it today, was shown to St. Catherine, she said, "Now it must be given to the whole world."

Archbishop of Paris, Hyacinthe-Louis de Quélen

The first Medal produced was given to Archbishop de Quélen of Paris, as requested, and the preliminary batch was distributed by the Sisters of Charity in the Paris region, during a second wave of a deadly outbreak of cholera in 1832. The graces that promised to flow through Our Lady began.

At the grade school in the Place de Louvre, an eight-year-old girl named Caroline Nanain was the only child in her class not wearing the Medal—and the only one to catch cholera. After the sisters gave her a Medal, she recovered straightaway and returned to the classroom the very next day.

In the diocese of Meaux, a pregnant woman in the small town of Mitry-Mory was deemed a hopeless medical case, but after receiving a Medal, she suddenly returned to good health and had a successful delivery to the amazement of onlookers. In the same village, a crippled child, who had received no help from "famous doctors," began to walk the day the Medal was laid on him.

On November 21, 1832, a sixteen-year-old boy was bitten by a dog and was suffering from either epilepsy, according to some, or rabies, according to others. In either case, epilepsy was incurable and rabies, at the time, was lethal. Through the gift of the Medal, the boy immediately recovered.

Conversions were reported in droves as well. On June 13, 1833, a Daughter of Charity applied a Medal to a solder from Alençon who was "mad with rage and blaspheming." Contrary to all expectations, he began to pray and composed himself for his impending death with peace of heart, even going as far as to say, "What grieves me is that I have come to love so late and that I do not love more than I do."[42]

Archbishop de Quélen made use of his Medals immediately, and he wasted no time in having a statue "on the model shown to the Sister" made for his bedroom. One of the graces granted to him through the use of the Medal occurred in 1836. The Archbishop was grieved that a Monsignor de Pradt, former chaplain to Napoleon, had become an unlawful bishop. This Monsignor had accepted his office from the hands of the Emperor, not the Holy See, and now he lay dying, defiant in his stance and unreconciled with Catholic Church. Archbishop de Quélen had tried to see him in person on several occasions but had been rebuffed. In faith, he tried again, and this time decided to carry a Medal with him. Miraculously, he was allowed in to see the apostate bishop, who was so touched by God's grace during the visit that he repented and confessed his sins. The next day, Monsignor de Pradt received the Sacraments from the hands of the Archbishop and died in his arms. This so moved the Archbishop that he became an enthusiastic promoter and protector of the Medal for the rest of his days.[43]

When the first production of Medals disappeared, new ones poured out liberally from the minting presses, inundating France and beyond. By 1836, more than fifteen million had travelled around the world,[44] as images of Our Lady of the Immaculate Conception and of the Medal emerged in a plethora of cultures and contexts. Even Pope Gregory XVI, who received a package of Medals in the Vatican in Rome, placed one at the foot of the crucifix on his desk and began distributing them to his visitors. The rapid spread of the Medal was as astounding as the miracles attributed to it.

In February 1836, the Archbishop of Paris instituted a Canonical Inquiry, which concluded that the Medal was of supernatural origin and the wonders worked through it were genuine. The inquiry helped to spur the Holy See's eventual institution in 1895 of a feast day in honor of the Medal, which continues to be celebrated every November 27. The inquiry was also a significant aid in the process of Sr. Labouré's future canonization.[45]

By 1842, *one-hundred million Medals* had reached the furthest corners of the Earth.[46] Along the way, this sacramental from heaven received a new name. At first, it was called simply the Medal of the Immaculate

Conception. But in little time, it became known as the Miraculous Medal, due to the unprecedented number of extraordinary cures, conversions, divine acts of protection against imminent dangers, and other miracles attributed to it. In 1833, Fr. Jean Marie Aladel ended up writing a ninety-page book called *The Miraculous Medal: Its Origin, History, Circulation, Results*, which went into four editions within the year. The former restrainer of the message was now spreading the story far and wide. Expanded editions of nearly 300 pages were published in 1835, 1836, and 1837. An eighth printing from 1842 was over six hundred pages, and a ninth edition from 1878, printed after Sr. Labouré's passing, also contained Fr. Aladel's biography of the saint he had once doubted.[47]

As the Medal took the world by storm, Sr. Catherine listened with great interest and rejoiced in hearing of the many graces washing over humanity, especially the most famous Miraculous Medal conversion of all time, that of Alphonse Ratisbonne. Ratisbonne was a young, socially prominent, anti-Catholic Jewish man of great wealth, with blood ties to the Rothschilds, who became transformed into a fervent disciple of Christ—his experience sent shockwaves through the Church.[48]

All the while, Sr. Catherine remained hidden. When the first Medals were distributed among the sisters, she received hers just like everyone else. Not even the Mother Superior of her convent, much less the Archbishop of Paris or Pope Gregory XVI, were aware of her identity as the Rue du Bac visionary. The Holy Father is known to have said, "To think of keeping a secret for forty-six years—and this by a woman, and a Sister!"[49]

In 1860, when Catherine was fifty-four, Fr. Etienne appointed thirty-seven-year-old Sr. Jeanne Dufès, as her Superior over her at the Enghien house. "I am sending you into the house of Sr. Catherine Labouré," he told Sr. Jeanne, "where she leads a hidden life." This phrase may have made the new Superior wonder if Sr. Catherine was "the one." The arrangement was new for Sr. Labouré, who as custodian of the elderly occupants of Enghien, had been the de facto superior of that home. The two women felt a natural antipathy toward each other, and their tempers were quick to flare. But, according to Sr. Dufès, "There is this different between Sr. Catherine and myself that, while we are both very quick, she conquers her quickness at once, but with me, it is hard and long."..."I do not know how she is able, in an instant, to capture such absolute calm."[50] While other sisters were impressed by Sr. Labouré's capabilities and piety, Sr. Jeanne Dufés was unimpressed and said she preferred "a different kind of sanctity to that of Sr. Catherine."[51]

For the next sixteen years of Sr. Labouré's life, Sr. Dufès' harsh treatment of her would perfect her hard-won virtue of humility. Sr. Jeanne Dufès would reprimand Sr. Catherine severely, at times, and for things of

The Enghien Hospice in Reuilly where Sr. Labouré worked and lived the last 46 years of her life

trivial importance. One of the nuns, Sr. Charvier felt bound to tell Sr. Dufès of her astonishment at seeing the Superior scold a venerable Sister so vehemently for the smallest things. Sr. Jeanne replied, "Let me be. I feel compelled to do it." Against the rule of the order, Sr. Jeanne would humiliate Sr. Catherine in front of several of the sisters, and Sr. Catherine would kneel at her feet, with a humble word or none at all. Afterward, Sr. Catherine would often go to the chapel, then return to knock at the door of the Sister Superior in order to ask in a pleasant tone for some permission or another. In this way, she showed Sr. Jeanne that she bore no grudge because of the reprimand she had received.[52]

While Sr. Catherine did her best to ensure that nothing distinguished her from the others in her community, it became apparent to some that there was something different about her. This surfaced during the Paris Commune, for instance, when in 1871 an anti-religious, communist government briefly seized power in the French capital. For two months, from March 18 to May 28, the nuns lived in constant fear as danger surrounded the convent. Only Sr. Labouré, who was told forty years earlier that her community would be protected, showed calm and confidence. She even fearlessly distributed Miraculous Medals to the solders of the Commune when the revolutionaries invaded their retirement home and expelled the nuns.[53] "The Virgin will watch over us,"

she reassured the sisters. "Nothing bad will happen to us."

Yet there was reason to worry. Between May 24 and May 26, seventy hostages of priests and lay people were murdered, including Archbishop Darboy, as Our Lady had foretold. And on Ascension Thursday, May 18, the communist revolutionaries broke into the Church of Notre Dame-des-Victoires and perpetrated horrible sacrileges. Even the graves were pried open and the remains of the saintly Father Desgenette were scattered over the pavement, and his head paraded around on a pike. When Sr. Catherine heard of this sickening demonstration, she said with a stern brow: "They have touched Our Lady. They will go no further."[54]

Acting as head of the house, when the Sister Superior went into hiding, Catherine told the nuns that the house would be preserved, and they would all return in one month, by May 31 to be exact—not to worry. And events transpired exactly as she said they would.

It was only at the end of St. Catherine's life, years after Fr. Aladel's death, that she felt compelled to reveal her identity to her Sister Superior, Sr. Dufès. "I will not live much longer now," she said to Sr. Jeanne. "I think the time has come to speak—you know what about."

Moved, her Superior responded, "My good Sr. Catherine, it is true that I suspect very strongly that you received the Miraculous Medal, but, through discretion, I have never spoken to you about it."

"Very good, Sister, tomorrow I will ask the Blessed Virgin's advice in my prayers," Catherine said. "If she tells me to tell everything, I will do so. If not, I will keep silence."

The next day, Sr. Catherine spoke to Sr. Dufès and relayed to her much of what happened forty-six years earlier in the Rue du Bac chapel. The Sister Superior felt herself several times wanting to throw herself at Catherine's knees, to beg pardon for having known so little of her. She held herself back, but could not prevent herself from murmuring, "You were highly favored."

"Oh," Sr. Catherine replied, "I was nothing but an instrument. It was not for me that the Blessed Virgin appeared. I did not even know how to write! It is within the community that I learned what I know. And if the Blessed Virgin chose me, an ignoramus, it was in order that no one should be able to doubt her.'"[55]

Sr. Labouré's last few days on earth tell us much about how she lived and what mattered most to her. She wanted it known after her passing that "The Blessed Virgin has promised graces every time that someone prays in the chapel [of Rue du Bac]—above all, purity of spirit, purity of heart, purity of will ... pure love."

As her body weakened, Sr. Catherine asked for prayers for the dying, which were recited around her bedside. "Aren't you afraid of dying?" asked Sr. Dufés.

Sr. Catherine's blue eyes of seventy years took on a thoughtful look of wonder. "Why be afraid of going to meet Our Lord, His Mother, and St. Vincent?"

A few days later, on December 31, 1876, Sr. Jeanne Dufès was still by her side, continuing to make up for years of undue treatment toward the hidden but famous visionary of the Daughters of Charity. Sr. Catherine turned to her quietly and said, "I shall not see tomorrow."

"But tomorrow is New Year's Day!" Sr. Jeanne responded. "This is no time to be leaving us!"

But Sr. Catherine repeated, "No, I shall not see tomorrow." On her bed were piles of Miraculous Medals that she was putting into small bags for the sisters.

At about 3:00 p.m., Sr. Catherine rallied with sweat on her brow to welcome a visit from her sister Tonine's daughter, Marie-Antoinette Duhamel, who arrived with her two little daughters and another niece. She happily gave them the presents she had prepared: sweets, chocolate ... and a handful of Miraculous Medals for their mother.

The only authentic photograph taken of Sr. Catherine Labouré, the year of her death, 1876

As soon as they had left, Sr. Catherine collapsed on her pillow. Little packets of Medals fell from her hands and scattered all over the bed. "My dear Sr. Catherine," Sr. Jeanne teased her, "don't you know it's December 31? Now I ask you, is this the sort of day on which you ought to be frightening us like this?"

But come 6:00 p.m., Sr. Jean began to believe that the visionary was slipping away. Saying the opposite of what she saw happening, she blurted out, "Come on, don't worry. You're on the mend!"

But Sr. Labouré was not worried. She calmly repeated: "I shall die this very day."

The sisters who had gathered around her bed continued to say prayers for the dying. Sr. Jeanne Dufès, with great tenderness, said, choking back tears, "So, you want to leave us ..." Sr. Catherine did not reply. The sisters repeated the invocation of the Miraculous Medal: "O Mary, Conceived without Sin, Pray for Us Who Have Recourse to Thee." Gently, without a moment of agony, or struggle to breathe, Sr. Catherine gently went to sleep.

At 7:00 p.m., a slight smile swept across Sr. Catherine's face, and none of the normal signs of dying appeared—only two large tears that rolled down her cheeks. Someone closed her eyes. It was the end.

Thirty-three years earlier, Sr. Catherine had written the following words while on retreat:

> *Mary loved the poor, and a Sister of Charity who loves the poor [...] will have no fear of death. No one has ever heard that Sisters of Charity who really loved the poor had terrifying fears of death. Quite the opposite [...], such sisters have been seen to die the gentlest of deaths.*[56]

By the time of Sr. Catherine Labouré's passing to the next life in 1876, over a billion Miraculous Medals had been distributed around the globe.[57] In France, the Miraculous Medal was a familiar item to all, and an English bishop had written as early as 1855: "Except for the Holy Cross, no other Christian symbol was ever so widely multiplied, or was ever the instrument of so many marvelous results ..."[58]

Sr. Labouré's body was buried on January 3, 1877, and disinterred in 1933, fifty-six years later. It was found completely incorrupt. The doctor overseeing the exhumation, upon finding that the body was so flexible, thought to open the Sr. Catherine's eyelids. When he did, he was startled. Not only did her blue eyes open easily, but they appeared clear and beautiful. Just like that of the founder of her order, St. Vincent de Paul, Catherine Labouré's body is a continuing miracle to this day. It lies in a glass reliquary under the very spot where Our Lady appeared in the chapel at Rue du Bac in Paris, revealing the glory of a pure and guileless soul that once graced the earth.

July 27, 1947, Pope Pius XII canonized Sister Catherine Labouré, declaring her to be called by the Church what she was, and had long been—a saint.

The incorrupt body of St. Catherine Labouré in the Chapel of the Motherhouse at Rue du Bac, Paris, France

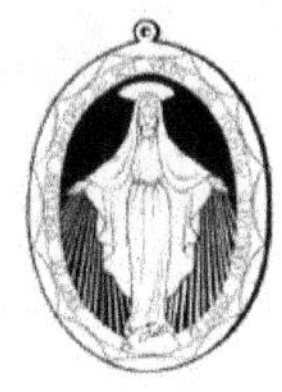

THE MIRACULOUS MEDAL TRAVELS AROUND THE WORLD

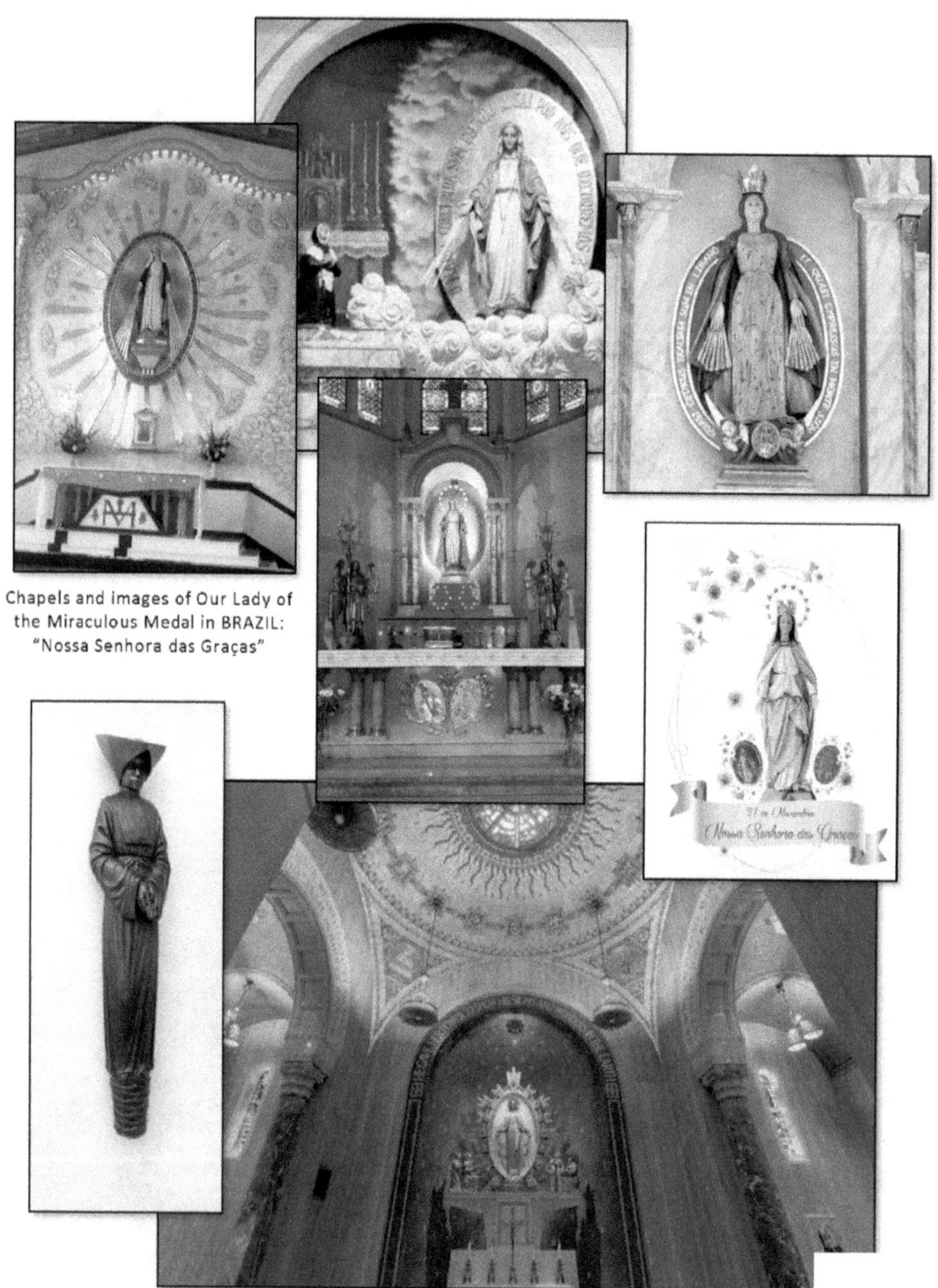

Chapels and images of Our Lady of the Miraculous Medal in BRAZIL: "Nossa Senhora das Graças"

Basilica of the National Shrine of the Immaculate Conception, Washington D.C., UNITED STATES OF AMERICA

Miraculous Medal Shrine, Philadelphia, Pennsylvania, UNITED STATES OF AMERICA

Niagara University, New York, UNITED STATES OF

Miraculous Medal design from PORTUGAL

Miraculous Medal altar in Bydgoszcz, POLAND

Image of St. Catherine from Krakowski Street in Tarnow, POLAND

Painting of Catherine Labouré as a novice, Warsaw, POLAND

Pictures from Our Lady of The Miraculous Medal Shrine In The Village of Ramalloor, Kothamangalam In Kerala, INDIA

Painting from SPAIN of the Miraculous Medal and St. Vincent de Paul

Image from SPAIN of Catherine's second apparition

Pictures from SPAIN celebrating scenes from St. Catherine's

Our Lady's apparition holding the globe, painting from SPAIN

Old Miraculous Medal, minted in SPAIN

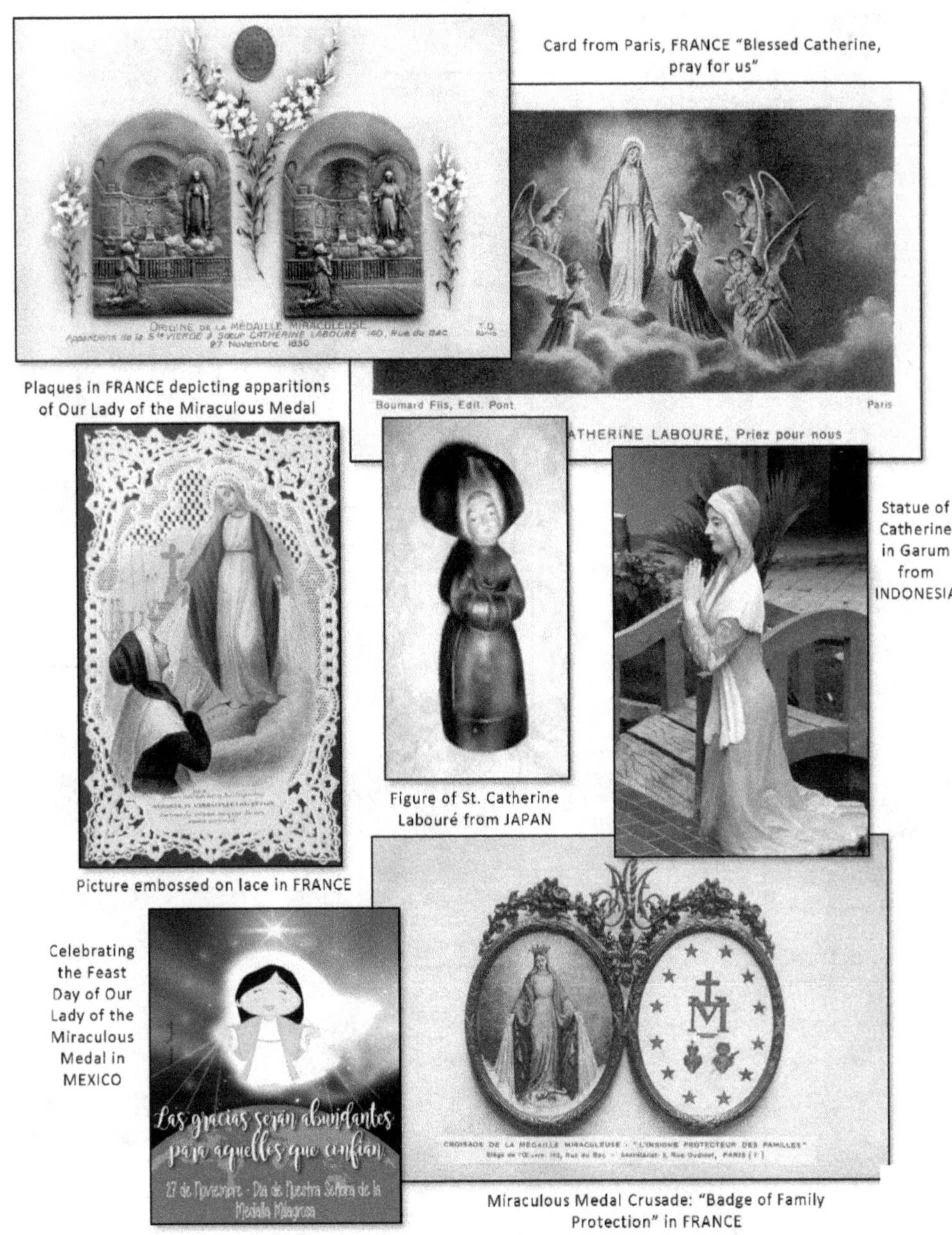

Card from Paris, FRANCE "Blessed Catherine, pray for us"

Plaques in FRANCE depicting apparitions of Our Lady of the Miraculous Medal

Statue of Catherine in Garum from INDONESIA

Figure of St. Catherine Labouré from JAPAN

Picture embossed on lace in FRANCE

Celebrating the Feast Day of Our Lady of the Miraculous Medal in MEXICO

Miraculous Medal Crusade: "Badge of Family Protection" in FRANCE

Painting from Nitra, SLOVAKIA

Holy card from IRELAND

Painting in Istanbul, TURKEY, in the Daughters of Charity House

Church dedicated to the Miraculous Medal, Pilis Csaba, HUNGARY

From a painting in ITALY by Morgari

Card from BELGIUM with French text from Sr. Catherine's decree of beatification (1946)

Our Lady of the Miraculous Medal Church, New Cristobal, PANAMA

Wood carving in Pilis Csaba, HUNGARY

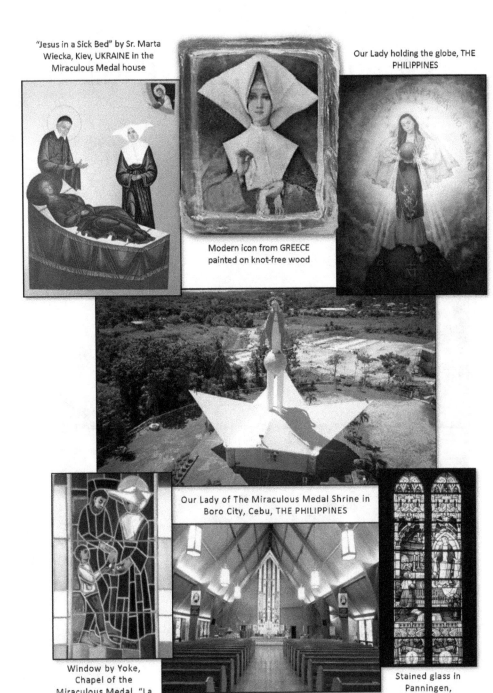

"Jesus in a Sick Bed" by Sr. Marta Wiecka, Kiev, UKRAINE in the Miraculous Medal house

Modern icon from GREECE painted on knot-free wood

Our Lady holding the globe, THE PHILIPPINES

Our Lady of The Miraculous Medal Shrine in Boro City, Cebu, THE PHILIPPINES

Window by Yoke, Chapel of the Miraculous Medal, "La Providence," Fribourg, SWITZERLAND

Our Lady of The Miraculous Medal Church, Toronto, Ontario, CANADA

Stained glass in Panningen, NETHERLANDS

STORIES OF PROMINENCE

ALPHONSE RATISBONNE (1814-1884)

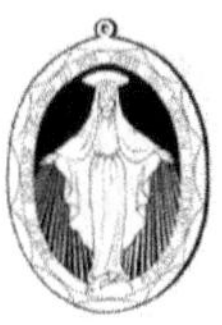

Alphonse Ratisbonne was Jewish in name only. He was a French Freemason[59] who had no belief in God. Being the ninth child of a rich and charitable family of bankers from Strasbourg (Alsace, France), who were related to the Rothschilds and allied to other affluent Jewish families, he was distinguished in the world for his social position.[60] While sadness gripped him as a child when he lost first his mother and then his father, he was left with siblings who loved him, and placed in the care of a very wealthy and generous uncle, who denied him nothing: not horses, nor coaches, nor excursions. Alphonse wrote:

> *My uncle scolded me for only one thing: "You are too fond of Les Champs Elysées,"[61] he said to me affectionately. He was right. I thought of nothing but pleasures ... I had a notion that people came into the world simply to enjoy themselves.[62]... There was a fearful void in my heart, and I was not happy, though I possessed everything in abundance, in profusion.*

Ratisbonne was inherently intelligent and earned a law degree in Paris. Although terribly rich, he was free from the love of money for its own sake. He was known to do such things as let the driver of his hired carriage fish through his wallet and help himself, without bothering to see what had been taken.[63]

In 1841, when he was twenty-seven, Alphonse got engaged to a young Jewish girl, Flore, who was his niece; she had been promised to him when they were both children.

> *Something was still lacking, and this something I found ... in her I beheld the fair promise of my future life and the satisfaction of all my hopes ... It would not be easy to imagine a young girl more gentle, more amiable, more charming ... the look of my fiancée awakened within me a mysterious sense of human dignity and worth; I began to believe in the immortality of the soul. More than that, I began, by a kind of instinct, to pray to God. I thanked Him for my happiness; but for all that, I was still not happy. I could not analyze nor account for my feelings.[64]*

One of Alphonse's older brothers, Théodore Ratisbonne, had converted to Catholicism in 1827, when Alphonse was thirteen. Soon afterward, Théodore entered the Jesuit priesthood and practiced ministry in Strasbourg—a shameful defection, said Alphonse, *"before the inconsolable gaze of his family ..."*

> *My brother's conversion, which had been considered an unexplainable madness, gave me reason to believe in the fanaticism of the Catholics, and I was horrified by them. I only hated one member of my family: my brother Théodore. His habit disgusted me, his presence annoyed me, and his words, serious as they were, ignited my anger.*[65]

With one of their sons as though dead to them, the Ratisbonne family's hopes lay in the young Alphonse, who was destined to receive his uncle's estate and assume his responsibilities in the family's banking business—though he found the office setting stifling and business irritating. His passion was the regeneration of poor Jewish people.[66] Alphonse was one of the most zealous members of a society founded fifteen years earlier by one of his brothers, which provided jobs for young Jews.[67]

Before Ratisbonne's wedding, which was delayed until August 1842 because of the young age of his fiancée, who was only sixteen, it was decided that Alphonse would take an extended trip "to beguile the time of expectation."[68] He mapped out a journey of nine or ten months travelling to the East,[69] visiting some of the most remarkable cities of Italy along the way.[70] Of his journey, he wrote:

> *Before arriving at Naples, the ship put in at Civita Vecchia, the port of the Papal States. The cannon on the fort boomed loudly ... I inquired the meaning of these warlike sounds in the peaceful lands of the pope. I was told, "This is the Feast of the Conception of Our Lady!" I shrugged my shoulders and did not disembark.*

Anything involving the Catholic faith or Our Lady held no interest for Alphonse. When the ship docked at Naples, he remained there a month and filled his journal with bitter words against Catholicism and its priests. *"They seemed to me out of keeping with that magnificent country."* Ratisbonne's next ship sailing to Malta wasn't able to leave, which meant that he would stay in Italy for New Year's Eve.

> *I was alone at Naples; no one to congratulate me and wish me well, no one to press to my heart. I thought of my family, of the festivity and joy with which my uncle always kept that day; I began to shed tears, and the lively gaiety of the Neapolitans deepened my sadness. I went out to shake off my importunate melancholy and followed mechanically in the train of the crowd. I reached the Place in front of the palace and found myself, I know not how, at the door of a church. I went in. I think a priest was saying Mass. I remained there, leaning against a pillar, and my heart seemed to open and expand in a new atmosphere. I prayed after my own fashion, without taking any notice of what was going on around me; I prayed for my fiancée, for my uncle, for my deceased father, for the loving mother who had been taken from me so early, for all who were dear to me; and I asked of God some inspiration, some intimation of His will, which might guide me in my projects for improving the condition of the Jews—projects which haunted me incessantly.*
>
> *My sadness passed away, like a cloud which the wind breaks up and disperses; and my heart was filled with an unutterable calmness, with a consolation such as I should have felt if a voice had said to me, "Your prayer is heard."*[71]

Since Alphonse had to change his travelling plans, Neapolitan family friends tried to persuade him to travel to Rome; but there was nothing, or so he thought, that would interest him in that city. His fiancée had even sent him instructions from his physician positively forbidding him to go to there because of a widespread malaria outbreak. But something caused Alphonse to end up there. Unsure how this happened, he later wrote: *"But how did I go to Rome? I find it impossible to explain, even to myself."*[72] ... *"I must have missed my way, for instead of going to the bureau of the Palermo boats, as I intended when I left my lodging, I found myself in the bureau for Rome."*[73]

Ratisbonne planned to stay in the "Eternal City" only a few days and return to Naples. As he was touring Rome, he heard someone call him. It was Gustave de Bussières, an old schoolmate and childhood friend. Alphonse was glad to see him since his solitude had begun to weigh heavily on him. Gustave was a zealous French Protestant, who had endeavored several times to persuade Alphonse to embrace his Protestant faith. But the latter was immovable, and the two friends, after useless discussions, usually closed with a renewal of their own infallibility. "Fanatical Protestant!" shouted one; "Callous Jew!" retorted the other.[74]

Gustave invited Alphonse to eat at his father's house, and when he entered, Gustave's older brother Baron Théodore De Bussières was walking out. Ratisbonne knew that the Baron was close friends with his brother, Fr. Théodore Ratisbonne, and a recent and zealous convert to the Catholic faith. Therefore, he disliked Baron Théodore De Bussières intensely.[75] But, since the De Bussières had travelled to Sicily and Asia, places where Alphonse had set his sights to go, he mentioned an interest in speaking with him at some point—though he later wished he had shut his mouth.

The interior of the Basilica of Santa Maria in Aracoeli, Rome

Alphonse paid a goodbye visit to Baron De Bussières before leaving Rome, only out of propriety, and cursing his promise to do so. The Baron knew that Ratisbonne was Jewish and received him with affectionate eagerness. Their conversation naturally covered the various places of interest in Rome that the young French traveler had visited, and then their words drifted into a religious discussion. Ratisbonne did not disguise his real sentiments. Without hesitation, he expressed his animosity toward Catholicism and his unalterable attachment to Judaism, responding to the Baron's arguments with frigid politeness, a smile of pity, or new protestations. He did say to De Bussières, however:

"A rather odd thing happened to me the other day. While I was looking around at the church of Aracoeli on the Capitol, I felt suddenly seized by an emotion I couldn't understand. The guide, seeing my agitation, ask me what the matter was and if I wanted to go out into the open air, adding that he had often seen strangers similarly affected."

Théodore Renouard de Bussièrres

Seeing the Baron's eyes well with tears of delight may have prompted Ratisbonne's next comment; he added that the emotion was most definitely not a Catholic emotion, but purely *"religious."*

"Besides, as I came down from the Capitol, a melancholy spectacle rekindled all my hatred of Catholicism. I passed through the Ghetto, and as I saw the misery and the degradation of the Jews, I said to myself that, after all, it was a loftier thing to be on the side of the oppressed than on that of the oppressors."[76]

The Baron tried to persuade Alphonse to share his own Catholic convictions, but the young Israelite retorted: *"A Jew I was born, and a Jew I shall die!"*[77]

"Since you are so confident in the strength and stability of your understanding, promise me to wear something that I will give you," Baron De Bussières invited.

"Let me see it first; what sort of thing is it?"

"Only this Medal." The Baron held up a Miraculous Medal. At the sight of it, Alphonse threw himself back in his chair with a gesture of mingled indignation and astonishment.

"But," said the Baron quietly, *"as you look at things, this should be an indifferent matter in your eyes, while it will give me a great deal of pleasure."*

"Oh, I will not refuse you," Ratisbonne exclaimed with a hearty laugh. *"I shall at least show you that people have no right to accuse us Jews of obstinacy. Besides, you are furnishing me with a charming chapter for my notes and impressions of my travels."*

Ratisbonne went on mocking the Medal and the Catholic faith. Meanwhile, De Bussières told his two little daughters to put the Medal on a cord. They did so, and gave it to their father, who hung it around Alphonse's neck.[78] Recalling the moment, Alphonse later wrote:

> *No sooner was this agreed to, than it was accomplished, and I burst out laughing as I exclaimed: "Ah! Ha! I have now become Catholic, Apostolic, Roman." It was the devil who prophesied through my mouth.*[79]

Encouraged by this first success, Baron De Bussières pushed the matter still further. Handing him Saint Bernard's invocation, the Memorare, he tried to get Alphonse to ask for the favor and protection of Mary. This time, the exasperated Ratisbonne refused. A new outpouring of blasphemies spewed out of him.

"I combated his reiterated refusals with the energy of desperation," recalled the Baron. *"An interior force urged me on."* He asked Alphonse to write down a copy of the prayer and recite it each morning and evening.

Ratisbonne, finally convinced that resistance was useless, agreed and walked out of the house murmuring to himself: *"What an unreasonable fellow! I wonder what he would say if I were to plague him with reciting Jewish prayers!"*[80]

The front door slammed shut. Baron De Bussières and his wife looked at each other for some time without speaking a word. Distressed by the anti-Christian invectives they had been compelled to listen to, they united in prayer to ask God's forgiveness for Alphonse and asked their two little daughters to say an Ave Maria at night for his conversion.

In the following hours, Ratisbonne read the Memorare and read it again, trying to find what on earth made the Baron give it so much worth.

Because of this, he unintendedly memorized the prayer and began repeating the Memorare mechanically, like a tape looping through his mind:[81]

> *Remember, O most gracious Virgin Mary, that never was it known that anyone who fled to thy protection, implored thy help, or sought thine intercession was left unaided. Inspired by this confidence, I fly unto thee, O Virgin of virgins, my Mother. To thee do I come, before thee I stand, sinful and sorrowful. O Mother of the Word Incarnate, despise not my petitions, but in thy mercy hear and answer me.*

Meanwhile, De Bussières became completely absorbed by the idea of winning Ratisbonne to Christ. He resolved to prevent, at all costs, the young Israelite's departure from Rome. Not finding him at the Hôtel Serny where he was staying, he left a note for Alphonse, asking him to come by again. That evening, the Baron spent his scheduled hour in Adoration of the Blessed Sacrament in the company of friends whom he begged to join him in praying for Alphonse's conversion.

Ratisbonne, however, had already fixed the day of his departure, January 16, and stopped by the next day: *"Well, I hope you have forgotten your yesterday's dreams. I have come to say good-bye to you; I am off tonight."*

"My dreams!" said De Bussières. *"The thoughts that you call dreams occupy me more than ever. And as for your going away, we will not speak of that, for you must absolutely put it off for a week."*

"Oh, that is impossible. I have reserved my place."

"What of that? We will go together to the office to say that you have changed your mind and are not going."

"Oh, now this is going too far. Most decidedly I leave tonight."

"Most decidedly you will not leave tonight, even if I have to lock you up in my own room."

Under the pretext of a very imposing ceremony in St. Peter's Basilica at the Vatican, Baron De Bussières pressured Alphonse to stay a few days longer. Dazed by his pertinacity, Alphonse agreed.

That evening, De Bussières went to dine with his older friend, Count De La Ferronnays, whose Breton region in France is known for its uncompromising faithfulness to Catholicism. De La Ferronnays was the former French ambassador to the Holy See and Minister of Foreign Affairs, and a man of great virtue and piety. Over dinner, the Baron shared his desire to see Ratisbonne converted and asked for the Count's prayers for him. De La Ferronnays shared with the Baron the confidence that he had always felt under the protection of the Blessed Virgin, even when the cares and distractions of political life had scarcely permitted him the time he desired to devote to his faith.

"Keep up a good hope," De La Ferronnays said to him. *"If he says the Memorare, he is yours, and many others with him."* Twenty-four hours later, on the 17th of January, the Count went for a walk to the church of Santa Maria Maggiore, where he spent a long time in prayer. There he recited dozens of Memorares for the conversion of Alphonse Ratisbonne. Then that same night at 11 p.m., Count De La Ferronnays, whom the Baron loved as his own father, died suddenly of a heart attack.

Pierre Louis Auguste Ferron, Count De La Ferronnays (1777–1842)

The Baron, though heavy-hearted, continued to pass the days showing Alphonse various religious antiquities in Rome, but Ratisbonne didn't show the slightest sign of a happy change. Filled with hope against human hope, De Bussières allowed no opportunity to enlighten his new young friend to escape. He showed him the Basilica Santo Stefano in Rotondo, with its circular colonnade and frescoes of thirty-four scenes of atrocities inflicted on Christian martyrs, each accompanied by a descriptive text and the name of the Roman

Basilica Santo Stefano in Rotondo (The Basilica of St. Stephen in the Round), Rome

emperor who ordered their execution. But Alphonse only looked disgusted, asking, *"What of the atrocities that Christians have inflicted on the Jewish people?"*

Baron De Bussières could not obtain a single consoling response. He brought Alphonse to the church of Aracoeli for a second time, but Ratisbonne felt nothing and answered the Baron with cold witticisms. All the while, Ratisbonne was astonished by the imperturbable calm with which De Bussières persevered in trying to convince him. The Baron's tranquility was incomprehensible to him, as he felt more aversion to the Catholic faith than ever.

Scala Sancta (The Holy Stairs) in Rome

De Bussières did not even hesitate to express his belief in the eventual triumph of his cause. On the 19th, they passed by the Scala Sancta, twenty-eight stairs reputedly brought to Rome from Jerusalem by Saint Helena in the fourth century, and watched pilgrims climbing them on their knees. These steps, which Catholic traditions says led up to the praetorium of Pontius Pilate, were climbed by Jesus Christ Himself on his way to trial during his Passion. The Baron bowed his head in reverence and declared aloud, "*Hail, holy staircase! Here is a man who one day will ascend your steps on his knees.*" Ratisbonne let out a disconcerting peal of laughter.

When they parted ways for that day, the Baron went immediately to prostrate himself beside the remains of his friend, the Count De La

Ferronnays, begging his assistance in obtaining what he had already prayed for when on earth.[82]

Ratisbonne's visit to Rome was finally drawing to a close. He said of that day:

> *On Wednesday, the 19th, I found myself with Lord Bussières once again. He seemed sad and his spirit broken. I was to leave on the 22nd for Naples, as I had reserved the ticket once again. In the meantime, I kept thinking about the invocation of Saint Bernard with a curious impatience. At midnight, between the 19th and the 20th of January, I awoke with a fright. I saw before me a large black cross without the body of Christ. I made an effort to part this image from me, but I could not avoid it. Wherever I turned, there it was before me.[83] Finally, I fell asleep again, and the next morning on awakening, I thought no more of it.*[84]

The following day, Alphonse stepped into a café in *Piazza di Spagna*, the Spanish square, and when he walked out at 1 p.m., Baron De Bussière's horse carriage happened to pass by. Alphonse agreed to climb in. De Bussières was on his way to the nearby Church of Sant'Andrea delle Fratte, to make arrangements for the funeral of his dear friend. He suggested that Alphonse wait for him briefly in the carriage outside, and then they could go on their intended stroll. But Ratisbonne preferred to go inside.[85]

When they entered the church, various decorations were set for the next day's funeral Mass. Alphonse asked about their meaning. The Baron shared that they were memorial decorations *"for a friend I have just lost, and whom I loved very much, De La Ferronnays. His sudden death is the cause of the depression of spirits you may have observed in me the last day or two."* He asked Alphonse to wait for him a moment, while he said a few words to one of the monks regarding arrangements for the funeral.[86] Alphonse decided to look around and walked along the right-side aisle, since he could not cross over to the left side, due funeral preparations blocking the central nave.

When the Baron returned only ten to twelve minutes later, he did not find Alphonse where he had left him. Ratisbonne recalled what happened:

> *The Church of Sant'Andrea seemed to me small, poor, and forgotten; I felt as if I were alone in it. There were no works of art to draw my attention. I walked about aimlessly, without seeing anything to arouse a thought. I can recall only that a black dog sprang into my path, bounding to and fro, impeding my progress ... but soon he was gone.*
>
> *Then the church itself seemed to disappear; and I saw nothing at all ... or I should rather say, O my God, that I saw one thing alone! How can I speak of this? No! Human words cannot even try to convey what is beyond expression...*[87]

The altar above which Our Lady appeared to Alphonse Ratisbonne in the Church of Sant'Andrea delle Fratte in Rome. In English: "Saint Andrew of the Grove," as the church used to be amidst a tree grove

When De Bussières returned to look for Alphonse, he seemed to have disappeared. After much searching, the Baron found him on the far-left side of the nave, on his knees. He approached his new friend, but wasn't heard; he touched him, but could not distract him; he touched him again, but still no response. He spoke a third and fourth time, and at last, Ratisbonne turned to him. With his hands joined and his face bathed in tears, he exclaimed, *"Oh! How the Count De La Ferronnays has prayed for me!"*[88] Of that moment, Alphonse recalled:

> *[At first], I didn't know where I was. I didn't know if I was Alphonse Ratisbonne or not. I was so entirely changed that I did not know myself. I seemed to seek to identify myself, and to fail in the effort. The most glowing joy pervaded my heart ...*[89]
>
> *When Mr. de Bussières recalled me to myself, I was in tears and unable to answer his question ... But I seized the Medal, which was on my breast, and I fervently kissed the image of the Virgin ... Oh! It had indeed been she! I was not able to speak; I did not wish to discuss what had happened; I felt within me something so solemn and so sacred as to require me to ask for a priest.*

The Baron lifted up his young friend, who was completely overcome by a heavenly visitation. *"I was quite petrified with astonishment,"* said De Bussières. *"I felt what people feel in the presence of a miracle ... I led him, or rather almost carried him out of the church. I asked him what the matter was, and where he wished to go."*

The conversion of Alphonse Ratisbonne

"Lead me," Alphonse replied. *"Lead me where you please ... After what I have seen, I obey."* Not being able to say more, he grabbed his Miraculous Medal, covering it in kisses, and amidst his sobs, said, *"How good is God! What a plentitude of gifts! What joy unknown! Ah! How happy I am, and much to be pitied are those who do not believe!"* Then he burst into tears at the thought of schismatics and unbelievers. The Baron brought Ratisbonne back to his apartment, and despite his repeated questioning, could get nothing from him but exclamations, broken by guttural sobs.

"Do you not think I'm crazy?" he asked the Baron. Then answering his own question, he said, *"No. I am not crazy ... I know well what I think and what passes within me ..."*

The Baron recounted: *"Ratisbonne declared that he would not explain himself until after he had obtained permission to do so from a priest ... 'for what I have to say can only be said when I am on my knees.' I took him immediately to the Church of the Gesú, to Fr. De Villefort."* Ratisbonne never could explain how, being left in one of the side aisles before the mystical experience, he was afterward found in the other, since the central nave was obstructed.

Fr. De Villefort, a Jesuit priest, welcomed Alphonse tenderly and tried to draw out an explanation from him. Ratisbonne took the Medal in his hand again and covered it respectfully with kisses, mingled with a shower of tears. Endeavoring to overcome his emotion, he exclaimed with joy, *"I have seen her! I have seen her!"*[90] He continued with difficulty, interrupted from time to time by sighs of emotion:

> *I had been in the church but a moment, when suddenly I was seized with an inexplicable fear. I raised my eyes; the whole edifice had disappeared from my view. All the light seemed as if it were concentrated in one chapel alone, and in the midst of this brilliance, upon the altar, there stood the Virgin Mary, as she is shown on the Medal—beautiful, glorious, and embodying at once both majesty and kindness. A force, which I could not resist, drew me toward her. The Virgin made a sign with her hand that I should kneel, and she seemed to say, "It is well." She did not actually speak to me, but I understood all.*[91]

Ratisbonne earnestly entreated that the apparition of our Holy Mother should be kept secret. He longed to bury himself in a Trappist monastery and occupy himself exclusively with the things of eternity. He also believed his family and friends would think him insane, and he preferred to escape entirely from the world and its opinions and judgments.[92]

Fr. De Villefort, however, considered it wiser not to yield to Alphonse's fear and desire for secrecy. Such a miracle, he felt, should be proclaimed for God's glory. Ratisbonne, in obedience, let his preference give way to the priest's discernment.

> *O my god! I who but half an hour ago was still blaspheming! I who felt such a deadly hatred of the Catholic religion ... But all who know me know well enough that, humanly speaking, I have the strongest reasons for remaining a Jew. My family is Jewish, my bride is Jewish, my uncle is a Jew. In becoming a Catholic, I sacrifice all the interests and all the hopes I have on earth; and yet I am not mad—everyone knows that I am not mad, that I have never been mad! Surely, they must receive my testimony.*[93]

In the brief testimony that Alphonse had shared, Fr. De Villefort and the Baron were particularly struck by one phrase that encapsulated a signal grace: *"She did not speak to me, but I understood all!"*

Ratisbonne had previously been completely ignorant of the truths of Catholicism. He had never read a book on the subject, and his hatred of the faith kept him from examining the object of his blasphemy. He judged without hearing, despised without investigating.[94] Then through a sudden apparition, he was gifted not only with Our Lady's presence, but with the infused knowledge of the mysteries of the Catholic religion. *"He spoke of the Real Presence,"* said the Baron, *"like a man who believed it with all the energy of his whole being; but this expression is far too weak ... he spoke like one for whom it was an object of direct perception."*[95]

Already, Ratisbonne was filled with a holy desire to see the kingdom of Jesus Christ extended throughout the world. Already, he was prepared to shed his blood to bear witness to his faith as a disciple, recalling the sufferings of the Roman martyrs he had seen represented on the walls of

St. Étienne le Rond. Initiated into heavenly secrets, he was strengthened in love by the favors that the Immaculate Heart of Mary had conferred upon him.

> *I am asked how I attained a knowledge of these truths, since it is well known that I never opened a religious book, had never read a page of the Bible, and that the dogma of original sin, which is either denied or utterly forgotten by the modern Jews, had never for a single moment occupied my thoughts ... The only explanation I can suggest is that I was like a man suddenly roused from slumber, or rather, like a man born blind, whose eyes are suddenly opened ...*
>
> *I saw before me the fearful miseries from which I had been rescued by the mercy of God; I shuddered at the sight of my innumerable sins, and I was stupefied, melted, almost crushed by a sense of wonder and of gratitude ...*
>
> *I think I state the precise truth when I say that I knew not the letter, but that I grasped fully the inner meaning and the spirit of the Catholic dogmas. I rather felt than saw them; and I felt them by the indescribable effects they produced within me. The scene of these wonders was within my soul; and their impressions, ten thousand times more swift than thought, ten thousand times deeper than reflection, had not only shaken my soul to its foundation, but had, as it were, turned it round and given it another direction, toward another end, and in the power of a new life ... I found myself in some way like a bare and naked being; my soul was a "tabula rasa" ... The world had no longer any existence for me; my prejudices against Christianity were no more; the instincts and preconceived notions of my childhood were gone, and had left no trace; the love of my God had so entirely ejected and replaced every other love.*[96]

With Alphonse in tow, Baron De Bussières left Fr. De Villefort to go and give thanks to God, first at the church of Santa Maria Maggiore and then at the Basilica of St. Peter.[97] *"Ah,"* Alphonse said to the Baron as he warmly pressed his hands, *"now I understand the love with which Catholics regard their churches and the piety which leads them to embellish and adorn them! ... How good it is to be here! One would long to never leave! It is no longer earth; it is the vestibule of heaven."*

At the altar of the Blessed Sacrament, the Real Presence of Jesus so overwhelmed Ratisbonne that he was on the verge of fainting and the Baron had to lead him away, so awful did it seem to him to appear before the living God with the stain of original sin upon him. He sought refuge in the chapel of the Blessed Virgin. *"Here,"* he said to the Baron, *"I can have no fear. I feel myself under the protection of an unlimited mercy."*

He then prayed with great fervor at the tomb of St. Peter at St. Peter's Basilica. Baron De Bussières shared with him the conversion story of St. Paul, and Alphonse shed abundant tears. He was astonished by the *"posthumous bond"*—the expression he used, which united him to Count De La Ferronnays. He had expressed a desire to spend the night beside his remains, saying that gratitude made it his duty. But Fr. De Villefort, seeing that Alphonse was exhausted with fatigue, had prudently advised him to remain there no later than 10 p.m.[98] In these hours following his conversion, Alphonse begged the Baron not to leave him alone; he felt that he needed a trusted friend into whose heart he could pour out the overwhelming emotions of such a day.[99]

By the following morning, the news of Ratisbonne's astonishing conversion had spread throughout the city. Romans were anxious to learn more about it, curious about the circulating rumors, wanting to see the new convert and hear his account. When Ratisbonne and Baron De Bussières were again at Fr. Villefort's rectory, a military general named Chlabonski was introduced to Alphonse and said, *"Sir, so you have seen the likeness of the Blessed Virgin. Tell me all about it."*

"The likeness, sir?" exclaimed Alphonse, interrupting him. *"It was no image, but herself that I saw; her real self, in person, just as I see you now!"*

At first, Ratisbonne had been able to see all of Our Lady of the Medal of the Immaculate Conception, then his eyes were not able to bear the brightness of the heavenly light. Three times he tried to look at Our Lady's face. Each time, he was unable to raise his eyes beyond her hands. Just as on her Medal, torrents of graces flowed from them, like rays of brilliant light. He said of this moment:

I could not express what I saw of the mercy and liberality in Mary's hands. It was not only an effulgence of light; it was not merely rays I distinguished. Words are inadequate to depict the ineffable gifts filling our Mother's hands and descending from them: the bounty, mercy, tenderness, the celestial sweetness and riches flowing in torrents and inundating the souls she protects.

Baron De Bussières had the consolation of entertaining in his own home the new son that heaven had just given him; the young Israelite remained there until the retreat that preceded his baptism. In turn, Alphonse had the comfort and need of a confidant, someone who understood him thoroughly and to whom he could communicate the emotions of his heart. It was when he was alone with the Baron that he could give full vent to his feelings:

Alas! When my excellent brother embraced Catholicism, and afterward entered into the ecclesiastical state, I, of all his relatives, was his most unrelenting persecutor. I could not forgive his desertion of our religion—we were at variance, at least. I detested him, though he had none but the kindest thoughts for me. However, at the time of my engagement, I said to myself that I must be reconciled to my brother, and I wrote him a few cold lines, to which he replied by a letter full of charity and tenderness.

One of my little nephews died about eighteen months ago. My good brother, having learned that he was seriously ill, asked that the child be baptized before its death, adding, with great delicacy, that to us it would be a matter of indifference, while to himself it would be a veritable happiness, and he hoped we would not refuse. I was infuriated at such a request! ... I hope, Oh! Yes, I hope that my God will send me severe trials, which may redound to His honor and glory, and convince all that I am moved by conscience.

The new convert also read to the Baron parts of his letters to his bride, to his uncle, to all the members of his family. Over and again, he reiterated many proofs, which he felt should convince the most skeptical:

The weightiest inducements, the most powerful interests, bound me to my religion. A man has a claim to be believed when he sacrifices everything for a conviction, which must have come from heaven. If all that I have stated is not rigorously true, I commit a crime, not only the most daring, but the most senseless and motiveless. In making my entrance into Catholicism by a sacrilegious lie, I not only risk my position in this world, but I lose my soul, and assume the frightful responsibility of all those whom my example could induce to do as I am doing. And what interest can I have in this?[100]

From the moment that Ratisbonne requested the Sacrament of Baptism, he was under the care of the Father General of the Society of Jesus, who laid out before him the significance of the request. He urged him to weigh well the sacrifices he would be compelled to make, the serious obligations he would have to fulfill, the unique conflicts that awaited him, and the temptations and testing that a step like this would bring—for trials would surely come. Pointing to a standing crucifix on his table, the leader of the Jesuit order said, "Once you have been baptized, you must not only adore this Cross, which was shown to you during your sleep; you must carry it, as well." Far from discouraging Alphonse, this strengthened his resolve.

Photograph of Alphonse Ratisbonne

When the priests assisting him had wanted to defer his baptism, Alphonse protested, "*The Jews who heard the preaching of the Apostles were baptized immediately, and you want to put me off, after I have 'heard' the preaching of the Queen of the Apostles!*" Remarkably, he felt an almost physical repulsion of original sin, which he could no longer bear.

> *I had come out of a dark pit out of a tomb, and I was alive, completely alive ... I thought of my brother Theodore with inexpressible joy. But how I wept as I thought of my family, of my fiancée, or my poor sisters. I wept indeed, as I thought of them whom I so loved and for whom I said the first of my prayers ... Will you not raise your eyes to the Savior Whose blood blots out original sin? Oh! How hideous is the mark of this taint, and how does it alter beyond recognition the creature made in God's own likeness!*

Alphonse's wish was granted, and the date of his baptism was set for January 30, only ten days after his visitation from Our Lady of the Miraculous Medal. Following a one-week retreat at the Jesuit Church of the Gesú in Rome, the ceremony began. Cardinal Patrizi, Vicar of Rome, performed Ratisbonne's Baptism, Confirmation, and first Holy Communion before an immense audience, including all the higher ranks of Roman society. The Abbé Dupanloup, a French priest and one of the great orators of the time, who just happened to be in Rome, offered a lengthy and beautiful address in Alphonse's mother tongue, celebrating the infinite mercies of God and Mother Mary's miraculous protection of a child from France.[101] Abbé Dupanloup described the end of the baptismal Mass with these words:

> *Mass was then said and during it, Ratisbonne received his First Holy Communion. He went before the altar to receive the Sacred Host. This last grace caused his soul to overflow. Until now, he had been entirely the master of his emotion, but at this point, he was unable to control the strange new feeling of happiness that welled up within him, and all at once, he burst into sobs and had to be supported, half-fainting, back to his place.*

Alphonse Ratisbonne

Many of the local Romans in attendance kissed their rosaries in grateful love to Mary Immaculate. They pointed out to one another the Baron who had given the Miraculous Medal to the young Jew: "He is a Frenchman," they repeated. "Blessed be God!"[102] Ratisbonne's joy was palpable. Surrounded by a crowd eager to see, hear, and embrace him, he received everyone's congratulations with bounding happiness. At the close of the ceremony, Cardinal Patrizi led the new convert toward the house of the Jesuits. Just after they had left the church, Alphonse could not constrain his emotion and hugged the Cardinal tightly to his chest. An eyewitness related that when Ratisbonne finally retired to the same cell he had occupied during the retreat, his first movement was to prostrate himself before his crucifix.[103]

The city of Rome was in a stir. News of this miraculous event spread quickly all over Europe, especially in diplomatic and financial circles, where the Ratisbonne, De Bussières, and De La Ferronnays families were widely known. Interest centered especially on the Miraculous Medal, which until this time, had only the approbation of the Archbishop of Paris.[104] When news reached Paris and the Rue du Bac, the Sisters of Charity rejoiced openly, and Sr. Catherine Labouré treasured Ratisbonne's radical conversion in her heart. It was a major triumph of the Medal of the Immaculate Conception.

Another great consolation came to Ratisbonne when he and the Baron De Bussières were granted an audience with Pope Gregory XVI, a dream of Alphonse's that he never thought could come true. The Jesuit Superior General led them to the Vatican Palace, where they knelt before the Holy Father and received his blessing. The pope welcomed them with paternal tenderness, and His Holiness conversed at length with them. Ratisbonne said of the visit:

> *He was so exceedingly kind as to take us into his chamber, where he showed me near his bed, a magnificent picture of my dear Medal, a picture for which he has the greatest devotion. I had procured quite a number of Miraculous Medals. His Holiness cheerfully blessed them for me, and these are the weapons I shall use in conquering souls for Jesus Christ and Mary.*[105]

The pontiff gifted Alphonse with a special crucifix and had a special Church commission established to study Ratisbonne's astonishing conversion. Cardinal Patrizi was placed in charge of the inquiry, and twenty-five sessions were held between February 17 and June 3, 1842. In the findings of the commission, it was:

> *... pronounced and declared, the 3rd of June 1842, that the instantaneous and perfect conversion of Alphonse Marie Ratisbonne, from Judaism to Catholicism, was a true and incontrovertible miracle, wrought by the most Blessed and powerful God through the intercession of the Blessed Virgin Mary. For the greater glory of God and the increase of devotion to the Blessed Virgin Mary, His Emminence deigns to permit the account of this signal miracle, not only to be printed and published but also authorized.*[106]

A painting of the Virgin of the Medal of the Immaculate Conception, commemorative of the apparition of the Blessed Virgin to Alphonse Ratisbonne, was also placed in the chapel of Sant'Andrea delle Fratte, where the miracle had taken place.[107]

Alphonse's baptism was followed by a second retreat, after which he prepared to return to France. He would come back to visit Rome many times and would converse with Baron de Bussières, now his brother in Christ.

Only a few days after stepping on French soil, Alphonse felt called to express his thanksgiving to God, mixed with an urge to obtain his family's conversion. To this end, he set about erecting a chapel under the invocation of Mary Immaculate in the Providence orphanage in St. Germain, Paris. The cornerstone was laid on May 1, 1842, and the sanctuary completed on May 1, 1844. There, Alphonse often mingled his

The commemorative painting of Our Lady of the Medal of the Immaculate Conception in the Chapel of Sant'Andrea delle Fratte, Rome

prayers with those of the Daughters of Charity and their cherished orphans, underneath a beautiful picture of the Immaculate Conception placed above the high altar.[108]

While in Paris, Ratisbonne made several attempts to converse with the unknown Sister of Charity who had been given the Miraculous Medal by Our Lady in 1830. But he never got beyond Fr. Jean Marie Aladel, Sr. Catherine Labouré's confessor, who respectfully told Alphonse that the visionary insisted on remaining unknown.

When Alphonse had first returned home, he tried to convince his fiancée, Flore, of the truth of what he experienced. Up to that time, Flore had been a deist, but now before his eyes, she became an atheist, a blow that stabbed him deeply in the heart. On his knees in the chapel he had built—and everywhere he went until the end of his life—Alphonse prayed for Flore's salvation. Ratisbonne's uncle, who had raised and treated him like his own son, disinherited him and revoked his partnership in the family's bank.

Alphonse trying to win over his fiancée, Flore, but she could not accept his conversion to Catholicism.

Ratisbonne had previously said of his family, *"There are few families so happy as mine: the affection that reigns among my brothers and sisters verges on idolatry; my sisters are so good, so loving and so lovely."*[109] However, their love for their kin did not prove, at first, to reach beyond secular Judaism. After Alphonse's conversion, the family disowned him.[110] The same animosity he had felt toward his brother, Théodore, was now directed at him.

But Alphonse never stopped praying. Having been nourished and enlightened by the Jesuits who welcomed him into the Catholic Church, he entered the Society of Jesus and spent many years serving as a Jesuit. In 1847, he was ordained a Catholic priest and took the name of Father Alphonse Marie. When his Jesuit superiors repeatedly turned down his request to go to China as a missionary, he said his true vocation was to be an apostle, *"not a sixth-form master,"*[111] a term referring to the job of teaching teenagers studying for advanced school-level qualifications.

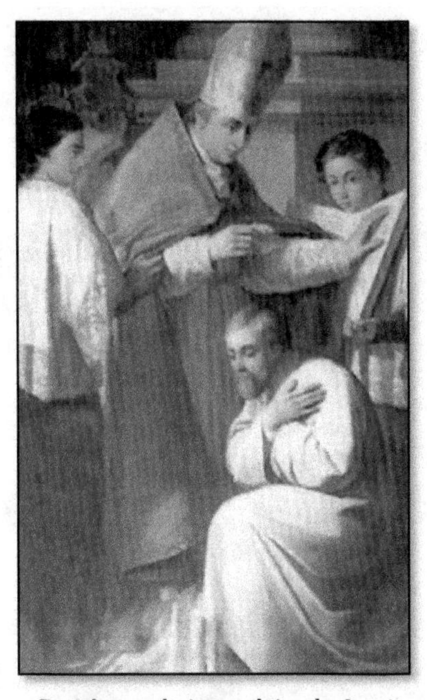

Ratisbonne being ordained a Jesuit priest and taking the name of Fr. Alphonse Marie

In 1852, with the permission of the Jesuit Superior General and of Pope Pius IX, Fr. Alphonse Marie left the Jesuits to join the work of his brother, Fr. Théodore. By that time, Fr. Théodore had founded the Congregation of Our Lady of Sion, an order dedicated to the conversion of the Jewish people. Fr. Alphonse Marie would write: "I recognized that the will of God in my Conversion and in my vocation to the priesthood obviously destined me to work for the salvation of Israel.[2]

Alphonse Ratisbonne (right) and his brother, Fr. Marie Théodore Ratisbonne

While his brother spread his congregation throughout France and England, Fr. Alphonse Marie moved to the Holy Land in 1855 to open a convent for the sisters of the congregation, and he never left. So great was Fr. Alphonse Marie and his brother's love for the people of their Jewish ancestry that they dedicated the remainder of their lives to the conversion and care of their souls.[112] In the Holy Land, Fr. Alphonse Marie would labor with a few companions from the Fathers of Zion for the

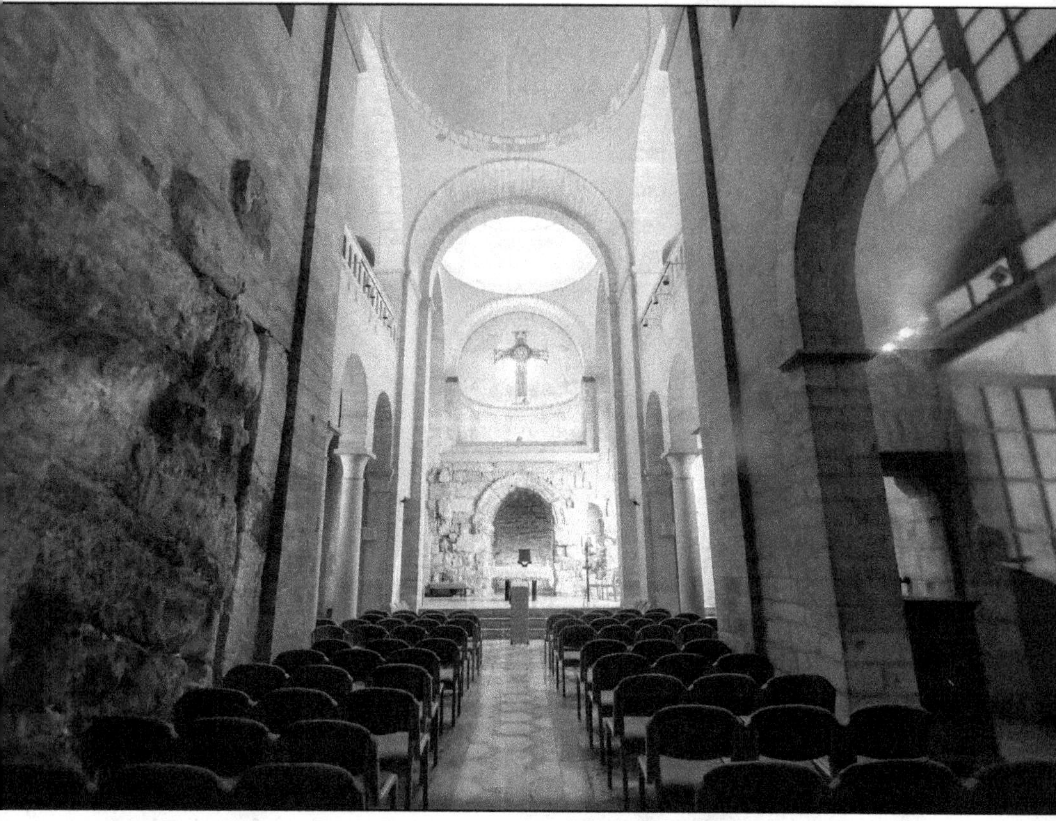

The Ecce Homo Basilica alongside the Convent for the Sisters of Sion, both built by Fr. Alphonse Marie in the Old City of Jerusalem

conversion of Jews and Muslims until his death. Among the converts of both priest brothers were a total of twenty-eight members of their own family.[113]

When Fr. Alphonse Marie first arrived in his ancestral homeland, he was deeply moved by the connections he saw to his Roman Catholic faith and his Jewish heritage, and desired to build a lasting presence of the Church in Jerusalem. One day, while walking along the Via Dolorosa, he met Mathias Marroum, a Greek interpreter and bureaucrat of the Austrian Consulate. Mathias showed him the ruins of Ecce Homo, which Turkish owners were ready to sell. Its land and ruins were believed to be the site of Pontius Pilate's residence, the Praetorium, with the very the stones of the pavement where Pilate showed Christ to the Jewish crowd, saying "Behold the Man!" ("Ecce Homo"). Alphonse quickly took advantage of the opportunity. Though he did not have the money to pay for it, no longer being a wealthy man, Alphonse strongly believed that he was directed and supported by the hand of God. He wrote:

> *In this sad and glorious work, everything is a miracle, and sometimes, when I am alone, I laugh out loud thinking of the singular instrument that God has chosen for such an enterprise.*[114]

Between 1858 and 1862, Fr. Alphonse Marie built the monumental Ecce Homo Basilica and a convent alongside it for the Sisters of Our Lady of Sion. On the convent grounds, he also built an orphanage and vocational school for girls, which the sisters ran.[115]

In 1860, Fr. Alphonse Marie built another Convent for the Sisters of Our Lady of Sion, together with a Chapel and another orphanage for girls. He set it on a hilltop in a village in the southwest outskirts of Jerusalem, called Ein Karem, the traditional place of Mary's visit to Elizabeth and the birth of John the Baptist. For boys, he erected the Orphanage of St. Peter, near the Gate of Jaffa bordering Jerusalem's Old City, as well as a school for mechanical arts. All of these institutions were open to children of every creed.[116] In 1874, Fr. Alphonse Marie began his last large project in Jerusalem's Rehavia neighborhood, the construction of the Ratisbonne Monastery.[117]

Ein Karem Convent Chapel

Many times, Fr. Alphonse Marie would voyage across the sea to Europe to raise the funds he needed. Of what he endured, he wrote:

> *It would fill volumes if it were necessary to tell of all the trips, letters, dangers, contradictions, fatigues, humiliations, and work that filled those first years. If I had not felt upheld with a special strength from on high, I would have lost courage a hundred times.*[118]

Photograph of Fr. Alphonse Marie with orphans in Ein Karem

By sheer force of character and an indomitable spirit, Fr. Alphonse Marie Ratisbonne, in the last thirty years of his life, established several institutions in the Holy Land. He died on May 6, in the month of Mary, 1884, the same year that his dear brother Fr. Théodore Ratisbonne died. Both were known for their exceptional virtues. [119] The last words that Fr. Alphonse Marie spoke were remarkable: *"All my wishes have been granted!"* At eight o'clock in the evening, as he lay in bed, motionless and silent, a visible light appeared and cascaded onto his face. He opened his eyes, which were now nearly blind. Those who witnessed this said that his eyes seemed full of life, and they expressed at first surprise and then delight. Fr. Alphonse Marie remained in ecstasy for three minutes.[120]

Perhaps Our Lady of the Medal of the Immaculate Conception, with her hands imparting rays of grace, had appeared to him once again. One thing is known for certain. She was there and eager to bring Alphonse Ratisbonne, her good and faithful son, to his eternal home.

ST. MAXIMILIAN KOLBE (1894-1941)

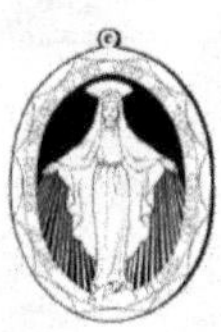

In 1917, during World War I, a Polish Conventual Franciscan friar named Maximilian Maria Kolbe was in Rome, working on his second doctorate of theology from the University of St. Bonaventure.[121] He walked outside to witness the celebration of the 200th anniversary of the founding of Freemasonry, the secret society that took upon itself the mission of ridding the world of Catholicism and Christian morals.[122] Brother Kolbe was compelled to watch as a long procession of Freemasons wound their way through the Eternal City toward St. Peter's Square.

Aware of their intentions, Br. Kolbe wrote of Freemasonry:

> *In the years leading up to the war, the masonic "sect"—disapproved of on several occasions by the Sovereign Pontiffs—governed in Rome, the capital of Christianity, with ever greater impudence. It did not even hesitate to brandish in the streets of the City during the festivities in honor of Giordano Bruno*[123] [(1548-1600) their chosen mascot, tried for heresy by the Roman Inquisition on charges of occultism and denial of several core Catholic doctrines], *a black flag showing the Archangel Saint Michael beneath the feet of Lucifer; still less did they hesitate to brandish masonic insignia beneath the windows of the Vatican. A reckless hand felt no repugnance in writing: "Satan will rule in the Vatican and the Pope will serve him in the uniform of a Swiss Guard," and other things of that kind. This mortal hatred for the Church of Jesus Christ and for His Vicar was not just a prank on the part of deranged individuals, but a systematic action proceeding from the principle of Freemasonry: "Destroy all religion, whatever it may be, especially the Catholic religion."*[124]

"Is it possible," thought Maximilian, as he stared at the Masonic procession passing by, "that our enemies should make such a display of force in order to defeat us, while we fold our hands on our laps and do nothing? After all, do we not have much more powerful weapons: can we not count on all of heaven, and especially on the Immaculata?"

Symbol of Freemasonry, the square and compass

Many years later, when asked to write about that time, Maximilian said:

> *When in Rome the Freemasons started coming out in the open daringly, flaunting their banners under the windows of the Vatican...the thought came of setting up an association committed to fighting Freemasonry and other servants of Lucifer. To make sure that such idea was coming from the Immaculata, I sought counsel from my spiritual director at the time, Fr. Alessandro Basile, a Jesuit, ordinary confessor of students at the College. Having obtained assurance from holy obedience, I decided to get down to work.*[125]

Freemasonry ongoing today: a Giordano Bruno meeting of February 17, 2022, in Rome in the outdoor square, Campo de' Fiori

Why would Maximilian look to Mary, "the Immaculata," as he affectionately called her, as the Church's key defender against the scourge of Freemasonry? This is explained by a visitation that happened shortly after he had made his First Holy Communion. It was a moment that would forever change him and bind him to his Mother in heaven. Growing up, his name was Raymond, and being a rambunctious, clever, and mischievous child, he had gotten into trouble. Wanting his own free-roaming chicken, he had been taking eggs from the kitchen cupboard and sneaking into the neighbor's henhouse to place them under one of the hens, hoping his eggs would hatch—until his mother found out.[126] "What will become of you?" she complained. The question struck the boy's heart deeply, and later that day, while praying before a statue of Our Lady in church, he asked her the same question, "What will become of me?"

The Blessed Mother suddenly appeared before him holding two crowns: a white crown for purity, and a red crown for martyrdom. She asked him if he wanted them, and Raymond responded, "Yes"—he wanted both the white crown and the red crown. After the apparition, his mother noticed a sudden and profound change in her boy: he was more meditative and solemn, and often found praying before a statue of Our Lady in their home.[127]

Raymond's attachment to Mother Mary also came from his family's strong religious convictions and fervent devotion to her. Raymond was the second of five children, two of whom died young and the remaining three of whom all became priests. In seminary, as in grade school, it was clear that Raymond had an extraordinary mind, excelling in all subjects and demonstrating a genius level in science, physics, and mathematics.[128] He also took a great interest all things military and in astrophysics. While studying in Rome, he even designed a spacecraft and tried to patent it.[129]

A photograph of Raymond, the young Maximilian Kolbe

At age thirteen, Raymond entered the junior Franciscan seminary with his older brother, and at sixteen, he thought of leaving to become a soldier to help save Poland from Russian control. But before giving anyone the news, his mother announced that she and her husband intended to enter religious life, since all their children were now in seminaries.[130] Raymond did not have the heart to change his

Where Kolbe would pray in Sant'Andrea delle Fratte

parents' plans, so he stayed on the road to priesthood. His mother went on to become a Third Order Franciscan,[131] and when World War I started, Raymond's father chose what his son had given up. He fought against the Russians for an independent Poland. In 1914, at the relatively young age of 43, Raymond's dad disappeared. There was evidence that he had been captured and likely hanged as a traitor by the Russians, a traumatic event for the twenty-year-old Raymond, who was now called by the religious name Maximilian, after his entry into the Franciscan novitiate.[132]

It was around this time, when studying in Rome, that Friar Maximilian stopped seeing humanity's prevalent struggle as a military one. He didn't like what he saw of the world; in fact, he saw it as downright evil. But the war in front of him, he decided, was a spiritual one. The world was bigger than Poland, and there were worse enemies than earthly ones. He would fight the battle, but with love, not the sword.[133]

To the left of the altar is a bust of Ratisbonne

On January 20, 1917, Br. Kolbe's superior in the house of Conventual Franciscan friars presented to the seminarians a meditation on the conversion story of Alphonse de Ratisbonne, involving the Miraculous Medal. Ratisbonne became a Jesuit priest after being not only a Jewish atheist, but also an anti-Catholic Freemason. This story inspired Maximilian so profoundly that he often visited the church of Sant'Andrea delle Fratte to pray before the very altar where Our Lady had appeared to and converted Ratisbonne.

Br. Kolbe believed he had discovered the perfect ammunition to fight the Church's enemies and save souls under the banner of Our Lady: the Miraculous Medal. Inspired, he decided to share with other friars his idea

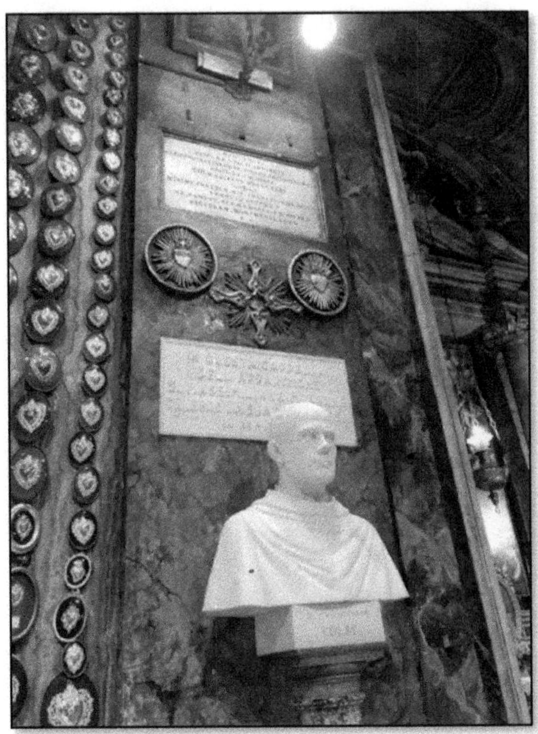

Could Br. Maximilian Kolbe have imagined that a bust of himself would one day be displayed to the right of the altar where he prayed in Sant'Andrea delle Fratte?

of concretizing his goal into an association called the Militia Immaculata (MI), "Army of the Immaculate One," the title being of no surprise.

As soon as he did so, Maximilian experienced his first severe symptoms of tuberculosis, the disease that would plague him for the remainder of his life. Kolbe recalled:

During a football game, blood started coming out of my mouth. I drew aside and lay down on the grass. Br. Girolamo Biasi, of blessed memory, took care of me. I spat up blood for quite a while. Soon after, I went to the doctor. I rejoiced at the thought that perhaps I was already nearing the end of my life. The doctor ordered me to go back [to the College] in a coach and go to bed. Medication could barely stop the flow of blood, which kept coming out.

After two weeks of doctor-ordered bedrest, Br. Maximilian was allowed to go outside.

When the clerics saw me, they cheered and were in high spirits, and brought me fresh figs, wine, and bread. Having had something to eat and drink, my aches and pangs ceased, and for the first time, I mentioned the idea of starting an association to Br. Girolamo Biasi and Fr. Iosif Pal, who had been ordained a priest before me, although we were attending the same year of theology. However, I stipulated that each of them should consult their spiritual directors first, to make sure that it was, in fact, God's will.[134]

It was. But the movement started off small and haltingly with six other friars who met, as Maximilian would explain…

…at night, in secret, in a locked, inner cell that was constructed by means of a temporary wall. In front of us there was a little statue of the Immaculata between two lighted candles ... For more than a year after that first meeting, the MI made no progress. In

fact, all kinds of setbacks piled up, to the point that members were uncomfortable even mentioning it among themselves. One of them even tried to convince the others that the MI was something useless.

Br. Kolbe is standing second from left with a few of the first members of the Militia Immaculata

It was then that, with wonderful signs of election, the Immaculata summoned to her side [to join the MI] *Fr. Antoni Głowiński, and ten days later, Br. Antonio Mansi, both victims of the Spanish flu. As for me, the condition of my lungs got worse: every time I coughed, I spat blood. That is when it all started to change. Having been excused from school, I took the opportunity to copy out the Program of MI ... In that early period of life of the Militia, our activity—besides private prayer—consisted in handing out Medals of the Immaculata, called "Miraculous Medals."*[135]

The Program of the Militia Immaculata, which Br. Maximilian wrote down while in his sick bed, was, in summary:

The original Statutes of the M.I.

"She will crush your head" (Genesis 3:15).
"Thou alone hast vanquished all heresies throughout the world" (from the Roman Breviary).

I. Object:

To work for the conversion to God of all men, be they sinners, heretics, schismatics, Jews, etc., in particular the Freemasons; and that all become saints, under the patronage and through the mediation of the Immaculate Virgin.

II. Conditions:

1. To consecrate oneself entirely to the Immaculate Virgin, placing oneself freely as a docile and generous instrument in Her hands.

2. To wear the Miraculous Medal.

III. Means:

1. If possible, to pray the following ejaculation at least once a day: "O Mary, conceived without sin, pray for us who have recourse to Thee, and for all those who do not have recourse to Thee, especially for the Masons and for all those who are commended to Thee."

2. To use all other valid and legitimate means for the conversion and sanctification of men, according to one's means, in the different states and conditions of life, as the occasions present themselves; this is entrusted to the zeal and prudence of each one. Particularly recommended, however, is spreading the Miraculous Medal.

N.B. These means are recommended only as suggestions and not as an obligation; not one of them obliges under pain of sin, not even venial sin. Our principal motive is to help the greatest possible number of souls to be united with the Sacred Heart of Jesus through the mediation of the Immaculata.

In his day, the words that Br. Maximilian used to describe non-Catholics were commonplace. Today, heretics would be called "fallen-away Catholics"; schismatics, our "Protestant brothers and sisters"; and Jews, our "elder brothers and sisters." But the message is the same—to bring them and all souls under the one true God, through Our Lady, and into one fold. The fact that Friar Maximilian Kolbe was in bed coughing up blood as he wrote down these statues, imagining a future of "Knights" conquering the globe for the Immaculata, is a testament to his indomitable spirit.

Fr. Kolbe's First Holy Mass was at Sant'Andrea delle Fratte (right side and ceiling view)

On April 28, 1918, approximately a year after his small, faltering association began, Br. Maximilian Kolbe was ordained in Rome to the Catholic priesthood. As the day of his ordination approached, Kolbe's health improved dramatically, and he attributed his strength to Our Lady's prayers and God's will. Of the Mass of Holy Orders, he wrote:

> *After the consecration I had tears in my eyes, but I needed to hold back my emotion to recite the prayers of the Canon with His Eminence the Cardinal. After ordination I went back home. What feelings! It should be acknowledged that the Immaculata has deigned to bring me this far. [...] On the following day, the 29th, I celebrated Holy Mass at the very altar where the Immaculata deigned to appear to Fr. Ratisbonne; what is more (against all hopes) the Mass of the Miraculous Medal.*[136]

That same year, Fr. Kolbe wrote down a prayer to his Mother in heaven, expressing his intimate love for His "Loving Mama," through words of total self-oblation.

June 1918:

> *May you be blessed forever, Lady and Queen, my Most Loving Mama, for you yet deign to think of me, so full of pride and self-love. At the Last Judgment, everyone will know that it was you who gave me everything, while I am nothing. May you be blessed forever, O Immaculata; therefore, I am all and totally yours, both soul and body; my whole life, my death, my eternity, belong to you forever; deign to do with me anything you please. I am fully satisfied. If it pleases you, deign to take me even this very instant. If you prefer later, then take me later. I am yours, my Loving Mother.* [137]

The Militia Immaculata soon experienced far-reaching and miraculous success. Three years after its first meeting in 1917, membership rose to over 400; by the beginning of World War II, the association had more than 500,000 members.[138] With its humble beginning of seven struggling friars, the Militia Immaculata continued to grow to where it stands today—on five continents and in forty-six nations. Every movement and organization within the Church, all religious orders, and individuals can join the MI, whose official membership is now over three million.[139]

Friars of the Militia Immaculata

Fr. Maximilian's overarching goal spurred him on with an intense resolve. "See, I am too fiery, am I not?"[140] he asked a fellow friar rhetorically, in an effort to push a matter forward.

M I
MILITIA OF THE IMMACULATA
"To win the entire world for the Immaculata and, through her, for the Most Sacred Heart of Jesus." - St. Maximilian Kolbe

Within the MI movement, he wanted Franciscan friars, wholly given over to Our Lord and Our Lady, to join in the thousands:

> *And when there will be 50,000 or more of us under the banner of the Immaculata, we will invite all our confreres in our Father St. Francis to "Climb higher," "closer" to St. Francis. And under the banner of the Immaculata, we will gather all those who profess the Rule of our Father St. Francis and will form an army that will wipe out the present kingdom of Satan. The leader of this army will be the Immaculata, and under her banner a great battle will be fought: we shall hoist her flags on the fortresses of the king of darkness. And the Immaculata will become the Queen of the whole world and every single soul, as foreseen by Blessed Catherine Labouré. And then we will keep good watch, so that no one tries to take our banners DOWN.*[141]

Fr. Kolbe was clearly aware that Saint Catherine Labouré, then still Blessed—not yet canonized, was known to have said: "Oh, how wonderful it will be to hear, 'Mary is Queen of the Universe ...' It will be a time of peace, joy, and good fortune that will last long; she will be carried as a banner, and she will make a tour of the world."[142]

Fr. Kolbe, third from left, pushing his holy agenda forward

Fr. Maximilian wanted to ensure that the Militia Immaculata would be under Our Lady's banner. For its emblem and shield, he chose the Miraculous Medal,[143] which all members were called to wear as an external sign of their consecration to Mary.[1] Fr. Kolbe gave specific instructions for the Medal's usage to those who joined the MI. The following is his exhortation and a warning that reveals the crown of purity Our Lady asked him to wear—a white crown that he never removed:

> *As soon as you receive your enrollment card with the Medal, you need to wear the Medal around your neck. When she revealed the Miraculous Medal, the Immaculata placed particular emphasis on that, and not without reason. To wear a Medal around one's neck, one must give up the plunging neckline that fashion now blithely promotes, despite the fact that it is the source of many a dishonest thought, of one's sinning and of the sinning of others. How many souls are damned because of it!*[144]

The Miraculous Medal should also be blessed by a priest, Fr. Kolbe said, "like any other medal."[145] And he advised that it never be taken off: "We wear it because the Immaculata urged us to do so and has promised her protection to those who do so. We sorely need such protection. Experience shows that when the devil wants to lead someone astray, the first thing he does is to make one find some pretext to lay aside one's Miraculous Medal. How powerful is the Immaculata's protection!"[146]

"Now in this era of the Immaculate Conception," he wrote, "the most Blessed Virgin has given mankind the 'Miraculous Medal.' Its heavenly origin has been proven by countless miracles of healing and particularly of conversion."[147] "The Miraculous Medal should be the weapon, the bullet, which the Knight of the Immaculata makes use of."[148] Fr. Kolbe imagined "that eventually there will no longer be a soul anywhere that does not wear the Miraculous Medal around their neck, penetrating hearts with more vitality through the living Word."[149]

Fr. Maximilian saw the Medal as an agent so powerful as to help usher in the Triumph of the Immaculate Heart of Mary:

> *Blessed Catherine Labouré—the fortunate nun to whom the Immaculata chose to appear in Paris, in the chapel of the Motherhouse of the Sisters of Charity and who, as an instrument of the Immaculata, has served to introduce and spread the Miraculous Medal everywhere—predicting the veneration with which the Immaculata would one day be recognized, exclaimed: "Oh, how nice it will be, how nice it will be to hear:* Mary is Queen of all the world![150] *And all her children repeat:* She is the Queen of each one of us."

[1] For a beautiful and efficacious consecration to Mary, please see www.MarysMantleConsecration.com.

What can we do to make this moment occur sooner?... Distribute her Medal wherever possible, even to children, so that they may always wear it round their necks, to the elderly and young people in particular, that under her protection they may have sufficient strength to reject the countless temptations and pitfalls that beset them in our times. Even to those who never come to church, who are afraid to go to Confession, who make a mockery of religious practices, who laugh at the truths of faith, who have immersed themselves in the mud of immorality, or who live in heresy outside the Church. Oh! to these it is absolutely essential to offer the Medal of the Immaculata and make them want to wear it, and at the same time, pray fervently to the Immaculata for their conversion. Some manage to give a Medal, even when someone does not want to accept it in any way. They sew one right into the person's clothing, hiding it well, then they pray, and the Immaculata, sooner or later, will show what she is capable of doing. The Miraculous Medal, then, is the bullet of the MI.[151]

Fr. Maximilian did not exhort others to do what he did not. Wherever life took him, he evangelized with the Medals. The same year of his ordination, on March 6, 1918, he jotted down, while passing through Marseille: "Everywhere, both in Czechoslovakia and in Austria, in Italy, and in France, everyone gratefully accepts the Miraculous Medal: even ticket collectors on trains, policemen, and other people. It means that the Immaculata can find a way to enter hearts. May this happen as soon as possible across the whole world!"[152]

On January 8, 1920, he wrote from Krakow to his friend, Fr. Petru Iosif Pal in Romania: "When you have an opportunity, I would like to ask you to let me have some Miraculous Medals. Of those that I received, I gave one to a Jewish woman, 4–5 to former Jews, one to a deaf-mute, and another to a poor sick man who was about to die."[153] On March 24, 1930, he wrote in his notebook, while stopping in Ceylon, Sri Lanka: "The medals promote benevolence. A Buddhist accompanies us; there is no one in church. Devotion of the inhabitants of Ceylon (Sri Lankans). A heavy gentleman gives me his address; on the streetcar; the Medals are very gladly accepted."[154] In the chapter that follows are consummate examples of how Fr. Maximilian Kolbe converted people to the Catholic faith through the Miraculous Medal, without apology and with love.

Friars constructing building in "The City of Mary"

Suffering from repeated headaches, one collapsed lung and the other permanently damaged, and sometimes coughing up blood, Fr. Kolbe pressed forward, undaunted in his mission. He founded two friaries honoring Mary Immaculate, both of which grew to become self-sustaining towns and centers of evangelization, where printed materials were published. The first, located near Warsaw, Poland, was called Niepokalanów, which translates, "The City of Mary." In 1922, there were only three members of Fr. Kolbe's friary dedicated to Mary Immaculate. In 1927, when Niepokalanów was founded, there were 18 brothers; in 1939, there were 762.

Friars living in Niepokalanów, the City of Mary

By 1936, Niepokalanów had an airport, medical facilities, and even its own fire brigade. The friary produced a daily newspaper and monthly magazine called "Rycerz," *The Knight of the Immaculata*, with circulations of 230,000 and over one million, respectively. (To give perspective, this is about four times more than the current paid subscription to *The Washington Post*).[155] The

Fr. Kolbe with the fire brigade of The City of Mary

The City of Mary, Warsaw, Poland

first cover of the magazine indicated its uncompromising mission, with Mary Immaculate framed by two large swords impaling snakes on books labeled "heresies" and "freemasonry."[156] All through the night before the magazine went into the stands, Fr. Maxi-milian had all of the workers gather in prayer before the Blessed Sacrament, The magazine still has a circulation of around 45,000 in Poland, and is available around the world in several languages.

Following Fr. Kolbe's wishes, *The Knight of the Immaculata* does not have a cover price and is made available to people who cannot afford a subscription.[157] As he once said, "If we do not have Catholic media, our shrines will one day be empty."

Friars working in a printing press in The City of Mary

OPŁACONO RYCZAŁTEM.

Rok I. STYCZEŃ 1922. Nr. 1.

Redakcja i Administracja:

KLASZTOR OO. FRANCISZKANÓW, PLAC WW. ŚWIĘTYCH 5, KRAKÓW (POLSKA).

Prenumerata na 1-szy kwartał: w Polsce 70 Mp. — w Ameryce 25 cent. am. — w Danji 1 Kor. d.
Numer pojedynczy: 25 Mp. (10 ct. am. — 40 öre.)

In 1930, after making a pilgrimage to the Chapel of the Miraculous Medal on Rue du Bac in Paris, Fr. Kolbe travelled to Japan, where he established a second monastery in Nagasaki, active to this day. *Seibo no Kishi*, meaning "Knight of the Immaculata" in Japanese, became the first Catholic monthly magazine in Japan and continues to be published.[158] He was advised not to purchase the land on the side of a hill in a poor area, where the monastery stands, but, as in many of his writings, he placed his plentiful trust in Mary. Defending his action, he wrote the following letter:

> *I read: "Help! Help!" but if the action was approved by Holy Obedience, you can rest fully assured that it is the Will of God and therefore also of the Immaculata. And if everything were to fall through later or if the superiors themselves at a later time were to change their minds, one may be completely untroubled about previous actions, for they conformed to Obedience then. That is, I think, the principle. [...] Since the land was in fact quite cheap and very well suited to an expansion, I bought it. Thus only the will of the Immaculata was accomplished. Therefore, the Immaculata too, from now on, must take care of it, for she cannot be illogical. One may thus remain unperturbed in spite of consequences. We have already moved, on May 16, to the Japanese Niepokalanów, that is, Mugenzai no Sono [or "Garden of the Immaculata"]. The current address is as follows: Mugenzai no Sono, Hongochi, Nagasaki, Japan. In addition, yesterday the whole debt for the land was paid off. It is on the side of a magnificent mountain...*[159]

Fr. Kolbe writing at his desk in Nagasaki, Japan

As providence would have it, because the monastery was on the side of the mountain facing away from Nagasaki, it was spared the devastation of the atomic bomb that the United States dropped on that city on August 9, 1945.

Fr. Kolbe's obedience and trust did not mean that everything always went smoothly, however. Yet he viewed even difficulties as a sign of the care of his Most Loving Mama. Such faith is shown in a letter he wrote to Fr. Antonio Vivoda in Padua, dated April 19, 1932:

One month has already rushed by and I have still not finished this letter—just imagine. Meanwhile, the dollars that I wanted to send you have "disappeared"; so I am not sending any money ... however, the Immaculata will take care of it—right? I understood from your letter that difficulties were not lacking; this is also the sign that it belongs to the Immaculata ...[160]

Again, in a letter to Fr. Florian Koziura in Japan on May 30, 1931, as in many of Fr. Kolbe's writings, his plentiful trust in God and Our Lady shines amidst strife and struggle. In sharing the various ways he was soliciting funds to purchase a printing press for the monastery in Japan, he engenders confidence:

Fr. Kolbe's winning smile during a friendly game of chess

Ah! I pleaded for money, but was told that there is no hope of getting something from the Congregation. Possibly only from the Holy Father directly. [...] However, the Immaculata knows everything: let us remain, therefore, completely at peace![161]

After establishing the Franciscan monastery in Nagasaki, Japan, Fr. Maximilian traveled to Malabar, India, where he sought, unsuccessfully, to found another monastery. In 1938, after health issues brought him back to Poland, Fr. Kolbe started a radio station, Radio Niepokalanów, and he set his sights on one day building a motion picture studio.

Then came World War II. In 1939, the Nazis occupied Poland. Fr. Maximilian's priestly life expanded from spreading the Gospel and devotion to the Immaculata to include helping his fellow Poles survive. He is credited with saving the lives of at least 2,000 Jews in his friary in Niepokalanów.

But Fr. Maximilian Kolbe was labeled as a "dangerous person." In 1941, the Nazis plundered all of Niepokalanów's buildings and destroyed the friar's printing equipment. Fr. Kolbe tried to restore whatever he could and even printed one more magazine.

Fr. Kolbe's establishment of a monastery and printing press in Nagasaki, Japan

On the morning of February 17, 1941, Fr. Kolbe dictated to Brother Arnold his most comprehensive essay on the Immaculate Conception, as the perfect "complement of the Holy Trinity," echoing the unique expression he used for his greatest inspiration and his life's love: The Immaculata. Moments later, at 11:50 a.m., he was arrested by the Gestapo. As he was being taken away with four other friars, he is famously known to have said, "Courage, my sons. Don't you see that we are leaving on a mission? They pay our fare in the bargain. What a piece of good luck! The thing to do now is to pray well, in order to win as many souls as possible."[162]

The plundered buildings of the printing press at Niepokaloanów

Fr. Maximilian Kolbe, at age forty-seven, ended up in the concentration camp of Auschwitz, prisoner #16670. Priests were treated with intense brutality, worse than the other prisoners, and Fr. Maximilian, still struggling with tuberculosis, was given extra work. While the Nazis' primary targets were Jews, eighty percent of Catholic clergy in Poland had been deported to death camps by 1939.

In Auschwitz, survivors reported that Fr. Kolbe calmed and comforted the other prisoners, and frequently gave them his meager food rations. When he was beaten by the guards, he never cried out. Instead, he prayed for his tormentors. A doctor in the camp, Rudolph Diem, recalled, "In view of the general animal instinct of self-preservation so evident in everyone else, his desire to sacrifice himself for others surprised and intrigued me." A young Jewish boy in the camp remarked, "He dispensed love and nothing but love."

Sometimes, under the cover of night, Fr. Kolbe would move from bed to bed and gently ask, "I'm a priest. Can I do anything for you?" Other times, prisoners would crawl across the floor at night to be near the bed of Fr. Maximilian, to make their confessions and ask for consolation. He whispered to those who came to him in despair, "Hate is not creative; only love is creative."[163]

In July of 1941, a man from Fr. Kolbe's barracks vanished, and as a punishment, the Deputy Camp Commander, SS-Hauptsturmführer Karl Fritzch, selected ten men to be starved to death in Block 13, to deter further escape attempts. Adding to the absurdity of evil, the man who had disappeared was later found drowned in the camp latrine.

The Auschwitz camp photographs of Franciszek Gajowniczek

One of the men selected, Franciszek Gajowniczek, exclaimed in anguish, "My poor wife! My poor children! What will they do?" Upon hearing his cry, Fr. Kolbe stepped forward and offered his life in exchange for the man who had a family. The commandant agreed. This meant that Fr. Kolbe would be led into the starvation cell.

A Polish man, Bruno Borgowiec, assigned to work in Block 13, gave an eye-witness testimony of the final days of Fr. Kolbe and his fellow prisoners, left cold and naked in a cement cell. If any of them approached the door asking for food, he recounted, that poor prisoner was immediately kicked in the stomach by the SS men. Falling backward on the hard floor, he was instantly killed, or he was shot to death.

"Fr. Kolbe bore up bravely, he did not beg and did not complain but raised the spirits of the others ... Since they had grown very weak, prayers became whispers. At every inspection, when almost all the others were now lying on the floor, Fr. Kolbe was seen kneeling or standing in the

The starvation cell in Auschwitz where Fr. Maximilian Kolbe was killed with a poisonous injection

center of the cell, as he looked cheerfully in the face of the SS men. Two weeks passed in this way. Meanwhile, one after another, they died, until only Fr. Kolbe was left." The authorities then decided to kill the Knight of the Immaculata with an injection of carbolic acid. "Fr. Kolbe, with a prayer on his lips, voluntarily gave his arm to the executioner."[164] On that day, the 14th of August 1941—the eve of the Feast of the Assumption of Our Lady—Fr. Maximilian Kolbe received his red crown.

Let us let ourselves be carried by the Immaculata; she will think of everything and take care of all our needs, of the soul and of the body. Let us give every difficulty, every sorrow to her, and have confidence that she will take care of it better than we could. Peace then, peace, much peace in an unlimited confidence in her...Above all, never let yourselves be troubled, never be frightened, never fear anything.[165]

—St. Maximilian Kolbe, canonized by Pope John Paul II on October 10, 1982

ST. MAXIMILIAN'S MIRACULOUS MEDAL CONVERSIONS

The primary reason that St. Maximilian Kolbe insisted the Miraculous Medal be shared and worn was for conversion. In his letters and writings for publication, the saint would sometimes share his stories of evangelizing through the Miraculous Medal, in order to inspire and guide Catholics to do the same.

In cases when others might throw up their hands or never even attempt to bring a soul to the Lord, St. Kolbe would roll up his sleeves and zero in. The most hardened soul in the room was not to be ignored. Holding Our Lady's banner high, St. Kolbe went to battle for souls, trusting that she would act through her Medal and far more than he. The accounts below by the hand of a great saint offer a treasure trove of insight and instruction for how to bring people to Christ through Our Lady.

WITHOUT "CLEARER EVIDENCE"

Article in Rycerz Niepokalanaj (The Knight of the Immaculata magazine[166])

January 1924, pp. 3-4

"Well, that one will never convert," complained a dying woman. I was trying to comfort her as best I could, telling her that our Blessed Mother can save even obstinate sinners, so her husband still had a chance to convert. He came to see his wife shortly afterward. An altercation with the driver announced his arrival. A young clerk, formerly a university student in law, but rather backward when it came to religious issues; he was, in a word, the very opposite of what would be commonly called "a progressive liberal." In my capacity as hospital chaplain, I somehow thought it my duty to take care of that poor soul, as well. In my spare time, therefore, I was glad to talk with him on issues of faith. However, his closing argument was: "I need clearer evidence." I gave him Fr. Morawski's book *Wieczory nad Lemanem*, well known among intellectuals. However, as I could see, he did not read it much. In fact, he carried around with himself immoral publications. When I spoke to him with greater resolve, he openly declared: "Father, I am a heretic." I could see he did not want to educate himself and despised good reading. What to do at that point? I entrusted the whole matter to the Immaculata, through the intercession of the virgin of Lucca, Gemma Galgani, who had died a few years before in the odor of sanctity and was already well known all over the world.[167]

Sometime later I was told that he would be leaving the next day, and shortly after that, I was informed that his departure would take place precisely the following night. To complicate matters, one of his relatives had come who was staying with him. In order to find him alone, I let him know that, later, I would be busy, so if he wanted to meet me it would have to be right away. And he did come. Starting from afar, I led our conversation into Confession, but the topic proceeded with difficulty. Suddenly, the door opened and his relative barged in, telling him to hurry up because it was time to go to the train already. So, after a brief goodbye, they left. I was left alone... "How will this matter end?" I said to myself. I knelt down and with few words, but fervently, I pleaded to the Immaculata through the intercession of Gemma. All of a sudden, I got an inspiration; I went out into the hallway. There I found his relative. "Excuse me," I said turning to him, "I have one more issue to attend to with this gentleman."

"But certainly, please go ahead," he said. My "heretic" was already leaving the room with his suitcase, so I invited him to my room. As soon as the door was shut, I took a Miraculous Medal and gave it to him as a souvenir. He accepted it out of kindness. Then I once again proposed that he go to Confession. "I am not prepared. No! Absolutely not," was his only reply. Yet...in that very moment he fell to his knees, as though he had been forced to by a higher power. His Confession began. And he wept like a child... The Immaculata had won even without "clearer evidence." Honor to her forever![168]

LETTER TO BROTHER IOAN GÂRLEANU

1 Rome P.b.J.C.
Krakow, September 25, 1919
Br. Ioan Gârleanu

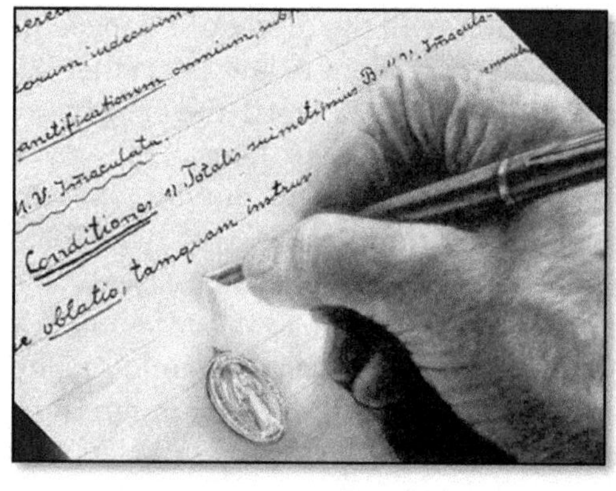

Dearest Friend,

I do not know if you received the letter that I sent you about a month ago through the Nazareth Sisters; anyway, now is a good time to write to you to again. I have not yet told you about the discussion I had on the train between Rome and Bologna with a Jew regarding the Catholic religion: that the Messiah already came, that the Messiah is Jesus Christ, the Blessed Mary is a virgin, that the afterlife exists, and so on. In the end, he promised to carry the Miraculous Medal that he had received from me, and he asked me to pray for him; and as I had recommended, he also said that from that day forward, he would pray to the Blessed Virgin Mary, so that if she was Immaculata and the Mother of God, she would convert him. You of the MI, pray for him on occasion, and if you have the opportunity, go visit him and show him some good books so that he might have the opportunity to deepen in the Catholic religion, which he seriously wants to know (he is a fabric merchant). [...]

On the train I met another person who openly denied the existence of hell, but confronted by the evidence of reasoning—I was invoking the

Immaculata continuously—he admitted in front of everybody the unsustainability of his argument, and accepted the Miraculous Medal, saying that it was the first religious sign that he had carried in his life. I am sorry that we live far apart. We exchanged addresses. Glory to the Immaculata.

We must fight; outside the College, the opportunity to act frequently occurs, even though there must always be time for prayer. How is the MI in the College? Here, there are 13 of us that have enrolled in the Militia of the Immaculata. In our short prayer, each one is free to add to the intentions what he wants, and this is done quite frequently among us. It would be a nice thing every month, for example, if the particular intentions for which we want to pray to the Immaculata were organized on cards (even anonymous, or with the initials of the people we want to be converted) and placed in a box at the feet of the Immaculata (for example, the statue), as a sign that we entrust her with them, and at the same time that everyone understands (once and for all) that, in praying our short prayer ["O Mary, Conceived without Sin Pray for Us Who Have Recourse to Thee"], we want especially to remember those whom we entrust to her, so that the Immaculata intercedes for them.

Moreover (if it seems appropriate to the Rector), sometimes it would be convenient to work through and examine together the following topics: the relationship of the Immaculata with our Order and with sinners; the method of discussion with nonbelievers, schismatics, etc.; the nature and spirit of the MI, etc.; the story of the Miraculous Medal, etc. Consider whether and to what extent you would like to do this, or rather, whether and to what extent the Immaculata would want this from you.

[...] I end this letter full of errors in every respect, since I have run out of space, and I hear the clock striking 10:15 p.m.; tomorrow morning I have to send the letter. Please send me your reply via the priest who lives in Via Mascherone 55, or one from the Polish college who must come to Poland.

Unworthy in our Father St. Francis,
Br. Maximilian M. Kolbe MI[169]

LETTER TO BROTHER GIROLAMO BIASI

Zakopane, January 25, 1921
Praised be Jesus Christ!
Br. Girolamo Biasi, Rome
[one of the first seven members of the MI]

My Dear Brother,

I write little because I am sick and still feverish. I continue to stay at the hospital as both chaplain and patient, and I will stay here until May (if the treatment goes well). In spite of everything, I am very well, because the life of MI members consists in letting oneself be guided where, when, and how our Heavenly Mother likes. Obedience, therefore. Our Holy Mother, sent me here; what more could I wish? I do not work on the MI anymore; that is, I do not manage it, because the Fr. Provincial [Alojzy Karwacki] told me to let everything go, even the leadership of the MI, and to concentrate on my health and getting better; so this is what our Mother wants. [...]

Not far from here there is a nursing home of university students, which is infamous for being irreligious. The Immaculata brought me among them by means of a clever subterfuge of mine, "sicut serpentes" [Mt. 10:16]: I held a series of apologetic but open discussions, so that each person could speak his mind. The fiercest objector said with conviction, at one point, "Logic is a game of words," and on another, "I cannot believe"; but after he failed a test on the philosophy of Schopenhauer, and with another book in his hand, he surrendered to the grace of God through the Immaculata, from whom he received the Miraculous Medal, and to his colleagues' amazement said publicly that he wanted to confess—and immediately did so. He has written to me now (because he went back home), commending himself to my prayers. Pray for him, too, and make others pray.

In the same house I was glad to baptize a Jew (a university student as well) and administered him the last rites (he was very ill). The day after, his mother came with his brother and made a scene, but it was too late. I also gave him the Medal. That is why I have incurred the hate of almost all the students, and when one of the women students asked the house doctor to call me (this was after I had been there already), he said that other priests might be invited, but this one [Fr. Kolbe], no, because he was

a. . . missionary. What a great offense, right? I would be very happy to die for such a fault.

When the Bolshevik prisoners were here (there were 40 of them), I requested some apologetic books (in Russian) from the library of the MI of Krakow, and I lent them those books, designating one of them to be the librarian. Several [prisoners] were persuaded that Jesus Christ had founded one Church, and some of them were persuaded that the head of this Church and the successor of St. Peter is the Pope. All accepted the Miraculous Medals; two Jews who were among the Polish soldiers guarding them also took Medals. Now everyone has left, and the Russians said, "When we look at this Medal, we will remember that it was given to us by a priest." Let us pray also for them and for that poor and wretched house of university students, that the Sacred Heart, to which it was consecrated by a lady [Jadwiga Bieniecka] who stays there, reign also in that place. I gave the Medal also to a Jewish woman who promised to keep it with respect: when we meet, she greets me with a deep bow.

Beyond this, I try to lend the books to the irreligious, and incite fervor in the good people, e.g., by means of "The Mirror of Spiritual Joys," or with some good words. Here are some of the actions that our Immaculate Mother is willing to do through me now. Meeting workers or others, if it is opportune and convenient and prudent, I stop and talk about the inadequacy of socialism, of the irrationality of nonbelievers, and about the happiness and truth in the practice of religion and faith. This is a bundle of news, which you can also communicate to Fr. Paolo [Moratti] and those who want to know how someone from the MI could work even without organizations. [...]

I would have much to write, but I cannot, or else my fever will go up. Let us pray, suffer, and work for the love of Jesus through the hands of the Immaculata. Soon—in Paradise.

Your very affectionate brother,
Maximilian M. Kolbe MC MI[170]

"THE VICTORIES OF THE IMMACULATA"

Article in Rycerz Niepokalanaj (The Knight of the Immaculata magazine[171])
August 1924, pp. 148–150

A few days ago, a lady came to me asking me to visit a sick person who does not want to go to Confession. Fr. H. had already been there to see him, and he had then sent that lady to me because his attempts had failed. "Does the sick person pray to the Virgin Mary by reciting at least one Hail Mary a day?" I asked.

"I suggested it to him, but he told me he does not believe in the Divine Mother."

"Please bring him this Medal," I said, handing a Miraculous Medal to her. "He may accept it out of respect for you and let you place it around his neck."

"He will accept it to please me."

"Good, bring it to him and pray for him; for my part, I will try to pay him a visit." And she left...

In the meantime, I met Fr. H., who told me: "I went to see that sick man as if he were an acquaintance of mine, yet I was quite unsuccessful. Would you please go there? I should add that the patient is an educated person. He has just completed his university studies in forestry."

Not long after that, that lady came back to report that the patient was getting worse and that his parents, who were there beside him, were hesitating to call for a priest because they were afraid that would upset him. I thought to myself: "The sick man does not want a priest, nor do his parents. Is it worth going, then?" Nonetheless, I did go, even though deep down in my soul I was tormented by doubts about the success of my visit. My only hope was the Medal that the patient was already wearing. I recited the Rosary along the way. After a difficult journey, I rang the bell at the hospital door. I was swiftly taken to the department for infectious diseases, where the patient had been admitted. I sat next to his bed and got into a conversation. I asked him about his health, but soon our conversation turned to religion. The patient voiced his doubts, and I tried to clarify them. During our conversation I noticed a blue string around his neck, which ran through the Medal. "He is wearing the Medal," I thought, "so the game is won."

Suddenly, the sick man turned to me and said: "Father, could you please come to the point?" "So you wish to go to Confession?" I asked. In response, a flood of tears shook his emaciated chest... His sobbing lasted for a good minute... When the patient had subsided, his Confession began. After receiving the Viaticum and Extreme Unction, the patient wanted to show me his gratitude by embracing and kissing me. Despite the danger of infection, I willingly gave him the kiss of peace. Honor to the Immaculata for this victory!!!

Next to him there was another sick person. At the hospital they had told me that he was near death also, yet he was not considering Confession. This is why I commended him to the Immaculata, through the intercession of Blessed Thérèse of the Child Jesus, who was recently beatified.[2] The next day I returned, ostensibly in order to visit the first sick person, but in fact wanting to see the other patient, as well. I sat down next to the first, but in the meantime, I had urged the nurse to ask the other if he wanted to take advantage of my presence. The sick man had not noticed me. So he answered impatiently: "The doctor says that I will be recovered in a week, and I am being bothered by a priest here." Without losing heart at such display of unwillingness on the part of the sick man, I struck up a conversation with him and sat beside his bed. Since the patient was stubbornly putting Confession aside, I took the "bullet" that we use in the Militia, namely the Miraculous Medal. The patient asked: "What is it?" I explained briefly. He kissed it, agreed to have it put around his neck, and... Confession began. Eternal thanks be to the Immaculata for such loving and merciful victories. M. K.[172]

[2] Sister Thérèse of the Child Jesus was beatified by Pope Pius XI on April 29, 1923, and canonized on May 17, 1925.

LETTER TO A READER OF RYCERZ NIEPOKALANEJ (THE KNIGHT OF THE IMMACULATA MAGAZINE)

Zawiercie Grodno
September 12, 1924

Dear Sir,

Please do not be discouraged by the fact that coldness and malice prevail, because the grace of God, through the Immaculata, is stronger. If they do not want to pay for Rycerz, then we will gladly send it for free, and the Immaculata will provide for finding the offerings for that place from somewhere else. The purpose of the Militia of the Immaculata is to conquer the whole world, all hearts and each person individually, for the Queen, not only of Heaven, but also of the Earth. To give true happiness to those poor unfortunates who seek it in the ephemeral pleasures of this world, this is our aim. You have to conquer even Zawiercie for the Immaculata: this is your place of battle. We must fight with our prayer, good example, and cordiality, with great gentleness and kindness, as a reflection of the Immaculata's goodness.

Those people who seek happiness outside of God are unhappy people who, wrapped up in sin and vice, are chasing happiness, looking for it where there is none and where they cannot find it. In addition, the Medal of the Immaculata is the weapon, or rather the bullet, that serves every Knight of the Immaculata. Someone could be the worst of all creatures, but if he agrees to wear the Medal, it must be given to him. We gladly send as many as are needed for free. You must pray for him, and at the right opportunity, through a kind word, try to bring him slowly to love the Immaculate Mother with all his heart, to take refuge in her in all his difficulties and temptations. He who begins to pray sincerely to the Immaculata, after a short time, especially on her feast day, will be persuaded to go to Confession. There is much evil in the world, but let us remember that the Immaculata is more powerful, and "she shall crush the head of the serpent" [cf. Gn. 3:15]. [...] May the Immaculata give you strength while you fight for her.

Br. Maximilian M. Kolbe[173]

ST. MOTHER TERESA OF CALCUTTA (1910-1997)

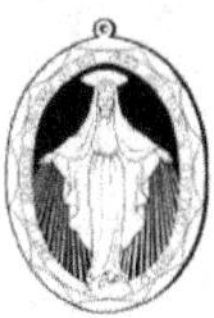

Mother Teresa at 18, born Anjezë Gonxhe in Albania

If St. Maximilian Kolbe was the foremost proponent of the Miraculous Medal in the first half of the twentieth century, another canonized saint would take up the charge in the second half: Mother Teresa of Calcutta. With the spread of the Missionaries of Charity, the order she founded in Calcutta, India in 1950, St. Mother Teresa played a key role in extending the graces of the Miraculous Medal to a world hungry for God.

In Mother Teresa's remarkable life of self-abnegation and radical charity, the Albanian-born nun, who lived from 1910 to 1997, personally handed out, by her own count, over forty thousand "Medals of Charity," as she often called Miraculous Medals.[174] Today, her sisters who minister around the globe in service to the poorest of the poor, wearing their signature white Indian saris with blue striped edges, continue to hand out 1.8 million Medals every year.[175]

Wherever Mother Teresa travelled, she attracted people of all ages and nationalities, whether poor or rich, Catholic or atheist—all wanted to meet this "living saint." To each of them she would give a Miraculous Medal—or two, or many. Mother Teresa would kiss the Medal before pressing it into someone's palm and briefly but firmly clasp their hand, as a clear expression of her love. This tiny present would create a crack in the armor of a person's isolation and egoism, and sometimes make miracles. Mother Teresa often showed how the Medal should be worn around the neck and explained that we can always trust the Mother of God, for she protects us—miraculously if necessary.[176] When it came to priests, she encouraged them to propagate the sacramental and to be devoted to Our Lady of the Miraculous Medal.[177]

Carrying her signature bag of Medals, Mother Teresa would often ask when visiting the poor and sick, "Where does it hurt?" Then taking a Miraculous Medal into her well-worn hand, she would gently press it onto that area on the person's body. "Let Our Lady kiss where it hurts," she would say. To engage the person in prayer of the heart, she would add, "Repeat after me: 'Mother Mary, be a mother to me now.'" As she repeated the phrase, stressing the word *now*, she would caress the area of the person's pain with the Medal beneath her fingers.

Several stories reveal how creative and confident Mother Teresa was in the power bestowed on the Miraculous Medal, when it was used in faith. She met several times with Pope John Paul II, with whom she shared a warm and profound mutual respect. During one of her visits to Rome, while referring to her Missionary of Charity's leprosy centers in India, she stated to the pontiff, "Holy Father, we need a saint for our lepers!"

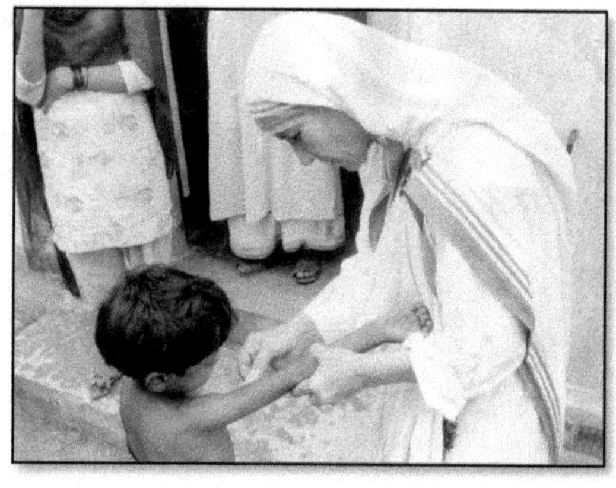

When the pope asked her whom she had in mind, she named Fr. Damian of Moloka'i. Fr. Damian was a Belgian missionary who lived among the lepers abandoned to live out their days in deplorable conditions on the Hawaiian island of Moloka'i. He cared for all of them until he himself was diagnosed with the disease, which took him to his grave in 1889.

With her characteristic candor and courage, Mother Teresa asked Pope John Paul II, "Do you know him, Holy Father?" He nodded in the affirmative. "Well then, why wait? When will you declare him a saint?"

But the pope was not able to do so because the Church required three certified miracles initiated by Fr. Damien's intercession from heaven; and while the priest's cause for canonization had begun, a miracle hadn't yet been documented. So, Pope John Paul II referred Mother Teresa to Cardinal Palazzini, the Prefect of the Congregation for the Cause of Saints, a distinguished papal advisor and known in the Vatican for his lively intelligence.

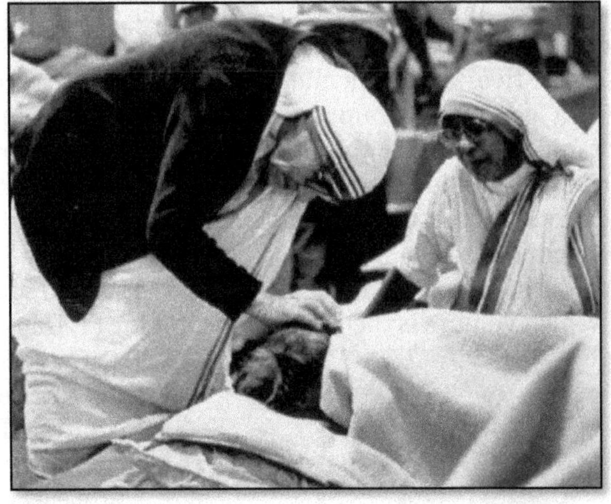

Accompanied by the entire staff of the Congregation, who followed him when they learned that Mother Teresa was in their midst, the cardinal introduced himself: "Mother Teresa, the Holy Father has sent me to you. What can I do for you?" Mother Teresa asked for Fr. Damian's canonization, and Cardinal Palazzini explained the problem with her request.

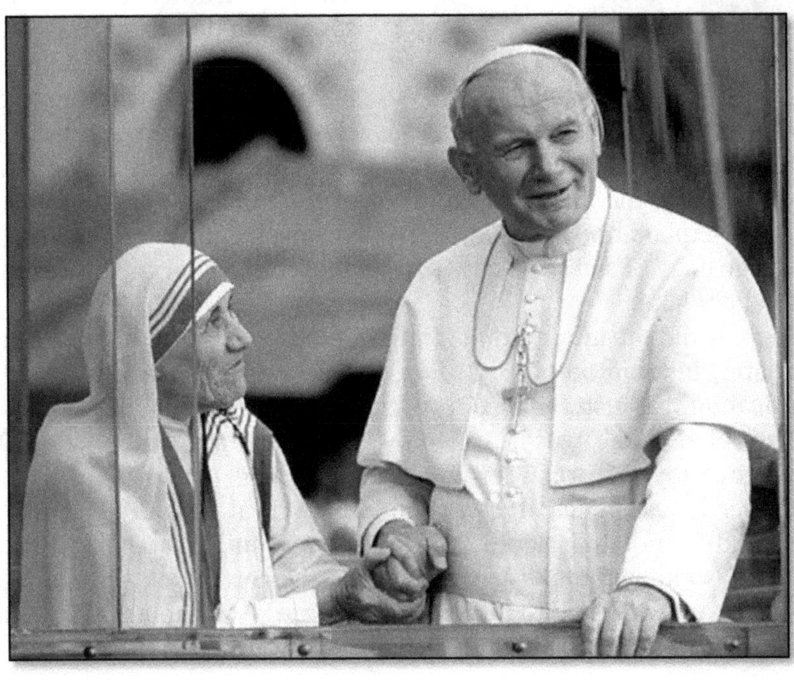

"That may be so," replied the diminutive Mother, "But in Holy Scripture it says... "She then held up a Bible and opened it to chapter 15, verse 13 of the Gospel of St. John. Reading to the startled cardinal, she said, "'Greater love has no man than this, that a man lay down his life for his friends.' And that's exactly what Fr. Damian did. Isn't he already canonized by the Bible? What are we waiting for?"

The two went back and forth, with Mother Teresa suggesting it would be a good opportunity to change the four-hundred-year-old Church tradition requiring three miracles, and the cardinal suggesting it would be easier for her to pray the miracles just happen. Cardinal Palazzini went on to show her the mountains of documents, hundreds of thick tomes, which had already been accumulated for Fr. Damian's beatification process. The determined Mother Teresa asked him three separate times, "Which volume is the most important for Fr. Damian's beatification?"

Gesturing toward the long and tall rows of archives, the cardinal continued to explain the complexity of the canonization process. But Mother Teresa only wanted the answer to her question. Finally, Cardinal Palazzini asked a staff member to climb a ladder to reach an old, heavy leatherbound book covered in decades of dust. As he began to describe why this particular book was important, she reached deep into her blue-gray carrier bag and pulled out a Miraculous Medal and a piece of sticky tape. Fastening the Medal to the front of the tome, she interrupted the cardinal's explanation and said, "So, we've done the most important thing. We can go now!" Then she left, with a perplexed cardinal and his bemused staff in her wake.

Not only did the miracle that Mother Teresa prayed for happen a short time later, but the number of documented miracles necessary for his beatification was also reduced from three to one. Fr. Damian de Veuster, the hero of Moloka'i, was beatified by Pope John Paul II on June 4, 1995, with an overjoyed Mother Teresa in attendance.[178]

Mother Teresa of Calcutta was confidently creative with her use of the Medal and did not limit her expectations to any single category of graces. She was also known to toss a Medal onto a property of choice in some of her "real estate deals" with the Virgin Mary, as the Missionaries of Charity continued to expand, or to kiss the Medal with a prayer intention attached.

"I was in London," she once shared. "We needed a house. The sisters recommended to me that it would be opportune to buy a certain house for many reasons. But there lived a tough man who did not want to sell the house at all. I told the sisters: 'Have faith. Tomorrow, I will go to see him, and I will kiss the Miraculous Medal of the Virgin, and then everything will be easier.'"

The next morning, Mother Teresa paid the man a visit. "At noon, that man came to see me and told me: 'I want to sell my house, and I also want you to be the ones to buy it.' The price was exact to ours. See, this is the work of the Virgin Mary."

In 1992, Mother Teresa decided to open a house in Baghdad, a city torn apart by Iraq's recent war with the United States. She searched for a suitable location, and when she found it, she left a Miraculous Medal on the premises. After a short time of waiting in faith, the property was hers, and there she founded a much-needed home for disabled and malnourished children.[179]

For Mother Teresa, "planting" Medals was a special kind of prayer and an act of faith. She would toss the Medal, which had to fall on and touch the ground. Then she prayed and waited in confidence for the desired result.[180] If it was the will of God, her prayer was answered through the intercession of the Blessed Virgin.

Gift-giving was another one of Mother Teresa's favorite prayers in action. Although the gesture of giving away a Miraculous Medal was something she did for tens of thousands of people, it was often perceived as a singular, unforgettable, and somehow miraculous event in the life of the recipient. Her tiny gift brought to life her famous quote: "Don't look for big things, just do small things with great love. The smaller the thing, the greater must be our love."[181]

Tony Magliano was one such person who considered receiving a Medal from Mother Teresa a uniquely formidable experience. The syndicated columnist on issues of peace and justice began an article in the *National Catholic Register* with the words: "Allow me to share with you one of the high points of my life—a short, yet deeply enriching encounter with a saint." He wrote of how when he was working with the Missionaries of Charity sisters, caring for HIV/AIDS patients at their Gift of Peace house in Washington, D.C., one of the sisters had told him, "Mother is coming." Elated, he immediately asked to join the reception.

A few days later, Mother Teresa got out of a car and walked toward the Gift of Peace house, and the sisters affectionately ran to greet their Superior General. Magliano stood back, waited, and watched. Then all who were present stood in a circle, while Mother Teresa with her head humbly bowed, walked up to each person and silently placed a Miraculous Medal in his or her hands.

When she approached Tony Magliano, he greeted her with the common word for hello in the Hindi language of India: "Namaste"; and she responded in kind. Then he asked her how she was doing in the only other Hindi words he knew, "Kaise hain?" ("How are you?") She replied, "Theek," which means "Okay." And that was it! This brief encounter with Mother Teresa and the Miraculous Medal, he said, "continues to spiritually enrich my life to this day."[182]

A helicopter pilot from Czechoslovakia was also profoundly touched by a similar incident. After disembarking from a helicopter ride from Bonn to Prague, the saint started handing out candies, chocolates, and her "Medals of Charity." First, she gave her gifts to the two pilots. One of them, visibly moved by this simple gesture, had tears in his eyes. "You know," he said, "I've been flying this helicopter for twenty-five years, with many great and famous people as passengers, but I have never received anything from anyone. Today was the first time: Mother Teresa gave me chocolate and a Miraculous Medal."[183]

In the 1990s, a seminarian named Brian Caulfield caught word that Mother Teresa would be visiting her Missionaries of Charity sisters in the South Bronx in New York, so he took the subway with friends and ended up waiting in a long line with everyone else who had learned of her coming. Eventually, he was directed to an auditorium and stood on a stage crowded with huddled nuns, priests, and laypeople from all walks of life. Suddenly, he felt a wrinkled yet strong hand grab his own and press something into his palm.

"God bless you," said the familiar voice he had only ever heard on television. Looking down, he saw Mother Teresa's tiny five-foot-tall figure, nearly dwarfed in the crowd surrounding her. Her hazel eyes, which looked up at his, were clear, engaging, and inviting. Brian held her hand and said, "Thank you, Mother."

On the subway ride home, a woman with her small boy, who was sitting next to Brian, noticed the Miraculous Medal now hanging around his neck alongside his crucifix. He explained to the mom how he had just received the Medal from Mother Teresa. "I could use a miracle," she said. Brian then expressed that he would like to give the Medal to her. She refused out of courtesy, but her little boy had no trouble accepting: "I'll take it!" As a seminarian seeking God's will, Brian felt called to keep only the grace of the moment for himself, so he took the Medal off of his chain necklace and gave it to the boy.

After arriving home, Brian shared what happened with friends, who marveled that he gave away what would likely become a second-class relic. The following day, as Brian was on his way to pray in front of an abortion clinic, an elderly parishioner from his parish crossed the street to tell him, "I saw Mother Teresa yesterday in the Bronx. For some reason, she gave me two Miraculous Medals. I tried to give one back, thinking it was a mistake, but she waved me away, saying, 'God will tell you who to give that one to.' Well, I was just praying as I was walking down the street, asking God who I should give the Medal to, when I saw you and thought that, as a seminarian, you should definitely have this Medal from Mother Teresa."[184]

"Uncle Hugo," a great devotee of Mother Teresa, provided the Miraculous Medals that she would hand out.

As with others who distribute the Miraculous Medal with great confidence wherever they go, Mother Teresa rarely knew in what ways its graces would travel. The full fruits of her giving were hidden in the mind of God, but she often got to see firsthand the special graces obtained—and to share the stories with others:

> *One of our doctors, an eye doctor, works a lot with our poor and is very kind to them. He dedicates two hours a day to them. During those two hours, he does not attend to anyone but the poor—everything for free: consultation, glasses, medicine.*
>
> *One day, he told me, "Mother, I have a malignant cancer, and in three months, I will die." He went to the U.S.A. and was told the same thing. He returned to Calcutta, and his family took him to the hospital. I went to visit him at the hospital. I took a Medal of the Miraculous Virgin, and I asked him to say, "Mary, Mother of Jesus, give me health." I asked his family to also pray to Our Lady. Despite being a Hindu family, they had to pray with great faith.*
>
> *After three months, at which time he was supposed to die, the eye doctor came to my house and said, "Mother, I went to the*

doctor, he examined me with X-rays, he did tests and found no trace of cancer. A true miracle!" He now wears a chain around his neck with the Miraculous Medal.[185]

Mother Teresa was well aware that on the Miraculous Medal, Our Lady of the Immaculate Conception is portrayed as not only distributing graces, but also crushing the serpent under her foot. With Medals in hand, Mother Teresa was never afraid to approach top political leaders, even when they were committed enemies of the Church. She knew the risks.

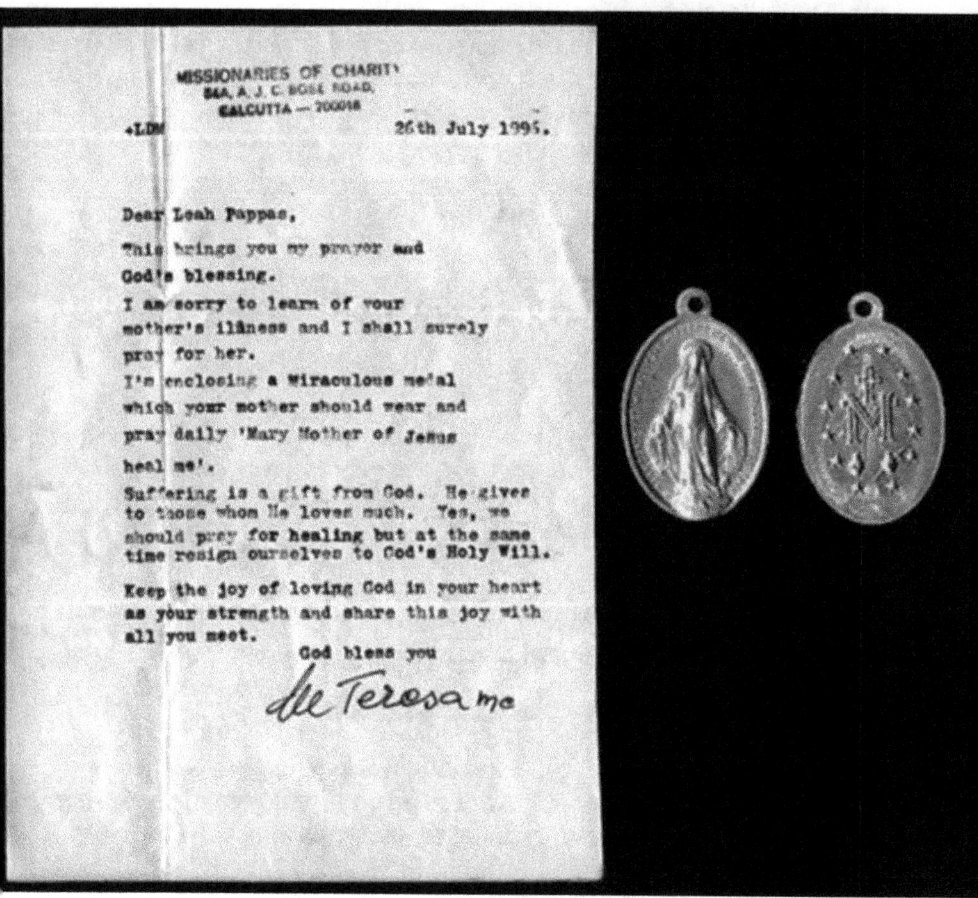

MISSIONARIES OF CHARITY
54A, A. J. C. BOSE ROAD,
CALCUTTA — 700016

+LDM

26th July 1995.

Dear Leah Pappas,

This brings you my prayer and God's blessing.

I am sorry to learn of your mother's illness and I shall surely pray for her.

I'm enclosing a Miraculous medal which your mother should wear and pray daily 'Mary Mother of Jesus heal me'.

Suffering is a gift from God. He gives to those whom He loves much. Yes, we should pray for healing but at the same time resign ourselves to God's Holy Will.

Keep the joy of loving God in your heart as your strength and share this joy with all you meet.

God bless you

M Teresa mc

She knew of failure. She knew that her Medal of Charity, ready to dispose great graces, could not soften the heart of someone who stood dead against what those graces sought to achieve; yet she never wavered in her one-track mind of doing good in faith.

When the saint traveled to Managua, Nicaragua in 1986 to request permission to build a house for her Missionaries of Charity, the country was governed by a Marxist authoritarian regime under the Sandinista ruler, President Daniel Ortega. As of this writing, the same leader is back in power and harshly persecuting the Catholic Church in Nicaragua. Ortega agreed to Mother Teresa's request to speak with him. She walked into a large, windowless room, alongside another sister and her friend and translator, Fr. Leo Maasburg.

On a raised platform at one end of the room stood a long desk, and behind it sat four masked men holding large machine guns. President Ortega sat between them. Before Mother Teresa could say a word, the dictator proceeded to give a fiery half-hour lecture about the legitimacy of the Sandinista guerillas, who in 1979 had overthrown the Nicaraguan government—which he demonized at length. With this victory, Ortega had maneuvered his way into the ruling junta and won the presidency in 1984.

Ortega's rant left him trembling with rage, and the silent air was thick with friction. Mother Teresa cut through it with the words, "Yes, yes, works of love are works of peace." The official translator clearly did not want to say this sentence. A dangerous tension mounted, and the sister decided to step in and say Mother Teresa's words in Spanish, which spilled out in a trembling voice.

Nicaraguan President Daniel Ortega on the far left speaking with Mother Teresa. Her bag of Miraculous Medals is on the table. She always came prepared.

Without waiting for the dictator's response, Mother Teresa stood up and asked him, "Do you have children?"

"Yes, seven."

"Do you have a wife?"

"Yes."

Then she took several Miraculous Medals out of her bag. After kissing them, she extended an arm up toward Ortega, who reached across the desk to receive each Medal from her, one at a time: one for his wife, one for each of his children.[186] "And here's one for you," she said, handing him the last Medal. "You need it!" Then she motioned with her hands that he should wear it attached to the cord already around his neck. With one holy stroke, Mother Teresa and the Blessed Mother had lifted the mood in the room from diabolical to delightful. Permission was granted the very next day for the Missionaries of Charity to have their first house in Nicaragua.[187] (In 1988, two years after Mother Teresa's visit, she was able to open the Immaculate Heart of Mary Home in Granada, Nicaragua, where the Missionaries of Charity sisters took in abandoned and abused adolescents and helped them reintegrate into society. In the Nicaraguan capital Managua, the sisters opened a nursing home for the elderly, a nursery for poor children, and started providing remedial education for at risk minors.)[188]

The town of Cuapa, 152 kilometers to the east, happened to be celebrating the Marian apparitions that had occurred there in 1980 and were subsequently approved by the Church only two years later. From Managua, Mother Teresa travelled in a police-led caravan along treacherous roads to attend the festival two-and-a-half hours away. When she arrived at the diocesan sanctuary built where the apparitions of Our Lady of Cuapa occurred, she was greeted by the visionary Bernardo Martínez, a humble sacristan who later became a priest. In honor of the Virgin's appearance there, Mother Teresa took off her sandals to walk barefoot on the holy ground. Bernardo proceeded to tell her the story of the apparitions, as she wrote it down, word for word.

Mother Teresa meeting the visionary of Our Lady of Cuapa, Bernardo Martínez, on the far left, during her visit to Nicaragua in 1986

A picnic was being held in a large meadow surrounded by dense woods. Several bishops supportive of the apparitions were present, including Cardinal Dario Castrillón Hoyos, the President of the Central American Bishops' Conference, and Cardinal Bravo, the Archbishop of Managua.

Mother Teresa, joining the picnic, sat down in the meadow amidst a large crowd. Suddenly emerging from the surrounding trees, one hundred heavily armed soldiers walked briskly toward the peaceful believers. Stopping just a few feet away, they pointed their guns threateningly at the mass of people, evidently intending to break up the gathering. Immediately, Mother Teresa stood up and walked directly toward them. Pausing in front of their menacing gun barrels, she looked down and started rummaging through her bag.

Then she proceeded to walk up to every single soldier, one at a time, and give him a Miraculous Medal. To make their hands free to receive them, the soldiers had to sling their weapons around their necks, which they did almost automatically. After Mother Teresa made sure each of them had a Medal, she invited them to eat with everyone at the picnic. The soldiers declined, but the picnic continued in peace, in spite of their presence.[189]

A few days later, the Missionaries of Charity were invited to live in Managua, and with the help of Cardinal Bravo, found lodgings in that city. In Nicaragua, they also ended up running a home for the elderly, a school for at-risk students, and a daycare center for impoverished families.[190]

Prior to the November 2021 election, President Ortega and his wife, Vice President Rosario Murillo, seized a fourth term of communist dictatorial power after imprisoning his seven leading opponents.[191] Desiring to rid the country of the Catholic Church and its opposition to his manner of governance, Ortega began an unprecedented persecution of the country's Catholic leadership.[192] Sadly, in June 2022, he expelled the Missionaries of Charity, who had graced Nicaragua with their good works for thirty-four years.

There is another true tale of twists and turns that revealed the daring and daunting nature of Mother Teresa's devotion to the Miraculous Medal. It all began when she heard that Pope John Paul II, in response to Our Lady's request in Fatima that Russia be consecrated to her Immaculate Heart, planned to consecrate the world on March 25, 1984, the Feast of the Annunciation. The pope asked that all bishops perform this consecration in their own dioceses; but who would do this in Russia? There was no Catholic bishop in the very country that Our Lady expressly mentioned she wanted to have consecrated.

Always a whirlwind of ideas and initiative, Mother Teresa prayed and had her sisters petition God for the conversion of Russia. Secretly, she sent rosaries, holy cards, and Bibles into what remained a communist country until 1991. She also prevailed upon her friend of thirty-three years, Bishop Pavol Mária Hnilica, S.J. (1921-2006), to buy bags of Miraculous Medals, which he had blessed by Pope John Paul II. She then had the Medals sent in "covert operations" to Russia and other communist countries.

But that wasn't enough. Mother Teresa possessed a fervent desire to see Russia belong to the Blessed Mother. The stakes were high. Unless that country was consecrated to the Immaculate Heart of Mary, and the Catholic faithful followed her request of the Five First Saturdays, as the Blessed Mother had said in Fatima, Russia would spread her errors and entire countries would be annihilated.

Mother Teresa formulated a plan. Communist Russia was inaccessible to religious communities, especially Catholic missionaries, and almost every form of faith and practice was persecuted and violently suppressed. She asked Bishop Hnilica if he was up for a dangerous mission: a Miraculous Medal needed to be brought into the Kremlin, the seat of

Russia's political power. It would be a gesture of consecration of sorts. She asked him to be the bold protagonist of her fearless plot.

Bishop Hnilica felt he was the least suitable person to attempt such a feat. He was considered "enemy number one" of the Communist Party in countries behind the Iron Curtain, and had even been condemned to death in Czechoslovakia because of his anti-communist activity. "Entering into the Soviet Union," he said, "was impossible for me, but I couldn't say no to Mother Teresa. Being with her, it was easy to get infected by her enthusiasm and courage." The bishop accepted the risk without any reassurance or hope that he could complete the task.

Pope John Paul II with Bishop Pavol Mária Hnilica, S.J.

With her secret agent on board, Mother Teresa set out to organize a James Bond-style adventure. She wanted Bishop Hnilica to be inside the Kremlin, praying in union with John Paul II at the precise moment that the pope recited the consecration in Rome. The bishop had the mission of leaving a blessed Miraculous Medal in the heart of Russian communist power. She felt that the journey needed much prayer in preparation. For an entire month, she and Bishop Hnilica and his chosen comrade for the mission, Fr. Leo Maasburg, prayed that their plans would work. She also asked the Missionaries of Charity to pray for a "particular intention," but no one in the world knew what they were up to.

Through her contacts in the Russian Consulate in Calcutta, Mother Teresa was able to somehow finagle a visa for the bishop, who was able to get two airline tickets. Bishop Hnilica and Fr. Maasburg were to go incognito as two tourists traveling from Calcutta to Rome via Moscow, where they would stop to visit the city's museums. At that time, a person could stay up to eight days in Moscow with a Soviet travel visa. Fr. Maasburg was not entirely optimistic either, letting slip before the trip: "Eight days in Moscow, twenty years in Siberia."

On March 23, 1984, Mother Teresa accompanied the two brave clergymen to the airport. Deeply moved, Mother Teresa grasped the hands of Fr. Maasburg and Bishop Hnilica, as they said their goodbyes. Then she gave her personal rosary to the bishop.

The pair flew on an Aeroflot jet via Bangkok to Moscow, and were the only ones to disembark at the Soviet capital in the middle of the night. At customs, security officers poked through their luggage and found not only

Bishop Hnilica's suspiciously large pectoral cross and several Vatican coins, but also a bag of one hundred Miraculous Medals. Bringing religious articles into the country was strictly forbidden.

Mother Teresa of Calcutta with Fr. Leo Maasburg

Thinking quickly, the bishop gestured in a friendly manner and asked the customs official if he liked the Medals and might want one. The man looked around furtively, then nodded and grabbed one. The priests were allowed to proceed further, until the bishop showed his passport to a soldier at the immigration desk. The soldier looked up at him suspiciously and began to ask him a slew of questions. Bishop Hnilica's heart began to race. He didn't let the soldier know that he understood Russian, so he began to speak in Italian, the language of his passport. The soldier didn't understand Italian and was visibly wary. He left his post to begin an investigation.

Extreme panic gripped the bishop, as the soldier picked up a phone at another desk and began dialing different numbers from the guardroom. At five o'clock in the morning, no one was answering. The minutes passed like hours as Bishop Hnilica waited in the outdoor immigration office in 23-degree weather. Shivering with cold and fear, he could already see himself deported to Siberia.

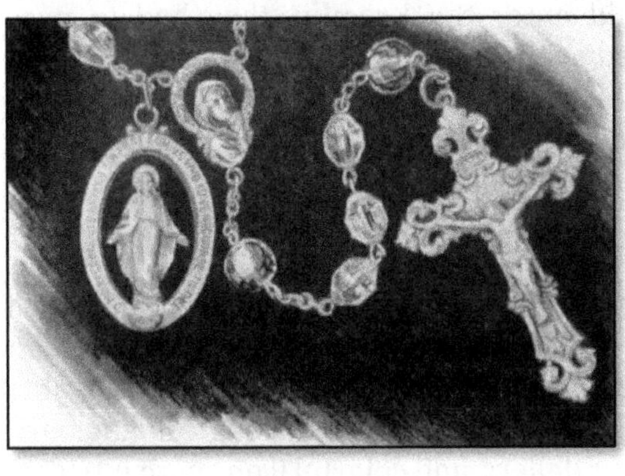

Pulling out Mother Teresa's rosary from his pocket, with a trembling hand, he secretly started to pray. Mother Teresa had said that his journey would be accompanied by her constant prayers, so he turned to God, saying, "Lord, let Your will be done! But remember that it is Mother Teresa who has sent me here."

Another hour passed. The solder, increasingly annoyed because he couldn't get ahold of anyone, asked the bishop once again if the passport was his. He nodded yes. The soldier stamped the passport reluctantly and finally let the bishop go to join a worried Fr. Leo, who had already made it through immigration and was praying intently in a corner of the airport.

On March 24, the vigil of the Feast of the Annunciation, the day Pope John Paul II would perform the act of consecrating the world to the Immaculate Heart of Mary, the two clergymen were providentially invited by Russian embassy staff members to join a group of diplomats on a tour of the churches in the Kremlin—exactly where Mother Teresa wanted them to be. The Kremlin, a citadel from ancient days, extended over an area of sixty-nine acres and was filled with ancient royal palaces and Moscow's former centers of worship.

The Cathedral of the Annunciation on the southwest side of Cathedral Square

The plan was that Bishop Hnilica and Fr. Leo would pretend to be tourists visiting the five churches of the Kremlin's Cathedral Square, which had been transformed into museums after the Bolshevik Revolution of 1918. They would enter and celebrate Mass in the cathedral of the Orthodox Patriarchs, the cathedral dedicated to the Annunciation, on the vigil of that very feast day.

Before the two clergy could enter the Kremlin, they had to pass through the inspector stationed at the entrance. But the guard objected to the small leather case in the bishop's breast pocket, which happened to contain their tiny Mass kit. The leather case would have to be handed over. Then Bishop Hnilica pulled out a Miraculous Medal, handed it to the guard, and gave a nod. They were suddenly waved through, Mass kit included.

During their tour, the priests passed through and admired the Church of the Archangel Saint Michael, the second largest in the Kremlin, and then they entered the Cathedral of the Annunciation. For a time, they were able to suspend their fears, as they admired the breath-taking religious art, majestic columns, glistening chandeliers, and colorful icons with intricate gold relief. Many tourists had flooded the Kremlin that day, which calmed their nerves and helped them feel more protected.

In his guidebook, Bishop Hnilica saw that there were thrones in the Cathedral of the Annunciation where the tsar, the tsarina, and the Orthodox patriarch of all Russia used to sit during their religious ceremonies. The bishop and Fr. Maasburg walked up to the patriarch's throne and decided that there, at the epicenter of Russian power prior to communism, they would celebrate Holy Mass.

Leaning against the throne, with tourists passing by, the priests began. They hid their photocopied prayers of the Mass and the pope's text of the consecration of the world, behind the large Communist Party newspaper *Pravda*—which in Russian means *The Truth*. Bishop Hnilica had the words of consecration in the Mass memorized and entered so deeply into prayer that the world around him disappeared. "At a certain point," he later recalled, "I found myself alone, and I began concentrating on celebrating Mass secretly. I carried out the consecration by memory using a piece of bread and some wine, which I had brought with me. This was an intensely moving and religious moment. A Mass had not been celebrated in this place for seventy-six years."

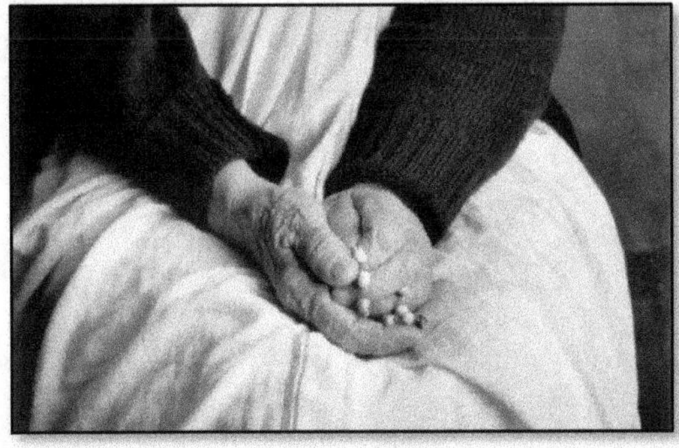

After their clandestine Mass and the prayers of the consecration of Russia and the world to Mary's Immaculate Heart, Bishop Hnilica decided that a Miraculous Medal should be hidden under the Russian patriarch's throne. Noticing a little crack in the wooden floor beneath it, he quickly dropped the Miraculous Medal into it and prayed that the current Orthodox patriarch, Alexy II, would soon be able to return to celebrate the sacred liturgy in that holy place.

Fr. Leo, meanwhile, remembered the assignment Mother Teresa had given him of planting Medals in the spiritual center of Moscow. He looked around attentively for the perfect hiding place and noticed that the carved stone coffins of several tsars stood slightly away from the wall. "My feeling," he said, "was that a Medal dropped into a gap behind a sarcophagus could surely bear fruit for centuries without being disturbed. While no one was looking, I threw the Medal behind a sarcophagus."

At that precise moment, the general murmurings of the tourists ceased and gave way to the "clink-clink-clink" of the Medal hitting the floor. In a split second, five agitated security guards descended on the spot and began searching for what caused the noise. For the next five minutes, Fr. Maasburg played the part of a highly disinterested tourist, as his heart beat wildly in his chest. But the Medal was too hidden for the guards to

Cathedral Square, the heart of the Kremlin.
From left to right: Dormition Cathedral (aka Assumption Cathedral),
Ivan the Great Bell Tower, and Cathedral of the Archangel St. Michael.

Interior of the Cathedral of the Annunciation

find. Today, it probably lies there in waiting for its next miracle, which is needed today more than ever before.

After Bishop Hnilica's and Fr. Maasburg's return from behind the Iron Curtain, Mother Teresa was delighted to receive a detailed account of their covert mission. Soon, doors in Russia opened miraculously for the Missionaries of Charity to begin work in that country, the first Catholic order to officially enter the Communist Soviet Union.

In 1988, after four years had passed, Fr. Leo traveled to Moscow to work with the Missionaries of Charity and met Mother Teresa in the airport. Full of enthusiasm, she greeted him saying, "I have asked the Blessed Mother to give us one house in the Soviet Union for each Mystery of the Rosary." At that time, there were fifteen mysteries, and obtaining permission to enter the Soviet Union was still extremely difficult. Fr. Maasburg gave an awkward smile in response and was guilty of thinking, "Oh dear, she's getting old and starting to imagine things."[193]

Nearly ten years later, in August 1997, two weeks prior to Mother Teresa's death, Fr. Maasburg travelled again to what was now the former Soviet Union. After giving a weeklong retreat in Moscow for the superiors of the Missionaries of Charity, he looked at a group picture to see that there were exactly fifteen superiors of fifteen houses. Each of the houses, still today, bears the name of a Mystery of the Rosary. Mission accomplished.[194]

In December 1988, when the sisters had not yet finished moving into their house in Moscow, Mother Teresa accepted an invitation go to Yerevan, Armenia in the Soviet Union. A major earthquake had killed over 30,000 people in the region, where most of the few faithful and persecuted Catholics in Armenia lived. She was asked to bring four of her sisters and one priest to minister to 600 injured children in a hospital built for 120. "Wait and see" was not Mother Teresa's motto, so they set off on Christmas Day in a snowstorm, with Fr. Leo in tow.

Stopping at Moscow's Sheremetyevo International Airport in sub-zero weather, wearing open-toe sandals, the sisters waited for their next flight, along with other travelers in a concrete KGB lounge. Fr. Maasburg witnessed how the sisters greeted everyone there with a warm Christmas smile. The slightest curiosity, meek smile in return, or questioning side glance warranted the gift of a Medal of the Bogoroditsa (the Mother of God in Russian).

Soon, every single person in that airport lounge on Christmas Day had a Miraculous Medal hanging on a chain or string around their neck or tucked in their briefcase.[195]

The missionaries' living conditions in Armenia over the next few weeks, which turned into months, "were the worst I have ever experienced," said Fr. Maasburg. Yet looking back, he described the time as "the most wonderful months of my life." The hospital, even the toilets, hadn't been cleaned in three years, the staff was overburdened and overwhelmed, and many of the children were injured to the point of death.

The sisters set to work: the hospital was scrubbed, the overtaxed nurses and doctors were encouraged, and the injured and traumatized children each received comforting caresses and Miraculous Medals. Whenever one of the children was dying, the young female doctors working in the intensive care unit would signal by knocking on the floor three times with the heels of their shoes. Fr. Leo, in the basement just below, would hurry up the stairs to the first floor. Ignoring the risk of being immediately expelled from the country, he would baptize the child in the last moments of his or her life.

The loving care of the Missionaries of Charity and the Miraculous Medals had such a healing effect on the children of Yerevan that many of them experienced inexplicable cures. One little girl was rapidly becoming increasingly paralyzed from a degenerative condition that affected her limbs and airways. Fr. Maasburg heard the triple knock and ran up the stairs to baptize her. Everyone waited for the girl to die—it could be only hours away. The following day, her lungs were no longer paralyzed, and she could breathe freely again. Three weeks later, she was dancing for the sisters in their chapel, thanking them for their prayers.

Reports of the little girl's miraculous cure traveled up the ranks of the medical community, reaching top officials in the all-controlling Moscow bureaucracy. In no time, a delegation of doctors and psychiatrists showed up in Yerevan, with instructions to learn what "healing method" Mother Teresa's sisters had used. The sisters showed them the Miraculous Medal and explained to the three physicians and psychologists, accompanied by a male intern, how to pray. Despite their atheistic governance and empirical training, they found the explanation satisfactory, taped a Miraculous Medal to a page of their report, and returned contentedly to Moscow.

The Soviet Union had an extremely high abortion rate, and Mother Teresa wanted to see that no child was ever aborted. Her axiom of action to save the lives of children was: "We fight abortion through adoption." In this spirit, the saint requested and was granted permission by Soviet authorities to select twelve children to care for from a list of the handicapped, who for the communists were considered expendable. On the list, the name in Russian given to the most seriously disabled children was "idiot"—which for the Soviets meant, "incapable of life."

"I will take all the children who are 'incapable of life,'" Mother Teresa said. So, the Missionaries of Charity took them in. They tried to bring those who could benefit from massage to a Russian masseuse, but like many Russians, the masseuse believed that disabled children were of no use to society and therefore had no right to life. One of the children providentially plucked from the list was a bad-tempered boy named Alexei. The sisters believed his

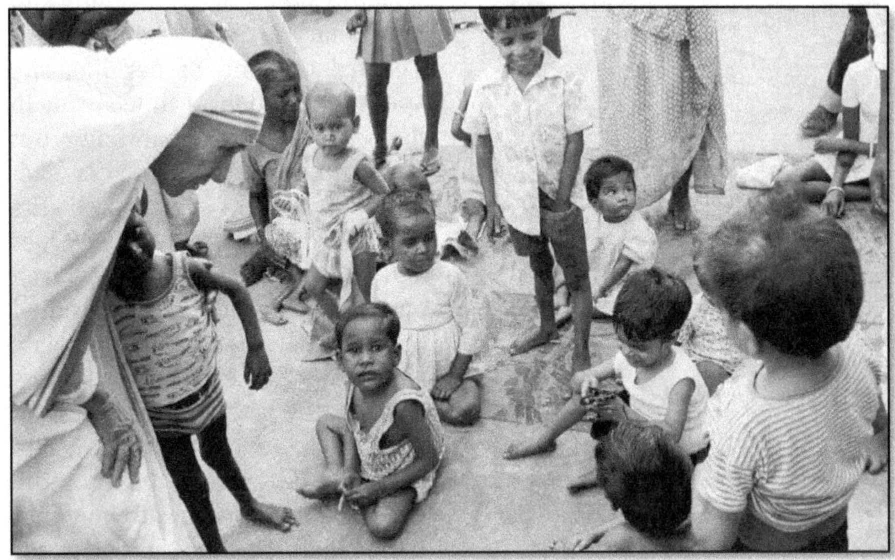

unhappiness came from his awareness that his birth mother had mistreated him and given him away.

As with all of the children in the care of the Missionaries, Alexei was given a Miraculous Medal on a string to wear around his neck. The sisters explained to him that from then on, the Mother of God would be his mother. In that moment, something miraculous happened. From that day forward, Alexei was often seen kissing his Medal repeatedly, and anyone who helped him get dressed had to kiss his Medal first, before they could touch him. His fierce temper and whiny temperament calmed, and he became the most well-behaved child at the midday meal.

The masseuse changed, too. She noticed the Medal one day and grew curious. The following day, the sisters gave her one, and from then on, she was content to massage the handicapped children who were brought to her. In particular, she treated Alexei with great care. A few years later, a family from Novosibirsk, a city in southwestern Siberia, came forward to adopt Alexei and was willing to go through the necessary and complicated adoption procedures.

This included a doctor questioning and examining Alexei. Using the English he had learned from the sisters, along with his native Russian tongue, the boy asked the doctor why he was asking "all those stupid questions." The doctor looked down at the certificate that stated Alexei was "incapable of living" and remained in thought for a few moments. Then he tore it up. This gave a green light for the adoption. Alexei grew up strong in the faith; he became a zealous altar server in Novosibirsk for Bishop Werth and went on to study at a Russian university.[196]

Mother Teresa, age 86, during her last visit to the Bronx, New York, in 1997

Over time, Mother Teresa of Calcutta's relentless travelling and missionary activity began to slow. Toward the end of her life, she spent a great deal of time sitting in her wheelchair, handing out Miraculous Medals. In her last days of travel, she visited the Bronx, New York in June 1997, at age 86. Able to do little else, a frail and sickly Mother Teresa cradled a basket of Medals on her lap, which her sisters kept refilling. With noteworthy reverence, she handed out her favorite sacramental, suggesting to the crowd flocking around her that the Medals be used as tools for spreading the Gospel message of love.[197]

Once back home in India, and when feeling up to it, she would sit in her wheelchair and receive visitors on the second-floor balcony of her Missionaries of Charity Motherhouse in Calcutta. To whomever she greeted, she gave a Miraculous Medal and invited them to pray and to trust in the goodness of God."[198]

Mother Teresa passed into the next life on September 5, 1997. Pope John Paul II waived the mandatory five-year waiting period to start her cause for sainthood, and the process began. Two miracles had to be verified before she could be canonized. One of them, fittingly, involved the Miraculous Medal.

In West Bengal, India, a woman named Monica Besra was taken into the care of the Missionaries of Charity with such an advanced tumor in her abdomen that doctors had no hope for her survival. Her last days in the sisters' home were spent in agony and exhaustion, as she could not sleep due to the intense pain.

On the day of the one-year anniversary of Mother Teresa's death, the sisters placed a Miraculous Medal, which had been touched to the body of the saint, onto Monica's stomach. The dying woman fell asleep, and upon waking up, her pain was entirely gone. Doctors soon discovered that her tumor had disappeared without a trace. After a thorough investigation, the healing was declared medically inexplicable.

Even death could not prevent Mother Teresa of Calcutta from finding a way to spread devotion to her most beloved sacramental, her Medal of Charity.

Monica Besra holds up the Miraculous Medal that helped to cure her

CLAUDE NEWMAN (1923-1944)

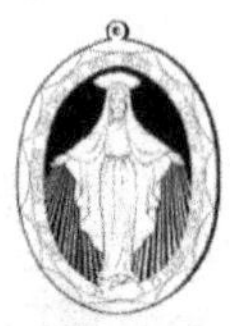

In 1943, at age twenty, Claude Newman was sentenced to die in the electric chair. Born on December 1, 1923, he was a powerfully strong and mentally challenged African-American farmhand, who worked on the Ceres plantation of Warren County, Mississippi. Born in Stuttgart, Arkansas, he grew up from the age of five with his grandmother, Ellen Newman, in the 500-person town of Bovina.

On December 19, 1942, in Bovina, Claude lay in waiting in a dark corner of the home of Sid Cook, his grandmother's estranged husband, an elderly farmhand who also worked on the plantation and was known to be abusive toward Ellen. There Claude stood with a gun in his hand, firmly intending to rob and kill him. As soon as Cook entered his home, Claude shoved a shotgun in Cook's mouth and pulled the trigger, blowing a hole through the back of his neck. After confiscating the old man's money, Claude immediately fled to Little Rock, Arkansas, where his mother lived. An FBI official apprehended and arrested him on January 8, 1943.

After a two-day trial in March 1943, Claude Newman was convicted of murder in the first degree in Mississippi's Warren County Circuit Court. It took the twelve-member jury twenty minutes to decide the case. Claude asked the trial judge, R.B. Anderson, to "go easy" on him, but the judge showed no mercy and replied that, given the brutality of the crime, he could only sentence Claude to death.

While Claude was spending time in Warren County Jail in Vicksburg, Mississippi, awaiting execution, he interacted with some of the other incarcerated men. One of them was a Caucasian man named Ralph Harris, serving three years for grand larceny. Ralph had been baptized in Greenville, Mississippi, and was a lapsed Catholic. Nevertheless, one day he gave Claude a small Miraculous Medal and urged him to wear it. Claude later explained this moment to a minister in the prison, Sr. Benna Henken, SSPS. "My cellmate was a Catholic from Greenville. When the guards came to take him to the penitentiary, my cellmate hung this little medal around my neck and said, 'Claude, pray!' I prayed every day."

Old Warren County Jail in Vicksburg, Mississippi

Before that moment, Claude had had no contact with Catholics and knew nothing about the Catholic faith. But when he received the medal, he was suddenly curious and eager to learn more about the figure of the woman on it. He said the Miraculous Medal made him feel that he just had to belong to the Church of the Miraculous Mother. "Then one day the thought came to me," Claude recounted to Sr. Henken, 'Why not call for a Catholic priest?' I did."

The priest called was Fr. Robert O'Leary, SVD, who served as chaplain to the County Jail in the mid-1940s. Fr. O'Leary reported that he first met Claude two weeks before the scheduled execution, when Claude asked for a Catholic priest: "On my first visit, I found

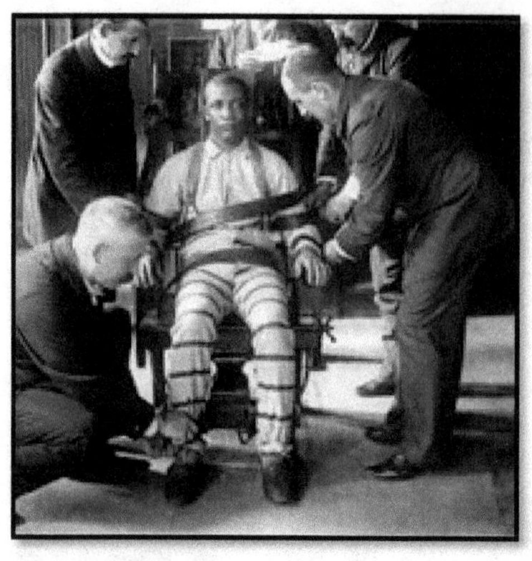

Claude desired to become a Catholic. As he had no contact with Catholics and knew nothing about the Catholic Faith, his request seemed decidedly strange."

Fr. O'Leary introduced himself to Claude and soon learned that the young farmhand was illiterate and knew next to nothing about religion. He had never been to school. The only way Claude could tell if a book was right-side-up was if the book contained pictures. He did not know who Jesus was. He did not know anything, except that there was a God. In no time, Fr. O'Leary, who served the African-American parish of St. Mary's Catholic Church, began catechetical instruction for Claude and was helped by two Holy Spirit Missionary Sisters, Sr. Henken and Sr. Michaeline Willsch, who also assisted him at the parish.

Claude was an inspiration to all of his catechists, especially the young priest of the Society of the Divine Word. Fr. O'Leary recalled that Claude "readily grasped Catholic teachings and understood them so well that one could not help but feel God and His Blessed Mother were his teachers." On January 16, 1944, just four days before his execution date of January 20, Fr. O'Leary baptized Claude Newman in the Warren County jail. That day, Claude's spirit resounded with great joy. He took the baptismal name "Claude Jude," with Sr. Henken as his sponsor,[199] and prayerfully entered into his First Reconciliation and First Communion. "Father," he

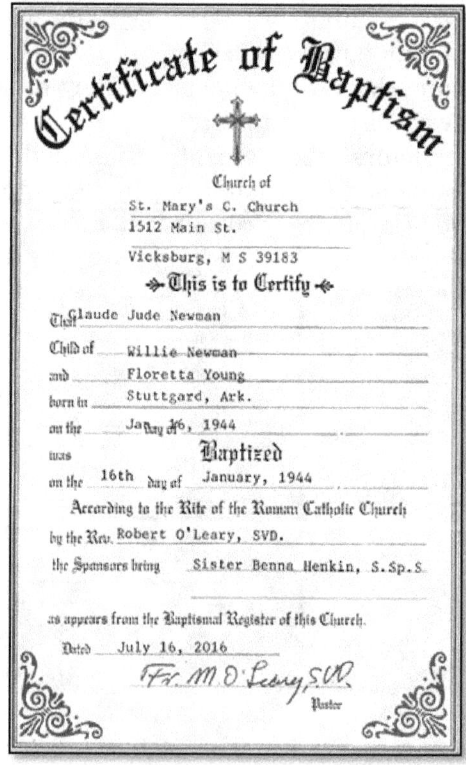

Certificate of Baptism

Church of
St. Mary's C. Church
1512 Main St.
Vicksburg, M S 39183

This is to Certify

That Claude Jude Newman
Child of Willie Newman
and Floretta Young
born in Stuttgard, Ark.
on the Jan 16, 1944
was Baptized
on the 16th day of January, 1944
According to the Rite of the Roman Catholic Church
by the Rev. Robert O'Leary, SVD.
the Sponsors being Sister Benna Henkin, S.Sp.S
as appears from the Baptismal Register of this Church.
Dated July 16, 2016
Fr. M O'Leary, SVD
Pastor

told the priest, "now I know that God loves me. ... I feel so happy and peaceful as never before. Oh, if only I could be executed tonight and go to God."

The sheriff and district attorney had petitioned the newly elected governor, Thomas Bailey, for clemency in Claude's case, but the governor upheld the sentence and scheduled a new execution date of February 4, 1944. Claude did not want this two-week delay, said Fr. Leary, as "It only prolonged the agony." While Claude waited, he "spent his extra days of life showing the way of Life to other prisoners."

Then the moment came for Claude to be executed. His time to die was scheduled for 7 a.m. on January 20, 1944. That very morning, Fr. O'Leary heard Claude pray, "Please Lord, help the other condemned men here." Just moments before his death, he wasn't cowering in terror, but thinking lovingly of those he would leave behind.

An immediate report in the local newspaper made simple mention of what was undoubtedly the dark and long minutes of a gruesome death that the Queen of Heaven surrounded with light. The first spark had already been lit with one inmate's gesture of placing a Miraculous Medal around another inmate's neck, enjoining him to "pray."

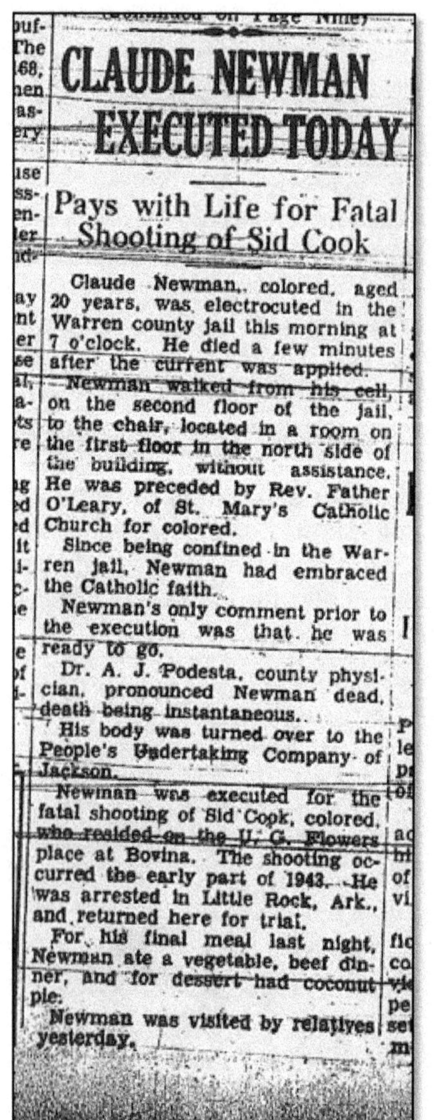

CLAUDE NEWMAN EXECUTED TODAY

Pays with Life for Fatal Shooting of Sid Cook

Claude Newman, colored, aged 20 years, was electrocuted in the Warren county jail this morning at 7 o'clock. He died a few minutes after the current was applied.

Newman walked from his cell, on the second floor of the jail, to the chair, located in a room on the first floor in the north side of the building, without assistance. He was preceded by Rev. Father O'Leary, of St. Mary's Catholic Church for colored.

Since being confined in the Warren jail, Newman had embraced the Catholic faith.

Newman's only comment prior to the execution was that he was ready to go.

Dr. A. J. Podesta, county physician, pronounced Newman dead, death being instantaneous.

His body was turned over to the People's Undertaking Company of Jackson.

Newman was executed for the fatal shooting of Sid Cook, colored, who resided on the U. G. Flowers place at Bovina. The shooting occurred the early part of 1943. He was arrested in Little Rock, Ark., and returned here for trial.

For his final meal last night, Newman ate a vegetable, beef dinner, and for dessert had coconut pie.

Newman was visited by relatives yesterday.

Claude Newman, colored, aged 20 years, was electrocuted in the Warren County jail this morning at 7 o'clock. He died a few minutes after the current was applied. Newman walked from his cell, on the second floor of the jail, to the chair, located in a room on the first floor in the north side of the building, without assistance. He was preceded by Rev. Father O'Leary of St. Mary's Catholic Church for colored.

Since being confined in the Warren jail, Newman had embraced the Catholic faith...For his final meal last night, Newman ate a vegetable, beef dinner, and for dessert had coconut pie. Newman was visited by his relatives yesterday.

Newman's only comment prior to the execution was that he was ready to go...

After Claude Newman's death, a prisoner named James Samuel Hughes was destined for the same fate four months later. Hughes faced execution for having killed a Deputy Sheriff who sought to arrest him for incest. The prisoner had impregnated his own 17-year-old daughter, Annabelle, while also having sexual relations with his other daughter, 16-year-old Esther.

The local *Vicksburg Evening Post* sent a reporter to cover Hughes's execution on May 19, 1944. Additionally, Associated Press stories of the execution ran in multiple newspapers, including the *Jackson Clarion-Ledger, The Evening Post* and Greenville's *Delta Democrat-Times*. They reported that he "was a member of the Holy Roller faith" and said that when Hughes was given a minute to utter his final words, he prayed peacefully for himself. Strapped to the electric chair, Hughes "looked calmly up at the few present and said in clear-cut tones, 'I'm not afraid to e official "shot trying to escape." The fliers, like most war prison- s, had made efforts to escape d had even mentioned them in ters to relatives.

AZIS REPORTED MASSING FOR COUNTER ATTACK

iders, Transports Con- aled Along Coast, London Paper Says

ONDON, May 19 — (AP) —The mans have massed gliders and sport planes in concealed hang- along the European coast in bers sufficient to drop at least airborne division on Britain, London Daily Mail said today, ting its information came "excellent sources."

e British do not rule out the bility of such a German coun- invasion. The enemy troops t be assigned to knock out centers vital to the Allied machine.

y last Saturday, Field Mar- Lord Ironside, commander of ome guards and former chief British imperial defense staff ed that "it is quite possible when we make our great in- , the Germans will make sort of effort to land in this ry."

Daily Mail said the Ger- aircraft reported assembled the channel coast included huge six-engined Dorniers, capable of carrying 150 men. aper mentioned medium glid- d Junkers 52 transports as the enemy array.

the Allies, Germany pre- ly is concerned with safe- ng her military secrets as n D-Day approaches. A Mos- roadcast heard here by the Monitor said Germany has led all visas to leave the and Germans reaching the office gave no explanation.

DNB agency announced in a ast from Berlin that the r force intended "to smash outh, Plymouth, Bristol and cks of London" — ports it ed as "bristling — positively ed to the bursting point— manner of invasion equip-

declared that "in these he entire Allied invasion l has to be concentrated." er Berlin broadcast con- previous neutral reports

ntinued on Page Ten)

with Mr. Fitz-Hugh and Mr. Sugg.

Two Executed This Morning In Local Jail

White Man, Negro Woman Pay with Lives For Murders

Two of Warren county's most sensational murders of recent years were avenged here early today in a double electrocution which took the lives of a middle-aged white man and a young negro woman.

The woman, Mildred James, went to the chair shortly before 4:15 a. m., and she was pronounced dead four minutes after she had taken her seat. She had been convicted of slaying Miss Nannie Conklin, aged spinster who lived alone in a rambling old home near the city limits.

James Samuel Hughes, convicted slayer of Deputy Sheriff S. J. Luckett, followed to the execution chamber at 4:25. He was pronounced dead at 4:35.

The woman made no statement as she sat calmly in the chair. She gave a fleeting smile to a Catholic priest as eye guards were made fast. Hughes asked mercy on his soul in a brief profession of faith in Christ. He was a member of the "Holy Roller" faith.

The James woman, first woman to die by electrocution in Mississippi, had murdered Miss Conklin at her home on McRaven avenue, but had failed to implicate two other negroes in the murder, was the first to die, walking calmly into the death chamber at 4:12 and seating herself in the chair unaided.

She only asked that the straps being placed about her waist be moved slightly to the right, as they were too tight in one place she said, and looked about her inquiringly as the leg straps were being fitted about her ankles.

As the eye-guards were being placed over her eyes, she looked up at a Catholic priest, which faith she had embraced several weeks before, and faintly smiled, then settled back into the chair to await the first shock which was applied at 4:14, and followed with the second and final one at 4:16 1-2 by executioner Watson. She gave only one quick, slight start as the current hit her the first time and relaxed as the body slumped slightly

(Continued on Page Ten)

and other dumps at Osela from where their long - range artillery has been operating in recent weeks.

Allied warships poured shells

(Continued on Page Ten)

"FREE SPEECH" ISSUE IN TRIAL DEFENSE CLAIMS

Opening Defense Statements Commence in Sedition Trial

BY KARL R. BAUMAN

WASHINGTON, May 19 — (AP) — Two words — "Free Speech" — will form the corner-stone of the many-worded defense in the mass sedition conspiracy trial.

This became apparent today on the basis of the first and still incompleted opening statement on behalf of the 29 defendants, accused of conspiring to establish a Nazi form of government in this country and to undermine the morale of the armed forces.

"Free speech is the paramount issue—the only issue," defendant Lawrence Dennis of New York told the jury.

Several defense attorneys reserved their opening statements until later in the trial to permit Dennis, to lead off. Dennis, described by the prosecution as "the Alfred Rosenberg of the (Nazi) movement in this country, who supplied ideas to other defendants," said he would require another hour to complete his statement when court reconvenes Monday.

Dennis contended the defendants had "nothing in common" except their opposition to Preident Roosevelt and his pre-Pearl Harbor foreign policy, and said it was only natural that the German leaders viewed with approval their efforts to keep this country out of war.

Dennis spoke after a new outburst had interrupted a day-long calm which contrasted sharply with previous tumultous sessions.

This uproar grew out of a protest by Prosecutor O. John Rogge to a long argument by Ellis O. Jones of Los Angeles for a mistrial.

Rogge said Jones was reading from a brief filed by Defense Attorney James J. Laghlin in another case and called this improper.

"I submit, your honor," roared Laughlin, "that that stamps him as the vilest insect. I take full responsibility for the brief and I have a right to give Mr. Jones information he asks for."

ter.

The b still wer of storm bombers many to 13 heavy planes y Nazis in ania, Be slavia, grounds.

NAZI F

Propa tentia Fro

B LOND new G mundeat hind the day the diate r offensiv the ene ed with

Hitler bombin of Row suggest pected the cen Russian the ne the Re the Am forces

Gern scatter potenti ery be Bay of ed its sance land.

Britis that co must be d roads erally area militar

A G Turkey floodin tem m ple of moved Europ

"It lied o an ov drama scale Ludw Berlin that into

confess the Lord Jesus Christ here tonight before man. May He have mercy on my soul, in the name of the Father, the Son, and the Holy Ghost.'"

When Hughes made his profession of faith in the Holy Trinity and asked for mercy on his soul, that was enough for Fr. O'Leary to absolve him of his sins, as he said, "in the last minute of his life."

Yet Hughes wasn't the only one whose soul was saved just before death. The article above tells of yet another conversion...

TWO EXECUTED THIS MORNING IN LOCAL JAIL:
White Man, Negro Woman Pay with Lives for Murders

Two of Warren County's most sensational murders of recent years were avenged here early today in a double electrocution which took the lives of a middle-aged white man and a young negro woman.

The woman, Mildred James, went to the chair shortly before 4:15 a.m. and she was pronounced dead four minutes after she had taken her seat. She had been convicted of slaying Miss Nannie Conklin, aged spinster who lived alone in a rambling old home near the city limits.

James Samuel Hughes, convicted slayer of Deputy Sheriff S.J. Luckett, followed to the execution chamber at 4:25. He was pronounced dead at 4:35.

The woman made no statement as she sat calmly in the chair. She gave a fleeting smile to a Catholic priest as eye guards were made fast. Hughes asked mercy on his soul in a brief profession of faith in Christ. He was a member of the "Holy Roller" faith.

The James woman, first woman to die by electrocution in Mississippi, had murdered Miss Conklin at her home on McRaven Avenue...was the first to die, walking calmly into the death chamber at 4:12 and seating herself in the chair unaided.

She only asked that the straps being placed about her waist be moved slightly to the right, as they were too tight in one place, she said, and looked about her inquiringly as the leg straps were being fitted about her ankles.

As the eye-guards were being placed over her eyes, she looked up at a Catholic priest, which faith she had embraced several weeks before, and faintly smiled, then settled back into the chair to await the first shock which was applied at 4:14, and followed with the second and final one at 4:16 1-2 by executioner Watson. She gave only one quick, slight start as the current hit her the first time and relaxed as the body slumped slightly...

Thus, in a continuation of the salvific graces flowing from the Miraculous Medal, Claude's selfless prayer for the souls of other condemned prisoners was answered.

SERVANT OF GOD, FRANK DUFF (1889-1980)

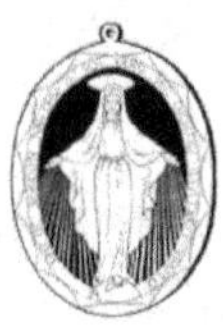

The standard of the Legion of Mary, containing the Miraculous Medal

On November 13, 1980, Cardinal Tómas O'Fiaich, Primate of Ireland, gave the sermon at Frank Duff's funeral Mass. He said that this single-minded Dubliner was regarded as "the man who made the greatest contribution to the life of the Catholic Church in this century." How is it that this Catholic layman from Dublin, Ireland, earned such a title?

Duff founded the Legion of Mary, which became the world's largest apostolic association of lay Catholics. Members are called legionaries and number about three million[200] active members and ten million auxiliary (praying) members in 170 countries, in nearly every diocese of the world.[201] Each branch is organized into a group called a praesidium.

The work of the legionaries is the sanctification of themselves and of the Mystical Body of Christ, through a close union with the Holy Spirit and through consecration and devotion to Mary. Members attend a structured weekly meeting and perform a statutory two-hour apostolic work, such as: calls to the elderly and homebound, visits to prison inmates, care of the youth, parish work, and evangelization. Their good deeds are supported by intense prayer and often the use of the Miraculous Medal.

Frank Duff in 1957

"When you understand what her motherhood is all about," Duff once said of the Blessed Mother, "you just know she's there, she's always close by. She's interested in absolutely everything you do and is ever willing to help you."

Frank's father: John Duff, retired at 42 due to typhoid fever

Frank Duff, the eldest of John and Susan Duff's seven children, was born in 1889 into a wealthy Catholic family who were churchgoers, but not particularly devout. Many of his family members suffered from ill health: his father, John Duff, had to retire early due to poor health; his sister Isabel lived with poor health for much of her life; one of his baby sisters, Laetitia, died in infancy, and her twin sister, Eva, maintained a remarkable holiness in the six months before her death from tuberculosis at age thirteen. "She is not for this world," thought Frank, as she was dying.

Frank's mother: Susan Leticia "Letty" Freehill

Frank's schooling was rigorous, and he had the intellectual capacity for it. From the age of twelve or thirteen, he was studying five languages: Irish, English, Greek, Latin and French. Lean, athletic, and unusually strong, Frank swam, biked, and played tennis and cricket. During a cricket match when he was twelve, a ball struck him, causing a permanent loss of hearing in his left ear.

John Duff handed down to Frank his trusty bicycle, when he grew too ill to ride it. (Frank never drove again after his brother's car exploded when he was at the wheel, and they narrowly escaped as young men.)[202] The young Duff soon began cycling through Dublin on his own initiative each Saturday to visit the pawnbrokers and collect six-pence each from them on behalf of the poor served by the St. Vincent de Paul Society.

In his visits to the ghetto, he always concerned himself with people's souls, as well as their material needs. Next door to the slum houses, Frank also saw that lived people who hadn't dipped below the poverty line, but who had fallen away from their faith. He decided, therefore, that he must start his own apostolate in order to evangelize them. Night after night, he

Photograph c. 1906/1907. Across top: Frank, Isabel Maud, Eva Lucy (died at 13), John Edwin, Alice Mary (on Frank's lap), and Sarah Geraldine (center front)

cycled or walked through the back streets of Dublin, alone, and became a familiar figure to everyone in the stacked tenement housing. Even the most lax of Catholics received him kindly, welcoming his prayers and chatty conversation and gratefully accepting his Miraculous Medals, scapulars, and holy water. Many returned to the active practice of their faith through Frank's gentle and persuasive appeals, and these sacramentals. Duff was kind to all, and now having discovered a whole world apart from the cultured, refined, and educated colleagues of his social upbringing, he came to also love his newfound friends in the poor. They would be his friends for life.

Filled with apostolic zeal, the twenty-five-year-old went to daily Mass (sometimes twice), prayed a daily Rosary and the Divine Office, and spent three out his four hours of daily prayer in various churches. His normal prayer schedule was astonishing. Duff joined forces with Sergeant Major and lay evangelist, Joe Gabbett, in combating the efforts of a proselytizing center that targeted poor and destitute Catholics. The center's goal: make

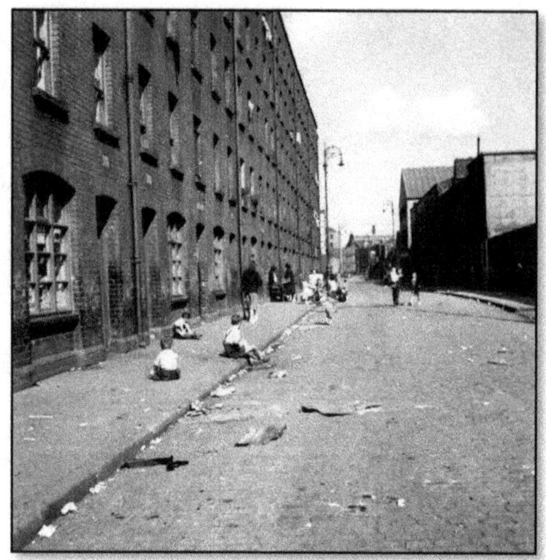

Montgomery Street (now called Foley street) in a tenement area of Dublin. From the 1840s until the 1970s, Dublin was blighted with the worst slums in all of Europe.

the Catholics abandon their faith in favor of Protestantism through the lure of a free meal, topped with a sermon. Gabbett rented the second floor of a large stable and named his enterprise the "Guild of the Immaculate Conception," where he served competing Sunday breakfasts and sermons for the poor, with Frank as his right-hand man. In one of the upstairs rooms, Gabbett adorned an altar with a statue of Our Lady of the Immaculate Conception as its centerpiece and called upon her intercession daily.[203]

When the Great War broke out in 1914, Joe Gabbett was appointed as the lay assistant to Fr. O'Loughlin, the chaplain to Portobello Military Barracks. He asked Frank to be his partner in this new task, and the two of them ministered to two thousand soldiers in a large barracks each week. Gabbett gave a sermon and then had the soldiers gather around a statue of Our Lady and sing a hymn to her. He led them in the Rosary and encouraged them to wear the Brown Scapular and Miraculous Medal. It was Frank's joy to hand out Miraculous Medals to all of the men and suggest, even insist, that the soldiers wear the Medal around their necks, putting their faith in Mary's intercession. The number of "captures" among the fallen-away Catholics was astounding!

Joe Gabbett

In 1916, at age twenty-seven, Frank wrote down the following prayer:

> *O, my God, my heart has been set upon the things that pass. But henceforth, I will give myself entirely to you. Give me the time, and faithfully do I promise now to serve you. Give me back the years that the worm and the locusts have devoured, that I may one day restore them to you full of achievement.*

O Jesus, I desire to become a saint—not that I may be great, but that you may be greatly loved.[204]

That same year, Frank wrote a booklet, "Can We Be Saints?" published by the Catholic Truth Society of Ireland, with the desire that everyone should know the answer was "Yes." (This classic is now available as part of the book, *Servant of God, Frank Duff: Founder of the Legion of Mary*) "In the heart of every right-thinking Catholic," Duff wrote, "God has implanted the desire to become a saint. ... Saints are the doctrines and practices of holiness made visible. If we frequent their company, we will soon imitate their qualities."[205]

By this time, Frank had made up his mind that he would never marry. Celibacy was for him an expression of his total commitment to God's work for him.[206] He also knew that his vocation was not to the priesthood or monastic life, though he greatly admired those callings.[207] Frank being known for his ready laugh and quick wit, said, decades later, when asked why he never married: "Why should I marry and make one woman miserable, when by staying single, I can keep dozens happy with hope!"[208]

When Frank Duff saw a need, he jumped into it with his whole heart. The Legion of Mary began providentially in just such a way. For four years, Frank had gathered monthly with a group made up primarily of young women, to organize outreach and evangelization to Dublin's poor. His local priest, Fr. Toher, also attended the meetings. When Frank discovered St. Louis-Marie de Montfort's book *True Devotion to Mary*, he felt he simply had to hold a special meeting to present and discuss the topic. Seventeen days later, the Legion of Mary was born. Duff would later write:

It is impossible to believe that the connection between the "True Devotion" meeting and the immediate emergence of the Legion from the next monthly meeting was a mere coincidence. There was too much supernatural design and too little human contriving. Nearly four years had gone by without incident until the "True Devotion" meeting was held. The moment it established in minds the true stature of Our Lady in the Christian system, things were ready for the Legion.

Frank Duff, circa 1915, age 26

At this first meeting of the Legion of Mary, a man named Matt Murray gave his usual report, including a moving account of his visit to the Dublin Union Hospital—such an apostolate was done by men at the time. Two women approached Frank and Fr. Toher to ask, "Would it not be possible for the ladies to do that same kind of work?"[209]

Always keenly interested in encouraging people's holy initiatives, Frank answered, "Yes, of course. Can you interest some more of the ladies in this work?" There was no precedent at that time for an apostolate of the laity of a pastoral nature. They were breaking new ground. At 8 p.m. the following Wednesday, September 7, 1921, Fr. Toher, Frank Duff, and thirteen women, most of them quite young, gathered in front of a makeshift altar. Placed on its center was the very same statue of Our Lady of the Immaculate Conception that Joe Gabbett had used. She was surrounded by flowers and candles, exactly as can be seen at any Legion meeting today.[210] The date of that first meeting, which gave birth to the Legion of Mary, "happened" to be the vigil of the Feast of Our Lady's Nativity.

The statue and altar used at the first Legion of Mary meeting in 1921

None of the attendants could have imagined that their humble meeting would one day turn into the largest Catholic lay organization in the world; yet Duff may have had an inkling of such a possibility, even then. In 1979, at age ninety, he shared in a video interview something that he had said to this first little group of members, just three months into the Legion's existence:[211]

> *The Legion from its first moment was in the hands of the Blessed Virgin, and building on that idea, I ventured on the prognostication to them that they would encompass the whole world. They thought it so funny that they must have consumed the best part of five minutes in uproarious laughter. Such was the respect with which my prophecy was treated.*

In recalling this moment, Frank burst out laughing.[212]

The Legion of Mary began as an apostolate for women and eventually expanded to include men. As the apostolate grew, it evolved into and came to maintain a disciplined structure, with divinely inspired guidelines and a focus on person-to-person contact through ministering in pairs. "The ordinary lay person down to the very simplest person is capable of apostleship," Frank declared.

Frank both knew and had seen, firsthand, the spiritual power granted to the Miraculous Medal to spur conversion. He therefore recommended that the legionaries make home visits, carrying always with them blessed Miraculous Medals as their "ammunition." They are gifts, he said, that make it very easy to enter into a religious conversation.[213] Frank's trust in his Mother in heaven to guide the way was extraordinary, and when it came to her Medal, Frank simply expected Mary's presence to reliably accompany the powerful sacramental.

With the Blessed Mother urging him to go out into the world, and his earthly mother ready with a warm meal when he arrived home late at night, Duff inspired some of his legionaries to tackle one of their first projects. Dublin's red-light district was one of the largest commercial sex centers in Europe, and Frank knew that if the Legion didn't tackle this work, no one else would. The Irish people considered prostitution an incurable social ill, part of humanity's fallen nature. But Frank and five sister members walked nervously down a slum road, gripping their crucifixes and Miraculous Medals, toward their destination—a brothel on Low Street, called Bentley Place. Their intention was to recruit the women for a retreat led by a Franciscan named Fr. Philip.

Frank's beloved bike now displayed in his home at 97 Phibsboro Road in Dublin. The sign on it reads: "His beloved bicycle: Note the Miraculous Medal which he attached to the handlebars."

Frank wrote of the experience in his book, *Miracles on Tap*, an adventure worthy of a blockbuster film: "There was a 'nest' of five of them in one room we entered. They were in one bed—the whole quintet! Some of their heads were visible; some were under the cover. Heads and legs protruded from the latter at every angle. It was almost fantastic; we could not guess how many people there were there..."[214] Yet, every single woman in that drunken tangle gave their promise to attend the retreat—the whole nest of them, as well as most every woman in the entire place.

The red-light district in the northeast of Dublin was nicknamed "Monto," slightly smaller than a square mile. It formed in the 1800s and flourished in its heyday with 1600 prostitutes until its closure in 1925 by the Legion of Mary, spearheaded by Duff.

After a retreat day of roller coaster drama, spiritual clashes, and dreadful fears, the Holy Spirit pierced the women's hearts, and one by one, all thirty-one of them entered the confessional. It was an astounding spirit-filled success! For Frank Duff, a thousand difficulties did not make one impossibility. As the retreat ended, an utterly exhausted, but exhilarated, Frank Duff immediately went to work again because he couldn't bear the thought of the women returning to their house of ill repute. With the aid of the local government and church hierarchy and religious whom he had convinced to help, the women moved to a new home and a new life in Sancta Maria Hostel in 1922.[215]

In each worthy endeavor Frank undertook, there were obstacles and trials, but his gift of wisdom provided guidelines to his success.

> *Never embark on an enterprise by considering all the difficulties you may meet or the opposition you may encounter. If you do so, you will never get anywhere. Of course, you will have to face difficulties and opposition, but those aren't the starting points. Instead, when a noble enterprise suggests itself to you, study it well, pray about it, but most of all, ask yourself: "Does God want this?" If you decide, under the guidance of the Holy Spirit, that God wants it, then follow it through and know that nothing on this earth can stop you, not because it is you that is involved but because it is God's work. And remember, God has to use whatever instrument is available to Him, even if that instrument is only you.* [216]

Duff also believed that signs guide us along the way, signaling what we are to do. When asked how he first learned to see signs, he replied, "from happenings." There had been, for instance, the "happening" of him coming across *True Devotion to Mary* in a used bookstore, just after he had heard about it through a St. Vincent de Paul brother. There was the encounter with Joe Gabbett, just when Frank was thinking of how to thwart the Protestant proselytizing center. There was Gabbett's request that Frank hand out Miraculous Medals, which increased Frank's faith in their power. And there was the unplanned date of the first Legion of Mary meeting on September 7, which fell providentially on the eve of the Feast of Our Lady's Nativity.

In Appendix 6 of *The Official Handbook of the Legion of Mary*, titled

Duff holding a large Legion vexillum (the standard and emblem of the Legion of Mary, which contains the Miraculous Medal)

"The Medal of the Immaculate Conception Called the Miraculous Medal," Duff pointed to signs of God's desire that the Medal be part of the Legion of Mary. He highlighted the Medal's historical inception and providential adaptation into the life of the Legion, even into its daily prayers and standard emblem. An excerpt from the handbook's Appendix 6, provides a good example, (bold text is added):

> *"Then the Blessed Virgin said to me: 'Get a medal struck after this model; those who wear it when it is blessed will receive great graces,*

especially if they wear it round their neck. Graces will be abundant for those who have confidence'." (St. Catherine Labouré)

Legionaries should greatly esteem this medal, *which has been prominently associated with the history of their organization. It was not the result of deliberation that a statue of the 1830 model graced the table at the first meeting, yet it effectively summarized the devotional outlook of the organization which came into life around it.*

The use of the medal in the work was then recommended. The invocation, which appears on the medal, commenced to be said at that first meeting, and now, as part of the Catena [a Legion prayer that incorporates the words on the Miraculous Medal],[217] *is recited daily by every member. The design of the medal is incorporated in the Legion vexillum [the standard and emblem of the Legion].*[218] *It is provocative of thought that the medal should in this manifold way insert itself into the Legion devotional system.*

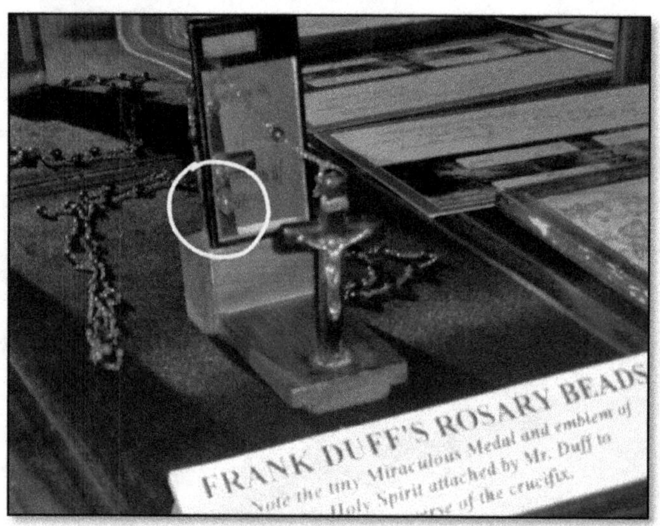

The Frank Duff's Rosary with a Miraculous Medal that he attached to the back of the crucifix (reflected in the mirror)

An astonishing circumstance is that it was at the precise moment of the centenary of the apparition to St. Catherine Labouré (which had special reference to France) that His Eminence Cardinal Verdier, Archbishop of Paris, opened the audience in which he gave his approbation and blessing to the Legion.

Thus, one can almost say that the medal has been assimilated by the Legion, so that the mission of the legionary includes that of the medal. ***The legionary is, as it were, a living Miraculous Medal, a humble instrument of Our Lady's graces to the world.***

A certain class of Catholics, anxious to show itself "advanced, intellectual," is found deriding this medal, as well as the other medals and the scapulars, as superstition. This attitude of disrespect for the sacramentals approved by the Church is a rash one. Likewise, it is against the facts, for there is no doubt that the use of the medal has been blessed in dramatic fashions. ***As legionaries are encouraged to regard themselves as soldiers, likewise should they look upon the medal as their special ammunition. To a certainty, Mary will impart to it a double power in the hands of her legionaries.***

By the enrollment ceremony one is made a member of the Association of the Miraculous Medal[219] *without any formal inscription in a register required. The member is entitled automatically to all the indulgences attached to the Association.*

The feast of Our Lady of the Miraculous Medal is celebrated on 27 November. [220]

Over the next few decades, the Legion of Mary spread worldwide through the efforts of envoys: legionaries who would dedicate years of their lives toward extending the work of the Legion into every corner of the globe. Duff and the accomplishments of the Legion of Mary came to be praised by five popes and innumerable church dignitaries. In 1930, Frank sat across from Pope Pius XI, who listened to him speak about the Legion for twenty minutes and then asked Duff a question: "What is it you wish me to do for you?"

The Duff meets Pope Paul VI at the Second Vatican Council

Frank had his answer memorized: "If we could say that it was the personal desire of Your Holiness that the Legion of Mary would spread over the whole world, this would be a great mode of propaganda for spreading the Legion."

There was a pause. The Pope then said: "With all my heart, I express that desire."

When Pope Pius XII succeeded him in 1939, Duff again asked for a meeting, and although ninety distinguished personages were awaiting the same favor and was told at first that there was absolutely no possibility of it, word came back to him that "The Holy Father will see Mr. Duff before anyone else in Rome!" The date was set for April 28. "Remarkable," said Frank. "That's the Feast Day of St. Louis Marie de Montfort!" When Frank found himself facing the pope on the other side of a large desk, he worried that he was too far away to hear the Holy Father due to his bad ear, and with a word of apology, picked up his chair, carried it around the desk, and placed it right next to the pope. During Pope Pius XII's reign of nearly twenty years, he ended up giving his unfailing and ardent support of the Legion of Mary.[221]

When Cardinal Roncalli was assigned to be the Apostolic Nuncio to France, he wrote to Duff: "...even though the bishops of France are divided on the question of the Legion, I am not divided. I am wholeheartedly in favor of it. Its method is right. *It seeks out the individual* in the spirit of faith and love, and that goes to the heart of the question." Ten years later, Cardinal Roncalli became Pope John XXIII, and two years after his election in 1958, gave the greatest possible approbation to the Legion of Mary when he declared: "The Legion of Mary presents the true face of the Catholic Church."[222]

Frank Duff (on right) with his good friend, Fr. Robert Bradshaw (center), who was also Duff's posthumous biographer and a Legion of Mary envoy to Iceland and Siberia

In 1965, when Duff was seventy-six, he was invited to be one of the few lay observers of the Second Vatican Council and received entry to its last session. Frank's greatest experience during his three-month stay in Rome was his private audience with Pope Paul VI, who said to him, "Mr. Duff, I want to thank you for your services to the Church and also to express appreciation for all that the Legion of Mary has done."[223]

Duff, in turn, thanked the Holy Father and assured him of the Legion's loyalty to him and to all priests, adding, "We look to our members to bear witness to this, even to the point of martyrdom." To that the Pontiff responded, "The Legion of Mary has served the Church faithfully, and the Church will protect the Legion."

During the Council, when Cardinal Heenan introduced Frank Duff to the 2,500 prelates who were present, all of them spontaneously rose to their feet for prolonged applause. They were saluting the man who had anticipated fifty years earlier the teaching of Vatican II, that the Church is essentially missionary and that the laity, as members of the mystical body of Christ, are called to help bring the Kingdom to earth, to be apostles to everyone with whom they come in contact.

Following the Council, when Frank was asked how he felt about the role of the Legion in the years ahead, he replied:

> *[As] I see things, the Legion has only now arrived at adult stature—only now. Up to the present, it has, in a sense, been in the cradle. Now it is a grown and armed soldier ready for the terrible fray that the next century is going to place us in the midst of.*[224]

In another prescient moment, Duff said:

> *The Legion stands up so well in that storm against the faith. The big reason for this is the Legion's devotion to Mary who is the torch of faith and who destroys all heresies. Another reason is the Legion's constant prayer for faith. One is emboldened to hope that the Legion is destined to play a key part in the supporting of the Church through the crisis of this spiritual winter and into a glorious spring.*[225]

On May 10, 1979, Duff and three legionaries were invited to assist at Pope John Paul II's Mass in his private chapel, followed by an Irish breakfast just for them. "Victory will come through Mary," the future saint told them.

One of the Legion members said to the pope, "Your Holiness, Mr. Duff will be ninety years old in a few weeks' time.

Pope John Paul II turned to Frank and said, "Well, you can consider yourself youth until ninety." Oddly enough, Frank took those words very seriously. As they were leaving the Vatican grounds, he said, "I know my time is very short."

Before saying his final goodbye, the Holy Father repeated, "Remember the words, 'Victory comes through Mary.'"

Frank did not forget them. The following year on October 25, 1980, fifteen years after Vatican II, Frank Duff, at ninety-one, was finally slowing down a bit. That day, he gave his concluding address at a Pro Christo Conference before hundreds of legionaries. His last public words were:

> *So we must think in terms of the apparently impossible: the conquest of the world of souls. Mary will make the dream come true.*[226]

Just two weeks later, on November 7, 1980, having attended two Masses that same day,[227] Frank wasn't feeling well and climbed into his bed in the afternoon. He was the last living member of his large family, whom he missed dearly. While sitting upright facing a picture of the Sacred Heart, he died peacefully.

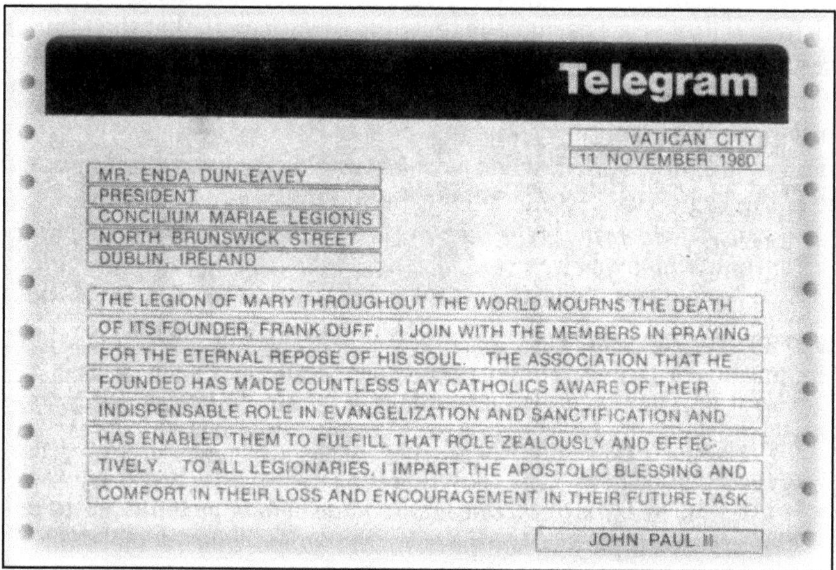

Telegram

VATICAN CITY
11 NOVEMBER 1980

MR. ENDA DUNLEAVEY
PRESIDENT
CONCILIUM MARIAE LEGIONIS
NORTH BRUNSWICK STREET
DUBLIN, IRELAND

THE LEGION OF MARY THROUGHOUT THE WORLD MOURNS THE DEATH OF ITS FOUNDER, FRANK DUFF. I JOIN WITH THE MEMBERS IN PRAYING FOR THE ETERNAL REPOSE OF HIS SOUL. THE ASSOCIATION THAT HE FOUNDED HAS MADE COUNTLESS LAY CATHOLICS AWARE OF THEIR INDISPENSABLE ROLE IN EVANGELIZATION AND SANCTIFICATION AND HAS ENABLED THEM TO FULFILL THAT ROLE ZEALOUSLY AND EFFECTIVELY. TO ALL LEGIONARIES, I IMPART THE APOSTOLIC BLESSING AND COMFORT IN THEIR LOSS AND ENCOURAGEMENT IN THEIR FUTURE TASK.

JOHN PAUL II

In July 1996, the Church began Frank Duff's cause for beatification. Fr. Bede McGregor, O.P., postulator for the cause of Frank's sainthood, shared the following story:

> *I remember once interviewing a man because I'm in charge of the cause for the beatification of Frank Duff—a man from the Morningstar Hostel, and he knew Frank Duff very well. And I said to him, "Now, are you prepared to say what you say under oath because it's no good to me unless you prepare to swear on the Bible that it's true." So, he said he was, he was, and I said, "What do you remember most about Frank Duff?" Now, this was a man who is an alcoholic, who had a tragic life, really, a tragic life, and he said an extraordinary thing to me. He said, "Father, Frank Duff was the only man I ever met who looked up to me." That is a tremendous thing to say—the reverence. Taking the dignity of a person, no matter how crushed they are in life. You know...you've got to believe that whatever you do to the least of my brothers and sisters, you do to me. That was his basic theology and practice, you know, so when I heard that, I said, "Now that's the kind of thing ... that's the kind of saint I like."*[228]

Frank Duff is now known in the Catholic Church under the title: Servant of God. The supernatural faith he possessed, a faith that moved mountains, combined with his apostolic zeal to evangelize, and his gift of imparting love and dignity, especially to the poor, has given the world a fresh and unique perspective on the use of the Miraculous Medal.

The following is Frank Duff's exhortation to members of the Legion of Mary, and to every Catholic. Frank realized, only too well, the sorrowful fact that Catholics, in general, do not speak about religion to those outside of the Church, and seldom enough to those inside of it. But now is the time to change that. May we take his words to heart, and with a bag of Medals in hand, step out in faith to do the most important work of all—that of bringing souls to Christ.

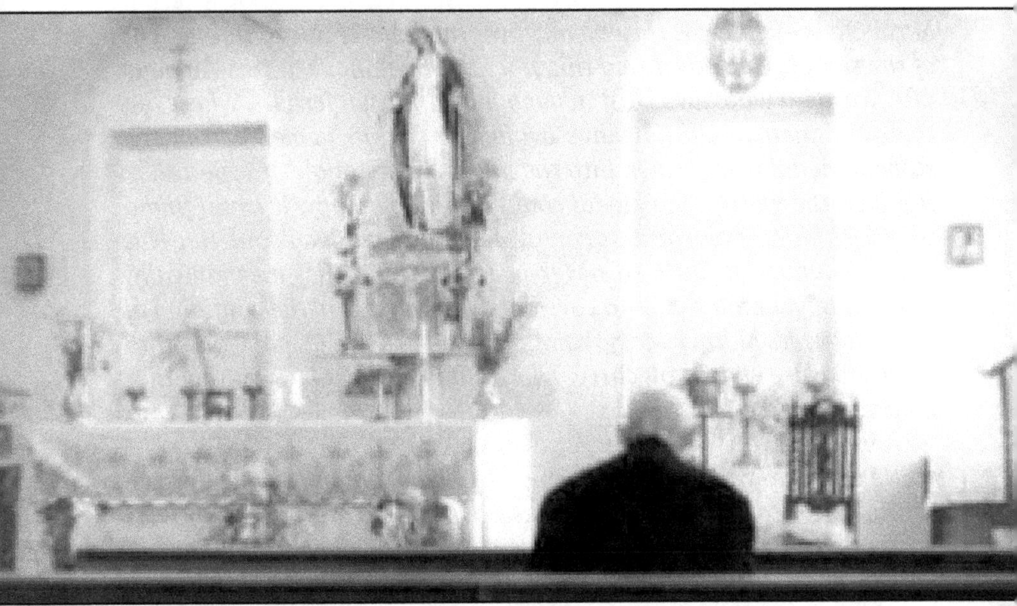

Frank Duff sitting alone in prayer in the chapel of the Regina Coeli ("Queen of Heaven") Hostel that he founded in 1930, which served destitute single women and unmarried women with children.

Faith is a divine, almost handleable quality. It can be used like money to buy things. But unlike money, it can increase in ourselves according as we bestow it on others. It is supposed to be communicated from one to another. Faith is passed on by giving and hearing ... Religious history is full of examples where unbelieving persons suddenly got faith from others who willed to give it to them.

You are privileged to see signs of this operation in connection with your use of the Miraculous Medal. The fact that this Medal works is uncontestable. There is not one among us who has not had startling evidence of its power to soften and to produce effects. The only valid explanation of its efficacy is that it is faith reduced after a fashion to visible form, which is precisely what a sacramental amounts to. It applies our faith to a particular purpose in a tangible way. Again, I use the analogy of money which conveniences us in purchasing. We are looking for something in the higher or spiritual order; we assign the Medal, so to speak, to that "purchase." Our faith puts itself forth through the Medal, and our desire is granted to us. The Medal almost enables us to handle grace, and I repeat that this is the idea of the sacramentals. Present the Medal to a person, and you have brought your faith into very close touch with him.

Some of you have heard the story of the Indian girl drowned in the Cowichan River. The body had been sought unavailingly for a week by the whole tribe. It came at once to the surface at the spot where a Miraculous Medal was thrown in, at the moment of the abandonment of the search. One day, I told this story to a legionary group. An hour afterwards, a watch was lost in a mountainside wilderness, where ten thousand men would not have availed to find it. Remembering the story, a Medal was thrown into the midst of the tangle of vegetation. It fell on the watch. The Medal could bring up a body, It could find a watch.[229] *More important, It can awaken life in a dead soul. But It is only a channel of faith, so never just give the Medal mechanically. Deliberately intend It to be a carrier of your faith and the confiding of that soul to its Mother Mary, whose image is on the Medal. Your faith is the treasure which you carry. Though it is yours, it is not altogether a personal possession.*

It is God in you.

He wants to widen His place in you, and at the same time, to issue through you to others. Indeed, these two things are bound up with each other. If we do not try to share our faith, it may dry up in us. If we do try to put it to a full use, it can become a vaster force than anything in nature, immeasurably greater than the atom bomb, more far-reaching than space travel.

Let us set that force at work on the most neglected cause of the day, conversion. Because conversion is the central idea of the Church and yet so neglected, effort directed towards it will draw omnipotence from on high. Listen, Our Lord Himself is speaking: "Have faith in God. Amen, I say to you, whoever says to this mountain: arise and cast yourself into the sea, and does not waver in his heart but believes that whatever he says will be done, that shall be done for him" (Mark 11:23). And Our Lord adds: "And nothing will be impossible to you" (Matthew 17:19).

Let us take Him at His word.[230]

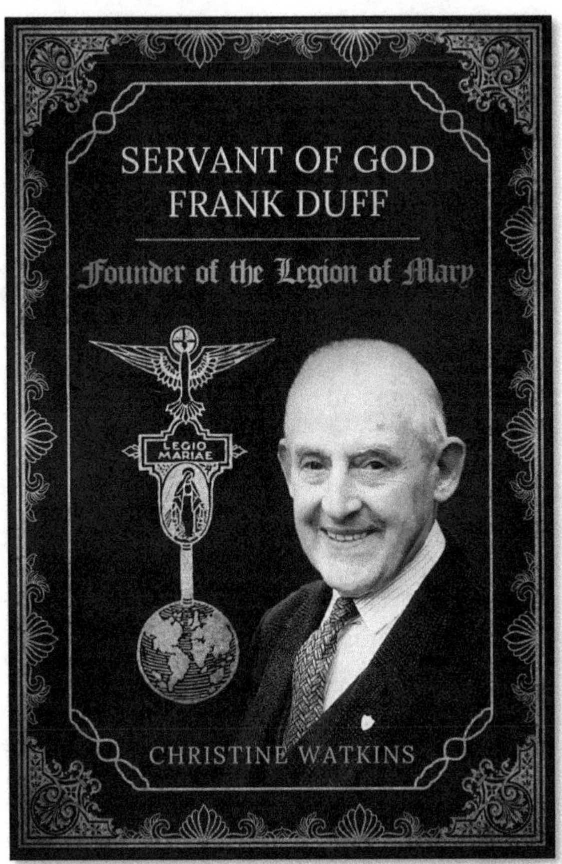

A deeply moving and inspiring biography of Frank Duff's life, available as a free e-book at www.QueenofPeaceMedia.com/frank-duff

SERVANT OF GOD, FR. JOHN HARDON, S.J. (1914-2000)

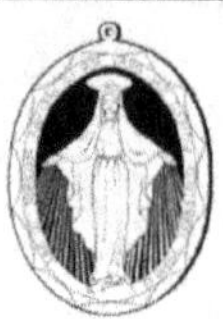

Servant of God, Fr. John Hardon, S.J., was a great intellectual in the Catholic Church. During his lifetime, he authored dozens of books on religion and theology, including *The Catholic Catechism* (1975), written at the request of Pope Paul VI, and the *Modern Catholic Dictionary* (1980). When in the early 1980s, Pope John Paul II instructed Mother Teresa of Calcutta to have her order evangelize the poor in addition to looking after their material needs, she told him she didn't know where to begin such an endeavor. The Pope referred her to Cardinal Ratzinger (the future Pope Benedict XVI), who called upon Fr. Hardon to instruct her Missionaries of Charity. To fill this need, he wrote a catechetical course for Mother Teresa's order, which was later adapted to create two catechetical home study courses for lay Catholics. In 1985, he founded the Marian Catechist Apostolate[231] an organization that uses these home study courses to form catechists throughout the world. Fr. Hardon's catechism pav ed the way for the Holy See's *Catechism of the Catholic Church,* promulgated by Pope John Paul II in 1992, for which he served as a consultant.

Fr. John Hardon was a prolific writer and professor for most of his life

Mother Teresa of Calcutta with Fr. John Hardon, on the right

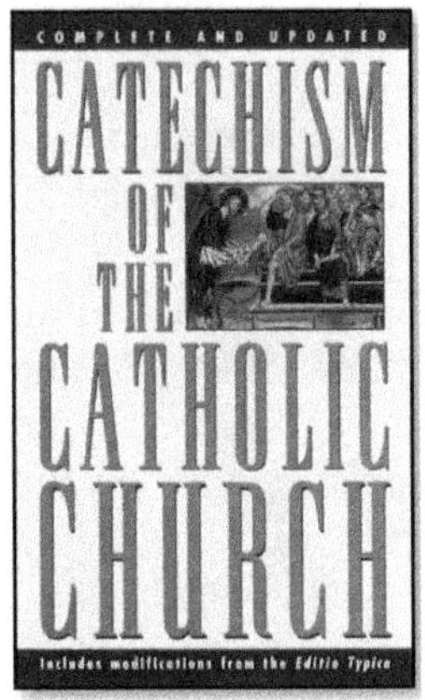

1992 Catechism of the Catholic Church

Fr. Hardon recorded nearly a dozen sets of audiotapes for Eternal Life of Bardstown, Kentucky, whose founder William J. Smith said that Fr. Hardon would write letters and books on his knees before the Blessed Sacrament. "Fr. Hardon was a master teacher. The two things that impressed me most were his holiness—he went to Confession every day, prayed for hours before the Blessed Sacrament every day—and still wrote prodigiously—and his encyclopedic mind. Once people met Fr. Hardon, they were hooked on him. For tens of thousands of Catholics, he was a very, very important person in their lives."[232]

Fr. Hardon was born amidst the iron and steel mills of Cleveland, Ohio. When John was only a year old, his father was killed in an industrial accident. His mother, Anna, a devout Franciscan Tertiary, worked cleaning offices, often at night, spending her days keeping an eye on little John. Her boy was willful and self-possessed, determined that no one was going to tell him what to do. "Yet as he grew," wrote John Janaro in his profile of Hardon in the book *Fishers of Men*, "he also became deeply devoted to his mother, and her religious sense—which filled the home and dominated John's upbringing—made its mark upon him. Upon entering the house John or his mother would always say 'Praised be Jesus Christ' to which the other would respond 'Now and forever. Amen.' There was a statue of the Virgin Mother of God, and always holy water by the front door."

John Hardon on the day of his First Holy Communion

Touched by God at a very young age, little John Hardon secretly asked to be a priest on the day of his First Holy Communion. He was only six years old. Two years later, on his Confirmation day, he asked for "the grace of martyrdom."[233] But John's martyrdom was not granted to him in death; rather it came to him in life.

Fr. Hardon praying before the Blessed Sacrament with Mother Teresa and her sisters

"The faith I had so casually learned," he said, "could be preserved only by the price of a living martyrdom. This faith, I was to find out, is a precious treasure that cannot be preserved except at a heavy price. The price is nothing less than to confess what so many others either openly or covertly denied."[234]

John was a profoundly spiritual man—"I doubt if there is any element in man's relationship with God that is more important than prayer"[235] —and a key part of the Lord's plan for his life was to introduce him to the power of the Miraculous Medal. Many times in Fr. Hardon's preaching, teaching, and lecturing, he told the following story, which often began: "One of the most memorable experiences that I ever had was with the Miraculous Medal. It changed my life ..."

Fr. Hardon as a young priest

In October 1948, when John was in the third year of his novitiate (or Tertianship), a year after his ordination and before taking final vows, he sat with other new Jesuit clergy, listening to a visiting Vincentian. The priest was talking at length, encouraging them to obtain faculties to enroll people in the Confraternity of the Miraculous Medal. Fr. Hardin remembered him saying, "Fathers, the Miraculous Medal works. Miracles have been performed by Our Lady through the Miraculous Medal."

"I was not impressed," recalled Fr. Hardin. "I was not the medal-wearing kind of person, and I certainly did not have a Miraculous Medal." Only because it didn't cost him anything, he wrote his name down on a list to receive a four-page leaflet from the Vincentians, with the then-Latin formula for blessing Miraculous Medals and conferring them upon the wearer. About two weeks later, his mail came with the leaflet for blessing and enrollment. He stuck it into the back of his priestly office book and promptly forgot about it.

In February of the following year, Fr. Hardon was sent to assist the chaplain of St. Alexis Hospital in Cleveland, Ohio, for two weeks. Each morning, he received a list of all the patients admitted into the hospital that day. With so many Catholics admitted, he could not visit them all immediately. Among the many patients was a boy about nine years old, who had been downhill sledding when he lost control of the sled and ran into a tree head-on. His skull was fractured, and X-rays revealed severe brain damage. When Fr. Hardon finally made the rounds to visit his room at the hospital, the boy had been in a coma for ten days. He could not speak or move his body and was being fed intravenously. There was no contesting the little boy's diagnosis: he would never recover from permanent and inoperable brain damage. The only question was whether he would live or die.

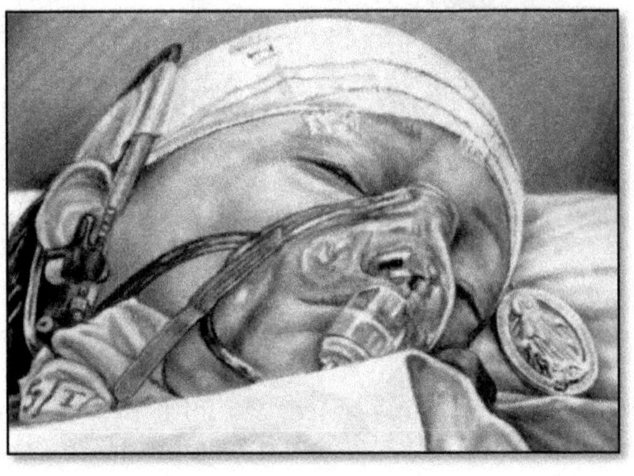

After blessing the boy and consoling his parents, Fr. Hardon was about to leave his hospital room, but then a thought came to him: "That

Vincentian priest. He said, 'The Miraculous Medal works.' Now this will be a test of its alleged miraculous powers!"

Not possessing a Miraculous Medal of his own, Fr. Hardon scoured the hospital workers to no avail. But something wouldn't let him give up. He persisted and finally a religious sister working night duty as a nurse gave him one that she found. Pulling out the leaflet from his office book, he learned that he wasn't supposed to just bless the Medal, but also put it around the person's neck with a chain or ribbon. He reached out to the sister again. Fr. Hardon shared, "So the sister-nurse found a blue ribbon for the Medal, which made me feel silly. What was I doing with Medals and blue ribbons?"

Persevering nonetheless, he asked the boy's father to hold the leaflet for investing a person in the Confraternity of the Miraculous Medal, and he proceeded to bless the Medal and say the prayer of enrollment.[236]

No sooner had Fr. Hardon finished than the boy opened his eyes for the first time in two weeks. The boy turned his head, looked at his mother and said, "Ma, I want some ice cream." Then he proceeded to talk clearly in perfect nine-year-old English to his father and mother.

Fr. Hardon and the boy's parents stood in stunned silence. After a few minutes, it dawned on them to call a doctor, who after examining the boy, told the parents they could offer him something to eat.

The next day, the boy received a series of tests. X-rays showed the brain damage was gone. Then still more tests. After three days, when every examination showed he had received a complete and miraculous restoration to health, the boy was released from the hospital.

"This experience so changed my life," said Fr. John Hardon, "that I have not been the same since. My faith in God, faith in His power to work miracles, was strengthened beyond description. Since then, of course, I have been promoting devotion to Our Lady and the use of the Miraculous Medal."[237]

FR. JAMES McCURRY, O.F.M.

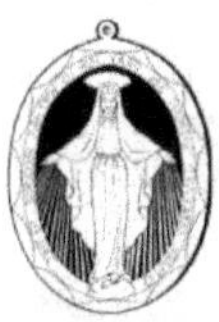

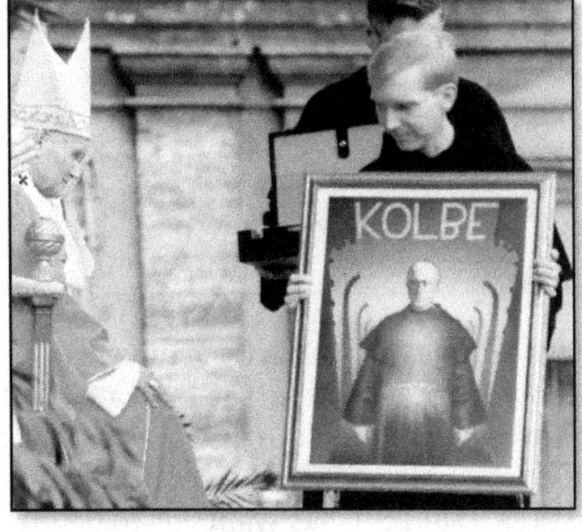

A great apostle of the Miraculous Medal is Fr. James McCurry, OFM, a Conventional Franciscan of Irish descent. He is the Minister Provincial Emeritus of the Franciscan Friars Conventual, Past-President of the Mariological Society of America, former National Director of the Militia of the Immaculata in the United States, and he has appeared regularly on The Eternal World Television Network (EWTN).

Fr. McCurry played a prominent role in promoting St. Maximilian Kolbe's candidacy for sainthood. Because of this, he presented picture of

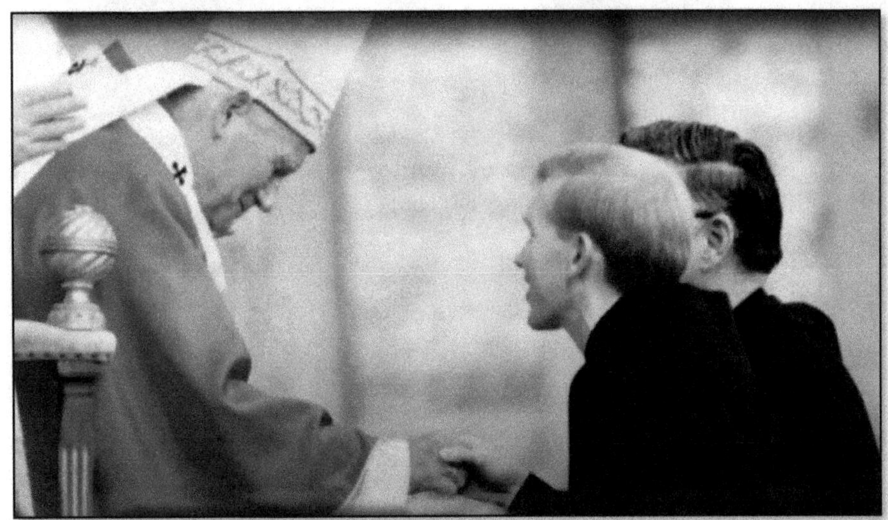

Fr. Kolbe to Pope John Paul II during the canonization ceremony on October 10, 1982, at the Vatican in Rome. Ready for the moment with his prepared speech, he said nervously, "Holy Father, I am Fr. James from America. Please pray that we might all be as consecrated to Mary as St. Maximilian Kolbe was."

The Pope responded by pointing a finger at him and saying, "You do that!"

Just hours before Fr. Kolbe's canonization, by a chance meeting inside St. Peter's Basilica, Fr. James also met Mother Teresa of Calcutta through a "chance" friendly chat, which developed into a friendship. For many years following, he provided retreats for her Missionaries of Charity sisters.

When Mother Teresa made her final visit in 1997 to the Missionaries of Charity convent in the South Bronx, Fr. McCurry approached her as she sat, delicate and feeble in a wheelchair. He realized that this would be the last time he would ever see her. With a signature basket of Miraculous Medals on her lap, Mother Teresa spoke her last words to him: "Jesus wants us to be joyful. Spread His joy."

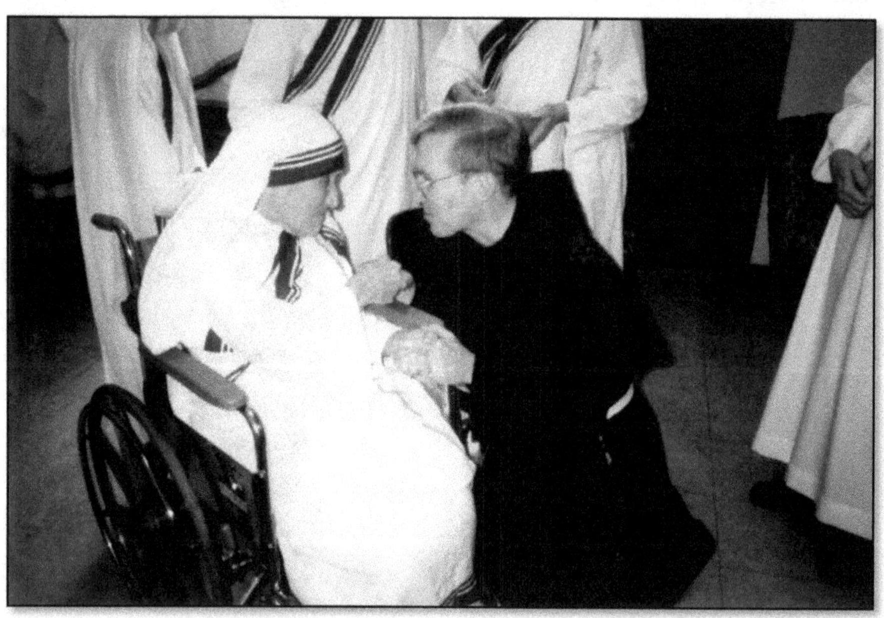

Fr. McCurry took Mother Teresa's words and Pope John Paul II's exhortation directly into his heart. Here in the priest's own words is one story that proves this:

In the early years after my Ordination to the Holy Priesthood, the Franciscan Order sent me to do doctoral studies at the University of Chicago. This was in the late 1970s. The closest Franciscan friary where I could reside was on the North Side of the city, while the University was situated on the South side. Hence, my daily journey to classes averaged an hour and a half each way – first on Chicago's infamous "L" (elevated train) to Garfield Boulevard, and then on a bus to Hyde Park.

Often while waiting for the bus after emerging from the Garfield "L" station, I would be approached by needy men or women begging me for money. As a poor friar with a vow of poverty, I normally did not have any extra money to give away. So, I began the practice of carrying in my trousers' pocket a small pouch of Miraculous Medals. I would always explain to the good soul in need, *"Sorry I have no money, but I'd love to give you this Miraculous Medal as a token of God's love for you, and a sign that I care."* I would then elaborate, as time permitted, with a mini-catechism lesson. First, I would explain that the front of the Medal depicted the Blessed Virgin Mary, who had been given the job by God to collaborate with her Son Jesus in crushing all the evils crawling across the world. Then I would show my new friend the reverse side of the Medal, pointing out the two Hearts of Jesus and Mary, with an assurance that these Hearts would always keep beating love for every person in this world.

This distribution of the Miraculous Medal outside the Garfield Boulevard "L" station became my daily mission of street evangelization. Only once did anyone ever refuse to accept the Medal from me. This happened when I offered it one day to a poor man with matted hair, dressed in rags, who had obviously been living on the streets for weeks, and whose body odor bespoke that fact. Moreover, he wreaked of the "devil's brew." Nearly overpowered by the smells, I nonetheless mustered strength, with Mother Mary's intercession, to offer him a Miraculous Medal. He looked at me gently, and I heard him whisper, *"Sorry, Father, I can't accept this. I don't know if anyone ever told you, but YOU have the WORST BREATH I've ever smelled!"*

On the first day of the second semester of my post-Ordination graduate studies at the University of Chicago, in January 1978, shortly after the noon hour, I alighted from the "L" (elevated) train on the upper platform at Garfield Boulevard. Still new to life in Chicago, I had not yet learned all the rules of survival in the "big city." One of those rules was to stick with the crowd. I normally have only three gears—slow, slower, and stop. That winter's day, for reasons known only to God, I was in third gear—the "stop" mode. Thus, all of the other passengers had already disappeared by the time I descended the stairs from the platform. Halfway down the stairs, I met on the landing a young man, who immediately asked me what time it was. I stopped, put down my briefcase, looked at the timepiece on my wrist, and replied to the tall lad, *"It's half past twelve."* He then pulled a gun out of his pocket and stuck it in my stomach.

Now, if you plan ahead what you will do if held up by a bandit, forget it. Everything happens so fast that you cannot possibly remember any strategy. So, I heard myself say to the young brigand: *"What seems to be the matter?"*

Then, trying to defuse the situation with humor, I added, *"I told you the right time, didn't I?"*

He was in no mood to be amused, and demanded, *"Give me your money!"*

Dressed in clergy attire, I said, *"But I'm a Franciscan; I'm normally the one who takes up the collection!"* Pitiless, he pushed me down. I stood back up, and once again, he pushed the gun into my stomach.

Now actually, on that particular day, I did have $50 in my pocket. It had been sent to me by our Province treasurer from Baltimore to use for the purchase of my university course books. (The fact that $50 would have sufficed for a semester's books in those days attests to how long ago this incident occurred!) Thus, I was in a moral quandary. I could not lie to the young gunman, because, if he shot me, I did not want to die with a lie on my conscience. On the other hand, I could not give him the $50, because I was more afraid of the old skinflint treasurer in Baltimore than I was of the Chicago thug. So, I had recourse to the oldest trick in our Catholic moral theology books—the "broad mental reservation." That is, one speaks the truth, but in such a way that it is heard differently than one intends. Hence, I weakly uttered to the gunman, *"But I have no money for you!"* The key phrase here was "for you." The $50 was not for him; it was for books! So, if he did kill me, at least I could have died without a lie on my soul.

The gunman and I had reached an impasse, facing each other in stalemate—with him still holding the gun in my stomach. I then remembered the pouch of Miraculous Medals in my left pocket, and thought to myself, *"If only I could give this poor creature of God a Miraculous Medal!"* Yet, I dared not reach for my pocket, lest the lad think I was reaching for his gun. Of course, all of this transpired in the flash of a few seconds. I was at a complete loss. At that moment, I felt inspired to invoke Our Lady. I silently prayed: *"Blessed Mother, if you want this gun-toting brigand to have one of your Medals, then you take over!"* Suddenly, I felt inspired to raise my voice and yell at the lad in a stern tone I had never used before: *"Listen here, don't you realize that we're brothers in Christ!"* I wish you could have seen his face change immediately. He blanched, and his whole expression softened. Shrugging his shoulders, he said to me, *"I guess you're right."* He put the gun back into his pocket and started to walk away, up the stairs from the landing to the "L" platform.

I thought to myself, *"Now's my chance,"* and I shouted after him, *"Wait a minute! Come back! Come back! I have something for you!"* He turned around and returned to me. By now I had taken a Miraculous Medal from my pocket. Handing it to him, I said, *"You mightn't have realized it, but just now there have been three of us present here: yourself, myself, and the Woman on this Medal. She is Mary, the Mother of Jesus Christ, and she has just prevented you from committing a sin—namely murder (and I wouldn't have appreciated that!). So please accept this Medal as a sign that you have a Mother in heaven looking out for you, you have a Brother in Christ, and a friend here in James* (pointing to myself) *who'll be praying for you.* He looked at the Medal, kissed it, and walked away wordless.

I never found out the gunman's name, but I have prayed for him ever since, nicknaming him "Dismas"—the good thief. Now, I relate this whole story, not with the slightest intent of self-importance. If it were James's own doing, I would be dead—my body six feet under, and with my name changed from James to "Peat"! Rather, I tell this tale of my attempted mugging in Chicago to glorify Our Lady of the Miraculous Medal. Not only did she save my life, but more importantly, she touched the hardened heart of a violent desperado, converting him into a "Dismas."

In all the years since that incident at the Chicago "L" station, every time I have walked down those stairs from platform to landing—or ascended them from landing to platform—I leave a Miraculous Medal on the banister. Invariably, it disappears, taken up by another needy passerby.

STEVE DAWSON

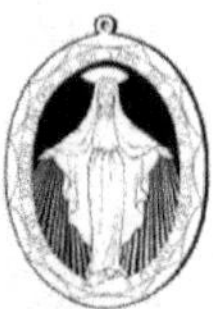

Steve Dawson was attracted to danger, like a child to Christmas morning. At age thirteen, he thought it would be a good idea—never having driven before—to steal his parents' car and push it to 120 miles per hour. Eventually crashing into a guardrail, nearly cutting the car in two, he said glibly to the policeman who arrived at the scene, "What seems to be the trouble, officer?"

Nothing was learned, and Steve fell precipitously into a life of party crowds, substance use, and thrill-seeking. After blowing up one of the toilets in his high school with a cherry bomb, he was immediately accused without proof of guilt. The staff simply knew he did it.

Steve's father was lawyer who worked long hours, and faith wasn't practiced in their upper-class home in Detroit, although his mother, a lapsed Catholic, went on a "search for church" when Steve was ten or eleven years old. After dragging him and his sister to different Protestant services every Sunday, until they protested, insisting they were Catholic, not so much to go to Mass, but to get out of going anywhere.

Wholesome entertainment bored Steve, who craved excitement. To satisfy this itch, he started off doing pranks, such as getting together with friends to soak tennis balls in gasoline, light them on fire, and roll them down a hill of green grass next to the railroad tracks. Then pranks turned into crimes in middle school, like stealing hood ornaments from cars—just for the thrill of it. His spurts of adrenaline reminded him that doing bad things tended to feel better than doing good things.

Early in life, Steve rejected the straight and narrow path, outright, in favor of a fun-filled rollercoaster spin—a ride that would turn sickening. He was expelled from his Catholic middle school, and after becoming enthralled with alcohol, marijuana and other drugs of recreation in high school, he was kicked out of there, too. This led to special permission to get his diploma by taking evening adult-education classes, which allowed him to sleep in and smoke during class breaks. He didn't mind. At seventeen, he was kicked out of his parents' home due to his out-of-control behavior. By age twenty-nine, his reckless behavior got him arrested dozens of times. He hadn't rejected God, at least not consciously. Faith just wasn't something he cared about.

At some point before Steve was suspended from high school, his mother returned to the Catholic Church of her youth. This happened largely because she developed a close friendship with Servant of God Fr. John Hardon, S.J. Praying daily for her wayward son to know the love of God, she had Masses said for him and asked her friends, including Fr. Hardon, to pray for his conversion.

Steve grew less and less satisfied with his life of "I'll do what I want, when I want." Nearing age thirty, he had filled his body with pleasure and his mind with thrills, even stolen from his parents…But in looking out for Number One, he ended up painfully agitated and teetering on desperation.

His life wasn't working—he had to admit. When Steve could no longer tread water and felt himself sinking in his self-induced quagmire, he started to give the notion of a God a chance. Researching different religions, he steered clear of Catholicism, especially since his father had been recently catechized and baptized by Fr. Hardon, and he certainly didn't want to be next.

Then Steve hit rock bottom. Instead of surrendering to thoughts of suicide, he got serious and challenged God: "Show me that You are real!" This dare from his depths inspired him to investigate God even further, even watch EWTN while drunk, and to probe the one religion he hadn't wanted to touch. Through his inquiry into Truth, Steve came to accept Catholicism intellectually. Then in time, he allowed his heart to catch up with his head—no doubt helped by the voluminous number of prayers sent his direction. And once Steve gave his life over to God, he was all in—body, mind, and soul. God joyfully took the reins, and Steve was given an unusual and superabundant shower of grace, which broke his bondage to his many sins.

Steve Dawson, sharing literature and sacramentals with passers-by

Desiring to help save people from experiencing the nightmare he had been living on earth, and the hell that could await them, he set out to evangelize. But he grew increasingly upset that Catholics, possessing the Truth that had saved him, were hardly sharing this pearl of great price. His fellow believers were largely ignoring the Great Commission of the Lord to "Go, therefore, and make disciples of all nations (Mt. 28:19)." It was a commandment, he realized—a non-negotiable, and the only way the Church could survive.

"Evangelizing is, in fact, the grace and vocation proper to the Church, her deepest identity. She exists in order to evangelize."

— *Evangelii Nuntiandi*, Pope Paul VI's 1 975 apostolic exhortation

The newly revived and on-fire Steve then learned of how St. Maximilian Kolbe had been inspired by the conversion of Alphonse Ratisbonne, and how the saint had used his "silver bullet" as a channel of grace for conversion. Now Steve, too, was inspired. Deciding to follow in the steps of St. Maximilian, he purchased 1,000 Miraculous Medals, had them blessed by a priest, and kept a daily stash in his pocket. Handing them out freely to strangers, he came up with a sidewalk introduction:

"Here you go. The Blessed Virgin Mary appeared to St. Catherine in

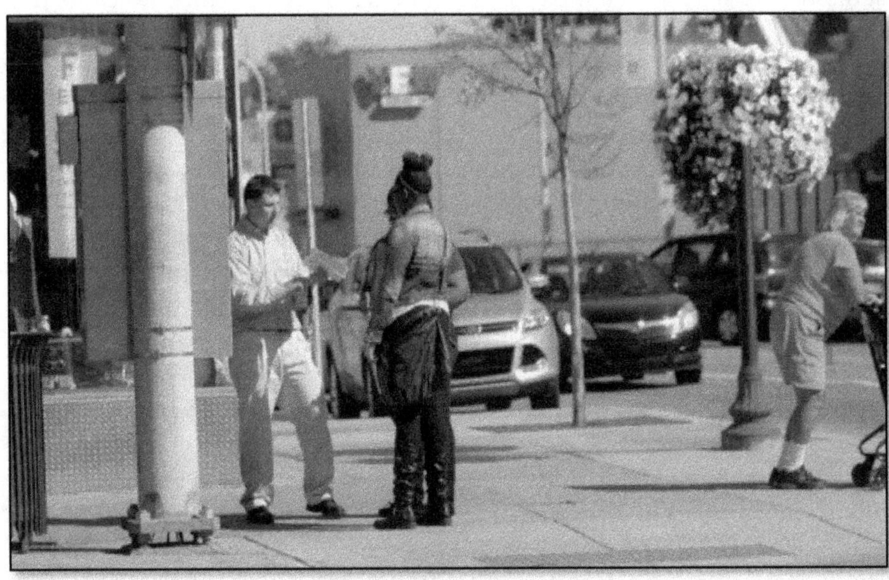

1830 and promised that whoever wore this Medal would receive great graces from God. So many miracles occurred because of it that it became commonly known as the Miraculous Medal."

The responses were nearly always kind—anything from "No, thank you," to "Great!"

Once, while at a dinner with friends, Steve gave a Miraculous Medal to a chatty young waitress. "I have a present for you," he said and dropped the "silver bullet" into her hand. She was Baptist, he learned, with a Catholic boyfriend. When Steve asked if she ever thought about becoming Catholic, she mentioned that she didn't agree with everything about Catholicism, one thing being its stance on abortion. Yet the conversation remained friendly. Before leaving, Steve handed her a model of a baby at ten weeks gestation, a Rosary, and a prolife pamphlet. The waitress graciously accepted them, and everyone at the table promised to pray for her.[238]

Three months later, Steve returned to the same diner with friends. The same waitress sat down next to Steve and said, "When you guys came in a few months ago, I had just found out I was pregnant. I was going to have an abortion, but after talking to you that night, I knew that God sent you as a sign for me to keep my baby."

The Lord had found a true disciple in a former hellion. God took the Miraculous Medal and Steve's fervor and inspired him to start what has become an overwhelmingly successful grassroots organization called St. Paul Street Evangelization. A seed began to germinate when Steve, his wife, Maria, and another couple decided to set up a booth at the Portland Saturday Market in Oregon and offer free Medals and Rosaries to the passersby. What began with four people has grown to network of over 200 trained street evangelization teams in the United States and abroad, with the support and accolades of notable clergy and lay evangelists. Hundreds of miracles of grace have since flowed through the friendly distribution of the Miraculous Medal, Rosaries, Catholic pamphlets—and heartfelt promises of prayer, in a world that is turning its back on God.

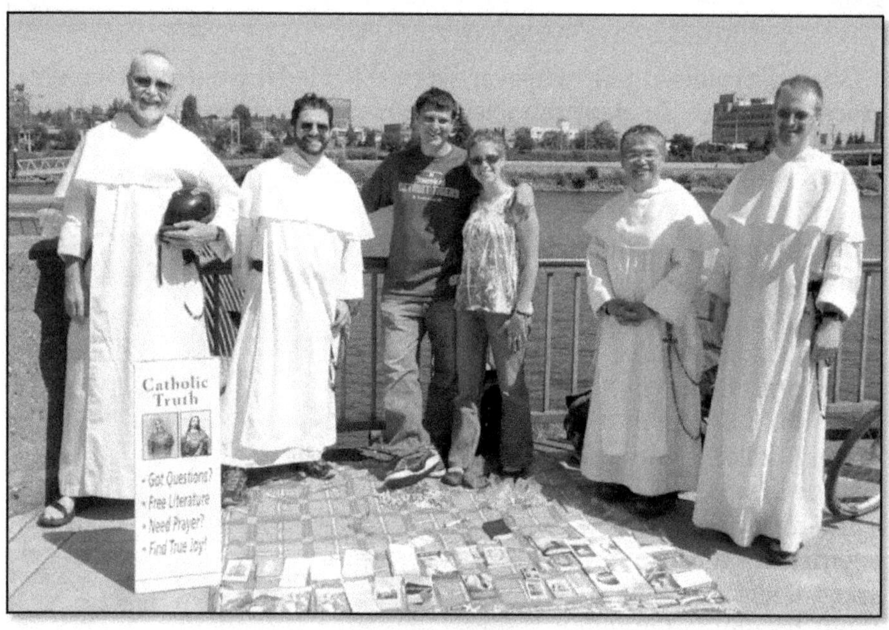

The reader is encouraged to get involved with St. Paul Street Evangelization. See https://streetevangelization.com and www.streetevangelization.com/medals.

FR. RONAN MURPHY

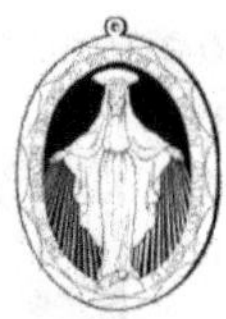

Ronan Murphy grew up in a nominal Catholic family of five children, one of them being his twin brother, so he jests that "There are two good-looking fellows running around in the world." In the Murphy family, it was expected that everyone would go to Mass as a Sunday routine, and that Ronan would attend Catholic schools, but he bore no interest in religion. The real god of his life was sports—and the partying that went with it.

On May 13, 1987, the Feast of Our Lady's appearance at Fatima, of which he had never heard, in a Marian year of which he was not aware, Ronan Murphy was on his lunch break from his job at American Express. As he was walking up Grafton Street, a busy shopping thoroughfare in Dublin City, Ireland, an exterior force stopped him outside of a Carmelite church. Then it turned him toward a jewelry store directly opposite the church entrance. As he gazed at the storefront window, the jewelry behind the glass suddenly disappeared before his eyes, leaving only a single, gold Miraculous Medal in the window. Ronan had never heard of the Miraculous Medal but understood, nevertheless, that the pendant was holy because of Our Lady's imprint. He felt immediately drawn to purchase it. When he entered the store, all of the jewelry reappeared.

Ronan possessed enough faith to take the Medal to the Carmelite church to have it blessed, and when he placed it around his neck, his whole life changed. In that moment, he was given an infusion of the basic tenants of the Catholic faith. He also received a special grace to love and devote himself to the Blessed Virgin Mary. Not having given her a second thought before, he now wanted to know all he could about her, and though he didn't know how to, he felt an inner desire to pray the Rosary. The only time that a "Hail Mary" had passed through his lips was when he was about six years old, and his mother had prayed a decade by his bedside.

A few days later, Ronan felt inspired to purchase a Brown Scapular. He didn't know what that was, either, but started to wear it, as well. He entered the Carmelite church, and this time, knelt before a statue of Our Lady. In a spontaneous prayer that welled from his heart, he consecrated himself to the Blessed Mother, without much of an understanding of what he was doing. The change in Ronan was so drastic that his mother commented, "I don't know where you came from!"

Ronan responded, "I hope, Mom, that you know where I came from, but my faith is a gift given to me on that thirteenth day of May."

Ronan soon learned, firsthand, that he who finds Mary finds Jesus. He went to Confession and began to attend daily Mass during his lunch break. No longer was Mass a Sunday habit, but the heavenly gift of receiving his God in Holy Communion. During one of his "church breaks" at lunchtime, Ronan heard a priest praying for emigrants, petitioning God that those leave the shores of Ireland might not lose their faith. "If I ever leave Ireland," Ronan told the Lord, "I promise You I will never lose my faith." That same day, he was invited to work at the American Express headquarters in England and accepted the new position. At twenty years old, he put his life in a couple of suitcases and moved to England.

Upon arriving on English soil, the first place Ronan went to in the Kemptown area of the English city of Brighton, was a Catholic church. There, two Irish priests welcomed him with open arms into the church of St. John the Baptist, which became his home away from home.

When Ronan was not at work at the bank, one could find him going to daily Mass, and praying his daily Rosary Divine Mercy Chaplet. In his prayer, a call to something more began to stir within him, but he felt unsure of what that "more" was... One day, while Ronan was in St. Mary's Pro Cathedral in Dublin for the Feast of the Immaculate Conception, two priests whom he had met in England four years previously, spotted him in the crowd and approached him in the middle of the church. "Out of four million people in Ireland," Ronan recalls, "they found me."

"We'd like to speak to you," they said. "Please see us after Mass." When the service ended, the two clerics took Ronan out to lunch, and the younger of them said to him, "You're still thinking of it."

No one had mentioned the word "priesthood," but Ronan knew exactly what he meant. "Father," he said, "God wouldn't call me. I had a big conversion five years ago, and you don't know the life I've lived."

The young priest responded, "Just try it."

"Yes, Father," he said before his mind could think otherwise, and immediately he felt the sensation of scales falling off the inside of him. For five years he had not let himself entertain the thought of priesthood, and suddenly his mind and heart opened to another world of belief, hope, and possibility. He had never felt so much peace in all his life.

Ronan entered seminary and one day in his first year of studies, he had another encounter involving the Miraculous Medal. He was walking home after attending Mass at his parish in Dublin, when he heard an interior voice telling him to turn around and go back to make a holy hour in the Adoration chapel. In seminary, he was not permitted to wear a priest collar, so he was dressed in casual clothes. No one could have known that he was a seminarian, yet as he was walking through the churchyard, a Missionary of Charity ran over to him and asked, "Are you a priest?"

"No, sister, but I hope to be one one day."

"Would you like to meet Mother Teresa?"

"Of course."

"If you get permission from your bishop to wear your collar, you can come in. I'll give you the address to the convent that you will be going to. It is where she did her novitiate before going to Calcutta in India." Mother Teresa had spent six months in Ireland during her time as a novice, and she was returning to that same convent to pay a visit.

Ronan received permission to wear his collar and arrived at the convent, along with about a thousand other people: bishops, cardinals, priests, religious and laity. When Mother Teresa entered the room, to Ronan she looked about half of half the size of him, but full of God. Everyone present fell silent. She walked around the room shaking everyone's hand, and briefly shook Ronan's hand, as well. There was no chance in such a large crowd for conversation with her. About 800 of the people formed a circle around Mother Teresa, and Ronan was on the periphery. He could not see her, but he could hear her quoting Gospel passages.

Ronan would have loved to have met and spoken with a living saint, but decided that since he couldn't even see Mother Teresa's tiny figure through the crowd, he would leave. As he started to walk out of the room, suddenly Mother Teresa stopped speaking. The room fell silent again. Ronan looked around to see what was happening. Suddenly Mother Teresa started bursting through the layers of people and ran after Ronan! He was not able to see her doing this, and there was no possible way that she could have seen him physically through the hundreds of people standing between them; yet in some way, she "saw" him.

She rushed up to Ronan, gave him a big hug and a kiss on the side of his cheek and said, You...I pray that you be a holy priest."

"Mother, I'm in the Marian Movement of Priests."

"Ah, I love the Marian Movement of Priests. You give me the list of all the priests in the Marian Movement, and I will have my sisters pray for them."

Ronan responded, "Well, that's impossible because there are about 120,000 in the world: cardinals, bishops, and priests. I'm afraid I can't give you a list of all of them."

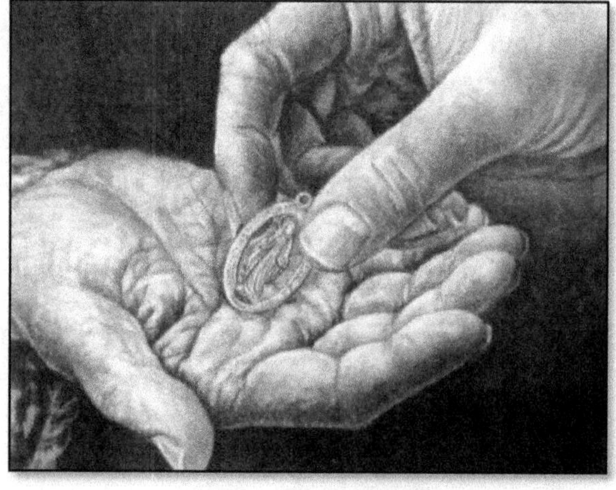

"I will have my sisters pray for them, but I will pray for you, that you will be a holy priest," and then Mother Teresa took Ronan's hand and placed a Miraculous Medal in it.

Ronan Murphy was ordained a priest in the Jubilee Year 2000 on the feast of our Lady of Fatima, on May 13, exactly thirteen years after the very day that an invisible force steered him toward a Miraculous Medal. Today, Fr. Ronan Murphy is what Mother Teresa prayed for...[239]

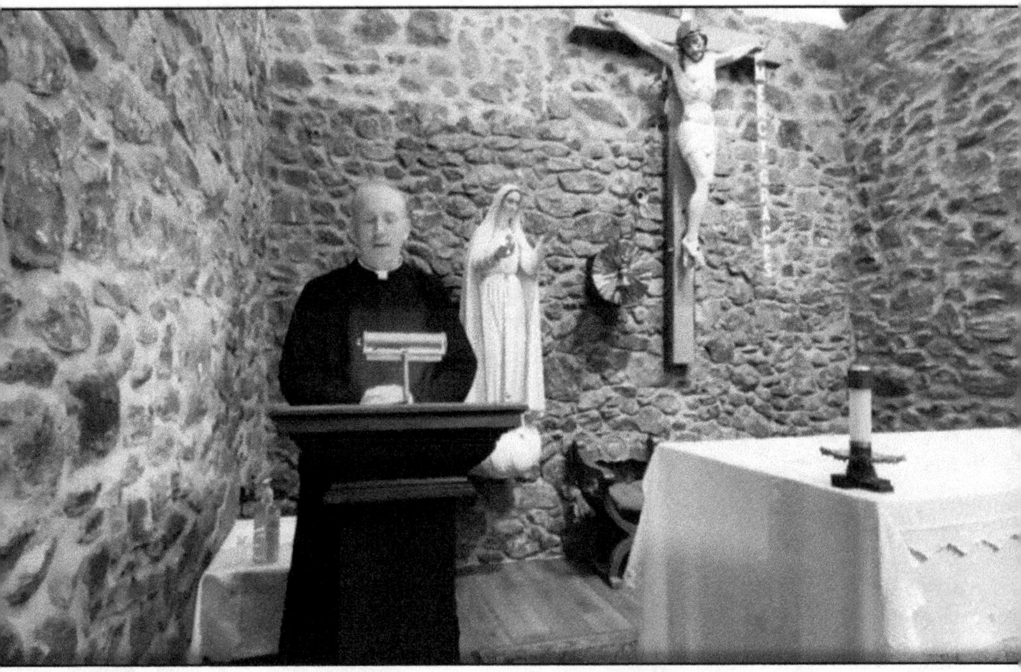

Fr. Ronan Murphy, preaching at The National Blue Army Shrine of Our Lady of Fatima on the Feast of the Annunciation

DEACON R. CHRISTOPH SANDOVAL

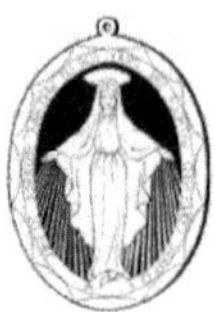

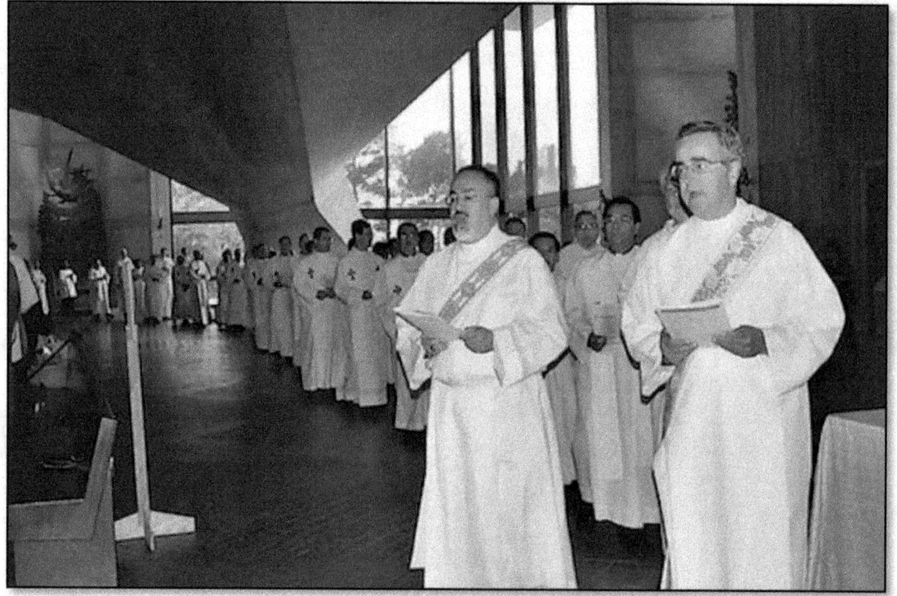

Christoph Sandoval en route to his ordination to the permanent diaconate at St. Mary's Cathedral in San Francisco, California. "The happiest day of my life."

In the summer of 2000, Christoph Sandoval was ordained a deacon for the Archdiocese of San Francisco. That same year, he asked his devoutly Catholic mother and his longtime close friend, Rafael, to journey with him to the Basilica of Our Lady of Guadalupe in Mexico City. Being from a poor, Latino/Hispanic barrio of Los Angeles, California, and having a grandmother whose family escaped the persecution and carnage of the Cristero War, he, like many faithful Mexican American Catholics, desired to visit his Holy Mother in his motherland.

On a high wall of the Basilica of Our Lady of Guadalupe, her miraculous image has been preserved on the tilma worn by the local Aztec convert to

The miraculous image of Our Lady of Guadalupe that appeared on the tilma of St. Juan Diego in 1531

Catholicism, St. Juan Diego, when she appeared to him on Mount Tepeyac in 1531. For the Latin-American people, Our Lady of Guadalupe is not simply an image on the tilma, as miraculous as this is.

[240] She is part her children's innermost identity. In the indigenous cultures of the time when Our Lady appeared, the tilma was the exterior expression of the interior identity of the person. By being visible on Juan Diego's tilma, Mary became imprinted in the deepest recesses of his heart—and in the hearts of all who come to her."[241]

The three excited pilgrims checked in at the beautiful Gran Hotel Ciudad de México near the Zócalo, the main square in Mexico City. The Zócalo is bordered by the largest cathedral in North America, with perhaps the longest name: the Metropolitan Cathedral of the Assumption of the Most Blessed Virgin Mary into Heaven. Together, they decided to peruse the artwork of painter Diego Rivera and then attend Mass at the Cathedral. Around 3 p.m., the hour of mercy, Christoph's mother grew tired. Being an older lady, she couldn't imagine walking another step. *"Can we go back and take a nap?"* she asked. So they returned to the hotel—Rafael and Christoph in one room, and his mother next door.

All three plopped onto their beds to rest, enjoying the luxury of not needing to be anywhere by any particular time. Deacon Sandoval lay face up, his eyes closed, and was about to drift off when he suddenly felt the presence of evil. Startled, he opened his eyes to see a massive, three-

The Metropolitan Cathedral of The Assumption of The Most Blessed Virgin Mary into Heaven in Zócalo square

Deacon Sandoval in the Basilica of Our Lady of Guadalupe

dimensional shadow figure, about ten feet tall, hovering over him. Pitch black with no visible facial features, the figure morphed itself into a threatening posture, with arms outstretched and fingers poised to strangle the new deacon.

Christoph called out the name, *"Jesus!"* and the ominous figure vanished. As he took a deep breath, he heard a knock at the door. It was his mother. *"Son, did you see that?"* Christoph let his mother in, and she began describing exactly the same dark figure he had just seen.

"We need to go see the Virgin as soon as possible," Christoph urged. Somehow, he recognized the figure as the evil entity that had been attacking him since he was a child. The hostile presence had come back again, but what was it so upset about?

Hopping into a taxicab the next morning, they took off in the direction of the Basilica of Our Lady of Guadalupe. There, like most pilgrims, they walked on their knees before the holy image of the Virgin, as a way of giving thanks for prayers answered; they went to Confession and received the Eucharist in both species, Body and Blood; and they wept with immense joy, awed by the gift of being in the presence of the miraculous image of their Mother, the Virgin of Guadalupe.

When Christoph and his earthly mother had finished their time of prayer at the Basilica, they headed back to the hotel. During the taxi ride, Christoph felt a benevolent force, all of a sudden, like a strong gravitational pull, tugging at him to get out of the vehicle. He told the driver to stop near the square next to their hotel. *"Mom,"* he said, *"I've got to walk the rest of the way. Meet me back at the hotel."*

As Sandoval walked down the street, he felt pulled toward the square in the historic center of Mexico City, and then to a building known as the Old Portal de Mercaderes, on the west side of the main plaza (otherwise known as the "Zócalo"). He entered the ground level first floor filled with jewelry stalls—Mexico being known for its gold and silver craftsmanship. Christoph continued to walk on, mysteriously pulled through the marketplace all the way to its far side. When he reached the end, he saw a large clock before him on the center of the back wall; and to his right, he caught site of a large woman dressed in red, standing behind a jewelry counter.

Directly below the clock were three girls, around age seven, with shoulder-length brown hair, all wearing bright white Mexican dresses. Christoph couldn't help but notice that each of them had an angelic countenance. The girls were standing side by side behind a brightly lit, glass, jewelry display case. Every other glass case in the market was loaded with religious jewelry and trinkets, but theirs displayed only three Miraculous Medals. The large, uniquely beautiful Medals were two inches tall and made of silver, with a delicate gold border and an image of Our Lady in gold relief. In Mexico, Our Lady of the Miraculous Medal is the second most important Marian devotion; but Sandoval, himself, had no personal devotion to "La Milagrosa."

The same force that had directed Christoph to that underground marketplace now pulled him toward the three girls, who stood behind their glass case, looking directly at him. As he approached them, the little girl in the middle said to him in Spanish, *"We've been waiting for you. We have a gift for you."* Handing Christoph the Miraculous Medal displayed in the middle, she said, *"We have three Medals. This one is for you. These other two are for your brothers and sisters."* Christoph put his hands in his pocket to look for money to pay her. *"No money,"* the girl responded. *"She wants you to have this. You will be needing it."*

The deacon thanked the girls and walked back in a daze to the Metropolitan Cathedral on the square. He sat through a Mass, then as is customary there, a priest walked through the congregation, carrying a large bucket of holy water, blessing everyone's religious objects as the faithful raised them high. Christoph held up his new Medal for a blessing. The moment that the holy water hit his face, his spiritual eyes were opened, and his curiosity woke from its slumber.

"What just happened?" Christoph wondered. He exited the Cathedral and ran across the square, then back through the doorway of the Old Portal de Mercaderes market. Rushing past the vendors, he arrived at the rear area where he had been just an hour before. He saw the clock on the wall and the woman in red on his right; but the brightly lit jewelry case and the three girls behind it were gone. Turning to the heavyset lady in red, he told her, *"I was here earlier."*

"Oh, yes," she responded. *"I remember you."*

"What happened to the three little girls and the stall that was here?"

"Sir, we have to keep that space open. There has never been anyone there."

Sandoval remembered seeing his grandmother wearing her Miraculous Medal around her neck throughout her life, but he had never worn one—until now. He was not unfamiliar with the unseen world around him; she was the one who had introduced him to it.

Christoph Sandoval, age 3

"We were always praying spiritual warfare prayers and praying against demons because of my grandmother's spirituality," Christoph recalled. His grandmother also had a devotion to the Five Sacred Wounds and would invite family members to pray the Chaplet of the Holy Wounds with her, contemplating and seeking healing through Jesus' suffering.

From a young age, Christoph said prayers that repel demons. But he also grew up beneath the shadow of a father possessed by the demon of alcoholism. As the first-born child, Christoph longed to get closer to his dad and to be shielded and protected by his love. Instead, he received his father's abuse. His dad loved the Los Angeles Dodgers baseball team, and on game days he would lie on the living-room floor with a pillow under his head, and watch the plays on television.

When little Christoph approached him, he would take an empty beer bottle and throw it at Christoph, aiming to hurt him. If Christoph came too close, his dad would physically strike him. Other times, his father would take off his belt and whip him with the full weight of the belt buckle. The more that Christoph's father lacerated him with a father-son wound, the deeper that Christoph entered the mystery of Jesus' scourging of the pillar. He later recounted:

> *As an adult, I came to understand that sometimes human beings take on the mystery of the punishment of the Sorrowful Mysteries. When my father whipped me, I was "tied" to the pillar. I had to sit still. What this left inside of me were post traumatic psychic wounds to my mind, and the soul wounds of rejection, abandonment, humiliation, betrayal, and injustice—piercing my heart.*

Growing up, Christoph contemplated, at times, whether he could escape the pain of his wounds. Try as he might, he was never able to untie himself from the pillar and the soul ties to his father's darkness, even when the beatings stopped. Over time, many of his wounds healed—but not all.

After returning to San Francisco from Mexico, Christoph told a priest friend the story of how he had received a Miraculous Medal from a trio of young girls who later disappeared. *"Until then,"* he told the cleric, *"I had never had a devotion to the Miraculous Medal; I had never even worn the Medal. Immediately, I placed the large Medal around my neck, and I picked up a book on the story of how it came to be."*

Deacon Christ Christoph Sandoval

"You are being called to Rue du Bac," said the priest.

"Let's go!" Christoph replied without hesitation.

Nine months later, Deacon Sandoval and his priest friend found themselves in Paris, along with thirty pilgrims Christoph had gathered to go with them. The highlight of his trip was spending time in the Chapel of Our Lady of the Miraculous Medal, one of the greatest shrines of Paris, more commonly referred to by its address, 140 Rue du Bac.

Sandoval delighted in being in the very place where his Mother in heaven had appeared to St. Catherine Labouré. He joyfully scanned the altar frescoes depicting the first apparition; he marveled at what God had miraculously preserved and was displayed for all to see: the incorrupt bodies of St. Catherine and St. Louise de Marillac, the cofounder with St. Vincent de Paul of the Daughters of Charity, as well as the incorrupt heart of St. Vincent.

Sandoval's priest friend had secured the privilege of celebrating the Mass for their pilgrims and anyone present in the Rue du Bac Chapel of Graces of the Miraculous Virgin (informally the Chapel of Our Lady of the Miraculous Medal). During his homily, he made mention of an investiture prayer for the Medal.[3] Deacon Sandoval assumed that after the Mass, his priest friend would say the investiture prayer for those who wished to receive it. But his friend refused. He recognized something in Christoph and said, *"No, this is a devotion given to you. You do the investiture for the people here."*

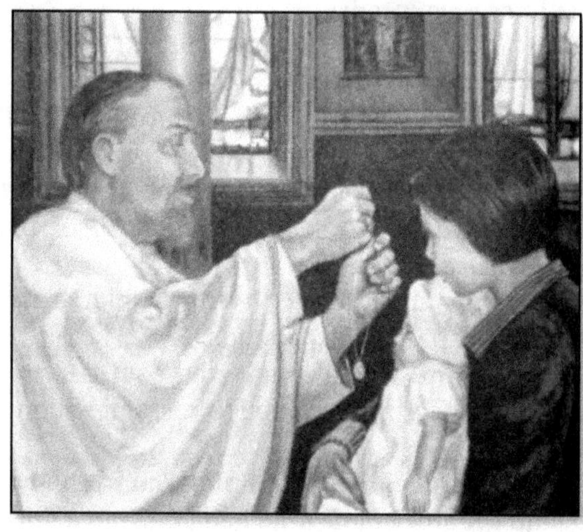

Christoph had brought with him many Miraculous Medals already attached to cords, and the thirty people in their group stepped forward, forming a line down the middle of the chapel aisle up to the sanctuary. For each person, one at a time, Deacon Sandoval said the investiture prayer and then placed a Medal around his or her neck. Then others in the chapel began to line up, people from all over the world—Africans, Asians, South Americans, North Americans, Europeans, and even people from Oceanic nations.

The scene looked like a gathering at the United Nations. The faithful in the chapel took off the Medals they were wearing and handed them over to the deacon for the special blessing. Unexpectedly, more people began coming in from the street. Sandoval ended up investing not only his own group of thirty pilgrims, but an additional one hundred fifty congregants and passersby. But he never tired of repeating the prayer, which was about

[3] See Appendix II, p. 327.

a half page long.[242] *"It was a pleasure and a grace to do it,"* he said of that day in the Rue du Bac Chapel.

> *And then I looked at the blue velvet chair. I realized that I was seeing the actual chair in which the Blessed Mother had sat. It had never been reupholstered.[243] I said to my friend, "I must touch that chair. This might be the closest I'll ever be to the Blessed Mother." But as soon as those words left my mouth, a horrific pain entered my chest, because I realized they were false. My words expressed a self-loathing, suggesting that I was unworthy of the Blessed Mother. But that was not true. She is my Mother, and my Mother loves me beyond my brokenness. I longed to be able to reach up to her and let her hold me.*
>
> *Everyone in the chapel saw me investing people with the Medal, so when I snuck toward the chair—which you're not allowed to do—no one stopped me.[244] They probably thought, "We'd better leave that devotee of the Blessed Mother alone. It's best not to fool around with an "Apostle of the Miraculous Medal."*

With the excitement of a child running toward his mother in anticipation of a warm embrace, Deacon Sandoval reached out and touched the blue velvet chair. In that moment, the material world vanished for him, and the arms of his Mother held him in the perfection of a profound peace.

> *I felt like a child reaching for his mother's hand, and I felt the comfort and the love of the Blessed Mother for me, an unworthy servant. It was a moment of beauty. It was five seconds that lasted five hours. This took me and launched me into the invisible universe in which I operate.*

What happened next took Christoph by surprise. In the blink of an eye, he sensed another presence with him, alongside Mother Mary, someone he did not expect. It was Joseph.

> *And then I remembered something very interesting about the Blessed Mother. Who was her protector? Certainly, the Eternal Father and the Holy Spirit, but there was another protector, a human being: St. Joseph. He was the man who presented the model of masculinity to Jesus. The Father's gift to Joseph was his paternity, his fatherhood, the one who protects the innocent, the one who faces the fire, the one who confronts the world, the flesh, and the devil. He is the shadow of the Eternal Father.*
>
> *When I reached out to touch Mary, Joseph, unexpectedly, reached out to touch me. And the more I thought about it, the more I realized that since I had no role model for masculinity, or for fatherhood, he was the one being given to me to emulate. He was calling me forth to be like him. What I loved about that was he was*

quiet, but with a powerful faith and virtues. He was a receptacle of the Eternal Father's gifts.

That moment was an awakening for Christoph, a personal Pentecost. A great spiritual light came over him and through him, and the gift of tears washed away the suffering he had endured at the hand of his biological father. As with the gift of the Medal, his spiritual eyes were not at first opened to see its full significance. He was only beginning to understand the mission unfolding before him.

Despite being a diabetic, with the pain of diabetic neuropathy and acute vertigo, Christoph never tired of voyaging to holy sites around the world. After a couple of years working in different ministerial capacities in San Francisco, especially with those grieving and with life-threatening Illnesses, he seized the opportunity to travel to see the statue of the mystical mother of Spain: the Black Madonna. "La Moreneta," as she is called, which means "the little black one," stands within the basilica atop the high mountain of Montserrat.

Deacon Sandoval did not dare to take the little tram up to the Spanish mountaintop, should his vertigo cause him to tumble out of it. Instead, he rode in a cab up a steep winding road to the stunning Basilica of Montserrat and the Abbey of Santa Maria, situated before jagged rocks that ascend majestically behind them. There he spent seven hours as a pilgrim in prayer and in awe.

Deacon Sandoval learning from the renown Vatican exorcist, Fr. Gabriel Amorth

Priests were present to offer Confession, and Christoph noticed one small cleric, off to the side, walking slowly with a cane and led by an attendant. He soon realized the man was blind. Little did Christoph know, however, that the diminutive priest could read souls. The priest sat down, and Sandoval sat down across from him. Without any introduction, the priest said to him in Spanish, *"Oh, so you've come to a blind man so you can learn how to see."*

With few words, the priest ignited within Christoph a calling to heal people from past wounds and free them from spiritual bondage. *"When God takes away your human sight,"* Christoph noted, *"He gives you another way to see. And sometimes that way to see is through the eyes of faith, the eyes of the soul, and the eyes of Christ, to be able to impart the gift of sight to those who wander in darkness."*

This priest was able to "see" into people's wounds and bring light, healing, and wisdom to them. He could also see, through the eyes of the spirit, that the deacon before him was being called to do the same. That day, Christoph traveled back down from the mountaintop with a prayer in his heart: *"Lord, let me see people's pain and suffering through Your eyes, so that I can know and understand it. I cannot see it through my own eyes. They are too weak."* And thus began the process of Deacon Sandoval's ministry of healing and exorcism.

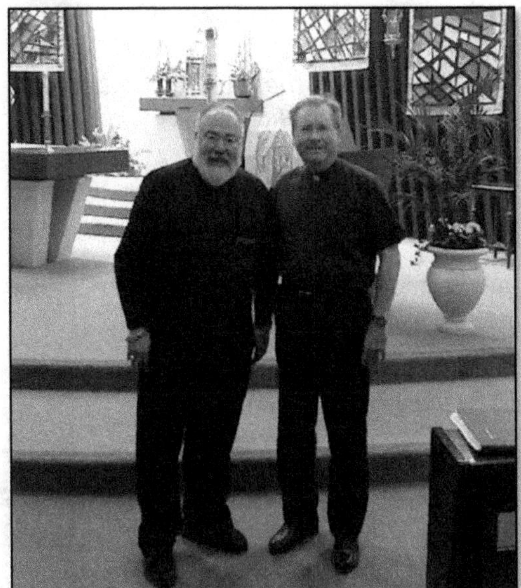

Deacon Sandoval with exorcist Fr. Gary Thomas, subject of the movie, "The Rite"

Following his pilgrimage to Montserrat and the Black Madonna, Sandoval was invited to Rome for exorcism training at the Vatican. entitled the "Exorcism and the Prayer of Liberation." There, he learned from the famous Vatican exorcist, Fr. Gabriel Amorth. *"He was like a little child, simple, with a sense of humor—gentle, but powerful in those moments when he needed to be,"* the deacon said of Fr. Amorth.

Christoph also met Fr. Gary Thomas, the exorcist for the Diocese of San Jose in California, who was also well known—in his case, for being the subject of the book and Hollywood movie, "The Rite: The Making of a Modern Exorcist." Initially, Fr. Thomas asked Sandoval to learn from Fr. William (Guglielmo) Lauriola, the exorcist emeritus of the Archdiocese of San Francisco. Then he started sending cases to him.

Deacon Sandoval receiving a blessing from exorcist and mentor, Fr. William Lauriola of the Archdiocese of San Francisco

"Father," Christoph told Fr. Thomas, *"I'm a deacon. I can't do the Rite."*

"Don't break the rules," said the exorcist, *"but as Fr. Lauriola told you, you have the gift."*

As Sandoval began to free people from emotional pain and spiritual oppression, he marveled at how the Lord was giving him insight into their wounds. Uniting the marks of his own hidden wounds with the wounds of Jesus Christ, he was helping people heal. The scriptural passage of 1 Peter 2:24 came alive for him with greater meaning:

> *He Himself bore our sins in His body upon the Cross, so that, free from sin, we might live for righteousness. By His wounds you have been healed.*

Sandoval could not perform the Rite of Exorcism, which is assigned to one priest per diocese around the world—the Rite being the last seven to ten percent of the healing and deliverance process. Therefore, he had to find ways that he could exercise the ministry as a deacon. *"When I'm with a person who has a spiritual affliction, I have to think out of the box—'I cannot do the Rite, but I can do this instead'—I have discovered prayers of healing and deliverance that a person like myself is able to do."*

Archbishop Salvatore Cordileone celebrating an Ash Wednesday Mass at the Metropolitan Cathedral of St. Mary of the Assumption with Deacon Christoph Sandoval next to him on the right

The Archbishop of San Francisco, Salvatore Cordileone, became aware of Deacon Sandoval's skills and asked him to assist with exorcisms in the Archdiocese. He was assigned the position of pastoral associate at the Metropolitan Cathedral of Saint Mary of the Assumption (the mother church of the Archdiocese) and as the right-hand assistant to the official archdiocesan exorcist. In addition, Christoph became the director of training and ongoing formation and development for the archdiocesan healing and deliverance team.

It was at this time in Christoph's life, when his ministry was well underway, that the words from one of the angelic girls in the Mexican marketplace rang in his memory: *"We have three Medals. This one is for you. These other two are for your brothers and sisters ... She wants you to have this. You will be needing it."*

> *I realized that I was supposed to be a disciple of the Miraculous Medal, just like the Daughters of Charity, Maximilian Kolbe, and others, because it is a shield of maternal protection for the soul.*

Deacon Sandoval understood that the Blessed Mother wanted to bestow her gifts to protect souls and combat the enemy—to help him conduct spiritual warfare. As he further discerned how the battle takes place, he realized how this gift of the Blessed Mother's protection would be extremely helpful, even decisive.

The first thing Christoph began to do for those brought in for exorcism or deliverance was to weaken the demonic presences afflicting them through the investiture ceremony and consecration prayer of the Miraculous Medal. Then he included the investiture ceremony and consecration prayer of the Brown Scapular, and guided his deliverance team to wear both sacramentals.

> *In the intersection between the visible universe and the invisible one around us is where we do the battle. It's almost like doing a bullfight, and the picadors come to weaken the creature. So, the Blessed Mother weakens demons for Jesus, the Exorcist, to step in.*

Deacon Sandoval didn't stop his efforts there. He was determined to bring the Blessed Mother's gifts to the wider community of the Archdiocese of San Francisco. He helped to organize yearly Rosary Rallies in front of St. Mary's Cathedral. For the third annual event, Archbishop Cordileone stepped forward to say the investiture prayer for the Miraculous Medal. Christoph looked out over a vast crowd. His heart expanded with joy at the sight of approximately five thousand people, all wearing the Medals that he had acquired and distributed to them. *"These other two,"* the angelic girl had said, *"are for your brothers and sisters."*

> *The Blessed Mother came to one of her sons to equip him for the fight ahead. But I am not the only one. To all who are called, and especially to anyone who has received Holy Orders, I say, "Get up, get armed, and join the battalions. Let us not forget our battle cry!"*

> *O Mary, Conceived Without Sin, Pray for Us Who Have Recourse to Thee.*
> *O Mary, Conceived Without Sin, Pray for Us Who Have Recourse to Thee.*
> *O Mary, Conceived Without Sin, Pray for Us Who Have Recourse to Thee.*

Deacon Christoph Sandoval speaking in front of St. Mary's Cathedral in San Francisco, preparing to invest approximately 5000 people with the Miraculous Medal

Postscript: On Saturday, May 27, 2023, shortly after Deacon R. Christoph Sandoval reviewed this story for publication, he sent to the author a final punctuation mark: "I report that I was just appointed to be Chaplain for the new chapter of the Legion of Mary at the Metropolitan Cathedral of Saint Mary of the Assumption. The Legion promotes both the distribution and investiture of the Miraculous Medal worldwide. Our Lady's wonders never cease..."

ZACHARY KING

The story of Zachary King is not an easy one to tell, to read, or to swallow. It exposes great evil in our world today, should all that Zachary says be true. Certainly, more of the dark underbelly of humanity is being revealed each day, and much of what used to disgust and shock runs wild in mainstream media and culture. As horrible and shocking as tales like Zachary's are, they can be for our benefit, "so that we might not be taken advantage of by Satan, for we are not unaware of his purposes (2 Cor. 2:11)." But beware. Do not read this story if reading about iniquity causes you harm. Even though the worst scenes of Zachary's life have been omitted or summarized, enough is said that could cause serious upset, the devil being what he is: pure evil.

This story is not like any other in this book. It navigates corridors of wickedness and provides a few sinister details along the way, thereby revealing how far downward God and the Blessed Mother are willing to descend to reach a soul. It also answers the questions—Will the Light of the world and the Immaculate Conception give up on a human being, even if that person sits at the feet of Satan, doing his bidding for years on end? Does God still love someone who twists himself into ugliness beyond human recognition? Is the Miraculous Medal able to touch the heart of a person who has done, been, and caused some of the worst evil imaginable? While it is important for us understand how Satan's wiles can trap a soul, it is even more critical that we know this: our Heavenly Mother can reach down through the hand of someone holding a Miraculous Medal and snatch a soul from the fiery floor of the deepest parts of hell.

For those who feel called to plow forward, rather than skip over Zachary's story, be reassured that to remain in the dark regarding nefarious affairs in our world is to allow the darkness to grow. To shine light onto the darkness is to heed the call of Christ. As Ephesians 5:11-13 reminds us: "Take no part in the fruitless works of darkness; rather expose them, for it is shameful even to mention the things done by them in secret; but everything exposed by the light becomes visible, for everything that becomes visible is light."[4]

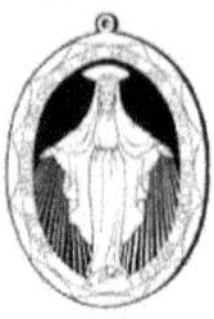

Zachary wanted magic to be real. He was a short kid, a bit nerdy, of Puerto Rican and Native American descent, living in an upscale neighborhood in South-Central Florida in the 1970s. His parents owned a restaurant and a movie theater, which devoured most of their time, and their remaining hours were spent with their other son, who suffered from cerebral palsy, Asperger's, and severe learning disabilities. Zachary's life fell through their cracks.

Little Zachary and his brother

Beginning in the fourth grade, bullies loomed large in Zachary's school life: they would spit on him, push him into lockers, shove his face down in the water fountain, and dump his entire body into a garbage can—all because he was small. Zachary complained to his teacher and his parents protested to the school, but they were never believed.

Clever and imaginative, little Zachary King wanted to escape into a world he could control. Every weekend, he played the game Dungeons and Dragons, reading the spells on the cards and choosing the role of the wizard or sorcerer. Superman could fly and levitate, and people in fantasy movies had superpowers. Maybe he could get them, too.

On Zachary's first day of fifth grade, a boy sidled up to him and said in a hushed tone, "Meet me in the bathroom at the first break." So, at 10:20 a.m., Zachary walked into the school bathroom—and so did forty-nine other kids. "We're going to turn off the lights and chant this phrase about Bloody Mary," the boy announced, "and if we do it right, the spirit of a 'burn victim' is going to appear in the mirror." Suddenly, fifty ten-year-

[4] The author understands that this material is explicit and outlandish and makes no claims of veracity, but invites the reader to discern for themselves.

olds were in total darkness. Together, they chanted the incantation. As soon as they finished, to their horror, a snarling face with dark, charred, shiny skin, faced them in the mirror. Extra skin stretched from top to bottom on the sides of its mouth, partially covering its angry teeth.

Forty-nine kids ran out of the bathroom, screaming in terror, trampling each other—one of them injured in the stampede. But there was one boy who stayed behind, mesmerized and enthused. "I did this. *I* did this!" Zachary thought to himself. He did not realize he was standing alone, staring at a demon.[245] Zachary would continue this game in his personal bathroom, so as not to get caught, and made the scary image appear in the mirror about twenty-five times a day.[246] Little did he know that he had already entered into "magick" with a "k"—the spelling that Aleister Crowley, an early founder of modern Satanism, gave so that satanic magick would have its own name.

Zachary wanted to be certain he possessed real powers, so he chanted a spell from Dungeons and Dragons, adding in words asking for money. The next day, money showed up. It happened again. Then Zachary tried something new. He stopped about halfway into the magick spell and inserted the "Bloody Mary" chant. This time, when the floating face appeared, he chanted the rest of the money spell, hoping to harness whatever force the burn victim might have. The next day he found ten hundred-dollar bills in a large, unpaved parking lot. This was no coincidence. Magick was real.[247]

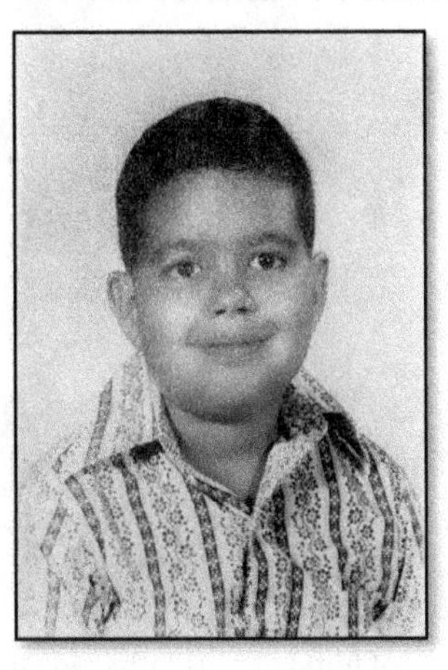

Zachary's parents never saw any of the money. The piggy bank in his room was two feet tall, and the clothes he would buy blended in with what already hung in his giant walk-in closet.

There was something else that Zachary's parents did not know about. In the sixth grade, when Zachary was eleven years old, his teacher gave him a pass to go to the bathroom. When he opened the bathroom stall, he was startled to see one of the female teachers there behaving indecently. She told him to come in, close the stall door, and lock it—and then she molested him. Zachary had never learned anything about human sexuality from his parents or peers; he had no idea what was happening.

Afterward, the teacher told him the experience was his idea, that he wanted it, that he enjoyed it, and that he could have walked away—but stayed. She warned him that if he told anybody, he would find himself in very big trouble: he would go to prison, his parents would disown him, and he would be kicked out of school. She cautioned that he had no choice but to keep quiet. Since Zachary did enjoy the unfamiliar experience, and because she was a teacher who would never lie to him, he decided to never tell a soul.

Once home, Zachary immediately took a bath in the hottest water his body could stand, trying to rid himself of a sick and dirty feeling that he had never experienced before. But no amount of scrubbing made him feel clean. The dirtiness had seeped deep within him. After a few days of fruitless scrubbing and bathing, he even entertained the thought of drinking some of his mom's laundry bleach, not to hurt himself, but to make the "stain" go away.

One day, not too long afterward, a boy with whom Zachary used to play DND and whom he had not seen in a while, suddenly reappeared. The boy shared with him how he was now homeschooled and got to play DND all the time, in a big fun house with a group of people who believed magick was real. The place also had a fifty-inch projection screen TV, where kids could watch R-rated movies—even X-rated and XXX-rated ones. Zachary was intrigued, so he walked a few blocks from his home and was introduced to a sixth-grade boy's dream. In a house set up like a boys and girls club, filled with people of all ages, he found pinball machines, video games, an outdoor pool, a big barbecue pit, every science fiction and fantasy movie he could imagine, limitless potato chips, and his favorite food in the whole world—Snickers.

Zachary's parents, it turned out, knew most everyone at this "club." Their large Baptist church had many deacons, and a good portion of them frequented this unofficial "youth center." Many of the kids were ones they had seen at Zachary's school, and many of the adults were from around town, so they felt relieved that their son had a safe place to go.

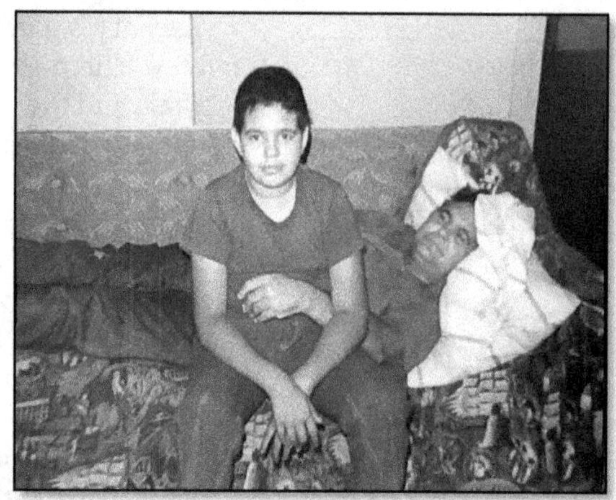

Zachary says this picture of him with his father must have been taken when he was 11, because "My dad didn't really like me after that."

Zachary felt relieved, too. He considered his parents the "No police," turning down his requests to do anything fun. "Can I go to the movies?" "No." "Can I go to this concert?" "No." "Can I have cookies?" "No." If he just looked at his dad. "No." So when Zachary suddenly found himself in "Yes

Land," he decided he would go there nearly every day; and the Yes's never ceased. If he wanted to go see a movie, "Yes." Or a concert, "Yes." "Pornography?" "Whatever you'd like, and help yourself to a beer in the fridge." Zachary also discovered that he enjoyed marijuana and the feelings that came from mixing acid with ecstasy, called "candy flipping." On weekend camping trips, he would pick a random pill from what was called a "salad bowl," and with elated anticipation await its unknown effects.

One day, he shared with one of the adults at the club his shocking encounter in the school bathroom. The man said in reply that what he went through was terrible—something that should never happen to anyone, "But you have the chance to get your power back. Now you can do that anytime you want. No one can tell you no. But if somebody wants to do that with you, and you want to say no, then you don't have to do it."

The club had already exposed Zachary to magazines and movies of children doing sexual acts. The man asked if Zachary would also like to do what he saw in the pictures "because there are people who like to look at it." Zachary did not imagine adult viewers, for he had always sat in a room watching child pornography with other kids. But "child pornography" was not the name being used. He was being offered the chance to be in "the movies."

"OK," responded Zachary, now age twelve. "I'm fine with that." Three young sisters taught him the ropes, and under the pseudonym "Tommy," he began doing photo sessions and two- to three-hour, pornography film shoots on the weekends—and sometimes after school. In no time, Zachary became addicted to sexual pleasure.

One day at Zachary's home away from home, an older kid said to him, "You know you're in a satanic coven, right?" Then the youth laughed and slipped away. Zachary thought to himself, "No, I'm not."[248]

Troubled, Zachary thought about the satanic movies he had watched, such as Rosemary's Baby and The Exorcist, which had creepy music and bad guys. "This isn't like that…is it?" He shrugged off the thought. But over the next couple of weeks, Zachary recalled how he had seen people coming and going—only at night—dressed in white robes and black robes with red, inverted pentagrams. He thought back to a particular sleepover when had gotten up in the middle of the night to relieve himself and had seen a man with white corpse paint on his face, wearing a black tuxedo with a top hat, and holding a wand. To Zachary, he resembled a member of the band KISS and had "the coolest look ever." Curious, he approached one of the adults the following day: "Hey, I saw this guy last night. Who was he?"

"You were dreaming. You didn't see that," he was told.

"Okay, so the adults are lying to me," he thought at the time. "One day, I'll find out what that was all about..."

Still unsettled, Zachary approached a club member and said, "Hey, you're gonna laugh, but I heard that this was a satanic coven. Crazy, right?" Then he waited for the man to burst out laughing. But, instead, the man looked at him and confirmed his fears: "Yes, it is."

Stunned and scared, Zachary asked, "Am I a member?"

"No. Would you like to be?" In that moment, Zachary thought of running out the door and never returning. But then he pondered what he would be leaving behind: everything he had become addicted to.

After counting the cost, Zachary stuttered, "All right, so what do I have to do?" Members told him there were thirteen steps in becoming a Satanist, and he had accomplished most of them already. Only couple of months later, after he turned thirteen, he would go on to complete the rest.

The night that Zachary took his second-to-last step, he was instructed to slice his left thumb (left, because it was closer to his heart). Then he was told to use the blood to sign his name on a five-page document. There were three statements that required his "signature":

The Blood of Jesus washes away all sin, but not mine. ________

Jesus died for everyone, but not me. ________

And on the final page:

I agree to sell my soul to the devil. ________

Zachary King signed all three, and the following day, in the presence of the entire satanic coven, all 150 members, he participated in a satanic ritual of initiation, donned a black robe, and denounced Christ.[249] The coven threw a party to celebrate.

Zachary did not tell a soul what happened that day. He figured the news might be received rather poorly. His parents had always insisted that he attended Baptist youth groups and services, and the coven had encouraged him to go, so as to appear "normal," but he grew disgusted with the church's pleas for money and refused to continue. Zachary was an official satanist now, a member of a coven that was a branch of the Ordo Templi Orientis (O.T.O.), also called Order of the Temple of the East or Order of Oriental Templars, an international "fraternal and religious" organization founded at the beginning of the twentieth century. Author and occultist Aleister Crowley was the coven's best-known member. Its other name was "Diablo Sex," signifying a coven focused on child prostitution, child pornography, and human trafficking.

Zachary's school picture at age 13 in 8th grade

Not long after his initiation ceremony, Zachary walked into a room in the "club," which he now called his coven, and sitting casually in a chair was the teacher who molested him. She spoke to Zachary sweetly, as though nothing had happened in the boy's bathroom two years earlier. "Would you like to sit with me?" she asked.

No!" he exclaimed and ran out of the room—and out of the coven. Zachary's mind raced: "She's probably been in the coven this whole time! They told me that what she did was atrocious and horrible, but they didn't prevent it or kick her out..." He thought back to a year earlier when they had told him he could get his power back by saying no to sex whenever *he* chose and by having sex whenever *he* chose. They said he could force himself sexually on anyone, whenever he wanted. He hadn't wanted to do anything that day in the school bathroom... but *she* did. He began to wonder... Did they use his desire to get his power back in order to put him in films? Did they know what the teacher did to him all along? Was he set up? He never shared his suspicions with anyone. That day, he felt like he was being raped all over again.

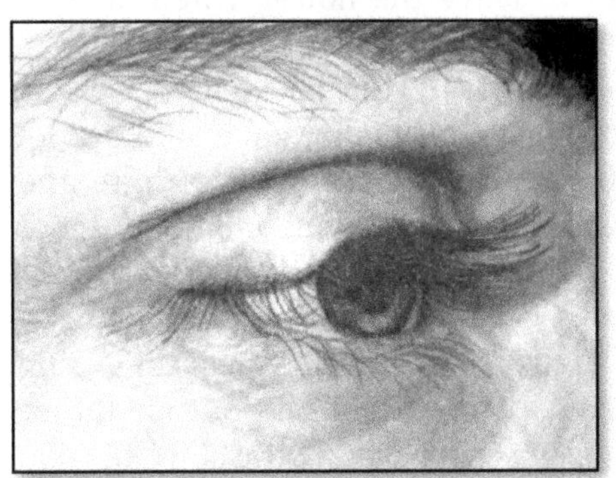

A familiar, sick, horrible feeling of abuse came over him, and it would not leave. Unable to cope, Zachary eventually decided to end his life. He did not understand which pills could kill him, so assuming any would do, he tried to overdose on Tylenol and aspirin, which caused him to throw up repeatedly and gave him a terrible headache.

After two weeks had passed, coven members reached out to him, saying, "Hey, we need to shoot some videos." Zachary did not want to return if the woman was still there, but a couple of his friends, who were also in "films," talked him into coming back. "If you're not comfortable with her, we'll tell them, and she won't be allowed in the house when you're here." Zachary decided to return and never saw the woman again.

After that, the coven members seemed especially nice to him, and his popularity in the movies grew. Letter requests came in frequently for more clips of the darker child named Tommy, since mostly white children were used for their lucrative sales of pornography photos, films, loops, and tapes. Over time, Zachary's suspicions faded. And so did what remained of his conscience.

When Zachary turned sixteen and grew a mustache, he aged out of child pornography. Suddenly, after four and a half years of "stardom," no one wanted to see him perform anymore. He graduated from being in demand and extremely popular to being just as unpopular as he had been before entering the coven. This stark and sudden rejection plummeted Zachary into a dark depression.

"What do I matter now?" he wondered. At seventeen, he decided to walk to Lake Okeechobee—to his favorite place along the peaceful shore. There, only a fence separated him from fish, snakes, turtles, even sometimes alligators. He planned to sit alone under the soaring birds and the sunny sky, and slice his wrist and drift away...

Zachary was in the kitchen about to leave the house, when his dad asked him where he was going. "I'm headed out," Zachary answered.

"Where to?" his father asked. "And what is in your backpack?"

"Stuff," Zachary grunted, trying to leave. But his father would not let him. Finally, his dad grabbed his backpack, yanked it off of him, and opened it up. Suspecting drugs, he was surprised to find a large butcher knife.

"What is that for?" his father asked.

"It doesn't matter," Zachary said tersely, still aiming to leave, figuring he would run away and find another way to kill himself. But his father grabbed him. And for the first time since Zachary was a little child, his dad hugged him. Zachary began to cry. Somehow, his father just knew. He sat Zachary down, spoke to him for a while, and said, "That's not the answer. We'll figure it out."

The moment, however, was never brought up again. Things quickly returned to abnormal.

Ever since Zachary's first attempt at suicide, it never crossed his mind that he was being used by his coven. No one there was going to tell him that he had been recruited by them, that they knew the coven member had raped him, that they were pedophiles who prompted the boy who had first invited him to the club to play Dungeons and Dragons. No one was going to admit to him that he had been handed every vice imaginable so that the coven could profit from his movies and pictures. Zachary figured he was simply being handed the good life.

Zachary at 15 or 16, when he aged out of "the movies"

It also never crossed Zachary's mind that anything he was doing was particularly wrong. One day, however, Zachary felt a twinge of conscience regarding abortion. One of his teachers had said in class that a fetus was a clump of cells, therefore abortion was okay, but he had seen otherwise, firsthand. His mind flashed back when he had first helped perform a ritual abortion on a "breeder": a woman who intentionally gets pregnant so the coven could perform abortions on her. The coven needed death in order to bring a certain councilman's wish to life. Because Zachary had wanted to do the official magick for the coven, he was required to get blood on his hands—the mother's or the baby's. Such services for hire required a strong spell, called a hex, which would offer Satan an abortion sacrifice, called a "blood-tie curse," pleasing enough for him to make the magick happen.[250] Zachary's legs had started to buckle and weaken beneath him from the shock of seeing what happens in a third-trimester abortion, also called a partial-birth abortion. These particularly heinous surgical techniques performed every day are too gruesome to mention here.[251] But seeing this did not stop him. The sense of strength and power he received afterward gave him a rush of invincibility, and he went on to assist and four or five more third-trimester abortions in high school.

Confused by his teacher's definition of abortion, Zachary asked his dad for his stance on abortion. His father, a huge and fearless man who had been a sniper in the U.S. Marine Corps, looked shocked and slightly scared that his son had said the taboo word. He answered that he thought that he was against it, but not necessarily in all cases—it depended upon why the woman would want one. "Okay," thought Zachary. "Then it's conditional. Abortion isn't wrong in every case."

When Zachary left home to attend Palm Beach Community College, renting an apartment in Lake Worth, Florida, he searched for another coven and found one advertised openly. A booth in the student union proudly displayed their "Satanic Club" sign. He joined, but to his disappointment, the club was just a group of kids away from home for the first time, who believed that the devil was about getting drunk and high and having sex, while still going to church on Sundays. He wanted the real thing—no kids clubs.

Zachary was still hurting from feeling rejected by his last coven, and by this time, was seeing a male counselor. Careful not to divulge too many details, he shared only that had joined a nefarious club, been popular and in demand with many sexual partners, but then no one wanted him anymore.

Zachary around age 19

After a couple years, the counselor said that it was time for Zachary to share with his parents what had happened to him in sixth grade. "My dad is not going to be receptive," he responded.

"They love you and they'll love you no matter what," the counselor reassured him. "I don't think you're right."

During his two-week Christmas break, Zachary said to his parents on his second day back home, "I need to tell you something," and sat them both down. Then he quickly scribbled something on a piece of paper. "What age was I when I went off the rails?" he asked. "What year did I turn into a little a_hole?"

Together, his parents responded, "Eleven."

Zachary held up his sheet of paper. On it was the number "11." "Let me tell you what happened to me when I was eleven years old," he began, and proceeded to tell them about the rape. Then there was silence. His mother stood up and walked out of the room. Silence. Then his father stood up and walked out, as well.

All Christmas break, words were shared about everything under the sun, but not that. The day before Zachary left to return to college, his mother came to him: "About that story you told me, as far as I'm concerned, it never happened." A few hours later, his father approached him: "I've been thinking about that story you told me. There are like 700 kids in your school, right?"

"Yes."

"Well, when I was growing up, the boys had crushes on the female teachers and would have loved to be laid by one of them. Out of the 700, she chose you." His father's compliment left him carrying a vague feeling of having been violated—again, and he couldn't understand why.

When Zachary returned to college, he searched for a real coven where he could belong. He got word that in his state of Florida, there was a giant satanic coven out to literally dominate the world, and he wanted to learn if such wonderful news could be true. Ever since he was a child, he had dreamed of ruling the world. Zachary picked up the phone and contacted his first coven, which was well versed in such matters. They confirmed that this major coven did, indeed, exist and was called Satan's World Church, or World Church of Satan. They worked with the Illuminati and in union with his old coven. Customers tended to ask one or the other for magick spells.

Zachary immediately called up the World Church of Satan, introduced himself, and was invited to one of their meetings. The "meeting" turned out to be 10,000 people packed and partying in a warehouse about the size of a Super Walmart. Marveling at the vast expanse of humanity from all walks of life, he caught sight of a man with white corpse face paint, wearing a black tuxedo, top hat, and carrying a wand in his hand. "That's the guy I saw! That's the coolest look ever!" Zachary grabbed somebody next to him and asked eagerly, "Who is that? What is that? How can I do that?"

"Well, who ran your coven?" the man asked him, in return.

Zachary shared how he had been part of a large coven with about 150 members and thirteen high priests and priestesses.

"Well," the man said, "we have over a million members, and we're run by a CEO and a board of directors. The people who do the official magick of the coven are called high wizards, and you just saw one."

"Can I be a high wizard?"

"I don't know. Nobody knows. The high wizard is handpicked by the devil."

Zachary realized he would need to get Satan's attention. Well aware of what was most pleasing to the devil—abortion, he began working with people in this new "church" who performed abortions, volunteering any time he could get blood on his hands.

When Zachary turned twenty, he transferred to a four-year college. In the midst of his studies for his Bachelor's degree in criminology and psychology, he received an unmarked letter in his mailbox. He was being called before the CEO and board of directors of the World Church of Satan.

No reason was given. In the past, certain persons summoned there were never seen or heard from again. In case he had done something they considered wrong, and they were planning to kill him, Zachary thought to himself, "I ain't going out like no sucker." He went out and bought a handgun with one hundred rounds of ammo.

Zachary was armed and ready. With his holstered gun in the small of his back, and his heart racing in his chest, Zachary entered the boardroom. Several top-level satanists motioned for him to sit down in a large, plush leather chair. One of the board members yanked on a rope hanging from a high ceiling, which opened curtain, revealing a display of about nine versions of the high wizard costume.[252] Then Zachary was shown several two-foot-square photographs depicting different ways to paint one's face. Finally, he was told, "Your magick is strong. You have been chosen to be the next high wizard. Are you interested?" They did not tell him why. Such knowledge was shrouded in secrecy.

"I'm not sure," Zachary responded, stupefied.

"Okay. Read this first before you decide. It's called the high wizard handbook." Zachary took the light blue and white book into his hands. The cover displayed a hokey cartoon image of a high wizard in his working costume. Zachary opened the book, which was filled with cartoon drawings. On the first page in large, bold letters, it read: "No one can tell you what to do. If somebody requests that you do a magick spell, you don't have to say yes. You can say no." The board members explained: "Even if the coven is paid money for the high wizard to do a hex, he decides whether to do it or not—no matter the amount given. It would be up to you."

Then Zachary was told he would travel throughout the U.S. and to other countries, drive fancy cars, stay at ritzy resorts, have women on his arms, and work with the elite: the most famous, powerful, and exceedingly wealthy people of the world. "This sounds like the funnest job ever," he thought to himself.

"Absolutely. I'll do this."[253]

It was 1987. Zachary King was now twenty-one years old and six-feet-three inches—no longer the small, weak kid bullied by his classmates. He chose an old-style tuxedo with top hat from the 1800s, added black to his white corpse face paint, and carried a cane—not a wand, which he thought looked foolish. With his new costume, he was raised to six-feet-ten inches tall. But he had gotten much taller than that. In his own mind, he now hovered over the entire world.

Within the world of Satanism, covens focus on different "specialties": political magick, sex magick, etc. Some covens follow Satan openly, while others deny the supernatural, yet still follow the devil all the same.[254] If a person is dissatisfied with a coven or wishes to change their focus, they can start another coven with a handful of people and become its high priest or priestess; therefore, outside recognition of satanic priesthood is negligible. A high wizard, however, is known by all to have great power because his (or sometimes her) magick has to prove itself. Ninety percent of his spells must be successful within ninety days, and not one day later—unless the spell is for something far in the future. Otherwise, he is considered a failure.

Zachary around age 21

Zachary had been practicing magick since he was ten years old, and his track record was nearly perfect. With tens of thousands of satanic priests in the world, but only one to ten satanic high wizards on earth at any given time, Zachary had achieved the ultimate grab of satanic power. He had gained the highest honor in satanic magick in the entire world.

The first gathering of elites that the new high wizard was expected to attend was the "Cremation of Care" event at Bohemian Grove: an invitation-only, eighteen-day event hosting 1,500 to 2,500 men (only), held every July in a privately owned Sonoma County forest in Northern California. Freemasons organized the event's security, and Zachary was personally invited by the Illuminati, who ran the affair. He was told that he would be rubbing elbows with society's billionaires, millionaires, presidents, politicians, monarchs, dignitaries, and rock stars, as well as with gay prostitutes and gay porn stars—homosexuality being very much a part of the whole experience.[255] No cameras allowed.

When working as the high wizard, Zachary had to wear his costume, and wherever he traveled, he was accompanied by a make-up artist, security detail, and secretaries. Zachary walked around the forest grounds with its outdoor amphitheater and thirty-foot-high concrete effigy of an owl, symbolizing wisdom because it can see in the dark, which towered at the head of the grove's manmade lake. Some people viewed the high wizard as a curiosity; others knew exactly who he was and what he could do. Zachary greatly enjoyed his assigned entourage, which was

"The Annals of the Bohemian Club," one of the books with pictures of past events, given to members only, who are sworn to secrecy. Estate sales sometimes put the books in the hands of the public.

"an ego-trip and a half." As he strolled by tents and trailers and through the outdoor and indoor eating areas, Zachary's secretary was there to write down any spells being requested by those they passed by, or to jot down anything he might need. If he was walking with his attendants on a collision course with someone approaching from the opposite direction, and that person got too close, his guards would tackle or taser the other person to the ground—at least give him a good threat. Why? Because one does not get too close to a high wizard without permission.

There were certain men, however, who had privileged access to Zachary, such as a certain well-known multi-billionaire who had used Zachary's services before. He sidled up to Zachary as he walked through a field and began to share with him his vision for the world: a smaller population and homosexual characters in every television show. Zachary questioned, "Where do I fit into your grand scheme?" The billionaire requested that all the major American television networks would have gay characters—men, women and children. But not just any gay characters. They also had to be the funniest, wittiest, brightest, prettiest, most handsome, caring and endearing—everyone's favorite. "I want you to do the spell work for me. But not just a regular spell. I want a hex." Those who asked Zachary for a hex knew that it required an abortion. Seeking more, the billionaire added, "I want all the TV stations, all the shows, everywhere..."

Each year at Bohemian Grove, long tables are set up in a round where the elite men are served their meals. Zachary says the tables were set up this way in the years he attended, and another area provided indoor eating.

Zachary pulled out his card and told him the coven would name a price. "I already have one," said the billionaire. The World Church of Satan received it was rumored to Zachary between a half billion and a billion dollars. Zachary performed the hex but thought the request was so far-fetched that his wish would never come true. It was the late 1980s, when homosexuality was considered taboo and vastly unpopular. Being openly gay was a social death sentence.

The Cremation of Care ritual and stage alongside the lake at Bohemian Grove

It was through the Bohemian Club that Zachary was introduced to the Illuminati—an organization that works with governments, corporate heads, actors, actresses, musicians, or anyone with windfalls of money who is willing to, for fame or for power, move Satan's agenda forward. The high wizard's role at Bohemian Grove was two-fold: he was to receive magick spell requests from Illuminati and others who asked him to push the right buttons or pull the right levers to make things happen, and to participate in their yearly "Cremation of Care." During this ritual play, which takes place at night, the high wizard, standing in a boat connected to a rail underneath it, floats across the lake between the owl effigy and the audience. With a tall pole in hand, he pushes himself along, passing by men standing around the owl, wearing white robes with hoods and carrying fiery torches. Then a mock sacrifice is performed. The high wizard leaves the boat to walk up to an altar, behind which, on the ground, lies a seven-year-old boy. The wizard lifts his arms menacingly, with one hand holding a curved

The Cremation of Care ritual at a later year

kris knife and swoops his hand down to pretend to slit the boy's throat, to enact a child sacrifice.[256]

The first time that Zachary attended the Bohemian Grove event, he fulfilled his role in the play, but was unprepared for what happened. As his arm swept downward with the knife, suddenly, the boy let out a hideous, blood-curdling scream and passed out. "How was the boy able to do that?" Zachary wondered. "Was his reaction on demand?" He would have to wait for the play to end to find out what had just happened. An effigy made up of sticks and twigs, in the shape of a human being, was then placed on the altar. The figure was set on fire, and the vast audience chanted the same fifteen-twenty-second phrase for about two minutes—Zachary does not remember the words. A man standing to one side of the altar shared, in a tone of spiritual authority, a concluding message: this ritual now ended all the bad luck of the year and would bring good luck until the following year, when it would be carried out again.

When the enactment ended, Zachary asked what made the boy shriek in terrible pain. A man explained that they had hooked up electrodes to his testicles and shocked him with a high and painful current. Before the play, Zachary had seen something similar to a baseball mitt covering the boy's private parts.

"And he just says yes to that?"

"Well, we told him it would hurt and he would probably pass out, but that we'd give him ice cream afterwards."[257]

In 1995, former President Bush gave one of the Grove's "Lakeside Talks" and used the occasion to say that his son, George W. Bush, would make a great president someday. (Dice, Mark, *The Bohemian Grove: Facts & Fiction*)

From 1987 to 1998, a total of eleven times, Zachary was invited to Bohemian Grove. At every event, he ran into many men the world would know: Republicans, Democrats, governors, Hollywood stars, pop stars, and presidents—past and future. He cannot say what has happened at the clandestine event beyond 1998.

In 1992 or 1993, after about five or six years into Zachary's high wizardry, Satan himself made it known to Zachary that he was pleased with his work. Zachary was called into the CEO's office, but when he arrived, no one was there, so he sat down. A man he had never seen before walked in. "I think one of us is in the wrong room," said Zachary, starting to get up to leave.

"No," the man instructed, "sit back down."

Zachary was incensed. He began to protest, when the man took one step toward the office door, fifty feet away, and was suddenly standing next to it, closing it shut. Then he took one step back in Zachary's direction and, within the blink of an eye, was standing in front of him again. Every second or two, the man's appearance morphed between five different looks, three of them being a sexually attractive Northern European male with blond hair in a tannish yellow suit. The other two looks were of a darker-skinned bald man with a goatee, wearing a long-sleeve Henley shirt and pants of the same tannish yellow, shiny black shoes, and a black belt with silver accents; and a man with a long robe of the same tan-yellow color, bearing a hideous face that looked like it had been devoured by a terrible case of leprosy. Zachary had to pay close attention to realize the person was never the same for long. The man extended his hand to Zachary and introduced himself as Satan. Zachary shook it. "I came to tell you that you're doing a good job," said the devil. Then he disappeared.

Zachary around age 21 in his Lake Worth, Florida apartment covered with rockstar posters

A year later, Satan paid another visit. As Zachary was poring over paperwork in the coven's office, his secretary stepped in to say he had a visitor. "But nobody knows I'm here," Zachary responded. Then in walked Satan, appearing just as he had the year before, but this time changing his look every minute or two. Zachary turned to his secretary and asked, "What do you see?"

"I see a man who is very nice, very polite, very much a gentleman."

Satan looked at Zachary and said, "C'mon. We're going to go out for ice cream." The secretary, acting smitten by the man, piped up that she wanted some too. "We'll bring back the perfect thing for you," the devil told her.

"Why are you taking me out for ice cream?" Zachary asked.

"Because today I'm meeting with all the high wizards and taking each of you out for ice cream."

"How many others are there?"

"Nine more besides yourself, and I've already seen eight of them."

Together, Zachary and the devil incarnate walked a block in silence to a nearby Baskin-Robbins ice cream store. Satan opened the door, and Zachary entered first. Satan ordered a cone of ice cream for himself, and a banana split for the secretary, while Zachary ordered a chocolate sundae. Gazing around, Zachary could not help but notice that everyone in the store was mesmerized by the man. When the two of them walked in, a woman, who was about to exit, checked out Satan head to toe, and even turned back to stare at him several times. The young man behind the counter, who appeared to be gay, started openly flirting with him. People standing in the queue for ice cream left their places in line to stare at him. When the two of them walked away from the counter to sit down, a couple offered to let them have their table, even though other tables were clearly vacant. "What are these people seeing?" Zachary wondered. "What is Satan projecting?"

But the foremost question in Zachary's mind was the purpose of the visit. It seemed bizarre to him that Satan was not asking for anything. Was ice cream the only purpose? This made no sense to Zachary, who kept waiting for Satan to tell him something of import. But the devil simply said, "It's been nice. I have one more guy to go." Then he disappeared without anyone noticing, leaving Zachary alone at the table with a half-eaten sundae and a banana split.

Taking such pride in his high wizard's accomplishments, Satan made sure that Zachary was present at another elite event so that his talents could be exercised for the most villainous of purposes. He would be invited to attend the yearly Bilderberg Group meeting—a highly secretive, invitation-only gathering for movers and shakers pulling the

Arial view of the Potsdamer Platz in Berlin, Germany

levers behind the world scene and advancing the devil's agenda, whether they knew it or not. The group was named after the Bilderberg Hotel in the Netherlands, where the first meeting took place in 1954. What may have begun with good intentions was now something very different. In 1991, Zachary travelled to Potsdamer Platz, a public square in the center of Berlin, Germany, where he spent a few days in a boardroom full of billionaires and people of influence, primarily from North America and Europe. About one-third of the attendees came from government and politics, and the remainder from finance, industry, labor, education, and communications.

Protesters of the Bilderberg Group outside the entrance to the Mariott Westfields Hotel in Chantilly, Virginia, where their annual conference was held in 2012

Of the 150 or so Bilderberger Group members, an elite core of about thirty people did not change—people who were truly out to rule the world. The larger group would vary according to the needs of this core group, of which about twelve were Illuminati. Every ego in the room was the size of the Potsdamer Platz building that they occupied, and so was Zachary's. Of the five gatherings the high wizard attended, he was always invited to join the boardroom discussions of the thirty power mongers, who held each other in disdain, and certainly did not like him. But they had to put up with the Halloween clown if they wanted what the clown could give them, and they had to pay a fortune to get it. The World Church of Satan expected hundreds of millions of dollars, even up to one billion

The Mariott Westfields Hotel in Chantilly, Virginia in Chantilly, Virginia, where the Bildergerg Group's annual conference was held in 2012

from the Bilderberger elite, before the high wizard would deign to cast a spell.

On the first day of the event, Zachary sat down at the boardroom's fifty-foot-long polished table, oddly juxtaposed with cheap vending machines, as well as catered food. He was pleased to see a metal ice bucket filled with his favorite drink, Dr. Pepper. Soon afterward, a man approached him asking for a ten-million-dollar deal. "You're boring," Zachary responded, and stood up and walked away.

Later, during a meeting with the core group, in walked a well-known billionaire (who will be referred to as simply Mr. G) with an entourage carrying dome-covered trays, each holding six to eight tall cups. These were filled with a smelly, foul-looking drink that was red, green, and lumpy. Someone in the room asked Mr. G for the name of the concoction. Loud enough for Zachary and most everyone to hear, he answered, "It's adrenochrome."

Zachary would only learn later what adrenochrome was: a chemical released in the bodies of trafficked children when they are tortured and terrified to death, literally.[258] Mr. G made sure everyone in the room had a cup. All were seated at the long table, except for two people who refused to sit down in the empty chairs on either side of the high wizard. Mr. G personally handed a cup to the high wizard. Then he announced to the room, "You'll thank me later. This will make you healthier and help you live longer. Drink up."

Everyone obeyed, swallowing the concoction with looks of disgust and repulsion, except for the high wizard, who pushed the drink away and took a sip of his Dr. Pepper. With an angry stare, Mr. G said, "Everybody in this room has to do what I say."

"Who do you think you're talking to?" Zachary retorted. Then Mr. G told everyone to stand up. So Zachary remained seated. Nonchalantly, he leaned back in his chair and propped his feet up on the table. This gesture incensed Mr. G. With his arms flailing, feet stomping, and voice rising, he yelled at Zachary, ordering him to obey. Zachary coolly asked him, "Is that your final answer?"

"Get up and take a drink."

With that, Zachary had had enough. He uncrossed his legs from the table, planted his feet firmly on the floor, looked Mr. G in the eye, and waved his hand in front of him. Mr. G suddenly froze. He could not move a muscle, except to speak. Zachary decided to leave him there and returned to his hotel. When he entered his suite, his room phone was ringing off the hook. He turned to his handler, Rich—the person who got him drugs, prostitutes, or whatever else his whims might dictate: "See if he's ready to apologize."

Rich picked up the phone, listened for a few seconds to the frozen billionaire, hung up and said, "I just got cussed out." Zachary took off his high wizard costume, then asked his makeup artist to remove his face paint and fill the hot tub in his suite. The phone started ringing again. Zachary unplugged it. He had planned to eat in the hotel, but taking Rich's suggestion that he capitalize on Berlin's nightlife, he got dressed in civilian clothes, dined out in a four-star restaurant, and explored the clubs in town for close to three hours. When he returned, he poured himself a drink, donned his pijamas, and watched TV for an hour. Then he had Rich plug the hotel phone back in. It was still ringing.

Rich answered the phone per Zachary's request, listened for a moment, and said, "He wants to know if you'll remove the spell on him." Six or seven hours had now passed since it was cast.

"Is he ready to say he's sorry?" Zachary asked.

"He says he's ready to talk to you." Zachary took the phone. This time, Mr. G made a very nice apology, even sounding convincing enough to have meant it. Satisfied, Zachary waved his hand, signaling the active demon to release him. Through the receiver, he heard a heavy sigh of relief as Mr. G's body collapsed into the boardroom chair behind him.

The Bilderberg event took place over a few days, and the main topic of that particular gathering was population control, the objective being to reduce the number of people in the world so that the New World Order could come into power and take over. Each day, the core members huddled together in smaller groups on one side of the boardroom table, plotting, planning, and jostling for who was in charge, while Zachary sat on the other side. The satanic wizard was their necessary evil. He was extremely adept at making things happen, either through pushing the right people and powers, or through his blood-tie curses. Zachary had fun with their contempt for him and every now and again would say to someone, "Hey, why don't you come over and sit next to me?"

"No, no thanks. I'm good."

Zachary attended four more Bilderberg meetings after the Berlin session. The end goal for the Bilderberg Group was to kill off major portions of the world's population because small, compacted populations would be easier to control. Each meeting followed a unique agenda mailed out to the participants in advance, but certain themes would resurface: the advancement of abortion, population reduction,[259] introducing world-wide viruses[260] and vaccines that would reduce the population and cause sterilization,[261] restrictions of access and travel,[262] paper body suits and masks to dehumanize,[263] the instigation of war, and psychological manipulation through that media[264] and the insertion of tiny robots [today known as nanobots] into people's bloodstreams, which would travel to the brain.[265] The attendees could agree on all these things, except for Zachary who thought it was all far-fetched.[266] But there was

A demonstration in Telfs, Austria, against the Bilderberg Group when their meeting was held at the Interalpen-Hotel Tyrol in Telfs-Buchen in 2015

another recurring scheme greatly desired by only eight-to-ten members.

"How much closer are we?" this huddled group asked each other at each meeting. "What's the technology now?" They were plotting to require human beings to have a chip or a code, something that could be inserted in the hand or the forehead—somewhere on the body that a scanner could easily access.[267] Anyone who refused to consent to it would not be able to participate in society: no bank, no food, no doctor, no life. Their goal was to implement this technology on a massive, worldwide scale. Zachary, knowing what comments would ensue, would sit back in amusement to watch the majority of the participants scoff at the smaller faction pushing tech implants: "Oh, c'mon, are you bring up that #$%^@! again?" "That'll never work." "Give it a rest." "You're taking up valuable oxygen."

The Interalpen-Hotel Tyrol in Telfs-Buchen Austria, which held the 63rd annual Bilderberg meeting

"It's not a mark," they would argue, but rather something administered permanently under the skin. If people didn't keep up with the latest technology, they would be left behind. "Right now, a technology is being developed to chip animals," one of them would insist defensively. "We could probably make that viable in humans."[268]

"There are going to be people who say, 'That's from the Bible,' and run away from it," argued the cynics.

But no one in their small group seemed to believe in the biblical prophecy of Revelation 13:15-18—the Mark of the Beast. They argued that even if some people might call it that, they would insist on getting the chip rather than watch their children die—or at least one parent would. "Christians will go along with it too," they said. "Survival over salvation."

Zachary wasn't so sure. The Baptist church he grew up in had been staunchly against the Mark of the Beast. Parents said they would hunt and kill their own food and never comply. "Then again," he thought. "It's easy to say you won't take something when your family isn't starving..."

During the break for lunch, this smaller group would often approach the high wizard to ask if he could convince people to take their "chip." I cannot do a hex that will make people do something against their will," he told them. "But I can do one that will predispose people to accept it."

Though Zachary could not fathom every Orwellian idea in discussion being successful—or even possible, this was the kind of power-broking he had always longed for: world domination.[269] He had set out in college to join a coven that wanted to rule the world, and here he was conspiring with the most powerful people on the planet. He knew that to continue scheming with this top echelon of the world's elite and to have inside access to non-publicized dealings that few ever see or understand, or even want to believe, he would need to continue participating in abortions. If not, his power would greatly diminish, and his position would be forfeit. After twelve years as the high wizard, he had been 91 percent successful with his magick; but if he dropped two percentage points, he was gone.

Commonly, Zachary was escorted by a staff member into an abortion clinic before the clock struck midnight. In every clinic, he encountered a satanist who openly helped him—whether it be the director, doctor, nurse, receptionist, counselor, or security guard. The board of directors of his coven had told him that ninety to one hundred percent of abortion clinics had at least one satanist on staff, and his experience bore that out. The scenario made sense to him, for if satanists can be employed at a job that revolves around killing the innocent with impunity all day long, why would they *not* work at such a place? Zachary had assisted in 149 ritual abortions—not even close to the most abortions done by a high wizard—but three of them had failed. He wanted to know why. In those botched abortions when the babies had lived, was there a pattern?

Zachary thought back to one particular occasion, when he arrived during daylight hours with a satanic biker gang. His group went to work gesturing obscenely outside the clinic, baring naked body parts, cursing, and throwing their cigarette butts in the direction of the people across the street who were quietly praying and holding some kind of prayer rope or chain. Many of them had their eyes closed.

Zachary proceeded to the second floor where a breeder was waiting. The satanic doctor began prepping, while Zachary and his handler, Rich, grew curious to hear what those crazy people outside on their knees holding ropes were saying. Zachary cranked open a large jalousie window to listen and repeated what he heard: "Hail Mary, full of grace, the Lord is with thee. Blessed art thou among women, and blessed is the fruit of thy womb, Jesus." Rich repeated the words, "Holy Mary, Mother of God..." and the two of them burst out laughing. Being Protestants turned satanists, they both thought, "Really? Give me a break. Who can be the Mother of God?"

Then the doctor grew slightly indignant and told the breeder it would be five hours until she would be ready because she was not even dilated yet, although she should have been. The baby, he said, was not in the birth canal. This enraged the woman, who screamed that the baby was definitely already in the birth canal, and she told Zachary to check. "I'm not a doctor," he responded, which provoked her to start swearing at both of them: "Is this your first rodeo!?"

The doctor checked one more time. The woman was not even dilated. "We're wasting our time," he said. "We should reschedule." As Zachary motioned to Rich to leave, they suddenly heard the cry of a newborn.

Stunned, they looked down at a baby girl now on the examination table. But there was no possible way the infant could have gone from the womb to outside the woman in a few seconds. An attorney, a nurse, and a social worker came into the room to take over, which happens when an abortion becomes a birth, and the baby was whisked away from satanists and into the hands of a couple that wanted it her.

Scouring his required records for his abortions, Zachary noticed one common denominator, which baffled him. His three unintended live births all happened at clinics during the day, with people outside on their knees holding the small ropes. Then Zachary read through the paperwork of failed abortions of high wizards before him. He noticed that every unsuccessful abortion took place during the normal operation hours of a clinic when people were nearby praying on what was listed as "prayer ropes," "prayer beads," "worry chains," or some similar name other than the word "Rosary." But Zachary did not understand the connection.

The only thing Zachary knew about Catholicism was what his father had told him when he was eight years old and innocent. One day, when he was walking home from school, passing by a Catholic Church, he saw a man in a cassock, which looked to him like foot pajamas, and a nun who looked to him like pure love. Little Zachary spontaneously ran up to the nun and gave her a hug. She smiled, knelt down, and gave him a long embrace in return. Then, seeing that his friends had passed him and were now a long way off, he left her to run after them. The next day, as his dad was driving him to school and passing the Catholic Church, Zachary asked, "What is that place?"

His father responded, "Catholics. You can read the sign."

"What's that?"

"It doesn't matter. They're all going to hell."

Years later, Zachary would have another confusing encounter with Catholicism. The World Church of Satan got word that someone in their coven was receiving an exorcism from a Catholic priest. In full garb with an entourage of seven fellow satanists, Zachary went to rescue their friend from his first-floor apartment in a two-story complex in a Detroit ghetto. They were not there to kill or hurt the priest, but should he interfere, they would have to do whatever was necessary. However, every time they walked toward their friend's front door, an invisible barrier would repel them backward. If they shouted, their voices sounded like a whisper. Even the objects they threw to strike or break his window would hit something invisible along the way and drop to the ground.

Zachary then ordered one of his men to try to lower himself from the second floor and jump down in front of their friend's door to try and break in. Soon the man was hanging from a sturdy second-floor handrail, ready to drop to the ground six feet below. But when he let go and fell into the area that nobody could penetrate, he suddenly disappeared. When the man reappeared, he found himself on the roof of the building, wondering how he had gotten there. Meanwhile, Zachary was doing his best with his magick, but nothing was working.

Puzzled, Zachary sat down to rest near a dilapidated vending machine, when five or six of his guys bolted past him. "Run like hell!" yelled the last one. Zachary sprang up and sprinted with them toward their van in the parking lot. When he looked back to see why they were so scared, he witnessed what looked like a monster, about one hundred feet tall, wearing armor and carrying a flaming sword. Zachary's jaw dropped. Grabbing his top hat with one hand and his cane in the other, with his hair flapping in the breeze, Zachary ran with his men into the ghetto, as far away from St. Michael the Archangel as they could get.

The only other run-in Zachary had with Catholicism involved the one spell he refused to do. As the high wizard, he was asked to ensure that a road was clear so that a future pope could be murdered. Zachary knew nothing about any popes, except that Pope John Paul II was in a Marvel comic book he had when he was sixteen, and the man was "cool." For some strange reason, there was no question in Zachary's mind on this point: You don't mess with a pope.

Zachary had also been invited by his coven to observe one of their regular black masses (a half-hour to forty-five minutes long), but he did not understand the significance of its name, nor did he realize he was witnessing an inversion of a Catholic Mass. Eventually in the spectacle, coven members pulled out what looked like a vanilla wafer. "What's that?" Zachary asked his handler.

"Oh, some religions believe that's God." Zachary started laughing. "Who's worshiping that?" he thought. "Come on, vanilla wafers are good, but..." Then he witnessed the members abuse this wafer, doing horrific and salacious things to it, which confused him. In the end, they threw it into a fire. "Why desecrate something that meant nothing?"

Marvel Comics book: The Life of Pope John Paul II, Issue #1, 1982

About five years into his assignment as high wizard, Zachary had learned, by happenstance, that black masses were also performed by his coven in an extended form, for an express purpose. While working in his office at the Chicago headquarters of the World Church of Satan, Zachary was approached by a familiar member who asked if he knew of someone who could take over for Steve, who had the flu. Steve's job was to make a few calls each day to secure that certain members performed their scheduled black masses to consecrate all the abortions in their time zone to Satan and to the Antichrist.

"What?" thought Zachary, "the Antichrist?" He figured that the Antichrist was an eventual reality, but not necessarily alive and well in his time. "Why won't they tell me everything?" Zachary pondered. "Why am I learning this just now? After all, I'm the high wizard." The man had no further knowledge, and the coven never did tell Zachary anything more about the Antichrist.

Taking the member's request into consideration, Zachary said, "I could do that," not realizing that there were 24 time zones and that Steve would be sick for 4 days. The man handed Zachary a list of 24 people to call, one in every time zone around the world—including their alternates, in case someone did not answer. In a coordinated effort, the World Church of Satan was making sure that beginning at midnight, an approximately three-hour-long black mass would be performed on the hour, every hour of every day, one in each time zone, consecrating to Satan and to the Antichrist, all of the previous day's abortions. Thus, every abortion around the world, every day, is a consecrated offering to the devil and his right-hand man to increase their power.

All of the members who answered Zachary's calls were chipper and friendly men. They looked forward to doing an extended black mass, they asked with concern about Steve's health, and they spoke English, though often with a heavy accent. Only after Zachary had asked one man in Ireland, fifteen times, to repeat what he was saying, did Zachary realize that the man was speaking English.

Zachary was impressed with the devil's organizational framework of worldwide black masses enacted through his coven. But over time, he began to wonder if he was on the right side of the battle. Though Zachary had laughed at what he had perceived to be a "wafer" desecration, he was not an atheist. He believed in God. The question for him was: who was more powerful? God or Satan? Another question confounding him was whether or not hell was real. The Baptist Church had told him that Jesus defeated the devil on the Cross and that the devil was afraid of the Baptist Church. But Zachary had been on one of three teams that had split up 120 Baptist churches. Zachary's team had employed gossip, another team had caused monetary scandals, and the third had sent teenage girls to seduce church ministers—and then cry victim. Though Zachary was the highest authority in the coven regarding magick, he was not privy to all of its evildoing. He was relegated to his "post and department," like an office in a large complex that focuses on one aspect of the whole.

At times, however, when Zachary was present, Satan would speak through the mouth of the CEO of the World Church of Satan, and he would say who he wanted attacked, based on who was attacking him. He ordered infiltrations of the Catholic Church; he ordered propaganda supporting atheistic, communistic, and New Age speakers; he ordered attacks against the Baptist Church. But the coven shut down these latter operations in 1995 because the Baptists were no longer a threat: by then, they were procuring abortions, doing away with floor-length skirts for women, accepting Freemasons, and attending gay weddings.

If the Baptist Church clearly lacked the power to stand up to the devil, how right could they be in their teachings? Did hell really exist? Zachary was not sure until the devil clarified it for him. When the CEO of his coven was being actively possessed, Zachary thought his words were fairly honest. Through one of these possessions, Satan spoke directly to Zachary and said, "I'll see you later in hell."

But if hell was real, Zachary did not want to go there. He wondered if he had a choice. At age thirteen, he had willingly signed a document in his blood, selling his soul to the devil. But now at age thirty-three, after twenty years as a satanist and twelve years as a high wizard, he was growing weary of it all. His pleasure was disappearing. He had even gotten married at twenty-eight, for all the wrong reasons, to one of the women he had been sleeping with, but was divorced a year and a half later after catching her cheating. As his father had taught him, "If you get married and it doesn't work out, just divorce her."

Evil was losing taste, and reality was poking holes through his life of illusion and appearances. As a high wizard, he had partied with about twelve thousand musicians and helped twelve hundred of them sell their souls for fame; but after a time, creating another rock star had lost its appeal. In the public eye, he was a formidable man. He would dress in costume or suit up in Armani, and when traveling, he would stay at a condo in Atlanta, a high-rise in Manhattan, and a mansion in Calabasas with twelve fast cars to choose from, including a Lamborghini Diablo. If he needed money, he could access an eighty-seven-million-dollar account. But the coven owned it all. If someone were to visit him in his own home in the ghetto of Tallahassee, Florida, they would find a man with 265 dollars in his bank account, wearing flip-flops, cut-off jeans, and a T-shirt, staying in a cheap, dumpy apartment, and driving an old Nissan Sentra with dents.

Zachary had long relished knowing more than perhaps anyone about casting magick spells—his job for the coven, having spent much of his life gaining esoteric knowledge of his "craft." Now he wasn't interested in learning anything more. Cavorting in the world as the high wizard, he had felt like he was diving into a vast candy store, eager to sample every treat. But after years of indulgence, he had made himself sick. And there were those candies that were too sour, even for him. When Zachary had been offered the opportunity, as an adult, to sleep with children, he had no desire to. And he hated a certain man in the coven whom he was told would rape children to their death. While abortion hadn't bothered him, learning in 1998 that other branches of The World Church of Satan were terrorizing and killing children to harvest adrenochrome was also extremely sour candy, even for the high wizard.

"There are only three ways out of this," Zachary realized. "I could commit suicide, be killed, or die of natural causes, and all three solutions have me ending up in hell. With that thought, he knew he had to somehow escape. Yet every step of his life was watched. Even as the high wizard, he was required to write reports of his whereabouts and dealings. It seemed that any time he contemplated extricating himself, a coven member would drop by, hinting that he or she knew what was in his mind.

Then Zachary had an idea. He began pilfering small amounts of money—twenty or thirty bucks at a time—so the loss would go unnoticed. After a few months, he was able to acquire a stash of cash. In 1999, at the age of thirty-three, he scheduled a visit with a satanic doctor, the only kind he knew. The appointment was set for five p.m., the last slot of the day. But instead of exiting the interstate to go to the doctor's office,

Zachary, in a paranoid, cold sweat, drove right out of town, racing for his life until he could drive no farther.

That night, a strung-out high wizard slept in his car, which had run out of gas. The following day, he hitchhiked to the next town, sold his old Nissan Sentra for scrap metal, and bought a Greyhound bus ticket, in an attempt to escape to Canada. At the border, however, he was rejected. Canadian officials told him he could travel anywhere that Greyhound went within the continental United States. So he opened an atlas of the U.S., closed his eyes, and pointed his finger on a page. It landed on the Panhandle State. Off to Oklahoma he went, and for a year he lived off the grid under his new and first alias, Zachary Halston. He made sure nothing could be traced back to him or to his parents, whom he had not contacted for years.

When Zachary King was made the high wizard, it was for life, so he still performed his magick spells, morning, noon, and night, to which he was addicted. In order to survive and keep up his other addictions—marijuana, booze, and cocaine—which weren't cheap, Zachary worked at various odd jobs. Eventually, he bought a car and tried again to enter Canada, but was rejected once more at the border. With half a tank of gas in his car and eighteen dollars to his name, he drove to Burlington, Vermont. There he entered a homeless program and got a job his first day in town as a dishwasher at Nectar's restaurant and bar. That first job led to a position in security, which led to managerial work, which led to employment as a manager of retail stores.

On October 10, 2007, Zachary got married again. His wife, a Jehovah's witness, was fascinated by his expertise in magick and the beliefs and practices of the New Age—a sugar-coated version of satanism, which he had no interest in leaving behind. Yet Zachary also wanted somewhere to belong and a place that could keep him from going to hell, if such a place existed, so he started to pray to the God he never stopped believing in. He thought of going back to the Baptist Church because it was all he knew; but he also knew Satan's rule that if something was not attacking him, he pretty much left it alone. "Why be a Baptist, then?" he sighed to himself. "They wouldn't be able to help me."

Zachary had learned that Satan was focused full force on the Catholic Church, but that confused him because Catholics were all going to hell. He couldn't join them... His wife's religion claimed that Jesus and St. Michael the Archangel were the same person because each had an army in heaven, and there could not be two armies in heaven—that was nonsense to him. So he prayed that God would lead him to someone who would guide him in the right direction.

One evening in January 2008, Zachary did a spell before retiring for the day. It was such a common, daily practice for him that he could not later remember what the spell was for. The following morning, he went to work at his job as the manager for a mall's largest jewelry kiosk called Piercing Pagoda. A woman approached the counter and said she was looking for a pair of gold hoop earrings; Zachary showed her what he considered the perfect pair. The woman said, "You know, I'm shopping with my daughter, and I'm going to keep doing that. When I'm done, I'll come back." Being in retail, he knew that most people saying such meant, "I'm going to go find them cheaper someplace else." But Zachary saw that she had an honest face; he knew she would return. Three hours later, the woman came up to his kiosk and paid for the earrings. At the end of the transaction, Zachary handed her a receipt and said, "You know, if you call the 800 number on this receipt and take a survey, you might win a thousand dollars."

The woman said, "That's great. I've got something for you too," and she reached into her purse. Zachary's heart sank: "Oh no, she's going to pull out a Jack Chick 'Jesus Saves and You're Going to Hell' pamphlet, and then I'll have to drop to my knees and beg for forgiveness for my sins—which I can never do because I sold my soul to the devil when I was thirteen." But instead, she pulled out a tiny, oval, gold-colored piece of tin with the figure of a woman on the front and a cross with an "M" on the back. Working with precious metals, Zachary knew cheap when he saw it. Then his new customer said the strangest thing he had ever heard, even as a high wizard around high people. Looking him directly in the eyes, she said, "The Blessed Mother is calling you into her army."

Zachary had no idea who she was talking about and thought, "Isis? Gaia? This woman must represent some female deity cult." Baptist Christianity was all that he knew. Baptists had never told him the story of the Blessed Mother's words at the wedding at Cana because they do not drink. The only name they had for the Mother of God was Mary, and the only thing she was good for was giving birth to Jesus. Not only that, Protestants never blessed anything.

Holding up the cheap piece of tin, the customer said, "It's very powerful."

"Wait a minute now," thought Zachary, indignant. "At one point, and even now, I might be the only high wizard in the world, with power over seven billion people, and you're trying to tell me that this worthless piece of tin is powerful? No. Do I have a neon sign above my head that says, 'Crazy? Come here!'" Then it dawned on Zachary that she had her gold earrings, and he had her money. She had already made his day financially... so why was she still talking to him? He decided to tune her back in. Again, he heard her say, "It's very powerful."

"No, you don't," he thought. "You don't challenge me like that. I'm going to take that little thing in my hand. I'm going to clench my fist around it, and I'm going to feel that there's no power in it." He stuck out his open palm to receive the small object with the intention of tossing it on the ground or slamming it on the counter. "I don't care if she gets offended at my store," his mind raced. "I'm the manager... I'm the only manager that earns above my goal for the company. I'm the top salesman. I practice customer service second to none. My boss is a regional manager, and she's never going to believe that I was rude to this woman... because I am planning on being rude to this woman, because she's challenging me. I know what's powerful and what's not... I'm the high wizard!"

All smiles, the woman dropped the oval piece of tin into Zachary's left hand, and he clutched it, ready to tell her it was worthless—except that the woman, his store, and the entire mall completely disappeared from his sight. Suddenly, he was in a darkened void, standing on nothing and surrounded by blackness.

Then, without seeing her, Zachary heard the female customer's voice, and she started to name his sins. First, she described the magic spell he did the night before. "That's of the devil," she said to him. "You've helped split up over one hundred churches, and that's of the devil. You've assisted with over one hundred abortions, and that's of the devil..." She continued with nine or ten other sins he had committed, and after naming each of them, she added, "And that's of the devil." With each new sin that she mentioned, Zachary broke out in a cold sweat.

A feeling of terror gripped him. He did not have the power to know someone's sins, or hand them a worthless, gold-colored piece of tin and usher them into a darkened void. "Her magick is stronger than mine!" he panicked. He could no longer see anything, and even if he were able to, he could not attack her back with a spell. And what if he were to release the piece of tin and let it drop? Would he fall through this black void? Would he ever be able to find his way back home? Zachary imagined the cameras in the mall showing the manager of Piercing Pagoda suddenly disappear, never to be found again. In that moment, he thought he might die.

Then Zachary heard the customer's voice say to him, again: "The Blessed Mother is calling you into her army." But this time, Zachary knew instantly that the Blessed Mother was the Mother of God—a very strange revelation for a former Baptist. And in the moment that he understood who she was, the Blessed Mother herself appeared before him, bathed in light, and she smiled. Zachary was awestruck: "She was the most beautiful woman I had ever seen." He knew he did not deserve her smile. He was acutely aware of his 146 assisted abortions. The Mother of God then took him by his left hand, which was holding the Miraculous Medal, and she turned him around to see Someone standing directly behind him. It was Jesus in His Divine Mercy image.

When Zachary looked at Jesus, his feet immediately felt like they were on solid ground, though he was still suspended in the void. Jesus's left hand pointed to his heart, and His right hand was raised palm open. His face was radiant, and He looked pleased to see Zachary. Zachary was not aware of the Divine Mercy devotion. He only knew that rays of light were shooting out from Jesus and toward him: over him, under him, and through him. And he knew instantly that he had not sold his soul to the devil when he was thirteen years old. He was not the owner of his soul, Jesus was, and he could not sell something that he did not own. Zachary was also given to know that Jesus Christ was his Lord and Savior and that all his magick, his occult powers, his satanism, his involvement in the New Age—everything was fake and false promises; and he knew that everything Catholic was Truth. Never in his life had Zachary even walked into a Catholic Church. Never had he known of the Eucharist. But in that moment, he was infused with the knowledge that the True Presence of Jesus was in the Eucharist, and the Eucharist was in every Catholic Church.

Then the Blessed Mother spoke. "Your job," she told him, "is to help me end abortion."

Zachary opened his hand and was standing back at his store counter in the mall. The customer was still talking to him. She explained that she was Mary Ann Wickman, Fr. Joe Whalen's personal assistant in his St. Rafael healing oil ministry, and that Fr. Joe was the busiest person she knew. He was so busy, she said, that he didn't even have time to talk to her. While she was saying this, her phone rang. She looked at it and said, "This is Fr. Joe. I've got to take this call."

With that prelude, Zachary said, "Sure, go ahead." Fr. Joe, a seventy-something-year-old priest starting to go deaf, spoke like everybody else was going deaf, too. Zachary could hear his every word through Mary Ann's phone. Without any introduction, Fr. Joe said in a gruff voice, "Can you hand the phone to the young man you're talking to?"

Mary Ann handed the phone to Zachary, who was shaking from head to toe.

"Hello?" Zachary stuttered.

"Welcome to the Faith," said Fr. Joe. "Hand the phone back to Mary Ann."

Mary Ann received a couple more calls and sent her daughter out to their truck: "Bring this man one each of everything."

"Everything of what?" Zachary wondered. The daughter returned with a paper grocery bag filled with about 125 Lighthouse Media Catholic CDs, a bundle of pamphlets about why Catholics did this or believed that, and a Catholic Bible. Then Mary Ann wrote down for him where she attended Mass.

Zachary went directly home after work that day. When he walked in through the front door, he approached his wife, who was doing the dishes, and announced, "Hey honey, guess what? I'm Catholic now." He figured Jesus and Mary appearing to him had sealed the deal.

She turned around with a deadly stare and screeched, "Of all the things you could possibly do!"

The next morning, Zachary realized that something inside him had changed. He was forty-one years old and had been doing spells since he was ten. Nearly every morning of his life, he had woken up looking forward to doing one—whether it be simple or complex; then he continued them throughout the day and performed one without fail before bedtime. But that morning, his addiction to magick was completely gone.

That same day, Zachary decided he would attend a weekday Mass at St. Francis Xavier Church in Winooski, Vermont, and convinced his wife to go with him. From the moment of the prayer of consecration—the "epiclesis," through the distribution of Communion, Zachary saw someone clearly, standing in front of the priest wearing a white robe. It was the Lord Jesus Christ Himself. Extending from His heart were red and white rays that spread over the entire congregation. "Do you see that?" Zachary asked his wife.

"What?"

"That man up there on stage."

"That's the priest."

"No, the other guy."

"I don't see anybody else."

Zachary scoffed aloud, "That's because you're not Catholic."

Meanwhile, Zachary's wife, who wanted to remain a Jehovah's Witness, set out to prove that Catholicism was wrong and not the true Church. Diving into books on both religions, she discovered that though her religion had taught her that the first Christians were Jehovah's Witnesses, no mention of them could be found before the 1800s. She had also been taught that the word "Eucharist" was used for the first time in the

sixteenth century. But then she read St. Ignatius of Antioch's words about the Eucharist, and he died around 107 A.D.

This piqued her interest. As she pored over the Catechism, Catholic Bibles, books on the saints, Catholic spirituality, and early Church history, she sometimes read passages aloud, such as quotes from saints whom Zachary had never heard of. Halfway through, Zachary would finish the saint's sentence, verbatim.

"Oh, you've read this before," his wife would comment.

"No."

"How do you know what I was going to read?"

"I don't know." This pattern continued: Zachary's wife would start to read aloud a passage, and he would finish the sentence. This gift of infused knowledge hardly intrigued or enthralled her. Rather, she found it so annoying that she told Zachary he had to leave the room when she was doing her research.

After a couple of weeks, Zachary's wife realized that many of the Jehovah's Witnesses' claims were false, and the Catholic Church's claim to be the religion that Jesus founded was true. But when her husband first converted, she followed Zachary into Catholic churches only to be a supportive wife.

A couple of days after their first Mass, Zachary learned there was a thing called Perpetual Adoration, where he could be with Jesus anytime. He asked a parishioner if there was a line for that, or perhaps a sign-up sheet. "Or do you have to wait for your name to be called, and then you get to come in and see Jesus?"

"No, there's no line to get in. You just show up."

"That's insane!" thought Zachary. "You can go to see God anytime you want to? There's a line to go see Elvis, and he's been dead for over forty years. Clearly God is bigger than any rock star!" Zachary and his wife pulled into the church parking lot for Adoration. Their first shock was seeing that they were the only other car there. Zachary had gone to four Pink Floyd concerts, and it had taken seven hours for ninety-one thousand people to park and fill the stadium—some of them waiting outside so long that they began to cry or pass out. And then after the concert, it had taken all night for the people to leave. Pink Floyd was hardly God. Their second shock was opening the door to the Adoration chapel to see only one woman inside. Their third shock was to see the one person in the Adoration chapel turn and look at them like a deer in the headlights, pack up her stuff as fast as she could move, and say, "You cannot leave until someone else comes in." Then, bam! She was out the door.

Zachary sat down and thought, "Why would I leave? I'm in a room with God!" Not only did Zachary see the exposed Eucharist, but right in front of him, only ten feet away, was Jesus Christ. Divine Mercy Jesus in the flesh, the same figure he had seen at Mass, was standing on the floor in front of the monstrance. Red and white rays, which emanated from His Heart, extended over and through Zachary and the entire chapel. Zachary could see more clearly now His white robe, His green eyes. Jesus appeared about five feet nine inches tall. His blondish-brown hair flowed just past his shoulders, with an underlayer close to His neck, curled in such a way that looked to Zachary like dreadlocks. He wore a slight smile on His face, and His penetrating eyes looked directly at Zachary.

In the Lord's presence, Zachary felt a love so intense that he wanted to cry. Never in his life had anyone's love for him come close to this. Falling in love for the first time with someone who loves you back couldn't touch what Zachary was feeling. This was a million times more tender, comforting, joyful, ecstatic—all that true love is. Not only did Jesus appear, but He also began to speak to him, taking a few steps to His right or left, sometimes gesticulating with His hands. Zachary could see the wounds in His feet and in the center of His palms.

The experience left no doubt in Zachary's mind concerning the Real Presence of Jesus in the Eucharist. Zachary would sit in Adoration anywhere from one to eighteen hours a day, and every time he did, he felt Jesus was healing his soul. "One of the reasons I would stay for so long was because there was no other place on earth that felt that good." This grace of seeing Jesus Christ for the entire time he would spend in Adoration lasted for the next two years. Zachary was receiving so much instruction that early on, he started bringing notebooks—ones he has kept to this day. "I could ask anything I wanted, and He would genuinely answer me." There were also long moments of beautiful silence. "When you're in a room with Someone Who truly loves you, and you love them, neither of you has to say a word."

Two or three weeks after Zachary's St. Paul-like conversion in the mall, Mary Ann brought Msgr. Richard Lavalley from St. Francis Xavier Church in Winooski, Vermont, to Zachary's home to bless it. By this time,

Zachary's wife had warmed to Catholicism. Zachary had made a point to ask Mary Ann what she had experienced in the mall. She said she did not call out any of Zachary's sins, nor did she fall into a dark void, but handed him the Miraculous Medal and spoke to him of its power as he stood behind the jewelry counter.

Msgr. Lavalley began by asking Zachary to write down what he wanted to confess and gave him the ten commandments as a guideline. "Just list the facts," the priest told him. "It doesn't have to be War and Peace or Ivanhoe." Zachary listed off in the confessional every sin he could think of and was then given his penance of saying prayers. Finally, he received the priest's prayer of absolution for his sins. Afterward, Zachary nearly floated out of the confessional. "I felt like I was on top of the world. I didn't realize I'd had the weight of the world on my back, until I no longer did."

Zachary was received into the Catholic Church in May, the month of Mary, in the year 2008, and so was his wife. Eager to remain in a state of grace twenty-four hours a day, he went regularly to receive the Lord's mercy and healing in the Sacrament of Reconciliation, attended Mass daily, and sat for many hours before the Blessed Sacrament. "Finding out that Jesus was legitimately in the Catholic Church was the greatest day of my life. It was the best-kept secret of all time."

Zachary's spiritual gift of seeing Jesus standing with the priest at Mass remained with him for over a year. With every subsequent celebration of Holy Mass that he attended, Jesus was there, standing alongside the priest—at one time hovering above him—with red and white rays pouring forth from His Heart over the whole congregation. This taught Zachary that whether the priest's homily was engaging or boring, long or short, his words true or specious, and whether the people in the pews were kind or cold, Jesus's Real Presence was on that altar, and He was there to give all of Himself—Body, Blood, Soul, and Divinity—at every Mass. Jesus so infused Zachary with spiritual knowledge that he knew, unreservedly, that Catholicism had the fullness of Truth. He also knew, without a shred of doubt, that the greatest gifts from God to mankind, in the times in which he was living, were the Eucharist, Confession, and the Blessed Mother.

Late in 2009, Zachary and his wife moved from Burlington, Vermont to Sarasota, Florida, where they stayed for a couple of years. From there, they moved to Lehigh Acres, Florida, to live with and assist Zachary's elderly parents with whom he had resumed a relationship in 2007. Zachary's mother was suffering from Lewy Body dementia, and his father could no longer be her caregiver, having nineteen ailments, a walker, and no license to drive.

Serving and living with his parents was both rewarding and difficult. A turning point came two years into their arrangement when Zachary got into a shouting match with his father. In his agitation, Zachary blurted out, "Imagine my joy when you told me, when I was nineteen, that I'd won the rape power ball." His father didn't know what to say. Zachary broke the silence: "I love you dearly, Dad, but you make it hard for me to like you."

"Likewise, I'm sure," his father shot back. They stared at each other for a moment and then reached out to shake hands. They never fought again.

In 2014, Zachary's father was actively dying, and Zachary posed the question, "Dad, I know you're Baptist, but do you really want a Baptist funeral? I can give you a Catholic funeral."

"Yeah, do that. That's fine."

Zachary reeled with surprise. His father wasn't one to change his opinion after a belief had grabbed his mind. "But, Dad, you told me all Catholics were going to hell."

"Well, I've learned some stuff since then. I shouldn't have said that." Zachary doesn't know what opened his father's mind and was afraid to ask, should he reverse his opinion.

Zachary's mother died six months after his father. She received a Catholic funeral, as well, having returned to the Faith of her roots with Zachary's encouragement and help. In her final years, she and Zachary got along wonderfully, even when she no longer knew who he was. She had always enjoyed singing silly songs and doing goofy dances, and in her dementia believed that this was her job. When she would suddenly break out in a performance of one of her musicals, Zachary would say, "Ok," Mom, can I dance with you?"

"Sure!" And the two of them would dance around the room, with her thinking she was getting paid for it.

In Zachary's newfound love for Catholicism, he was forever evangelizing, and his time spent in Lehigh Acres, Florida, was no exception. Fearless in spreading the Gospel, he followed the Blessed Mother's lead.

Living with and caring for his parents had come with stress, and when he had first moved in, he caught sight of a massage center advertised near his parent's home, which to his relief, did not outwardly display anything New Age or sexual. Though the town had only two main streets, it had four Santeria shops, being heavily influenced by the New Age. Zachary walked into the massage establishment, and the masseuse behind the counter asked if he wanted chakra balancing, Reiki work, and his crown massaged.

"None of that, please," he answered, asking that nothing New Age be involved. The masseuse agreed, and because she seemed honest, Zachary trusted her. In preparation, she asked, "Can you please take off all your necklaces?" Zachary proceeded to remove his chain, which carried his Miraculous Medal, along with a St. Benedict Medal and a Crucifix, leaving on his Brown Scapular. Clearly fascinated by his array of sacramentals, the woman carefully put them into a pile on a shelf mounted on the wall next to the massage table.

After the massage, Zachary reached for his medals and noticed that all of them were in the pile, except for the Miraculous Medal, which was no longer on its chain. "Well," said Zachary to the masseuse, "maybe Mary wants you to have it. If you find it, it's yours." This was the very same Miraculous Medal that had been handed to him by Mary Ann Wickman: the small, oval, gold-colored piece of tin that had spurred his mystical conversion.

Zachary King, ecstatic to be Catholic

The masseuse looked for the Medal over the next couple of days, embarrassed to have somehow mysteriously lost it. Though she had been in the New Age her entire life, she reached out in desperation to Mary: "I've never prayed to you in my life. I'm not Catholic, but I'd like to find this man's Medal. If you can direct me to where it is, I promise I will give it back to him." Searching once again, she sensed Mary guiding her to where it was: between the carpet and the wall, and there she found it. Calling Zachary, she shared the good news and explained how the discovery happened. "If Mary directed you to where it was," Zachary told her, "then she wants you to have it." Seizing the moment for evangelization, Zachary engaged her in conversation. The woman asked, "Where do you go to church?"

"I go to St. Rafael, the only Catholic church in Lehigh Acres." Zachary then led her to first sit in Adoration. She went and afterward told him that it was the most calming, joy-filled room she had ever been in. He explained why. Then she began going to Adoration before work, and again afterward. Eventually, she attended Mass, joined RCIA, and entered the Catholic church.

From Lehigh Acres, Zachary moved to Wichita, Kansas, where he currently resides, and was overjoyed to find that the Diocese of Wichita had over 140 Adoration chapels. Before the Blessed Sacrament, Zachary felt he was home. In Adoration was where the Lord continued to heal and teach, guide and correct him.

It was in an Adoration chapel in Burlington Vermont, a few years earlier, that heaven had set fire to Zachary's primary calling—that of helping to end abortion. One day, when Jesus stood in the flesh, before the Blessed Sacrament, Zachary spoke candidly to Him: "Hey, you know Your mom told me that my job was to help end abortion, but I don't know what to do." The Lord responded by telling him to wait. Some time passed, and then, suddenly, the Blessed Mother appeared standing to the left of Jesus. Zachary could see from the look on their faces and eyes that they greatly loved each other. "That was her Pride and Joy standing next to her." In the presence of the Blessed Mother, Zachary felt like a warm blanket of immense love had drifted over him. She said only four words to him, yet they were profound: "Use what you know." Then she was gone.

What Zachary knew was Satan's world. He had been educated in satanism for over twenty-six years. Pondering Mary's words, he thought back to the few times his actions of evil had been defeated. Immediately, he recalled the paperwork he had thumbed through from past high wizards, when he was searching for clues regarding his three failed abortions. The people kneeling with ropes! They were praying the Rosary! The battle against abortion, he realized, was first and foremost, spiritual warfare. Ephesians 6:12 outlined his battle plan: "For our struggle is not with flesh and blood, but with the principalities, with the powers, with the world rulers of this present darkness, with the evil spirits in the heavens."

Zachary searched his mind for what else he knew. He had learned that the devil and satanism thrived on blood sacrifices. Just as God had made blood a binding agent in agreements, contracts, and covenants, so too Satan, who apes God, was using blood in a binding manner. Zachary had seen, for instance, that demons were attracted to a person who cuts themselves, once blood appeared. Cutters, knowingly or not, were making a blood contract with a demon, and therefore with Satan, by exercising their free will in causing a blood sacrifice: themselves. In the act of cutting, they moved past the point of temptation and teetered between oppression and obsession, heading toward possession.

The same dynamic was happening with abortion. Whether it was through abortion "medication" or a procedure in a clinic, bloodletting with the intention of killing one's offspring, attracted evil. Abortion was a free-will blood sacrifice of an innocent child, made in God's very own image. Most of the women taking a morning-after pill or lying on an abortion clinic table were not fully aware of what they were doing. Somewhere along the line, Satan had fed them a lie. Sin and the obfuscation of truth were the devil's starting point. Zachary knew that the woman did not have to be aware of what she was doing for Satan to receive great power from her choice. "Now they are influenced by demons—and demons know how to be clever, deceptive, and violent. They are very seldom gentle. But remember, too, that most of these people are victims. They are missing a part of themselves. Those that have had abortions are missing their children."

Zachary saw the devil's power growing as satanic consecrations of all the abortions were being offered each day, in every time zone, bringing a continuous stream of Satan's power into the world. With every human sacrifice of abortion, demons were unleashed from hell into the wider world to do their work of death and destruction. When Zachary read Mother Teresa of Calcutta's words upon accepting the Nobel Peace prize in 1979, he knew exactly what she meant on the spiritual level, when she said: "And today the greatest means, the greatest destroyer of peace is abortion... because if a mother can kill her own child, what is left for me to kill you and you kill me? There is nothing between."

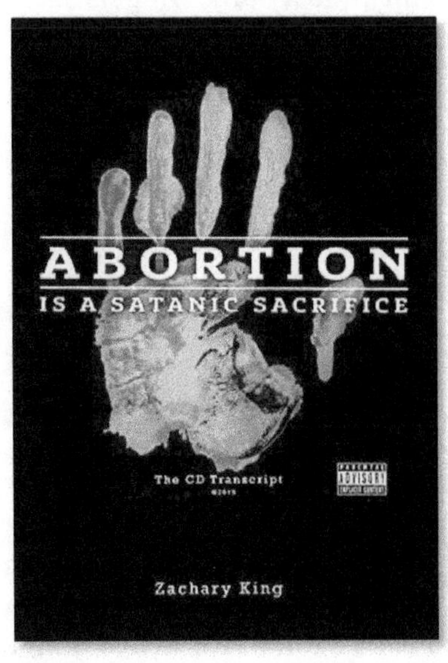

Zachary, being a poster child for God's mercy, was positioned by the Blessed Mother to speak of uncomfortable truths. He began to give talks, and large crowds came to hear him speak. He produced a CD and book made with the title: *Abortion is a Satanic Sacrifice*. At first, he was one of the only voices shining light on what remained hidden in the shadows; but then satanists themselves began openly and shamelessly proclaiming their agenda. Soon after Roe v. Wade was overturned by the U.S. Supreme Court on June 24, 2022, the following was announced on The Satanic Temple's own website: "The Satanic Temple is launching TST Health, the first-ever religious abortion clinic network. Samuel Alito's Mom's Satanic Abortion Clinic ... will launch in New Mexico on February 14, 2023. The telehealth clinic will provide virtual appointments and guidance for those who wish to participate in TST's Satanic Abortion Ritual in states where abortion has been banned."

The coven had named the clinic in mockery of Catholic Supreme Court Justice Samuel Alito, who authored the opinion overturning Roe v. Wade, and mentioned on their website that Alito should have been aborted: "In 1950, Samuel Alito's mother did not have options, and look what happened." The Satanic Temple, they announced, hopes to expand its abortion operations into other states as part of its campaign to claim abortion as a religious sacrament protected under the First Amendment and federal law. Operating under the motto, "Thyself is Thy Master," they have already succeeded in becoming a federally recognized religion (even though they do not believe in Satan or the supernatural). Suddenly, the world was being made aware of what Zachary had known for decades.

After Zachary's conversion, the devil commanded a demon to attack him almost daily. "Angels and demons," Zachary has commented, "commit to what they are commanded to do, and that is all they know. If an angel is told to guard someone or something, he is going to guard it until Jesus tells him not to. If the devil tells one of his demons to attack someone or something, he is going to keep attacking it until the devil tells him not to. He is like a high wizard addicted to magick."

Zachary's wife witnessed the crucifix around his neck being pulled up and off him, and then thrown on the ground. Others have seen his feet get swept from underneath him, knocking his six-foot-three frame onto the floor. Zachary has been followed by Freemasons who banned him from speaking in Medford, Wisconsin—something he is proud of. "Do not fear the biggest idiot in the room," Zachary tells people. "He had salvation in his hands. He was in heaven, and he threw it all away. If I'm hiding under a rock because I'm scared, who is hiding next to me? Who else is crawling under the rock not wanting the bright light to shine on him? If I'm hiding, the devil is already close to me. But if I'm walking down the center of the street in broad daylight, holding the Blessed Mother's hand, will the devil be next to me? No. There are so many people who don't want to attract the devil's attention by taking a stand in spiritual warfare, and I tell people, having been a victim of bullying when I was a kid, that not hitting the bully back doesn't stop him from hitting you."

"When I tell my story," Zachary has shared, "I've been accused of attention-seeking and exaggeration and simply making stuff up. I truly wish I was. The damage and hurt that I've caused in my life is unimaginable. I just hope to make it to the lowest rung of purgatory. I think, if anything, that I under-exaggerate because I don't want my story to seem sensationalized. You don't have to exaggerate to make Satan worse than what he is. He's bad enough all on his own. Whose idea was it to do human trafficking, adrenochrome, child pornography? Fabricating, lying, and deceiving people is Satan's realm, and I've been working hard over the last fifteen years to help Jesus and Mary defeat him. Even the smallest lie welcomes the devil. Scripture reminds me that I should expect persecution. Satan attacks me daily, and Jesus told His disciples to expect adversity. Most people have never heard a story like mine or walked hand-in-hand with Satan for twenty years, so my life is hard to believe and difficult to accept. I say to people, 'If you doubt what I'm saying, go to Adoration and ask Jesus face to face.' I've told many people to do that, and they have all come away with a lot of peace."

Christians have also accused Zachary of not showing love and compassion to those who have received and are getting abortions. Zachary feels, however, that he is not attacking people, but Satan. "I absolutely have sympathy for those who have had abortions, whether they understood what they were doing or not. I helped murder 146 babies who never got to worship God, love their mother, cure cancer, have their own babies, or experience the good and bad that life has to offer. And they all died nameless. One hundred forty-six is not just a number; each one is a child missing from our world." The grief buried deep within Zachary's soul due to his part in the loss of so many children was something he carried for years, until he attended a Rachel's Vineyard post-abortion healing retreat[270] and experienced a life-changing healing. More profoundly than ever before, he entered into the Lord's unfathomable mercy. Not only that, he felt the love and forgiveness of the 146 children he had helped to abort.

In 2012, Zachary received an email from someone who said he seemed arrogant when he was giving talks, answering questions, or even when responding to emails. Zachary asked his wife, "Am I arrogant?"

"No," she answered. But the accusation bothered him greatly. He called his friends and a few priests to ask if he seemed arrogant to them, and everyone responded, "No." Still unsatisfied, Zachary said to God, "I don't want anyone to ever accuse me of being arrogant again. You know I want to be humble. I want this virtue, but can you ease me into it? Please don't just hit me upside the head with humility." Zachary does not know if the following happened because of God or because of the devil, but the very next day, both of his retinas detached. Since then, he has been 93 percent blind.

Another sudden dose of painful humility came when Zachary's wife told him in 2016, after eight years in a civil marriage and nine months of traveling with him on an international speaking tour, that she wanted a divorce. He was shocked. He was in love with her. "I'm Catholic," he responded. "I'm married for life." Crushed by his wife's desire for a divorce, Zachary went through an annulment, which was granted because their private marriage ceremony with Msgr. Lavalley had not included any witnesses, nor had their marriage ever been consummated due to a health issue, invalidating it canonically. Zachary's first marriage was annulled, as well.

More humility came with the need for a wheelchair, kidney dialysis treatments, and on March 1, 2020, the amputation of Zachary's right foot due to gangrene. Zachary's blindness, he says, above his other disabilities, is what remains most humbling. "I know that there is a lot of wasted suffering in the world," Zachary has said. "But not right here. All my suffering... I offer up."

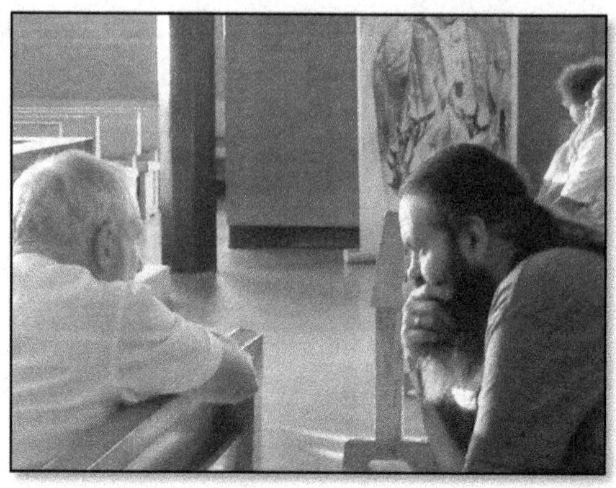

Zachary King speaking with Fr. Rory Morrissey while on an eight-day speaking tour in Auckland, New Zealand in 2016

Meanwhile, Zachary fell in love again. On March 25, 2023, he married a lovely, faithful Catholic woman, named Guadalupe; not only is he smitten with her, but with her three children as well, who call him Dad with great affection.

None of Zachary's sufferings and setbacks, however, have quelled his resilient spirit: "Working for God is infinitely better than working for the devil!" Every morning, Zachary wakes up around 4 a.m., prays four Rosaries, and throughout the day, prays four more. This is an unusual amount, but he has found that his blindness aids him and calls him to prayer. For two years, Zachary was involved with St. Rafael ministries, then the Blessed Mother told him he had to start his own ministry, which he launched in 2010: All Saints Ministry (see www.allsaintsministry.org). In 2023, he added All Saints Ministry Podcast "To hear answers to your spiritual warfare questions."

People from around the world began to ask Zachary to give his testimony. Others sought out his help when dealing with spiritual warfare in their personal lives. In time, Zachary began to assist in the ministries of several exorcists—all of whom have been thankful for his rare knowledge, mental clarity, and strong spirit—which has helped free people from Satan's wiles. One day in Venice, Florida, when Zachary was assisting Msgr. Anthony LaFemina in an exorcism, Satan, speaking through a possessed nineteen-year-old man, snapped the boy's head to the right, stared at the former high wizard, and snarled, "Zachary King is not welcome in this exorcism. He's a liar and a traitor." Afterward, a participating priest said to him, "That totally gives you street cred."

Testimonies of lives changed and minds enlightened, too many to mention, have followed in the wake of Zachary's conversion, and he has a list of references and recommendations from priests.[271] As just one example, Auxiliary Bishop Joseph Coffey of the Archdiocese for the Military Services in the United States has said, "I have heard the conversion story and have personally met Zachary King. I thank our Blessed Mother in her role in bringing about his dramatic conversion, and the Lord for going after this lost soul. Zachary is now committed to ending legal abortion and bringing about a Culture of Life. I applaud and deeply appreciate his good work."

One commenter who viewed one of Zachary's online video interviews, summarized his impact well: "This is a difficult interview to conduct and to listen to, but I greatly appreciate Zachary King's candor. I believe he's the real deal, and I believe he has made himself right in the eyes of the Lord. The importance of this interview is the following: 1) it gives insight to those young kids who are thinking about following a similar path, 2) it gives a heads-up to adults about things that are out there and how they seduce your children into the dark side, 3) it gives insight into how Satan works and how he convinces people to join him through empty promises, and 4) ultimately, how Jesus is ALWAYS there to SAVE you when you are ready to meet and know Him."—Norrin Radd

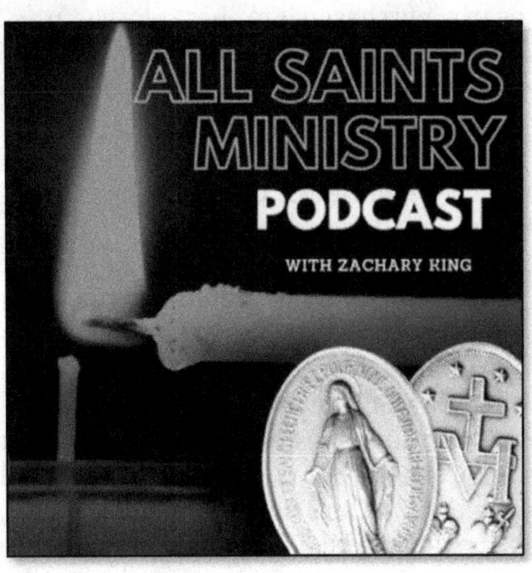

Zachary would add to that: "Everything you're scared to talk to your kids about… the devil is waiting in the wings to do it for you. If you don't tell them a Catholic description of uncomfortable topics, then their friends and Google will be their teacher, instead of you."

Taking advantage of his ability to reach hearts and touch souls, Zachary has made sure that wherever he goes, Miraculous Medals travel with him. A generous volunteer acquires Medals for him, a few thousand at a time, so that he can give them away in plenty. When Zachary sits at a conference table, people often come forward to grab just one Medal. Zachary will then offer a challenge: "You only have one friend? One relative? One person you know who is not Catholic? Take a handful!"

In 2015, when Zachary gave his testimony in Oakland, California, at the North American Congress on Mercy (NACOM) Conference, he brought five hundred Miraculous Medals with him for the taking. His speaker table also displayed beautiful rosaries with special stones, crafted by his wife at the time, who charged only for the beads. A woman approached their table and started to cry. She wanted one of the beautiful rosaries, but did not have the money to pay; her tears quickly dried when a priest nearby purchased it for her.

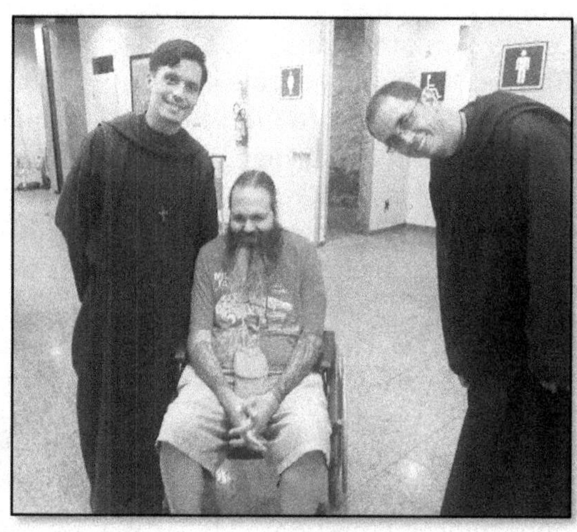

Zachary invited by Brother Emanuel Maria and Rafael Maria from the Hesed Institute for a speaking tour in Fortaleza, Brazil, June 4-June 11, 2016

Later, the woman returned to the table with her ten-year-old daughter, who was humbly and openly expressive of her belief in everything Catholic. The girl mentioned to Zachary that she would love to have a blessed Miraculous Medal. "Mother Mary is so beautiful," she remarked, and her eyes glanced down to see that all the Medals had been given away. Zachary, knowing her mother could not afford to buy one from any of the conference vendors, put his hand on his chest and clasped a large, stunning, sterling silver Miraculous Medal, which had been gifted to him. Removing the Medal and its silver chain from around his neck, he reached out, hung it around the young girls', and said: "I think this Medal has found a new home."

Five years later, the girl's mother sent Zachary an email saying her daughter was currently visiting convents and attributed her desire to enter religious life to the man who gave up his precious Miraculous Medal for her. The daughter wanted him to know that his generosity had made her want to live a life of generosity for others.

Zachary was finding it natural to evangelize, especially through the Miraculous Medal, but at times when he would sit before the Blessed

Zachary King interviewed in Brazil in 2016 by Programa Viver Pela Fé

Sacrament, the Mother of God would remind him of the mission she had entrusted to him, and repeat her instruction: "Do what you know." While sharing and promoting the Catholic Faith was intrinsic to his ministry and spirituality, Zachary could not ignore this calling that was upon him. "What is it that I know?" he pondered. He knew that to shut down abortion mills filled with demons, people needed to fight a spiritual war. Blood sacrifices occurring on the properties were essentially consecrating them to Satan, forming a "satanic bubble." Abortion clinics were therefore protected, in many ways, by the demons that inhabited them. Zachary set to work educating and inspiring people to "pop" that bubble and reclaim the ground for God—to weaken the evil happening in clinics and reach the people involved.

Zachary also knew that Catholicism provided the greatest spiritual weapons available for the fight. The Eucharist, exorcism prayers, the Rosary, fasting, and sacramentals were keys to victory. He set to work shutting down abortion mills through the coordinated efforts of priests and lay persons. To date, forty-nine clinics have closed, thanks to his efforts. Priests have processed with Jesus in the monstrance and with people praying the Rosary, circling clinic buildings or their street blocks, with a picture of Our Lady of Guadalupe held high: the miraculous image of the Blessed Mother pregnant with Jesus. People have fasted for several days, Masses have been said on the clinic properties, Miraculous Medals have been handed to the abortion clients, and priests have directed exorcism prayers at the clinic buildings.

Zachary believes Catholics must now fight smarter. Demons draw most of their power from the abortion industry; abortions literally feed them. Satanists, who know this, coordinate daily consecrations to Satan of abortions in every time zone, thus offering the seventy-three million

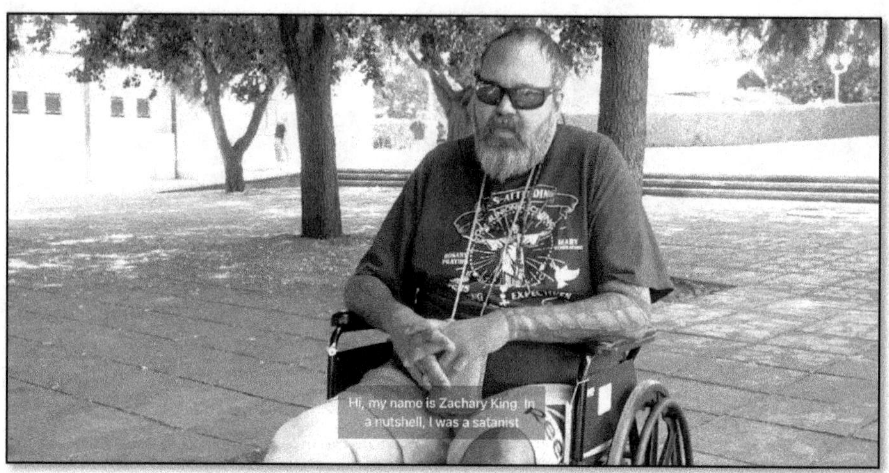

Zachary King speaking on Mary TV, July 24, 2021

children aborted worldwide each year.[272] When Zachary says abortion is a satanic sacrifice, he knows why, and he is fighting for these consecrations to be nullified. There is only one way to do this that he knows of: through the Holy Sacrifice of the Mass. Priests, through the authority of the Church, possess the ability to cancel out these consecrations of abortions. Zachary is, therefore, calling all priests to say daily Masses for this intention in their time zones by signing up at www.ourladyofguadalupesarmy.org. This simple effort will starve the demons of their main source of human sacrifice from which they feed and gain their power.

"React against evil by standing up," Zachary encourages. "Never say die, never give up. Don't stop praying. Get as close to the Blessed Mother as you can. She is going to help crush the devil's head one day in the future, and we should look forward to being there to see it."

If anyone doubts the possibility of such a grand victory over evil, just look at what the Blessed Mother was able to do with one small, oval, gold-colored piece of tin.

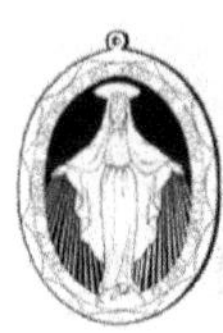

Zachary King's book, *Abortion is a Satanic Sacrifice: The CD Transcript*, is available at his website, www.allsaintsministry.org. To support Mr. King's ministry and help end abortion, click on the top right corner of www.allsaintsministry.org, Donations are greatly appreciated and what make his life and soul-saving work possible.[273] You will be rewarded for your generosity by being enrolled, along with your entire family, in the Perpetual Mass Association of the Canons Regular of St. John Cantius, and thus receive ongoing graces of protection, blessing, conversion, and salvation.

MORE THAN A MEDAL

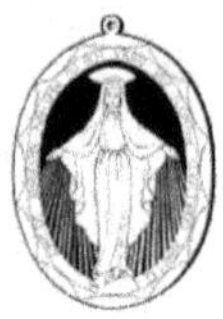

THE MIRACULOUS MEDAL IS A SACRAMENTAL OF THE CATHOLIC CHURCH

Though not mentioned overtly, it is to be assumed that the Miraculous Medal "starring" in every chapter of this book was blessed by a priest beforehand. Otherwise, the Medal would not carry the grace of a sacramental.

There are four forms of sacramentals, as explained in the Catechism of the Catholic Church (#1671-1673).

1. Ceremonies associated with the sacraments
2. Blessings and consecrations outside the sacraments
3. The religious use of blessed and consecrated objects
4. The blessed and consecrated objects themselves

Therefore, sacramentals of the Miraculous Medal are all of the following: the investiture ceremony or prayer (see Appendix II), a simple blessing by a priest, the use of the Medal, and the object itself. All sacramentals are visible reminders of a beautiful invisible reality. For instance, when a demon sees a blessed Miraculous Medal pendant around a person's neck, he does not see a Medal; he sees the Mother of God. It is the prayers and presence of Our Lady, herself, not the little piece of metal, that brings about the effects of grace—and God is ever present with her.

God has shown in Scripture how He sometimes chooses the things of the earth as vehicles for His power, precursors to the Church's use of physical sacramentals. Examples include grace acting through water, bones, mud, blood, the mark of "X", a bronze serpent, the Lord's cloak, and cloths or aprons that touched the skin of St. Paul. (See 2 Kings 5:10, 2 Kings 13:20-21, John 9:6-12, Exodus 12:13-28, Ezekiel 9:4,6, Numbers 21:9, Luke 8:44, and Acts 19:11-12, respectively.)

Some of the more well-known physical sacramentals of today are Miraculous Medals, rosaries, scapulars, St. Benedict medals, crucifixes, and holy water. The first two and forms of the third are sacramentals designed and instituted by the Blessed Mother herself, when she came from heaven to earth in apparitions.

THE MEDAL'S EFFECTIVENESS ALSO DEPENDS UPON OUR PRAYERS AND SACRIFICES

The reader will also notice that, preceding every outpouring of grace through the Miraculous Medal described in this book, there was a period of prayer and sacrifice. Recipients of these graces also displayed a purity of intention and fervency of belief, which often comes with suffering, bewilderment, contention, or strife.

The experience of Hidilyn Diaz, a female weightlifter who became the Philippines' first Olympic gold medalist, shows a similar pattern. Standing on the trilevel platform during the national anthem ceremony at the 2020 Summer Olympics, Hidilyn lifted up Our Lady's Miraculous Medal from around her neck. "Thank You, Lord!" she repeatedly shouted. The faith-filled athlete, who also set a new Olympic weightlifting record, later explained in an interview that the medal "is a sign ... of my faith to Mama Mary and Jesus Christ."[274]

In anticipation of her competing at the prestigious event, Hidilyn and her friends prayed the Miraculous Medal novena. Long before then, she had dedicated herself to years of strenuous training. Born into a poor family, the fifth of six children, Hidilyn would accompany her father after school to sell fish and vegetables on the street or at the local market. Many nights, her family had nothing more to eat than rice mixed with soy sauce. In her free time as a youth, she started lifting weights made from plastic pipes and homemade concrete weights cast in old tin cans, and people who noticed her dedication and talent began to help. Hidilyn's Olympic victory at age thirty was hard won—a beautiful mixture of human striving and divine blessing.

SACRAMENTALS ARE NOT MAGIC

Sacramentals are not man-to-God, or man-to-Mary, transactions based on an attitude of "I'll give you what you want, if you give me what I want." Hollywood actor and comedian Jim Carrey, beloved for his ability to make us laugh, has expressed this common misunderstanding of how the sacramental of the rosary, for instance, works. Though raised Catholic, Carey fell into a sinkhole of existentialism and New Age beliefs, such as the occult practice of Transcendental Meditation. His misinterpretation of a grace received as a child ultimately led him to promote the law of attraction, the belief that a person can bring into their life whatever they focus intently on.[275]

This notion began when Carrey was in second grade at a Catholic elementary school in Canada. "When I want something," a substitute teacher told him, "I pray to the Virgin Mary and ask her to ask God for it. I promise something in return, and I get whatever I want."

A light bulb went off in the mind of little Jim, whose family was poor at the time. "I need a bike!" he thought, promising the Blessed Mother that he would say a Rosary in return.[276]

Recalled Carrey: "I went home, and I prayed for a bike, and two weeks later, I walked into the living room, and there was a brand-new Mustang bike with a banana seat and chopper handlebars sitting in the middle of the living room. I said, 'What's this?' And they said, 'You won it in a raffle!' And it turns out, I won it in a raffle that I never entered. A friend of mine went into a sporting goods store and put my name into the raffle, as well as his. And that was two weeks later. I've kind of been doing that a lot ever since."[277]

Jim Carrey treated the gift from the Blessed Mother as something that he had manifested into being through his initiation of an exchange. He misunderstood the nature of grace.

The Miraculous Medal should not be seen as an amulet or good luck charm, or as a contract, investment, or transaction. It cannot be bought or controlled in any way. "Repent, and believe in the Gospel" is the necessary biblical attitude.

But if a person's sights are elsewhere, or their ears are deaf, or sin is their friend, then even the Creator of heaven and earth—Who can throw mountains into the sea—cannot move that person's heart. At play is a dance between God and the human soul. Even Jesus' death on the Cross cannot save someone who refuses His love. A small, blessed Medal from the Blessed Mother cannot break open a lock on a door that someone has stubbornly closed.

GRACE CANNOT BE CONTROLLED

God and Our Lady know much better than we do which graces to send and when. We cannot predict how the graces obtained through use of the Miraculous Medal will flow, and we are often unaware of what Mary has done for us. Did she help prevent our child from getting hit by a car or bullied at school? Did we stifle a lie, or perform act of charity, when we otherwise would not have?

Simply because a desired grace was not received does not mean that the Medal did not have great effect. Most of the graces obtained will be known only in heaven. One example comes from the life of Babe Ruth, who though he died in 1948, remains the greatest baseball player of all time. The charismatic Ruth was the first American sports superstar, who routinely garnered headlines across the country for both his on-field exploits and his off-field celebrity.

Ruth's fame earned him the names the Sultan of Swat and the Bambino, but his upbringing was harsh, poor, and obscure. "Looking back to my youth, I honestly don't think I knew the difference between right and wrong," he wrote for an article received by Guideposts magazine on the day of his death at age 53.[278] "I spent much of my early boyhood living over my father's saloon, in Baltimore—and when I wasn't living over it, I was in it, soaking up the atmosphere. I hardly knew my parents."

By age seven, little George Herman Ruth Jr. was so unruly—roaming the streets, drinking, skipping school, and breaking laws—that his German immigrant parents decided to place him in St. Mary's Industrial School for Boys, a reformatory school for orphans, delinquents and "incorrigibles" run by the Xaverian Brothers. Being an "incorrigible," Ruth resented authority, but he did learn there that God was the Boss of all his bosses—a truth that never left him. There was also another authority figure he admired: a 6-foot-6-inch, 250-pound man called Brother Matthias, who poured his heart into Ruth and introduced him to baseball. The Bambino never forgot the time he watched Brother Matthias smack a ball nearly 350 yards, leaving him dumbstruck. Eyeing the boy's raw talent, Brother Matthias coached him for hours in St. Mary's big backyard.

Ruth attributes his career in baseball to Brother Matthias, who left a lasting impression upon him: "He could have been successful at anything he wanted to in life—and he chose the Church."

Ruth went astray during his career, living a life of debauchery, chasing women, hot dogs and beer,[279] but always coming back to prayer. In Guideposts, he wrote:

> *As far as I'm concerned, and I think as far as most kids go, once religion sinks in, it stays there—deep down. The lads who get religious training, get it where it counts—in the roots. They may fail it, but it never fails them...*
>
> *In December 1946, I was in French Hospital, New York, facing a serious operation. Paul Carey, one of my oldest and closest friends, was by my bed one night.*
>
> *"They're going to operate in the morning, Babe," Paul said. "Don't you think you ought to put your house in order?"*
>
> *I didn't dodge the long, challenging look in his eyes. I knew what he meant. For the first time I realized that death might strike me out. I nodded, and Paul got up, called in a Chaplain, and I made a full confession.*
>
> *"I'll return in the morning and give you Holy Communion," the chaplain said, "But you don't have to fast."*
>
> *"I'll fast," I said. I didn't have even a drop of water.*
>
> *As I lay in bed that evening, I thought to myself what a comforting feeling to be free from fear and worries. I now could simply turn them over to God. Later on, my wife brought in a letter from a little kid in Jersey City.*
>
>> "Dear Babe," he wrote, "Everybody in the seventh grade class is pulling and praying for you. I am enclosing a medal which if you wear will make you better. Your pal–Mike Quinlan.
>>
>> P.S. I know this will be your 61st homer. You'll hit it."
>
> *I asked them to pin the Miraculous Medal to my pajama coat. I've worn the medal constantly ever since. I'll wear it to my grave.*[280]

The boy in the seventh-grade class was hoping, as was Babe Ruth, that the Miraculous Medal would help him live many more years. After his operation, during a short-lived reprieve from illness and pain, Ruth wrote in his 1947 autobiography, "I've got to stick around a long, long time. For above everything else, I want to be a part of and help the development of the greatest game God ever saw fit to let men invent—Baseball."[281]

Though Ruth died a year later, Mary's hopes for him did not. He carried the boy's gift of the Miraculous Medal to his grave, along with graces that he perhaps never expected.

MIRACLE STORIES

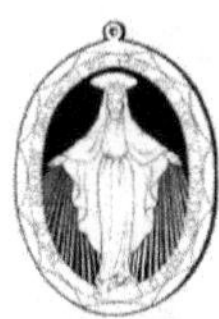

Our Lady requested that her Medal be worn around the neck. Her exact words to St. Catherine Labouré were, "Great graces will be given to those who wear it with confidence." Yet it appears that with the combination of her prayers, God's mercy, and the endless creativity of the human mind, the Medal has been effective through other uses as well.

What follows in this book is a collection of short and true testimonies involving the Miraculous Medal, presented in three sections: Stories of Healing and Deliverance; stories of Protection; and stories of Conversion and Grace. Some were preserved in a collection published by Fr. Jean Marie Aladal—the self-same priest spiritual director of St. Catherine Labouré, who doubted and persecuted her, then became the greatest defender and propagator the Miraculous Medal in her day. Others were collected by a German priest and prolific writer from Munich, Fr. Karl Maria Harrer (1926-2013). Still others were selected from sources and interviews conducted by the author. In certain cases, names have been changed for the sake of anonymity or to add color to the testimonies from of old, when names were sometimes reduced to initials or pronouns. Together, all of these stories reveal that no matter the century or the place, Mother Mary, through her Medals of grace, watches carefully over her children.

STORIES OF HEALING AND DELIVERANCE

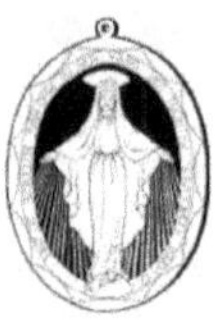

THE DIVINE SURGEON
(ÉLISE BOURGEOIS, FRANCE)

In a letter dated March 4, 1842, the Mother Superior of the Daughters of Charity in Troyes, France, shared this story of her experience with eighteen-year-old Élise Bourgeois, who was employed by the sisters in their workroom.

Élise was suffering severely from an anchylosis in the knee, and for seven and a half months, had been in excruciating pain. Her leg had shrunk two inches, and she could not put any weight on it without wincing. To go anywhere, she needed to lean on a cane or a kind person for support.

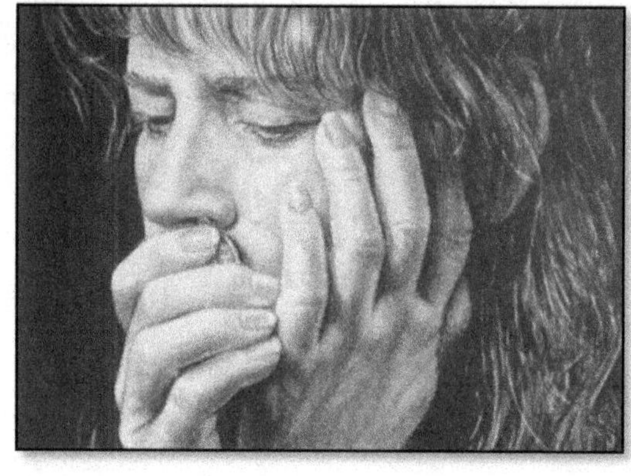

On April 8, 1841, the Superior had gotten word of an inspiring healing that had just happened. A Christian Brother, about to undergo a foot amputation, had been cured solely by the application of a Miraculous Medal when his sufferings were greater than usual one night. The Superior reproached herself for allowing the poor girl to suffer for so long without the sisters thinking once of turning to the Blessed Mother. She told Élise to put all her confidence in Mary Immaculate, apply the Medal to her knee, and commence a novena with her companions.

All of Tuesday night, Élise's sufferings were tremendous. It felt to her as if every bone in her knee was dislocated, and the next day, she still had no rest from the pain. When she woke up the following morning, she was taken to the convent chapel for Mass. At the elevation of the Host, she immediately felt something like the touch of a hand on her knee. This "touch" started replacing and shaping her bones into their natural position, and then began lengthening her shrunken limb!

At first, Élise's mind could hardly catch up to what was happening to her body, and she didn't dare venture to put weight on her knee. At the end of the Mass, when receiving the final blessing, she rested her weight on her afflicted knee, in spite of herself. To her amazement, there was no pain whatsoever; her knee felt completely normal. The Lord Jesus had healed her. She remained for some time in the chapel with her astounded friends, and together they said prayers of the deepest gratitude, thanking the Blessed Virgin for obtaining this great favor from her Son.

Élise then walked up to the Mother Superior to share the news of the miracle and asked for permission to walk over to the cathedral for Confession. The Superior granted it reluctantly, scarcely able believe what she was seeing. "How could Élise not be suffering in the slightest," she wondered, "when for seven and a half months, she had not been able to walk about at all?"

News of the miracle soon spread throughout the city of Troyes, and several people came to see the healed girl. Élise also requested permission from the Superior to go to the home of one of her uncles. The uncle had a neighbor who refused to believe a miracle had taken place. But after seeing Élise, the neighbor became perfectly convinced and said that in thanksgiving, a *Te Deum*[282] should be chanted in the cathedral.

"I forgot to say," added the Mother Superior in Troyes, in her letter of this story, "that our physician had seen this young woman two months before her recovery and pronounced the disease incurable. I had also had her examined by a surgeon, who ordered much blistering,[283] but without expecting a cure. Accompanying this letter are the signatures of seven Sisters of Charity and twenty-three other individuals, witnesses of the miracle."[284]

HEALING FOR ALL THE MEMBERS
(MADAME PÉRON, FRANCE)

Madame Péron lived on Rue des Petites-Écuries, No. 24, Paris, France. She dictated her story for transcription on February 26, 1835, in the presence of Sr. Marie of the Daughters of Charity, who was a witness to her healing. The following is adapted from this firsthand account.

Mrs. Péron was bedridden for nearly eight years, due to considerable hemorrhaging and consumption[285]. In all that time, she had only eight days of relief from her pain and was unable to help her husband in supporting the family. Her movements were slow and feeble, and the nourishment she was able to take in only seemed to worsen her sickness.

After so many years, Mrs. Péron's husband lost courage in trying to help her and was almost in despair. "As for myself," Mrs. Péron recalled, "seeing that medicines had no effect and cost us a great deal of money, I dispensed with doctors, and was a long time without one, having resigned myself to a slow death."

A neighbor, Madame Pellevé, insisted that Mrs. Péron call upon a Sister of Charity, and she relented. Though Mrs. Péron had always practiced some devotion to Mary, she hadn't received the sacraments for years and had only gone to parish functions occasionally, when her sufferings and occupations allowed for it.

The following morning, Sr. Marie from St. Vincent de Paul's Parish paid Mrs. Péron a visit. Trying her best to console her in her sufferings, she brought a much-needed respite of good cheer into the home. Sr. Marie also sent for another physician, but he quietly told her that the patient's case was hopeless, and Mrs. Péron should be sent to the hospital to spare her family the sad spectacle of her death.

Upon hearing the despairing news, Sr. Marie felt compelled to give Mrs. Péron's soul special attention. After several questions, she asked her if she had gone to Confession. Blushing, Mrs. Péron answered, "No." The sister begged her to go, but she replied, "When I am cured, I will." Dissatisfied with her evasive answer, Sr. Marie pressed further...but Mrs. Péron pushed back: "Sister, I don't like to be hounded with things of this sort. When I am cured, I will go to Confession." She knew this answer grieved Sr. Marie, but it didn't stop the sister from continuing to pay visits and giving her kind attention as her malady worsened.

One Sunday night in October 1834, a chill of death came over Mrs. Perón. She was no longer able to speak. Plans were made to recite prayers for the dying. When her husband touched her forehead, which was covered in a cold sweat, he presumed she was dead and called out to their eldest daughter, "Euphemie! Alas, thy mother is dead!" Euphemie ran to her mother's bedside, and they began to wail with grief. Their cries were so loud as to wake up their neighbor, Madame Pellevé, who came over to the home to console them.

After placing her hand on Mrs. Péron's heart, Madame Pellevé exclaimed, "No, she is not dead! Her heart is still beating." She then called on Sr. Marie to come over immediately.

The sister soon arrived. Sitting next to Mrs. Péron's bedside, Sr. Marie asked her, "Do you love the Blessed Virgin very much?" The dying woman was able to say in a faint voice: "Yes, sister."

"If you will love her very much, I can give you something to cure you."

"Oh! Yes, if I shall soon be well." These words came out of the sick woman's mouth, though she had been convinced death was near.

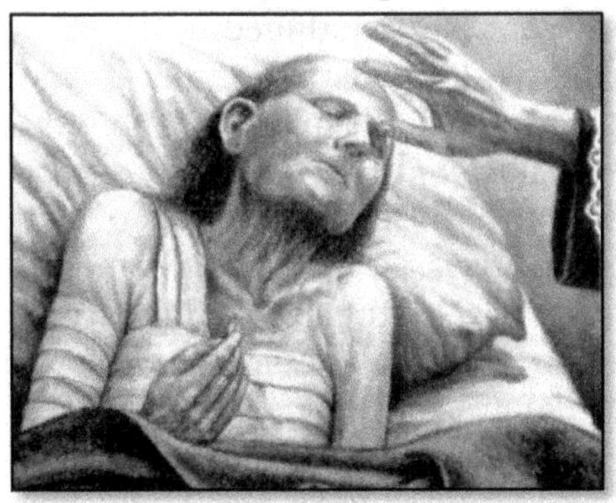

Sr. Marie told her, "Take this Medal of the Blessed Virgin, who will help cure you, if you have great confidence in her."

The sight of the Medal filled Mrs. Péron with joy. She took it and kissed it fervently, truly longing to be healed. Sr. Marie urged her to repeat daily the invocation to Mary written on the Medal: "O Mary, conceived without sin, pray for us who have recourse to thee."

Mrs. Péron shared, "She then put the Medal around my neck. At that instant, there passed through me a new and strange feeling, a general shift in my whole body. A current flowed through all my members. It was not a painful sensation. On the contrary, I began to shed tears of joy. I was not cured, but I felt that I was going to be, and I experienced a confidence that did not come from myself."

After Sr. Marie left the home, Mr. Péron, who had remained motionless at the foot of his wife's bed, said: "Put all your confidence in the Blessed Virgin. We are going to say a novena for you." Toward the end of that evening, his wife was able to raise herself up in the bed, which was astonishing, considering her years of near immobility.

On Tuesday, Mrs. Péron requested some broth. Remarkably, her strength returned—it returned in full! She had been cured! Only two days later, on Thursday, she wanted to go to church to thank God and the Blessed Virgin. Despite the family's concerns, Mrs. Péron insisted that she go alone, and there, she ran into Sr. Marie, who did not recognize her. Mrs. Péron took the sister by the hand.

"Oh!" Sr. Marie gasped. "It is really you!"

"Yes, sister. It is I indeed. I am here to go to Mass. I am cured!"

"And what has cured you so quickly?" asked Sr. Marie, lost in astonishment.

"The Blessed Virgin, and I am going to thank her."

From that time onward, Mrs. Péron enjoyed good health. Not only that, she soon chose a spiritual director and went to Confession and became a true disciple of the Lord. Her greatest happiness was receiving the Sacraments with frequency, to be close to Jesus. According to Sr. Marie, "Two things awakened her tears, the recollection of her past life, and gratitude for her twofold recovery. Nor is this all; the Blessed Virgin seems to have chosen this family for the purpose of displaying in it the wonders of her power of intercession before God."

The graces did not stop with Mrs. Péron; they continued to fall upon the family, who now turned to God daily with prayer and thanksgiving. One of her daughters, age sixteen, entered a life of deep prayer and piety after her mother's recovery, and her husband started to wear the Miraculous Medal, experiencing many of its blessed effects.

Another of their daughters, Hortense, who was six and a half years old, had great difficulty speaking. Though she was bright, she could scarcely finish a word due to a congenital defect. "Why do you not send her to school, instead of keeping her home all day?" asked Sr. Marie.

"You hear how she talks," answered Mrs. Péron, who did not like to have her child's infirmity exposed. But she yielded to Sr. Marie's wishes, and little Hortense was sent to the sister's parish school. Her imperfect speech did not improve, however, and sometimes it would take Hortense five minutes to pronounce half of a word.

Sr. Marie deeply pitied the little girl and spoke to her mother about a novena for curing the defect. "Cure Hortense? Sister! It is impossible. It is a natural defect!" Sr. Marie insisted, and they hung a Medal around Hortense's neck. That Saturday they began a novena, which consisted of daily Mass and reciting a few prayers in honor of the Blessed Virgin, and the little girl took part in all of it.

For several days there was no change. Then on Thursday, as Hortense was leaving church after Mass, she began to speak as distinctly and easily as anyone! Those who first heard her were dumbstruck. The news soon spread, and people came from all directions to hear Hortense's perfect speech and to see if this truly was the same girl they had known.

In thanksgiving for so great a gift, the family consecrated the child to Mary on the 21st of November, the Feast of the Presentation of Mary, in the same chapel where the Blessed Mother appeared to St. Catherine Labouré. In commemoration of this momentous grace in her life, Hortense promised to wear only blue and white, the colors of the Blessed Mother, until her First Communion.

"She cherishes her brass Medal so highly that she would not exchange it for one of silver or gold," Sr. Marie wrote. Whenever little Hortense was asked if she loved the Blessed Virgin, she responded as only a six-year-old could, "Oh! Yes, I love her with more than all my heart!" Mr. Péron continued to delight in hearing his daughter speak, and asked her if she could leave her Medal with the family to take care of it. Hortense responded, "For sure, papa, if you would like that, but I promised the Blessed Virgin, the day of my consecration, that the Medal should never leave me, but should even go down with me into the tomb when I die."[286]

A SIGN MADE OUT OF MEDAL
(ESTHER ZIEGERT, GERMANY)

In September 2000, Esther Ziegert of Dachau, Germany (once home to one of the first and the longest-running concentration camps built by the Nazis) called out to Mary, and she gladly entered therein. Eighteen years earlier, Esther had returned to the Catholic Faith, after which she saw the hand of God change her family for the better. But her husband still stood in the middle of the family, rooted like a strong tree—in unbelief.

A few years after her husband's retirement, he was afflicted with almost unbearable pains that reminded him of an earlier attack of pleurisy. For twenty-four hours, the family tried every means to provide relief for his sufferings, but their efforts were futile. Mr. Ziegert spent two agonizing nights without sleep. The doctor could not assure him of an exact diagnosis until the following day at the earliest.

Mr. Ziegert decided to spend the third night in the chair in front of their television. Mrs. Ziegert prepared pillows and blankets for her husband, and because his pain was so excruciating, she reached for the Miraculous Medal. "I saw that a chance had come," shared Esther, "to point him to the living God of love and to the Blessed Mother's work." Attaching the Medal with tape to the back of the blanket, she had him lean back so that the painful place on his back would touch it. Then she secured the blanket with a pillow and prayed fervently for her husband's healing and conversion. "I also asked the Blessed Mother for a sign that the healing would take place through her intercession. This was important to me for the sake of the one who did not believe, so that he would learn to believe."

The next morning, Esther Ziegert's husband woke up happy, healthy, and pain-free. He rejoiced and the family rejoiced with him. Mrs. Zieger's joyful thanks rose up to God in heaven. A short time later, Mr. Ziegert's ecstatic mood was punctured by a scare. When looking in the mirror, he noticed a strange red mark on his back in the spot that had once been so painful. He showed it to Esther. The mark was as red as a deep burn, and with the shape and markings of the Miraculous Medal! Mrs. Ziegert received her sign, and Mr. Ziegert's pain never returned.[287]

IN THE LAND OF TURKEY
(RELATED BY FR. LE LEU, TURKEY)

In the country of Turkey, in the cities of Smyrna, Angora, and Constantinople, which today are called Izmir, Ankara, and Istanbul, respectively, Miraculous Medals were distributed in great quantities. Dated March 16, 1835, this letter sent from Constantinople by the missionary priest, Fr. Le Leu, a Lazarist, shares evidence of their great impact:

> *It has been a long time since I proposed writing you something about the Medal. In my eyes, one of the greatest miracles it has ever worked is the rapidity of its propagation and the confidence it inspires. By our demands upon you for Medals, you may judge their effect in this country. We could dispose of thousands and yet not satisfy the innumerable calls we have for them. At Smyrna, it is the same. We had occasion to send a few into the interior of Asia, and the Blessed Virgin showed herself no less powerful or beneficent there than in Europe.*
>
> *At Angora [the capital city of Turkey], an old man was deprived of the use of all his limbs and had neither walked nor worked for years. He lived in frightful poverty and sighed for death because he was especially grieved at being a burden for so long upon his family in indigent circumstances. (In this country, there are numbers of Armenian families very devoted to the Blessed Virgin, and this was one of them.) He had no sooner heard of the Miraculous Medal, than he sought the happiness of obtaining and wearing it. In these countries, the Faith has retained its primitive simplicity; this recipient of a Medal did not content himself with praying before it, or hanging it around his neck, but he kissed it with profound respect and applied it to the affected parts. The Blessed Virgin cannot resist such confidence, and the good old man instantly recovered the use of his limbs. He now works and supports himself.*
>
> *Here is another incident. A young woman belonging to a respectable and very pious family had been prey to a disease for a long time, the nature of which neither the French, Greek, nor Turkish physicians could understand. The symptoms were extremely violent pains in her side, which prevented her from walking, eating, or sleeping, and which sometimes disappeared, only to return with renewed violence.*
>
> *Having heard of our Medal, this lady felt interiorly compelled to employ it for her recovery, but believing herself unworthy of obtaining a direct miracle, she asked the Blessed Virgin of the*

Miraculous Medal to enlighten the physician and make known to him the proper remedy.

She then traveled to the countryside. At the end of several days there, she saw her physician and was astonished to hear him exclaim when he saw her, "Madame, good news! I have found the remedy for your disease. I am sure of it; in a few days, you will be perfectly well. I do not know why it is, but your case has constantly occupied my mind since your departure, and by a careful study of it, I have at last discovered the cause of the disease and the manner of treating it."

The lady recognized, at once, that this knowledge came from above; she had not implored Mary in vain. Today, she is in excellent health. It was from the mouth of her mother that I received these details. "O Monsieur," exclaimed this good mother, "How happy I am about my poor daughter's recovery! It is the Blessed Virgin who has restored her to me. If you could only get me a few more of these Medals; I am overwhelmed with requests for them."

The physician, himself, published the details I have just given. So persuaded is he of the efficacy of the Medal that he calls it his final remedy and advises his patients to wear it whenever he is at a loss concerning their maladies. And the Blessed Virgin has rewarded his faith, for one of his own daughters, a most pious person, but in miserable health, has just experienced its beneficial effects.

I could mention numerous other incidents, as many conversions as cures, but one more will suffice for today:

Not long ago, the mother of a family had every symptom of an attack of apoplexy; she had already lost consciousness, when her son, a very pious young man, who wore one of these Medals, took it off his neck and put it around hers. He then ran for a doctor and a priest. On reaching the house, all three were astonished to find that she had quite recovered.

That evening, the son asked his mother for the Medal, and she returned it, but a moment after, she was stricken with another attack. The protection of the Blessed Virgin seemed to have been withdrawn with this sign of her power. He immediately put the Medal on her neck again, this time to remain, and she has been well ever since.

Oh! Do not delay, I beg you, in sending us the Medals we have asked of you.[288]

A GENEROUS GIFT FOR A GENEROUS SOUL
(MS. CATHARINA, SWITZERLAND)

In July 1824, Ms. Catharina, a twenty-nine-year-old Swiss woman, said goodbye to her family. She and some of her generous companions were traveling from where she lived, near the shores of Lake Geneva, to one of the large cities in southern Italy. There they would dedicate themselves to the service of the sick and poor. After a few months in the novitiate in a religious house devoted to works of charity in that city, she came down with a debilitating, wasting malady, which physicians were at a loss to define. Twenty-two months of ineffectual treatments went by, and her Superiors hoped she might heal if she returned to her home country of Switzerland to live among family. It did nothing, and doctors finally discontinued their visits.

After six years of living with this unknown and devastating illness, Catharina had improved only to the point of walking a few steps beyond her bedroom and stepping outside for a few minutes on occasion. Then from 1830 to 1835, she was no longer able to leave her couch of suffering, except for a few instances. Many times over the course of those five years, Catharina was on the verge of death. When a priest visited her family home, she was able to hear his words and mentally aware of his presence but could respond only with slight physical movements. The home became a school of holiness, where Christians might study the price of the cross and the heroism of patience.

Finally, it came time for Catharina to receive the Last Sacraments. For a total of eleven years, with her parents and siblings nearby, she had lived a life of suffering. Now it was time to say a different and more difficult goodbye to her family. But at that last hour, she conceived a hope of perhaps getting some relief through the Miraculous Medal. However, she mistrusted the possibility of an extraordinary cure, so only out of obedience did she begin a novena with that intention. Her sole task was to repeat, three times a day, the invocation: "O Mary, conceived without sin, pray for us who have recourse to thee."

On Wednesday, April 24, 1835, the second or third day of the novena, Catharina felt an irresistible desire to get out of bed. It was still very early in the morning. A little child assisted her in getting dressed. Finding that her limbs were supporting her, Catharina began to think that something miraculous must be happening. Filled with joy, she thought of announcing the news to her mother, who was in an adjoining room. She got up, walked across her room and down the hallway, and stood in her mother's doorway. Suddenly seized with fright, she turned around and walked back to her bedroom. It seemed too marvelous to be true.

Reassured by her newly restored strength and the ease with which she returned to her bedroom, she overcame her fear. Retracing her steps, she sought the embrace of her mother, sister, and brother. Catharina's unexpected appearance filled everyone with great emotion and abundant tears. Joy and gratitude overwhelmed them as they reached out to touch her, as if to prove to their senses that what they were seeing was real.

A clergyman who often visited Catharina soon heard rumors of her recovery, but gave no credit to them. Shortly thereafter, he met her mother on the street, and she burst into tears at the sight of the priest, unable to find words to express the cause of her emotion. Suspecting good news, he went immediately to the family home to see Catharina for himself. There, the miracle he couldn't deny was standing before him, and he and Catharina united their voices in prayers of praise and thanksgiving.

From then on, Catharina would arise at about seven o'clock in the morning, attend Mass, employ herself in various duties during the day, and take half-hour to hour-long walks. Her healing caused an extraordinary reaction in her area of Geneva, Switzerland. Many eyes were fixed on her. People sought out her presence, seeking inspiration, hope, and a deeper faith from one whom God had cured through the intercession of Our Lady of the Miraculous Medal.[289]

THE BLIND SHALL SEE
(ROSALIE DUCAS, BELGIUM)

On November 9, 1835, four-year-old girl Rosalie Ducas of Jauchelette, near Jodoigne in Belgium, was struck with total blindness. This happened without the slightest warning: no disease, no weakness. She had been in perfect health. Suddenly, the least amount of light hitting her eyes and the smallest whiff of air touching them was so painful that her face had to be kept covered with a folded cloth. The poor child's sufferings, night and day, were heartrending.

The priest of Jodoigne-la-Souveraine, who lived less than a half-league away, gave Rosalie's mother a Blessed Medal of the Immaculate

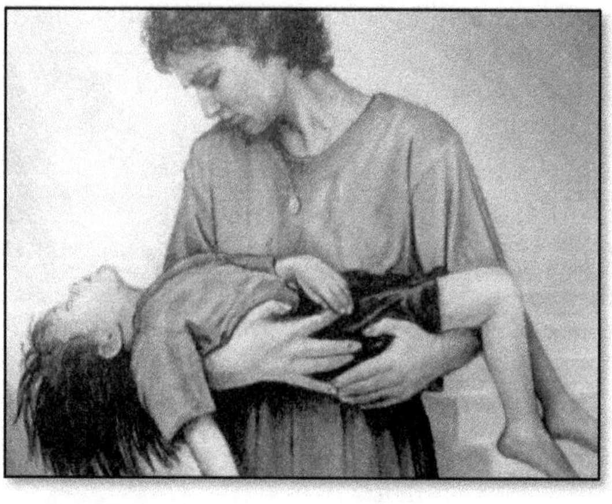

Conception. She received it and began to pray a novena. On June 11, 1836, another Medal was placed on the child's neck around six o'clock in the evening. At midnight, the little girl ceased her moans. On the fourth or fifth day of the novena, she opened her eyes. Her mother and father redoubled their prayers to the Blessed Virgin. On the ninth day, toward evening, the child recovered her sight entirely, to the great astonishment of the neighbors and all who had witnessed her sufferings, and with the joyful confirmation of the priest of Jodoigne-la-Souveraine.[290]

ARMED WITH FAITH
(OFFICER WAGNER, AUSTRIA)

In the year 1867, Officer Wagner in the garrison at Gratz, Austria, suffered from a serious wound in the right arm. He was brought to the general hospital there so that he could be under the special treatment of Dr. Rzehazeh, an eminent surgeon. The latter exhausted all of his skill, but in vain. After a few weeks, he saw that amputation was necessary to save the officer's life.

Learning of the doctor's decision, the patient was deeply grieved. He had never spoken of God and had accepted a Medal only out of courtesy. But now he seemed to experience a genuine satisfaction when the Daughters of Charity caring for him told him they would implore the Blessed Virgin on his behalf. In the days immediately preceding the operation, Officer Wagner frequently repeated the invocation engraved on his Medal: "O Mary, conceived without sin, pray for us who have recourse to thee."

The danger was now imminent, and the amputation, which couldn't be delayed, would take place the following day. A Sister of Charity came to visit him in the evening. Perceiving that the young officer was expressing confidence in continual prayer, she suggested that that he lay the Medal upon his afflicted arm and let it remain there all night. Officer Wagner gladly implemented her suggestion. That night, his sufferings were less severe than usual.

The next day, Dr. Rzehazeh, while waiting for his assistants, carefully examined the officer's wounded arm. He touched it, he probed it, and to his great astonishment, discovered that amputation was not necessary. The officer was overcome with happiness. The other doctors, arriving for the surgery, confirmed this surprising change. When Officer Wagner found himself alone with the chief surgeon, he secretly shared the reason for this wonderful change. "I believe it's this small Medal that I put on my arm throughout the night." The surgeon (notwithstanding the injunction of secrecy), could not refrain from telling the sister, "I believe the Sisters of Charity have engaged the good God in this case." And Officer Wagner soon left the hospital with a new arm and a new faith.[291]

A DOCTOR AND HIS MEDAL
(DR. SCHWEIZ, SWITZERLAND)

As a small boy, the Swiss physician, Dr. E. Schweiz, had been introduced to the Miraculous Medal by his mother. In 1983, he wrote of why he still thanks her, after so many years of life, for entrusting him with this treasure.

After forty years of practicing medicine in Switzerland and trusting in the power of the Miraculous Medal, Dr. Schweiz has helped many patients. He shared a little about how he has used it in his practice. When he applies bandages to broken bones or sutured wounds, he never forgets to include a Miraculous Medal and asks Mother Mary to ensure that his work is beneficial. For his patients who are bedridden, whether children or adults, he places the Miraculous Medal under their pillows. He has had patients with pneumonia and pleurisy who were healed in record time.

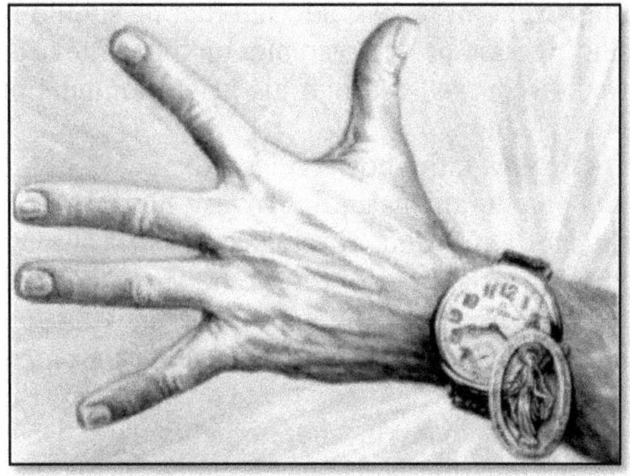

On one particular emergency call, Dr. Schweiz arrived arrived at the scene of a reserve officer who had been cleaning his pistol and fired a shot, hitting himself in the heart area. He was still unconscious. The doctor noted a small open wound in the front left of the chest with slight bleeding, pallor in the face, difficulty breathing, and other worrisome complications. He immediately called an ambulance and while they waited, he attached a Miraculous Medal to the officer's watchband, gave a wrist injection, and prayed fervently to the Blessed Virgin to help save him.

The ambulance arrived and took the officer to the hospital, where he would have to undergo surgery. He was immediately X-rayed, which revealed a large bruise. When the area was punctured, half a liter of blood flowed out. But after that, to everyone's surprise, the bleeding stopped altogether. There was no need whatsoever for an operation.

Two weeks later, the young man came to see Dr. Schweiz at his practice. He was completely recovered and well. "Doctor," he said, "when you gave me the shot in my wrist, I immediately felt better and could breathe!"

"His confession delighted me," said Dr. Schweiz, "but I told him that this improvement probably did not come from my injection, but from my taking refuge in the intercession of Our Lady of the Miraculous Medal."[292]

THE DUTCH BOY
(FRANÇOIS WENMAKERS, THE NETHERLANDS)

On April 25, 1836, François Wenmakers, a fourteen-year-old carpenter's apprentice in Holland, fell from a height of about sixteen feet. His head was partly crushed, and he suffered from an almost complete paralysis of the lungs, larynx, and esophagus. He was left unconscious, unable to swallow liquids or take in any food or medications. His parents, in their shock and grief, hung a Medal of the Immaculate Conception around their son's neck.

One of the physicians, worried over François' fixed stare, immovable limbs, and muteness, advised that he should receive Extreme Unction.[293] Another doctor declared him on the verge of death. As the days passed, it was discovered through his brief moments of lucidity that he was also nearly blind.

On May 4, the boy received the Last Rites. Now seeing that there was no hope for any natural recovery, his parents began a novena in honor of the Mother of God. Three days later, at about six o'clock in the morning, François asked his mother if the Medal around his neck was blessed. She answered yes, assuming his question was the effect of delirium. But then he kissed the Medal and, for the first time since his fall, sat up. "Something tells me," he exclaimed, "that I must get up...that I am cured!"

Astonished, his mother immediately called his sisters and a friend, who rushed into the room. Seeing that François strongly persisted in declaring himself cured, they persuaded his worried mother to let him rise. He did indeed get up, and pointing to a picture in the room, representing the

Miraculous Medal, he said, "It is this good Mother who has cured me." From that moment on, the boy's health was perfectly restored.[294]

PRAISE IN A PRISON
(VALDOMIZO MANUEL DO NASCIMENTO, BRAZIL)

On January 6, 1962, the Sisters of Mercy, decorated the altar in a cell-block prison chapel in Sao Paolo, Brazil, where a manger still graced the sanctuary. It was the Feast of the Epiphany, and a Mass was about to begin, followed by a distribution of sacramentals. The celebrating priest was a great devotee of the Blessed Mother. After his homily, the Father picked up the Child Jesus from the manger, gave him a kiss, and announced to the inmates that they would receive gifts of Miraculous Medals and the Green Scapular.

When Mass ended, the priest walked through the rows, followed by Sr. María, who distributed the gifts to the prisoners who desired them. As Sister María walked by an inmate named Valdomizo Manuel do Nascimento, a Protestant who for twenty-two years could walk only with crutches, she asked if he also wanted a Miraculous Medal. He answered yes.

"Beg for healing from the Blessed Virgin," Sr. María told him. Inwardly, Valdomizo prayed for healing. Immediately, he felt a tingling rush through his body, but did not move and remained silent.

A fellow prisoner, only ten feet away, watched as Valdomizo suddenly stood up and walked freely over to meet him—without crutches. Other inmates, clearly shaken, moved to support Valdomizo, but the healing was real and instantaneous. Valdomizo laughed and wept, calling out, "I am cured!" A wave of wonder and excitement crashed over everyone present that day.

Several doctors, when questioned by the director of the prison infirmary, confirmed that only a miracle could explain the healing. The following day, the director communicated the event to all the prisoners of the other cell blocks, exhorting them to follow the good example of that subdivision.

The happy Sr. María, mediator of the miracle, wrote on August 15 of that same year: "Today, several sisters were in the prison to attend the consecration of a statue of Our Lady of the Miraculous Medal in the chapel. At the beginning of Mass, all the prisoners sang a very beautiful Hail Mary. In the pavilion with 600 prisoners in attendance, 500 received Holy Communion, 150 for the first time, and 13 received Holy Baptism." The wave of the miracle of the Medal had also washed many of her wayward children back to her Son.[295]

MOTHER OF ALL
(NAIMEH MA'LOUF, THE HOLY LAND)

Just outside the walls of the Old City in Jerusalem is a German-speaking community of Benedictine monks, who come from different nations. I, Brother Gerhard, am one of them. We live in Dormition Abbey on Mount Zion, which is said to mark the place where Mary, Mother of Jesus was assumed into heaven. Some time ago I was sent from Munich various booklets of the small publication, Erlebnisse mit der Wunderbaren Medaille heute, *which greatly impressed me and inspired me to recommend the Medal at my first opportunity. And it soon came:*

On June 4, 1968, a young woman named Naimeh Ma'louf travelled to our Abbey to request prayer for her mother, who was scheduled to undergo surgery the next day at the Nazareth Hospital in Jerusalem. Considering her mother's advanced age, a second hernia operation put her at great risk. I handed Mrs. Naimeh a Miraculous Medal, encouraging her to place it under her pillow, and to pray and trust in Our Blessed Mother. Here is what transpired:

When Naimeh arrived at the hospital in Jerusalem around 10 a.m. on June 5, she learned that her mother had already been in the operating room for two hours. Fearing for her well-being, she began praying the

Rosary aloud, despite the taunts of one of her mother's hospital roommates, a Protestant woman named Im Salim. "Why do you pray to Mary?" she ridiculed. "She is a woman like you and me. She can't help you. You have to pray to God yourself!"

Naimeh was not put off and said, "You are wrong, Mary is not an ordinary woman. She is the Holy Virgin, the Mother of Christ, the Mother of God. We are sinful people. But she is our Mother, too. She can and will help us. And she will help my mother." Then she confidently continued to pray aloud with great fervor.

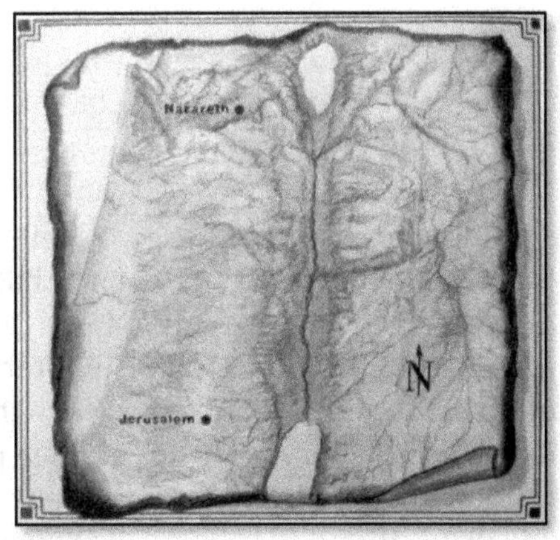

In the meantime, the operation ended, and Naimeh's mother was transferred back to the hospital room. As a result of the anesthesia, she was still unconscious. A long recovery was expected, and she wouldn't be able to walk on her own for some time. Naimeh knelt at her bedside and prayed the Rosary. She also placed the Blessed Medal of the Immaculate Virgin under her mom's pillow. Not an hour had passed before her elderly mother awoke and sat up. She felt so well that she stood up and walked around without help, to the great astonishment of the patients and the nurses.

Im Salim, the Protestant woman, turned to Naimeh and said, "You are a saint! I kiss your feet and ask you to pray for me, too, just as you prayed for your mother."

"If you want me to pray for you," replied Naimeh, "you must pray with me. Give your heart to the Blessed Virgin, and you will see that she will help you, too." She invited Im Salim to first learn the Hail Mary, and then the entire Rosary. By 3 p.m., they were both praying each decade of the Rosary together, slowly and devoutly. Naimeh fastened the Medal to the sick woman's hospital gown, and encouraged her to say, "Holy Virgin, help me!"

Im Salim was paralyzed on the right side and could not move her hand or foot. Her mouth was distorted, and her right eye twitched constantly.

She had been in this condition for five to six months and had already spent thirteen days in the hospital. At around 4 p.m., she suddenly noticed that she could move her hand and foot again. She exclaimed to her sister, who had come to visit her, "I am healed! Come and see. I can move my limbs again!"

"See now how the Holy Virgin helps!" remarked Naimeh, joyfully.

Im Salim said in reply, "I will now also venerate the Holy Virgin as you do. I wish to see a priest of your church, who honors and loves the Blessed Mother. I want to become Catholic."

News of the two miracles travelled to other rooms in the hospital, and Naimeh Ma'louf came to spend that day and the next praying for and dispersing the Miraculous Medal to other patients in distress. By the evening of June 5, through the intercession of His Mother, the Lord had miraculously healed not only Naimeh's mother, a Roman Catholic, and Im Salim, a Protestant, but three other patients, as well. A Maronite woman no longer had kidney stones, a Greek Orthodox woman could suddenly eat and drink after two months of expelling what entered her, a Greek Melkite woman was healed of osteomyelitis (inflammation of the bone marrow).

The last miracle was that of a Muslim woman named Rasmije, who was hemorrhaging, and for twenty-three days had suffered a high fever. When she heard about the healings that had taken place, she asked for Naimeh to come and see her. She told her that she, too, loved the "Virgin" and asked for a Miraculous Medal. In Islam, Mary's virgin motherhood is recognized under the honorary title "EI Adra"—"The Virgin." Naimeh placed a Medal into Rasmije's open hand, which lay motionless on her nightstand, for she was too weak to even close her fingers. Kneeling by her bed, Naimeh prayed the Rosary while Rasmije murmured repeatedly, "Yes Adra—O Virgo!" Three hours later, her temperature returned to normal, and her bleeding stopped.

On June 5 and 6, in the year 1968, in the land of her Son's death and Resurrection, the Blessed Mother came to visit through her Medal and wanted to prove herself as the common Mother of all.[296]

CURSES TO KISSES
(TOMASZ, PRUSSIAN POLAND)

In 1865, a man named Tomasz, notorious for his unsavory character, was brought to the Hospital of Beuthen in Prussian Poland, which was run by the Daughters of Charity. As soon as he burst through the front doors, he was blaspheming. Since the sisters were told by the physician that he had but a few days to live, Sr. Joasia, who was assigned to attend to him, offered him a few words of consolation, trying to turn his thoughts to his soul. His response was to curse at her.

After a few days of receiving foul insults in response to her suggestion that Tomasz return to the Church and the Holy Sacraments, Sr. Joasia said to him, "My friend, since you will not listen to me, I will ask my Superior to come see you."

"Let her come," he replied. "If she were to tell me to hang myself, I would obey her, but as for Confession, she may talk about that as much as she pleases. I shall never yield." He followed these words with such a stream of blasphemies that Sr. Joasia left his side with a very heavy heart.

"Have you given him a Medal?" the Mother Superior asked Sr. Joasia, after she had explained the patient's predicament.

"A Medal?" questioned Sr. Joasia. "He would throw it away."

"Ah, well, we must put one under his pillow and entrust him to prayer, for it is useless to talk to him. Tell him only that I said he is not worthy of going to Confession, and I forbid his doing so."

As soon as Sr. Joasia left the Superior to see the unruly patient, the Superior dropped to her knees and began repeating the Memorare. In a few short minutes, Sr. Joasia returned, this time, shedding tears of joy. "Ah, Mother," she said, "he wishes to confess. Just after I put the Medal under his pillow and recited the Memorare for him, I delivered your message. 'Indeed!' he said to me, rising from a sitting position. 'Well, I would just like to see the person who could prevent it! Tell your Superior that tomorrow morning at eight o'clock, I am going to pay the priest a visit.'"

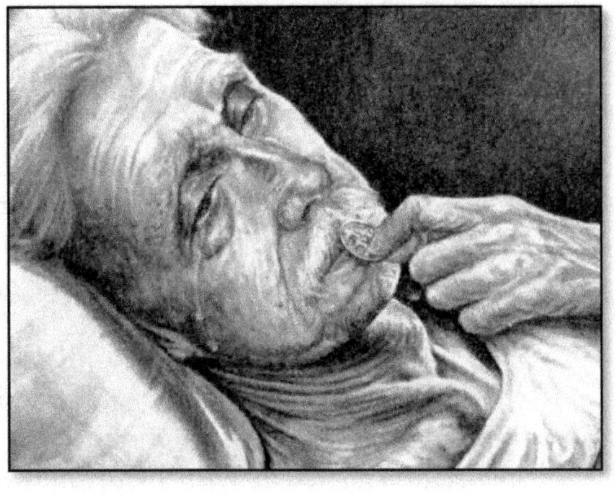

The Sisters of Charity felt a little troubled concerning a confession apparently dictated by the spirit of defiance and contradiction, but their fears soon dissipated when Tomasz returned to his sickbed bathed in tears. He had just been to Confession and Holy Communion, and Jesus had reached his heart through the Sacraments. Asking the sisters' pardon for his past misconduct, he begged them to implore the Blessed Virgin to let him live eight days longer so that he might weep for his sins. This favor was granted to him, and daily he wetted his pillow with tears. At the end of the eight days, while praising God in a faint voice and pressing the Miraculous Medal to his lips, Tomasz died.[297]

THE "MIRACLE PENNY"
(CHANG, FORMOSA)

In the late 1800s, the Franciscan missionary to East Asia, Fr. Cölestin M. Nardon, was among those who knew and loved a little boy in kindergarten named Chang.

One morning at 11 a.m., it was lunchtime at the Churngli Kindergarten school on the island of Taiwan, known by the name Formosa in the nineteenth century. Those students who lived nearby walked to their houses for lunch, and those who lived a farther distance away were driven through the busy streets, dropped off at their homes, and returned to the school's front door.

Little Chang deboarded the school van that stopped in front of his home and walked across the street to eat lunch with his family. Before he could reach the front door, a speeding motorcycle hit him, and he fell backward onto the ground. Blood oozed from a large wound in his head, and he was taken immediately to the hospital.

For five days, Chang lay unconscious. Medical science failed to help him. The little boy appeared comatose, and his parents looked on with heartbreaking sadness at their dying child. "Even if he were to wake up," said the father, "he would still be mentally crippled for the rest of his life because of the severe concussion." They were Buddhist, as was their child, and no star of hope flashed in their minds.

Fr. Nardon wrote:

> *My Chinese missionary sisters came to the hospital to visit little Chang, who had suffered an accident and was their pupil in kindergarten. When they saw that all the injections no longer helped, and that there was no longer any way to save the child's life, they placed the Blessed Mother's "Miraculous Medal" under the head of the unconscious child and prayed. Then it was as if an invisible hand was laid on the little one's round head: a slight trembling of the eyelids offered hope, and then his bright eyes opened and looked up with joyful amazement at his father, mother, and the sisters. His senses returned at the same moment, and his little hands and feet moved. His head wound closed up, and from the little one's sensible speech, no mental disturbance was inferred. The little boy was saved, yes, completely restored, wonderfully healed by [the graces obtained by] the ever-good Mother Mary. The joy of the parents was indescribable. Gratefully they acknowledged the wonderful help. And how thankfully the little one hung on to the "miracle penny," holding it tightly in his little hands, clasping it*

in his little fist, never wanting to let it go. With touching, childlike tenderness, he lifted it to his face. When he saw the cross on the sister's chest, he said fervently: "Sister has Jesus—I have Holy Mother."

It is easy to understand that the pagan parents not only allowed, but even wished that their child, given back by the Mother of God, should become Christian. Soon he will be baptized, and, we hope that his parents will also join him. Mary, the Mother of God, as the "New Eve," is also the Mother of humanity, the Mother of all, and she is happy to help everyone."[298]

THE MACANESE DEMONIAC

(YOUNG MAN, MACAO)

From a letter written by a French missionary in Macao, China, dated August 25, 1841:

A widow in Macao, China, had only one son, who, like herself, was raised in their local folk religion. One day, she watched him suddenly fall under the power of the devil. Tormented, and not in his right mind, her son began running through the fields wildly, uttering lamentable cries. People fled from his presence, and anyone who tried to stop him was immediately seized and thrown to the ground. This traumatic change in him left his poor mother in despair, nearly dying of grief.

A Macanese man, with a lively Christian faith, happened to see the possessed young man and was moved by his sufferings. He told those who were trying to restrain him to stop their efforts and stated that he would be able to quiet and restore him. His claim astonished those around him. But they did as the man requested, fearing for his safety.

The Christian wore the Miraculous Medal around his neck. Taking it into his hands, he approached the possessed man, and showing the Medal to him, commanded the demon to flee and leave him in peace. The demon obeyed instantly, and the young man, freed from the evil spirit, prostrated himself humbly before the miraculous image, not knowing what it was. The Christian told him to get up and walk with him, as he held up the Medal in his hand. This acted like a magnet for the freed man, and in this way, he was led back to his mother.

As soon as the young man reached her, he called out, "Mother!" to her immense joy and consolation. "Do not cry anymore," he said. "I am freed from the demon. The bad spirit left me as soon as it saw this Medal."

The change in her son was so great that the mother wasn't sure if she was in reality or a dream. The Christian reassured her that what had happened was real, adding that her son would not experience this again, if they renounced their idols and became Christians. She promised sincerely, and they immediately began to divest their home altar of its false gods. Then the Macanese Christian man left them, once assured that they would continue to learn about the faith that had saved them.[299]

PEACE OF MIND
(ST. JOHN GARBRIEL PERBOYRE, CHINA)

In 1838, Fr. John Gabriel Perboyre, the Apostolic missionary to China wrote letters regarding his experiences in that country with the Miraculous Medal. The following is his correspondence dated August 10, 1839, when he was working in the mission of Chayuankou, in the province of Hubei, which is part of the region of lakes formed by the Yangtze kiang (blue river). Fr. Perboyre was arrested a month later for the practice of his Catholic religion. After living out his faith generously during a year of "frightful tortures," he was martyred on September 11, 1840 by strangulation on a cross. On June 2, 1996, he was canonized and made a saint by Pope John Paul II.[300]

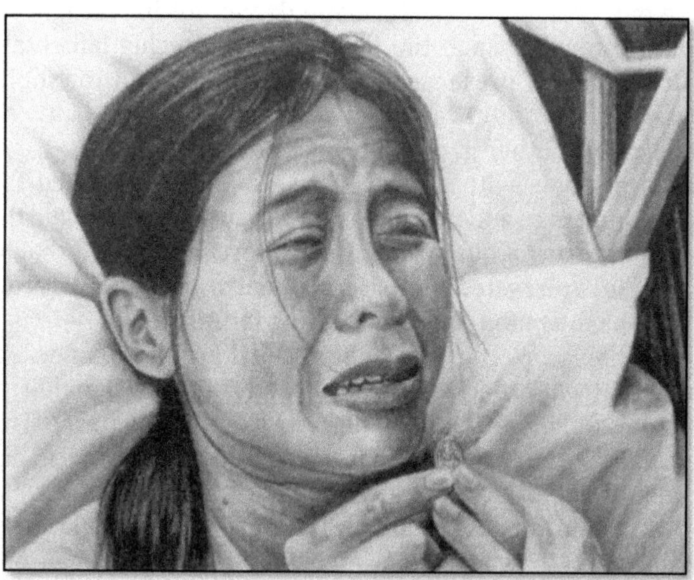

While I was giving a mission to the Christians of the Honan province, November 1837, they brought to me a young woman who had been afflicted with mental illness for about eight months, telling me she was very anxious to confess, and though she was incapable of the Sacrament, they begged me not to refuse her a consolation she appeared to desire so earnestly. Her sad condition of mind precluded

all thought of her deriving any benefit from the exercise of my ministry, but I heard her out of pure compassion.

In taking leave of her, I placed her under the special protection of the Blessed Virgin—that is, I gave her a Medal of the Immaculate Conception. She did not then understand the value of the holy remedy she received; but from that moment, she began to experience its beneficial effects, her shattered intellect improving so rapidly that, at the end of four or five days, she was entirely changed. From a complete confusion of ideas, from fears that kept her ever in mortal agony, and which I believe, were the work of the demon, succeeded good sense, peace of mind, and happiness.

She made her confession again and received Holy Communion with the most lively sentiments of joy and fervor. This special instance of Mary's generosity will doubtless surprise you little, you who know so well that the earth is filled with her mercy; but your hearts will be excited anew to fervent thanksgiving for this particular favor, which is the principal reason of my acquainting you with it.[301]

A HAIRY SPILL
(GABRIELE ELLMAN, GERMANY)

After a very busy day, Mrs. Ellman, exhausted and scatterbrained, was washing her little daughter Gabriele's hair in the evening. Getting ready to rinse away the shampoo, she grabbed, by mistake, the teapot filled with boiling water and poured the contents over Gabriele's hair. The girl let out a terrible scream, and rolled onto to the floor, whimpering and screaming. "It all happened so fast," recalled her mother.

At first, Mrs. Ellman couldn't process what she had just done, but soon realized that in her overtiredness, she had reached for the wrong container of water. Her husband, a doctor, came running, but despite his training and expertise, he had to watch helplessly as his child writhed in pain. Through Gabriele's wet hair, they could see her scalp form bright red burns marks. Then large blisters began to appear: second-degree burns! The mother and father carefully laid their daughter down onto a large pillow. Mrs. Ellman recalled, "I cannot describe how desperate I was at that moment. I could already see her beautiful hair falling out and her whole head covered with scars forever. And all was my fault!"

In her distress, Mrs. Ellman remembered the Miraculous Medal, which she always wore on her necklace. In her anguish, she repeated: "Please, dear Mother of God, help, please help," and she put the Medal on Gabriele's head over her hair. Her father then came with strong painkillers trying to at least offer some relief; the wound secretions were already

dripping from the blisters. But Gabrielle said, "Nothing hurts me anymore. I'm sure of it."

Mrs. Ellman thought to herself, "My good child is only trying to comfort me because she sees how desperate I am."

Again, Gabriele repeated: "No, I'm sure nothing hurts anymore, I don't feel anything at all," and then she fell asleep. Gabriele slept through the entire night without waking up, and in the morning, the Medal was somehow still in the same place on her head as the night before. The slightest movement should have caused it to slip off. When the little girl woke up, she again announced, "I can't feel anything at all."

When her parents looked closely, they observed that Gabriele's scalp had no redness whatsoever; it was entirely white. The large blisters were gone, and only her hair was left encrusted with wound secretions as thick as a millimeter. Mr. and Mrs. Ellman took hours to brush it out of their daughter's clumped hair. But not the slightest trace of her burns remained.[302]

DEFEATING DEATH AND THE DEVIL
(EMMETT, GERMANY)

In 1972, a Franciscan friar, Brother Kunibert, came to visit his seriously ill friend, Emmett, in the hospital. Doctors had not been able to give Emmett hope of a cure. His prognosis was terminal. Brother Kunibert told his evangelical Protestant friend that he had to go away for a fortnight. "When you come back," Emmett told him, "I will already be in the ground." But the friar responded to his sad goodbye with words of courage and hope, praying that God would heal him.

The following night, Emmett woke up suddenly. Standing at the foot of his bed were two figures—the devil and death. Deeply frightened, the terminally ill man's first thought was, "Now I will never see my friend Kunibert again in this life!" But then, a beautiful lady appeared and with a commanding gesture, chased the two sinister figures away from his bed. The woman was surrounded by vibrant light, and her hands extended out from her sides in a gesture of blessing. Then she disappeared. Immediately, the sick man felt completely restored to health. His inexplicable cure was confirmed with astonishment by the doctors, who examined him thoroughly the next day.

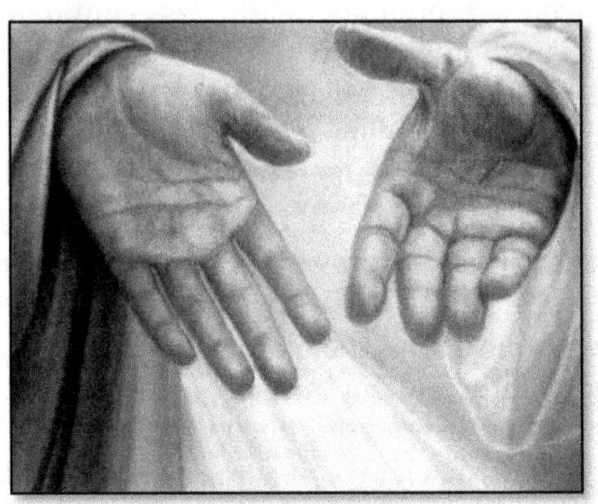

Emmett concealed his extraordinary nighttime experience, telling it to no one, not even his evangelical Protestant wife, as she would not have any context of understanding for it.

When Brother Kunibert returned, his first priority was to go the hospital to check on his friend. To the friar's shock, Emmett received him at the hospital room door—standing, healthy, and beaming with joy. It was his day of discharge. After Emmett recounted his strange experience during the night, Brother Kunibert pulled out and showed him his Miraculous Medal. Greatly surprised, the healed man confessed that the image of the lady on the Medal and her hand positions of blessing were exactly the same as how the beautiful woman had appeared to him. Brother Kunibert then shared *his* secret. Before he left Emmett's side, two weeks before, he had given his nurse a Miraculous Medal with the request that it be placed under Emmett's pillow.[303]

MEDAL OF DELIVERANCE

(CAMILA, PERU)

An elderly lady in Lima, Peru, named Camila, who had once been a pious young girl, lost her faith by reading bad books. For thirty-five years she hadn't received the Sacraments and wanted nothing to do with the Catholic faith. Over the years, she grew increasingly surly and sullen. Camila had been living with her sister, who suffered from an illness that lasted only five days, but took her to her grave. This embittered the old woman even more, and she vented her grief in blasphemies.

In 1877, a Sister of Charity, Sr. Rosales, gave the elderly lady a Medal of the Blessed Virgin. Camila accepted the Medal and wore it for several days. During that time, she appeared bothered and a little less confident in her skepticism toward Catholicism. Something within her kept urging her to lay the Medal aside, so she took it off and fell back into her habitual melancholy and hardness of heart, which gave her a strange and familiar comfort.

When Sr. Rosales paid a visit to Camila's home in Lima, she perceived these changes in her and inquired if she was still wearing the Medal. On receiving a negative answer, Sr. Rosales spoke to Camila about the dangers to which her soul was exposed without it, and the old woman promised to put it on again. Sr. Rosales, greatly interested in the poor woman's soul, offered up many prayers for her, and at the end of fifteen days, ventured to her home to see her again. Perceiving no change in her sentiments, the sister inquired immediately if she had put the Medal back on. The elderly woman, in her uncouth manner, didn't bother to answer, but made a telling motion with her head.

"What have you done with it, and where is it?" asked Sr. Rosales. Camila replied that it was in her wardrobe, and that she had made several ineffectual efforts to put it on again. The sister understood that the elderly woman's soul was under some kind diabolical influence, which was holding her aloof from what could reclaim her to God. She felt that now was the moment for prompt action. In a tone of severity, Sr. Rosales said to her, "Very well, since you will not wear the Medal, I will have to abandon you entirely." These words produced the desired effect. The old lady ran to the wardrobe and taking up the Medal, put it around her neck.

This gave Camila a new determination, and she soon experienced the sweet and powerful influence of Mary Immaculate. Within a few days, she was attending the Holy Sacrifice of the Mass and listening attentively to the Word of

God. From that time forward, Camila was entirely changed. She confessed and made her Easter Communion. The abiding sentiments of her heart changed from pain and bitterness to compunction and gratitude.

When going to church, the old woman wished to remain at the entrance, feeling unworthy to enter further into the sacred edifice. It was with the greatest difficulty that her friends could convince her to accept a place nearer to the altar. Mother Mary had brought her to Jesus in the Blessed Sacrament, and she knew that the sanctuary possessed the very presence of God. From the moment the Medal was first around her neck, Camila knew neither peace nor rest until she returned to the Church, she told Sr. Rosales. So great was the love of the Mother of God for her.[304]

"HOW IS THAT POSSIBLE?"
(MICHAEL, GERMANY)

On Shrove Tuesday, the day before Ash Wednesday—better known now as Fat Tuesday, little Michael suffered a terrifying accident near his home in Vallendar, Germany. While crossing the street, he was hit by a passing car, thrown to the ground, and dragged for about thirty meters. When his mother saw this, she collapsed in shock and agony, convinced that her boy was dead. From her angle of view, there was no possibility for her son's survival. But she did not see what other eyewitnesses did. They reported that something strange and miraculous had occurred during the accident. The child's head was held up as if by invisible hands, and his small body was pushed along by the car tire, but somehow not run over.

Michael suffered very serious injuries (a broken thigh bone and pelvis, fractured jaw, severe bruises and abrasions, and a destroyed optic nerve in his right eye), but he had miraculously survived. His family was convinced that the Miraculous Medal, which the child wore around his neck, had saved his life.

During little Michael's long weeks in the hospital, one of the injuries most difficult to repair was the fracture of Michael's temporomandibular joint, which in adults can be nailed together, but not in small children. Michael's head had to be put in a plaster cast, and his lower jaw set in a complicated brace. His food had to be administered through a small tube. During those trying weeks, his mother prayed a great deal to the Blessed Mother and repeatedly slipped a Miraculous Medal under his plaster head cast and pelvic cast, with a request for Mary's help.

After several weeks, the day came for Michael's head cast to be removed, to be replaced by a chewing apparatus. Every three months, Michael would have to have the facial contraption adjusted according to his bone growth for the next ten years!

In preparation for the insertions of the chewing apparatus, a current X-ray was taken. The chief physician of the dental clinic compared this X-ray with an earlier one. "How is that possible?" he exclaimed in amazement. Stupefied, the head doctor showed the other doctors the X-ray. Then he turned to little Michael and said, "Well you really are our little miracle child. Your joint fracture has healed so well that we can't even see the fracture site on the X-ray. We can spare you all the stress of the chewing apparatus."

How happy, relieved, and grateful Michael and his mother were when they heard this. Gone were ten long years of wearing an apparatus on his face and the ongoing painful adjustments that came with it. Now the boy was allowed to go home encased solely in his pelvic cast. For many years to come, however, Michael would still have to wear a black eye patch over his right eye. The optical nerve, normally about seven millimeters long, grows back very slowly, only half a millimeter per year.

At Michael's age, he would begin attending school the following year. But how could he learn to read and write with his injured eye? This was a great concern for his mother, but her trust in Mary was even greater. Applying a sticky substance to a Miraculous Medal, she placed it next to her boy's injured eye, and began to pray a novena to the Blessed Mother.

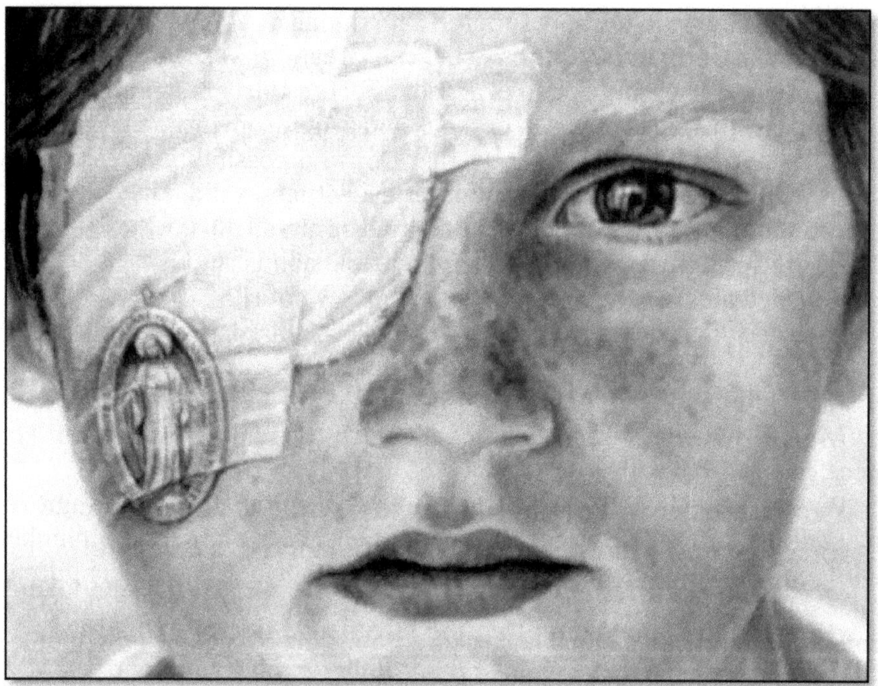

On the fourth day of the novena, Michael's paralyzed eye began to look slightly away from his nose, which had not been possible before. By the last day of the novena, the impossible happened again. His eye had completely healed and regained its sight! A few days later, when Michael was brought to the clinic, the doctors examining him were very much astonished, yet again. They stared at the little boy, dumbfounded, having no words to explain what they were seeing. The boy and his family experienced the inexpressible joy of another healing that was truly "miraculous." (February 11, 1994)[305]

BACK TO WORK
(G. GOTTFRIED, GERMANY)

G. Gottfried, a farmer's wife, spent long busy days throughout the year working with her husband in their barn and fields, while the housework was maintained by her sister-in-law. Often throughout her days, she sought consolation "in Our Lord God and His dear Mother." In addition to all the physical work she had to do, she suffered from a serious limb ailment. Her left leg was covered with painful varicose veins, some as thick as a finger.

As Mrs. Gottfried's pains increased, she was compelled to see a doctor, who diagnosed a high-grade phlebitis. To keep it from worsening, he prescribed bed rest. "How was the work on the farm to continue?" Mrs. Gottfried worried. Mr. Gottfried was no longer a young man, and to make matters worse, they were heading into a big harvest.

Mrs. Gottfried hid the doctor's orders from her husband and again sought refuge in Our Lord and Our Lady. She clasped the Miraculous Medal tightly in her hands and prayed the prayer that Mary desired be said with it: "O Mary, conceived without sin, pray for us who have recourse to thee." Then she placed the Medal on the inflamed part of her leg, pulled a rubber stocking over it, and followed her husband into the field. Repeating this "treatment" for a few days, she began to see improvement. After three weeks, the inflammation had disappeared, leaving only the pressure mark of the Medal and a sense of overwhelming gratitude.[306]

MOTHER TO MOTHER
(GIRL, BRAZIL)

In December 1994, Adriana traveled the long distance from her home in the city of Recife, Brazil, to the city of Paris, France, because she had learned that the Mother of God often did great things for those who petitioned her in the Chapel of Rue du Bac. At Adriana's side was her five-year-old daughter. The reason why Adriana traveled by plane across the

Atlantic was to ask for a miracle. Her precious little girl was terminally ill, and Adriana's specific wish was to sit her daughter down upon the very blue velvet armchair where the Mother of God had sat when she appeared to Sr. Catherine Labouré.[307] She would speak to Mother Mary as one mother to another, and after that, how could the Mother of God not ask her Son for help? After that, how could the Mother in heaven let her little girl on Earth just turn around and go home, the same as she came?

Adriana and her child finally arrived in Paris. They walked in through the entryway and into the famous Rue du Bac Chapel, a place of mystery and prayer. She recognized the details of the sanctuary she had seen so many times on postcards. Advancing ever so slowly and on her knees, Adriana moved forward along the stone chapel floor with her daughter. At last, she reached the sacred armchair. A cord separated the chair from the public, but for the Brazilian woman, this was no obstacle. Her child had not traveled across the Atlantic Ocean, and all the way to France to touch the chair only with her eyes! Yet, what should she do?

"Oh, wonderful," thought Adriana, seeing that Sisters of Charity were working in the sanctuary. "Sister, can the little one sit in the chair, please?"

"Sorry, but I can't allow you to do that, because if I did, everyone would ask to, and that would be impossible..." These words stabbed the mother's heart. The chair was necessary in her plan!

A little later, Adriana observed that the sisters had gone, and a new idea lit up her poor heart. She whispered to her daughter: "Listen. Now you go under the cord, and then crawl under the armchair. When you get there, reach out your hand to touch the place where the Mother of God was seated, and then come back again, very quickly—very quickly!"

The little girl didn't need to be told twice. She crawled on all fours under the cord. Then she lay her cheek on the blue velvet armchair and stayed there for a long while. Adriana remained transfixed. The little girl finally returned, moving very slowly.

"Why did you do that?" the mother reprimanded. "I told you to touch the chair only very briefly!"

"Mamma," replied the beaming child, "the woman told me to put my head on her knee."

Once mother and daughter returned to Brazil, it was confirmed by doctors that the little girl was completely healed. The news caused such a sensation in their diocese that the Archbishop of Recife picked up the phone to inform the Sisters of Charity on Rue du Bac of what had happened. In January 1995, three weeks after the miracle, he hand-carried to Paris all the medical reports and necessary evidence to confirm the five-year-old girl's cure. "I can verify," the Archbishop told the Mother Superior with whom he had spoken on the phone, "that the story I'm about tell you is true..."[308]

STORIES OF PROTECTION

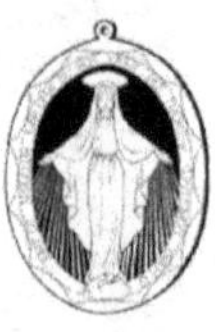

BULLET PROOF
(LENNIS FEWSTER, UNITED STATES)

Lennis Fewster had just gotten off work from her part-time job at the public library near Erdman Avenue in Baltimore, Maryland. It was August 9, 1989, and it was her birthday. As Ms. Fewster stood waiting at her regular bus stop around 1:30 p.m., she clutched a rosary in her hands and silently mouthed the prayers. She had long ago dedicated herself to praying a daily Rosary, being a member of the Blue Army, a world-wide apostolate dedicated to living the requests made by Our Lady of Fatima. And as a devotee of the Miraculous Medal, she was also known to faithfully wear the Medal and attend her parish's perpetual Miraculous Medal novena. Her favorite prayer from the novena was, "Ever while wearing it, may we be blessed by your loving protection."

Caught up in the contemplation of her prayer, Lennis hadn't noticed the young man approaching her. He tried to quickly grab her purse, but she would not let go of it. Suddenly, she heard a loud "crack!" Still, she refused to give over her purse. The thief punched her in the stomach and knocked her to the ground, finally getting what he was after. Ms. Fewster rose unsteadily to her feet and walked back to the library to get help. It wasn't until she stumbled through the front doors that she noticed blood. She had been shot in the chest.

Before that moment, Lennis had assumed, "he just set off a firecracker or something like that to scare me." Paramedics soon arrived and rushed Lennis to Johns Hopkins Hospital. "The doctor said the Miraculous Medal saved my life," she shared. "The Medal had been split in two by the bullet and the bottom half was imbedded in my chest." The bullet had bounced off the Medal and hit the ground. Police who inspected the scene of the crime retrieved both Ms. Fewster's rosary and the cartridge from the gun.

Lennis Fewster has kept the Miraculous Medal, burst in two. And with her rosary found by the police, she prays for the thief. She knows that what happened was much more than coincidence. "I learned that Mary is protecting me. The Lord isn't ready for me yet."[309]

THE BUFFALO HUNT
(GREG WILSON, KENYA)

Greg Wilson was planning a long trip to Africa. Before traveling there, he asked a Catholic acquaintance for "that little round thing that you always have with you." And he added: "As a Protestant, I don't think much of it, but I would like to have it, because on a journey of several months, you never know what may happen to you." His acquaintance, whose name was Stew, gladly gave him a handful of Miraculous Medals to take with him.

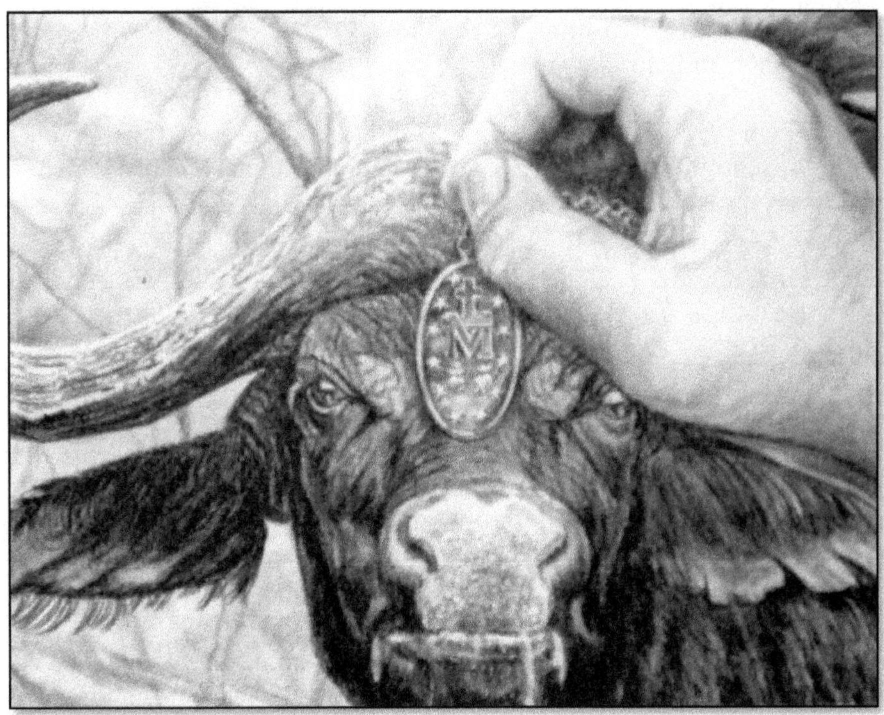

Months later, Greg's wife handed Stew a letter, which her husband had sent her from Mombasa, Kenya, describing a frightening experience he had undergone while on a buffalo hunt. Greg shot a buffalo without hitting it fatally, and the wounded animal raced towards him. Isolated from his local companions and with no rifle cartridge left, Greg knew he was a dead man. Panicking, he remembered the "Miraculous Medal" around his neck and grasped it in his hand.

At that very same moment, the buffalo stopped, halting in its frantic run. The animal glared at Greg with bloodshot eyes, so close that its breath brushed against Greg's face. He believed his last hour had come. Then the animal turned and trotted peacefully away, without harming a hair on Greg's head.

When the African natives, who had been watching from a distance, rushed to gather around Greg, they declared to him that a shot buffalo never spares its victim. They threw themselves on the ground and shouted that the great God had been with him, and they asked Greg for the remainder of his Medals, which he gladly gave them.[310]

IMPOSSIBLE LANDING

(PILOT JAKOB, AUSTRIA)

A pilot named Jakob fell ill, and while he was recuperating in the Rudolf Hospital in Vienna, Austria, he was given a Miraculous Medal. From that time forward, the pilot kept a Medal on him always. Years later, as Jakob was flying 2700 meters in the air, his plane malfunctioned, and he dropped from that height in a terrifying crash landing. Everyone in the Vienna district of Aspern who had seen the plane fall from the sky thought he must be dead—an unrecognizable body.

The pilot, however, crawled blithely out of his shattered plane! Except for a dislocated thumb, Jakob had miraculously suffered no injuries. He went to the hospital to have his finger bandaged. There, Jakob first told Count Pajascevich's nurse, and then many others, that when he sensed his plane was going to crash, he took the Medal in his hand and called upon the merciful Mother of God for help.[311]

"MARY, HELP!"
(FR. J. ROTH, GERMANY)

In 1940, Fr. J. Roth, who had venerated the Miraculous Medal and carried it with him since his childhood, was working in an industrial community of about 14,000 inhabitants in Germany. National Socialism had brought terror upon the nation. No priest was sure of his life. Fr. Roth recalls the day of May 3, 1940, Friday of the Sacred Heart, the day of the greatest miracle of his life:

> *Early in the morning at 4:30, we heard a thumping. The Gestapo took me and the second vicar to prison. I hid the breviary on my*

chest and carried some Medals in my pocket, as usual. We two priests were the first to be locked up in a small cell. By and by, there were thirty-five of us crammed tightly together. We were aware of what was about to happen. Next to me was a family man of six children, a merchant by profession. He was crying like a child. I remained calm and comforted him with the words, "Mary will help! Then I gave him a Medal. He pressed it to his lips, pleading, "Mary, help! Mary, help!"

We had to stand there for two long, anxious hours. I prayed and comforted as best I could. Then a truck stopped in front of the prison. SS men came to get us and told us to get in. Silently we obeyed. After a terribly worrisome hour, we reached the designated town. I prayed unceasingly to Our Lady along the journey, and father wept and prayed with me.

In this town, the truck stopped in front of a large hall. Several hundred prisoners were already standing inside. What were they expecting? No one spoke a word. We were joined by them. I knew what was in store for us now, namely transport to the concentration camp at Dachau.

What a wonderful grace was granted to me, for I was able to pray and pray, and the father of the family also prayed and begged Our Lady to have mercy on his children. I knew very well that we could only be saved by a miracle.

But I believed in the miracle, for I had often experienced how Mary had helped in hopeless situations through her Miraculous Medal. Now the moment was approaching when all the prisoners had to board the train to Dachau. All of them?—Two people were released, the merchant and I! For what reason? Ask the Immaculate Heart of Mary, which has power over hell.

And let us continue to trust in this Immaculate Heart, which loves us all so dearly and wants to help save us from eternal death—if need be, by a miracle.[312]

CALLING A TAXI
(WOLFGANG, GERMANY)

To get home quickly from the city of Munich, Germany, Wolfgang decided to grab a taxi. During the ride, he and the driver conversed about trivial things. Then the thought occurred to him: "Perhaps I should give the taxi driver a Miraculous Medal." But Wolfgang had reservations. He had no idea if this man was religiously minded or how he would receive it. Back and forth, Wolfgang tossed the notion about anxiously in his mind.

When the car slowed, arriving at Wolfgang's destination, he gave himself an inner push and took a leap of faith. "I'd like to give you this. It's called a Miraculous Medal. It is blessed and offers many graces for the one who wears and keeps it." To his surprise, the taxi driver accepted the Medal happily. Visibly pleased, he responded, "Yes, I'll gladly take it. I'll put it in my car right now."

About three months later, Wolfgang had to return to Munich and was about to cross the street when his eyes landed on a brand-new taxicab. Two ladies were stepping into it, and the driver was assisting them. As Wolfgang was thinking to himself, "I know that man," the driver looked his way and motioned for him to wait.

Hurriedly, the driver ran up to Wolfgang and said, "You're the one who gave me the Miraculous Medal, aren't you? I just wanted to tell you that I was in a serious accident a few days ago. A car crashed into me from the side with so much force that my car was totaled. Miraculously, nothing at all happened to me. I should have been injured or dead. I owe it all to the Medal. Thank you so very much for offering it to me." Then he ran back to the taxi, as quickly as he came, to get behind the wheel again.

At that time in Munich, Germany, there were about 2,000 taxi drivers deployed for service. Of all the people in the entire city and of all the taxi drivers, Wolfgang was gifted with meeting this particular one again and of hearing of this miracle of divine protection, all because of his small gesture of faith.[313]

A DEADLY TUMBLE
(FR. EDMUND POLTS, GERMANY)

As a men's chaplain, a Jesuit priest, Fr. Edmund Polts, drove many long distances in his Volkswagen. When he initially bought the vehicle, someone had given him two Miraculous Medals. "I stashed them in the glove compartment of the new car," he said, "and didn't really think about them after that." One day, two years later, Fr. Polts was driving at full speed on the highway, with a friend in the front passenger seat. A car sped up from behind, attempting to overtake them on a high bridge.

The reckless move caused the driver to crash into the priest's Volkswagen with tremendous force, throwing his car over the bridge. "The car overturned about seven times, over a distance of thirty-two meters," Fr. Polts shared. "The eyewitnesses to the accident all believed that the occupants were dead."

When the car came to a stop, the priest asked his companion if he had been hurt. "I'm all right," he replied. "It was then that we noticed that each of us had a Medal on our lap. They were struck with speechless gratitude. "We considered it a clear sign that we owe our lives to the Blessed Mother's special protection." Fr. Polts believed that that Our Lady had been watching over him from heaven, protecting his life and his priesthood in a moment of piercing the veil that exists between heaven and earth. Until that miraculous incident, the Jesuit father had not thought much of the importance of the Miraculous Medal. After that moment, he could never forget it.[314]

A CITY SPARED
(FRENCH PILOT, PARIS)

Why was Paris, the city of the "Miraculous Medal," saved from destruction in World War II? There is more than one story that tells how the capital of France was spared from ruin.

On September 3, 1939, mobilization of the military was announced in France. A pilot came to the Rue du Bac and asked for as many Miraculous Medals as the Sisters of Charity could give him. Eager to help, the sisters came to the door and poured what they had into his hands. The pilot then went up in his plane and scattered countless Miraculous Medals over the city of Paris.[315]

A few months later, on June 14, 1940, Paris fell to Nazi Germany. French military commanders "aimed at sparing [Paris] the devastation which defense would have involved. The command considered that no valuable strategic result justified the sacrifice of Paris."[316] The French, therefore, planned no retaliatory attack, thus sparing the city.

On August 23, four years later, Adolph Hitler gave the order by cable: *"Paris must not pass into the enemy's hands, except as a field of ruins."*[317] Explosives were laid at various bridges and monuments. (Later, the explosives were disabled.)

General Dietrich von Choltitz, commander of the German garrison, defied the order by Hitler to blow up Parisian landmarks and burn the city to the ground before its liberation. Choltitz signed a formal surrender that afternoon. Though Hitler did not completely give up on the destruction of Paris, with the Luftwaffe firing V2 rockets into the city from Belgium on August 26,[318] this did not deter the Free French General Charles de Gaulle from leading a joyous liberation march, on that very same day, down the Champs d'Elysees.[319]

The pilot's trust in Mary was apparently rewarded. After the war, the people of France and beyond spoke of the "miraculous preservation of Paris."

SAVED FROM RAPE
(SR. B. GRIEBEL, GERMANY)

Sr. B. Griebel (who shared this story in 1989) was employed as a young nurse at the St. Anna Höchstadt Hospital. On a day toward the end of October 1958, she arrived three minutes late to take the 8 p.m. train from Höchstadt to Burgkunstadt. The last train to take her home had already left. She was especially annoyed because that evening, a film about Mary's apparitions at Lourdes was playing for the last time.

Hoping she might find a ride to Burgkunstadt, she walked to the gas station next to the train station. Taking her rosary out of her coat pocket, she prayed. No car could be seen. In her naiveté, she stopped a car and asked the driver for a ride all the way to Burgkunstadt. "Please, get in!" the driver welcomed.

When he had driven for quite a distance, Sr. Griebel realized that the road led to Kronach. She asked the driver to let her get out of the car. He did not respond to her request, but drove into the nearby forest, with the intention of raping her there.

In her extreme mental and physical distress, Sr. Griebel inwardly called upon Our Lady for help and asked for her protection. When the stranger reached out and gripped his fingers around her neck, he received an electric shock from the Miraculous Medal and immediately withdrew his hands. Startled, he asked her what she was wearing around her neck. His stunned reaction gave her the chance to escape the vehicle and run into the forest.

Shortly thereafter, the man raped a girl on another route. Due to Sr. Griebel's having the exact description of the vehicle and the driver, the fiend was apprehended by the police.[320]

NOT THE SAME CITY
(THOMAS GREERTY, UNITED STATES)

In the year 2000, a lawyer named Thomas Greerty went on a pilgrimage with the Order of Malta to Lourdes, and along the journey home, he stopped in Paris to visit the Shrine of the Miraculous Medal. When Thomas left the chapel and was ambling along the slight upward incline of a walkway toward a main street, he passed by a couple of ladies in their 40s who were handing out Miraculous Medals with colorful brochures. In perfect English, animated with an elegant French accent, they asked where he was from.

"I'm from the San Francisco Bay Area," he told them.

Handing him a Medal and brochure, they said, "The Blessed Mother would like every person in the world to have this Medal. It is meant to be given to everyone—everywhere," they explained. "Mary said this to St. Catherine Labouré...It has real power through Mary's intercession." They were determined to make of Thomas, and every passerby, an apostle of the Miraculous Medal. "What is important to do," they insisted, "especially if you meet someone who is struggling, who is homeless, is to pin it on their shirt, or give it to them as a necklace."

"Do you know," the Parisian ladies asked him, "what really happened in New York City, when it became a different place—a better place?"

Thomas knew of New York City's transformation around the turn of the century. He had experienced it firsthand with his wife, Kit. Being married to a woman from New York, born in Manhattan, and raised on the North Shore in Queens and Long Island, he had often traveled there. In 1981, Thomas found the city to be a scary place with rampant crime. In 2001, the year that Mayor Guliani finished his eight years in office, Thomas and Kit returned to New York to celebrate New Year's Eve. They danced outside on the streets of Broadway, stood in the packed crowd midnight in Times Square, and walked at night wherever they wished without a care. "It was a different place," he said to the two women.

"It wasn't really Rudy Giuliani who did that," they responded.

"No? Who did it then?" he asked.

"Something happened there that was more than law enforcement could do. We know about this because we were part of it. In France, we know that, in many ways, New York is the capital of the world, and we wanted to make a difference. At the same time that Giuliani came into office, a group of us flew to New York, bringing *six million* blessed Miraculous Medals with us. We spread them all through the city's boroughs, and in particular around Manhattan, asking Our Lady to help bring the peace of the Holy Spirit to New York City."

"Wow," said Thomas. "That is amazing! What a stunning thing." These two women, armed with extraordinary faith in what Mother Mary could affect through her Medal, had flown across the world out of selfless care for a land and a people that wasn't their own. Thomas felt lifted, inspired, and empowered by their example.

"What we're supposed to do with this Medal is not emphasized," Thomas said to his wife, after he returned home from Paris. But now, he and Kit knew exactly what to do. They would become apostles of the Miraculous Medal for the remainder of their lives, and in large and small ways, they began to share thousands with the world.[321]

FROM THE GUTTER OF FREEMASONRY
(LYAM, FRANCE)

In 2006, Lyam, a tall brunet in his 20s, handsome, intelligent, and cultured, traveled from his home country of France to the pilgrimage site of Medjugorje in Bosnia-Herzegovina, where the Virgin Mary has allegedly been appearing since 1981. He came with a heart on fire with faith and overflowing with gratitude. Only a few months earlier, he had met an older gentleman, a 32nd-degree Mason—one degree lower than the highest degree a Freemason can attain—and the man was keen on Lyam entering Freemasonry.

Lyam agreed to enter a Masonic Lodge and was mentored by the gentleman over the course of several months. He became an invested and proud member of the largest secret society in the world, severing ties completely with his Catholic family and his Catholic faith. Then the older Mason shared with Lyam a couple of high-level Masonic books, ones that entry-level Masons are never privy to see. Lyam saw clearly that the content was evil and realized that he had immured himself in the tentacles of a disturbing trap. He decided to leave the secret society, but by then the damage was done. Lyam's mood had grown despondent. After he cut his ties with Freemasonry, his depression remained and even worsened. His feelings of desolation became so severe and debilitating that, one day, he made up his mind to end his life.

On a Sunday afternoon in Paris, Lyam walked to his car, which was parked next to a street curb. His plan was to drive to a certain spot and do away with himself. When he opened his car door, his eye caught sight of a shiny gold object below him in the gutter. Reaching down to pick it up, he noticed instantly that it was a Miraculous Medal. For Lyam, this was a sign. The grace of Light, reflected in the glimmer of the Medal in his palm, immediately penetrated his heart. He decided that instead of driving off to kill himself, he would drive to the nearest Catholic church. But when he arrived at the church doors, they were locked, and he was crestfallen.

While Lyam stood outside the entrance, wondering what to do with himself, a priest walked up and asked if he could be of any assistance. Lyam requested to speak to the priest, who graciously opened the church doors for both of them to enter. Not only did the priest listen attentively to Lyam's heartfelt confession in the Sacrament of Reconciliation, but the two ended up talking for hours. In the course of their conversation, the Father revealed that after he had locked up the church hours earlier and driven quite a distance away, he felt a strong urge to turn the car around go back, though he had no idea why he would do such a thing. And he found Lyam standing outside.

The same day that Lyam had decided to kill himself ended up being the same day that he decided to live; never again did the desire to die take up residence in his soul. He became a fervent Catholic and reunited and reconciled with his family. Lyam's pilgrimage to Medjugorje was his manner of saying thank you to the Blessed Mother, who came to him on his darkest day, and through a Miraculous Medal in the gutter, saved his life.[322]

BAD CHEMISTRY
(RHONDA BASEL, GERMANY)

While Ms. Rhonda Basel was working as an assistant laboratory technician, she reached up to grab a bottle from the top shelf in the lab room. That shelf contained a rack of bottles with highly dangerous contents: acids, alkalis, and liquids with a risk of explosion. A glass plate shifted. Rhonda gasped. The topmost bottles started to fall onto the second shelf, which pulled down the third shelf of thirty-six bottles of the most dangerous acids, all of which crashed to the floor.

Glass splinters flew and liquids splashed onto Rhonda's face and clothes. She screamed at the top of her lungs and lunged toward the door to try to escape, but in no time, a toxic steam permeated the laboratory, and everything became shrouded in a thick fog. The door was nowhere to be found.

Rhonda presumed her life was over, expecting at any moment that a massive explosion would blow up the room—and her. Her mind raced: "If I get out of this room at all, I will be badly hurt and hideously disfigured." Finally, the door opened from the outside, and helpful hands of the management and staff came to the rescue. They wanted to rush Rhonda to the doctor because her work apron, stockings, and undergarments had fallen off like burnt rags. As they covered her body, everyone assumed she was badly burned.

The lab was a terrible mess. The house fire brigade had to spend three hours cleaning the room and restoring order. After Rhonda had recovered somewhat from the shock, she discovered that she had not suffered the slightest burn. Medical treatment was not necessary. It was difficult for her to convince the others that she was not injured in the least. Many times, from various voices, the joyful words rang out, "A miracle has happened to you!"

It was then that Rhonda remembered that she was wearing something. She grabbed the chain around her neck and showed the bystanders her Miraculous Medal. Pointing to the picture of the Blessed Mother, she said, "This is where the miracle came from."[323]

IMPOSSIBLY ALIVE
(WILLI, GERMANY)

Willi was driving his parents' car to Nuremberg. Just before arriving in the city, a large long-haul truck pulled in front of him, and he had to hit the brakes. Suddenly, a smaller truck ran into the back of Willi's car and pushed him under the commercial truck. He heard a crash, and then fell unconscious.

His parents received a call from the police saying that their son had been in an accident. His car was totally demolished, but he was alive. Willi's mother, Agathe Mölkmer, cried out, "For God's sake, that can't be! If the car is so broken that it can't be driven anymore, then our Willi could not have survived, either!"

When Willi's father arrived at the scene of the accident, he saw Willi standing by his car without a wound. The car was scrunched together like an accordion, nothing but a lump of metal. Willi was shaking through every limb and pointed to the Miraculous Medal. His mother had tied it to the car's rearview mirror. He exclaimed with emotion: "That was my salvation!" The trunk of the car, the back seats, everything had been forced into the front of the vehicle. Willi untied the Medal from the wreckage and took it home with him. None of the bystanders could believe that the driver was not crushed dead. It was undeniably a miracle.[324]

ESCORTED HOME
(MS. SCHUBERT, THE SUDETENLAND)

In September 1938, the Munich Agreement granted Adolf Hitler a border area of Czechoslovakia, the Sudetenland, which was home to many ethnic Germans. (Five months later, Hitler violated the agreement and invaded the remainder of Czechoslovakia.[325]) From September 13 to 30 in 1938, martial law prevailed in Cheb, a city formerly called Eger in the Sudetenland. The Czechs were shooting at the Germans and fearful of the impending German takeover. The following is what transpired on a chilling day that September, as reported by Ms. Shubert, a schoolteacher and ethnic German living in Cheb.

Ms. Shubert was walking home one morning from her school. Even though there were no classes being held, she had to report to the school every day. This was a highly dangerous walk. Czechs were shooting and killing people in the streets, and they had just shot down a young boy nearby. The street that led Ms. Schubert home was deserted, but for one man, a Czech master baker, who opened his shop door to shout, "Now the Fräulein Kindergärtnerin (Miss Kindergarten Teacher) will be shot down!" By that, he meant her.

Ms. Shubert walked briskly, holding tightly in her hand a rosary of the Immaculate Conception with the Miraculous Medal and a picture of St. Joseph. Suddenly, a Czech man came running toward her frantically, struck her on the left shoulder with the butt of his rifle, and shouted, "Down, German girl!"

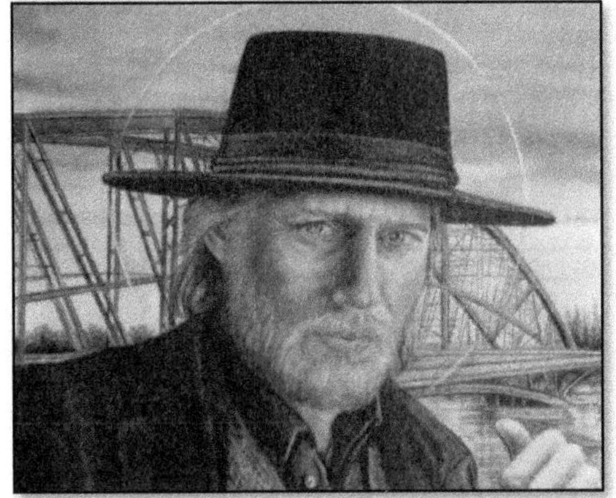

At the very same time, a distinguished older man with white hair and a beard, wearing a coat and a broad hat, suddenly stood alongside her and said to the Czech, "You mustn't hit this one; she's there for all the children and helps out." The Czech man took his rifle and ran away, as if possessed.

The unusual gentleman then took Ms. Schubert by the hand and escorted her. He taught her to pray the Rosary diligently and said she should always wear and love the Miraculous Medal. "Be careful tonight," he warned. "The bridge will be blown up [which later happened]. Take care, there are hand grenades all around the fence. Pray fervently to the Immaculate Virgin!"

When they arrived at her front door, the good man said, "Courage. I will not leave you; hold the Medal!" Then suddenly he was gone. Though the street was very wide, and one could see very far in both directions, no one was visible.

In the words of Ms. Schubert, "That good man was—and I will swear to this on my deathbed—St. Joseph.[326]

STORIES OF CONVERSION AND GRACE

HAVE WE PRAYED IN VAIN?

(MRS. WEBER, GERMANY)

Mrs. Weber had been praying ten long years for her daughter, Heidi, and her three grandchildren to return to the Catholic Church. Mrs. Weber's son-in-law, under coercion from his father, had insisted that he marry Heidi in a Protestant church, and their children were subsequently baptized and educated in that church.

Heidi, who had never wanted to leave her Catholic upbringing, suffered for many years under this forced participation, over which she had no control. It seemed that all of her and her mother's prayers were in vain. On the Feast of Corpus Christi in 1960, before the procession of the Real Presence of Jesus in the Eucharist, the grandmother held the hand of her ten-year-old grandchild, Marianne, who always asked the same question of her grandmother on such occasions, "Why can't I go with you in the procession? I want to have a White Sunday!"—her term for Sunday Mass.

A church friend, aware of Mrs. Weber's heartache, gave the little girl a Miraculous Medal and the grandmother three more Medals for her daughter and other two grandchildren, saying that the dear Blessed Mother would surely help.

Three months hadn't yet passed after the Feast of Corpus Christi, when Mrs. Weber came up to her friend, beaming with joy. Her son-in-law, after a quarrel with his father, had quipped to his wife: "Heidi, take our children and go to the Catholic priest. Order a Catholic ceremony for us." From then on, every Sunday was a White Sunday for Marianne.[327]

NOT AT EASE
(FR. DANIEL, GERMANY)

The following story illustrates how the Miraculous Medal is not a good luck charm. It cannot penetrate a hardened heart that stubbornly refuses God's gifts. To accept the flood of grace that the Miraculous Medal provides is an act of human free will—a freedom that God will never revoke or overstep.

A military priest, Fr. Daniel, worked as a chaplain in the big city of Bundeswehr, Germany, and looked after the patients in a hospital as well. During that time, he was able to prepare the dying for their moment of passing, except in three cases. Among those was an old woman with a seemingly indelible sinister look. The priest was giant in stature and normally unafraid, but around her, he was never at ease.

When the priest spoke to the woman about the Sacrament of Reconciliation, she spewed a stream of curse words at him. Perhaps the Miraculous Medal will help, he hoped, as he knew that with it the Blessed Mother had helped to convert an untold number of souls across the years. During rounds with the doctors, Fr. Daniel came to the bedside of the woman, who was seriously ill. While the doctors stood at the foot of her bed, asking about her condition, the priest slipped a Medal underneath the woman's pillow, unnoticed.

At that very moment, the woman, who was normally too ill to leave her bed, suddenly jumped up and screamed in a frenzy, "My bed is burning! My bed is burning! Away with that stuff! Away!" The doctors attempted to put her back onto the bed, but she threw the three men off of her, using inhuman strength. Then she fell back onto the bed, and cursing horribly, she died.[328]

I WISH TO BE LIKE YOU
(LEO, FRANCE)

In August 1862, in the town of Issoudun, France, a young man, Leo, age twenty-nine, was dying of consumption.[329] Every idea of religion that his friends and the Sisters of Charity nursing him offered was immediately extinguished in his heart. A Sr. Marie spoke to him very kindly, proposing to send him a physician, adding that she would supply all necessary medicines and nourishment. "I need neither doctors nor medicines," he replied to her. "I am going to die, and I ask only that you will let me die in peace."

Leo's poor wife, holding their little child in her arms, said to him in tears, "Accept sister's offer and perhaps you will recover," but he gave no answer.

Day after day, Sr. Marie returned to the Leo's bedside and was met with a frigid silence. As he grew worse, the sister's prayers increased, and she felt inspired to offer him a Medal of the Immaculate Conception. "Me...accept a Medal!" he exclaimed vehemently, "and what do you wish me to do with it? It would suit my wife or child well enough, but as for myself, I want no Medals!"

Sr. Marie withdrew from the fight for the time being, but returned to the charge the next morning. "Ah," she said pleasantly, "are you going to take the Medal today?"

"You know what I told you yesterday," Leo answered. "Besides, Sister, I am afraid of becoming imbued with your sentiments, should I accept it, for I perceive that you are much more unhappy than I care about being." With that verbal slap, a ray of happiness came across the sister's face. The patient then pried her with questions about religion and concluded, "After all, death will be a great relief to me; I have twice made an unsuccessful attempt at committing suicide. I suffer so much that I desire nothing but to die as soon as possible."

The next day, Sr. Marie asked her Superior to visit Leo and offer him the Medal. She held out a Miraculous Medal to him, and surprisingly, he not only accepted it, but after doing so, at last consented to see a priest. When Sr. Marie saw him next, he was completely changed and expressed his joy over the Father's visit and his desire to see him again soon. "Sister," he said, "I am too miserable; I wish to be like you."

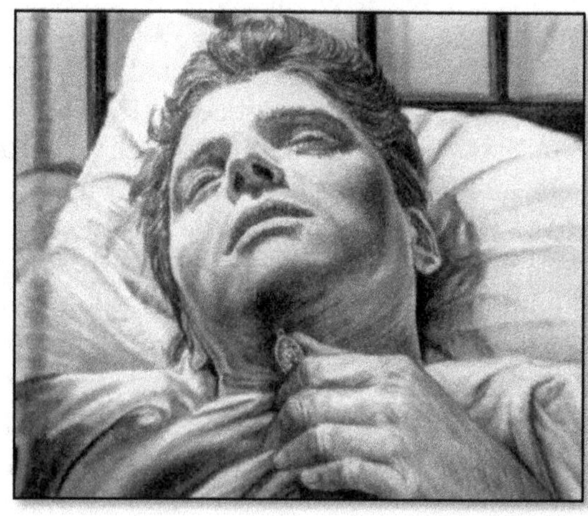

The priest did not delay in returning, and the suffering man, having made his Confession, asked for Holy Communion, which he had not received for many years. But the favor was denied him, his throat being so inflamed that he could swallow only a few drops of liquid. Leo's last days were sanctified by the most admirable resignation. No one heard him utter a complaint. He asked for one thing only, the visits of the priest and Sr. Marie, which alone seemed to afford him any consolation. And on the Feast of All Saints, with every sign of a sincere conversion, he breathed his last.[330]

A FREEMASON'S CRY
(CHARLES, A PROMINENT FREEMASON, UNITED STATES)

In 1865, in the great Charity Hospital of New Orleans, Charles, a very prominent Freemason, was admitted as a patient. There, he displayed his hatred of Catholicism in a thousand ways. Not only did he prevent Sr. Sarah, who cared for him, from offering any allusion to his salvation, but he also habitually repaid her kindness and attention to his physical sufferings with harsh and injurious words. Others who ventured to mention the subject of religion to him were met with taunts and jeers.

Several times, the Mason was at the point of death, but his disposition remained the same. At last, when Sr. Sarah saw that he had only a few hours to live, she stealthily slipped a Miraculous Medal under his bolster pillow and said interiorly to the Blessed Virgin, "My dear Mother, you know I have spared no effort to touch this poor man's heart, but in vain. Now I abandon him to you. It is you who must help save him. I leave him entirely in your hands and will try to divest myself of all anxiety concerning him."

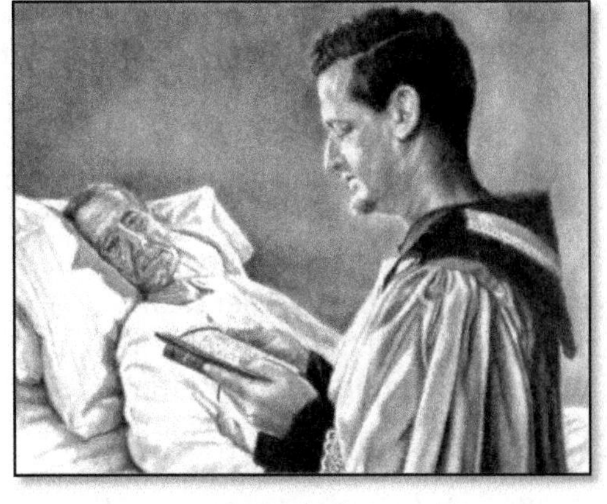

That evening, while making her rounds, the sister glanced at Charles and learned from the infirmarian[331] that ever since her last visit, he had been very calm and apparently absorbed in thought. When she asked the patient how he felt, she was astonished by his polite answer. Remembering that she had entrusted him entirely to the Blessed Virgin's care, Sr. Sarah did not say a word about his soul. Bidding him good night, she left the room.

At about nine o'clock that night, the patient called the infirmarian and asked for a priest. Knowing the Freemason's former bitterness, the infirmarian thought it was a cruel joke and treated the request accordingly. The Mason repeated his request but with no better success. Then he began to weep and cry aloud for a priest. All the other patients in the room went mute with astonishment, and the infirmarian, unable to resist his entreaties, left to get the chaplain and the sister. The dying man requested Baptism, which was administered immediately, and he received the Last Rites. Before the morning came, Charles had rendered his account to the Sovereign Judge. His body was interred with Masonic rites, but his soul, thanks to the powerful protection of Mary Immaculate, and the mercy of the Lord Jesus Christ, had been rescued.[332]

"GIVE THEM AWAY. GIVE THEM AWAY."
(OLGA AVILA, CALIFORNIA, UNITED STATES)

Olga Avila stared down at the smartphone in her hand. An offer popped up on her screen: "Would you like a free Miraculous Medal?" She tapped the button: "Yes." After reluctantly entering her contact information, she thought, "What have I done? Who knows what I'm getting into."

Three days later, on February 2, 2022, while sitting in church praying before Mass, Olga felt a tap on her right shoulder. Looking up she saw a sweet Hispanic woman in her thirties. "Our Lady wants to bless you," said the woman, and she handed Olga a Miraculous Medal. Wide-eyed, Olga took the Medal gratefully and held it to her chest with great love. "How many more would you like?" the woman asked. Olga declined the offer, but at Mass, an interior impulse prompted her to ask for more Medals so that she could give them away, not only to her family and close friends, but also to those beyond her immediate circle. The words, "Give them away. Give them away," echoed in her heart.

Olga learned that the woman's name was Lucy, and they agreed to meet up the following Sunday after Mass. In the church parking lot, Lucy opened the trunk of her car, and Olga wondered why. She expected to receive about four or five more Medals.

"I've got four hundred for you," said Lucy.

Olga knew at that moment that Our Lady was directing her steps on a new life path of evangelization. She began distributing the Medal at familiar churches, then in chapels of Adoration, and from there, she began traveling to unknown churches and handing them out to people as they exited Mass.

One day, a friend called Olga on the phone and asked, "How's it going regarding your distribution of the Miraculous Medals?"

"Well," she said. "I've been handing them out a few at a time, encouraging people to give them to others."

"That's great, Olga. I have a box of one thousand for you."

"A thousand!"

But she never did get that free one in the mail...[333]

PEDAL TO THE MEDAL
(LUCY, UNITED STATES)

Lucy sat in the passenger seat, white knuckling the car door handle, as her husband put the pedal to the floor, gunning the gas to 110 miles per hour. It was 7 p.m., and he was late to pick up his parents at the San Francisco airport. Weaving along California's Highway 101, he didn't notice the police car in his rearview mirror. "Alejandro!" shouted Lucy, as he sped around another car. "A police car is following us!"

They were newly married. Lucy was from Mexico, she hadn't yet received her U.S. visa, and in California, a driver speeding over 100 miles per hour can be charged with reckless driving. Lucy grabbed the Miraculous Medal hanging around her neck, kissed it, and said its prayer frantically, "O María, sin pecado concebida, ruega por nosotros que recurrirmos a ti!"

Red and blue lights flashed in the rearview mirror, and a siren sounded its alarm.

"Pull to the side of the road, please," boomed the cop's voice from the police car's loudspeaker.

Time froze. Alejandro stopped the car. They awaited their sentence. Lucy imagined herself and her new husband handcuffed and stuffed into the cop's backseat, and from there, who knew...

A young, brown-haired Caucasian man walked up to the driver's side of their car. "Show me your license." Then the officer asked for Lucy's ID.

"Sólo tengo una tarjeta de identificación de México." Alejandro translated for her, as she showed the officer her Mexican identification card.

"Do you know that you were going more than 90 miles per hour?"

"Yes."

"Did you know that you could have caused an accident?"

"Yes."

While Alejandro searched for his registration and insurance, Lucy continued to pray, and when she looked up at the policeman, she was amazed to see that a soft glow had formed around him.

"Where are you going?" the cop asked.

"To San Francisco to pick up my parents at the airport," answered Alejandro.

"Oh, that's good. You know what? I'm not going to detain you because you're going to pick up your parents."

"Oh, no? Sí? Gracias!" Lucy blurted out with gratitude, and started rummaging through her purse. "Tengo un regalo que quiero darte" ("I have a gift that I want to give to you"). This being the same Lucy as in the previous story, she normally carried many silver-colored Medals with her, but now neither she nor Alejandro could find a single one anywhere. They searched the entire car until Alejandro checked through her purse one last time and opened up her change pocket. "Ah, ha!"

By this time, even the cop was excited, figuring whatever they were looking for must have been worth the search. Lucy handed the Medal to the officer, and an intrigued look came over his face. "Oh, it's beautiful," he stated. "Now, let's go!"

"Wait, go where?" asked Alejandro.

"To the airport. I'm going to escort you so you can get there a faster way."[334]

ILLUMINATED
(WILLIAM, UNITED STATES)

At a Charity Hospital in New Orleans, a religious sister tried in vain for a long time to convince a Protestant man named William of the essential truths of Catholicism, but he was deaf to all her persuasions. One day she showed him a Miraculous Medal and related its origin. He appeared to listen somewhat attentively, but when she offered it to him, he scoffed in a tone of great contempt, "Take it away! This Virgin is no more than any other woman."

"I am going to leave it on your table," the sister replied. "I am sure you will reflect on my words." William said nothing, but to put it out of sight, placed his Bible over it. Every day, under the pretext of arranging and dusting his room, the sister assured herself that the Medal was still there.

Several days elapsed, during which the patient grew worse. One night, while lying awake racked with suffering, William perceived a brilliant light around his bed, though the rest of the room was enveloped in darkness. Greatly astonished, he wondered where it could be coming from. Despite his weakness, he succeeded in rising and turning up the gas heater, in order to search for the cause of this mysterious light. Finding none, he returned to bed. Then a few minutes later, he discovered that the luminous light was coming directly from the Medal.

Taking the Medal in his hands, the Protestant man held it for the remainder of the night. As soon as the sisters rang their rising bell (which was at four o'clock), William called the infirmarian and begged him to tell the sister that he desired to be baptized Catholic.[335] The chaplain, who had conversed frequently with William, was immediately informed.

"Impossible!" the chaplain exclaimed. Well aware of the Protestant's sentiments, he could scarcely believe him. Nevertheless, he fulfilled the patient's request, and finding William truly disposed and thanking the Blessed Virgin for making herself and the true Faith known, the chaplain administered the Last Sacraments. Shortly afterward, William died, filled with the consoling graces of God through the Sacraments of the Church, and the assurance of going home.[336]

A LIFE-SAVING ACT AND A SOUL-SAVING MEDAL
(GUGLIELMO, ITALY)

Four-year-old Guglielmo ran outside to play with his family's farm animals, his Miraculous Medal swaying and swinging around his neck. He was blessed to live in a small country home in Italy next to a small but deep body of water, which nestled itself among towering trees. His mother, Anna, yelled after him: "Wait for me!"

But he didn't hear her. How could he? The sky looked glorious, and the birds were singing a delightful melody. Skipping and dreaming of joining them in flight, he hopped from one rock to another around the pond.

Anna busied herself in the kitchen, putting away dishes, and looked out the window. Where had little Guglielmo gone? He should have been within her view, but she couldn't see him anywhere. "Where are you, Guglielmo?" she shouted. No answer. She walked outside, calling his name repeatedly. Still, no response. Her stomach turned, and she started to run.

Guglielmo couldn't swim. He had lost his footing, tumbled into the water, and was sinking to the bottom. As Anna ran toward the pond, her heart trembled. She feared the worst. But as she ran up to the water's edge, she was met by a rugged, haggard-looking man, dripping wet. She gasped. In his arms was her son, thoroughly soaked, but alive and well. Sighing, she thanked the man profusely and asked his name. "My name is Ademaro. I happened to be passing by here when I saw your son fall into the water."

Anna invited him into their home. After a supper meal, she reached over to her little son, took the Medal from around his neck, and gave it to Ademaro. Urging Ademaro to wear it, she said, "Please pray a Hail Mary each day to the Mother of God." Warily, he accepted the gift, and promising to pray daily, he left.

Ademaro had been leading a life littered with sin, and he didn't change his ways that day, except to say a daily Hail Mary, as he had promised. For years, his only home was the street, as he traveled from town to town, a vagabond living in waiting for his time to die. The years only ended up making him more bitter and cruel. No one desired to be near him, and he, in turn, despised mankind.

One day Ademaro was found on the street, far away from his homeland. He had fallen ill and was taken to the nearby hospital. The staff could do nothing for him, for he was hours from death. They called for a priest, and when he entered the hospital room, Ademaro began to scream and curse violently. But then he grew calm. The priest was from the town he grew up in, in another country entirely! He knew the same streets, the same townspeople, the same corner store.

The priest made every attempt to share the love of God in word and gesture with Ademaro, but his efforts failed. Ademaro would not believe that there was hope for him, having lived such a deplorable life. He challenged, "Give me now a sign that there is still hope for me. I don't believe you can do that." For a moment, all was silent. Expecting the priest to leave, Ademaro turned his back to him.

The priest stayed and noticed a chain around the back of Ademaro's neck. He inquired as to what it was and where it came from. Turning back around, Ademaro showed him the Miraculous Medal and told the story of how, back in his home country, he had rescued a little boy from drowning many years ago and received the Medal as a gift. The priest's face grew pale, and tears formed in his eyes.

Confused and upset, Ademaro asked why he was reacting that way. The priest seemed lost in thought. Seconds passed, and he responded: "The little boy you saved so many years ago was me. You saved my life once— and now God has sent me to save yours." Overpowered by the Holy Spirit speaking to him through the priest's words and by the near-impossible odds of their encounter, Ademaro's heart opened to receive the grace of God. Shortly after making a sincere Confession, he passed from this life and found his way home.[337]

"JUST STAY"
(SARAH, FRANCE)

October 1936, Sarah was sitting in her room when the telephone rang. The person on the line told her that there was a seriously ill man who needed her. Sarah was then told to write down an address. When she wanted to know more and asked who was on the line, the person hung up. As Sarah was not unfamiliar with helping people around town, she went to the man's home immediately, thinking along the way what reason she could use to justify her visit. Sarah never found out who called her.

Stepping into the apartment, Sarah found a distinguished gentleman of about fifty years of age, lying in bed, seriously ill with pneumonia. Apart from a nurse, whom the patient did not like, no one else was present. The sick man didn't act at all surprised by Sarah's visit and didn't ask her why she had come. When Sarah asked him what she could help him with, he said in a tired, desperate voice, "Just stay here!"

For about an hour, Sarah spoke with the sick man, endeavoring to engage him in a little conversation. Then she had to leave, as she had stopped by while also on her way to hear the lecture of a certain spiritual speaker. She asked the sick man if she could return the next morning. At first, he wasn't at all willing to let her go. But then he relented, asking her to come back as soon as possible.

The lecture had already begun when Sarah arrived, and the priest was saying the words, "And Christ stands by every deathbed waiting. He waits with open arms and is ready to forgive even the worst." These words, Sarah felt, were a finger pointing at her from above. Right after the lecture, she hurried back to her patient, who was clearly happy she had come. She noticed, however, that his condition had changed considerably and that his life would soon be ending.

Sarah didn't know how to help the man, so she started telling him about God. As she spoke, his whole face twitched, and he visibly struggled with himself. Finally, he shared the reason for his discomfort: he was a Freemason. He didn't have the courage to tell her earlier for fear she would then leave him. Sarah assured the man that she would stay to help him pass the time.

But now the situation became very difficult for Sarah. After all, she had just met the patient and knew nothing about him; she was terrified that her ineptitude might spoil everything at the last moment.

Come 9 p.m., she wanted to go home and come back the next day. When she told him this, he replied very weakly, "Just stay, just stay." Soon his shortness of breath increased greatly, and he could no longer lie down. Sarah sat him up in bed and had to support him continuously. In the meantime, she told him about the manger in Bethlehem and noticed how he listened with tears in his eyes. Time passed, and at the sick man's request, she sent the nurse to bed.

Then a time of severe suffering began for the poor man: shortness of breath, physical pains, and more. At the same time, he was afflicted with an indescribable fear, to such an extent that his whole body trembled. Sarah sat down next to him and leaned his tired head against her shoulder.

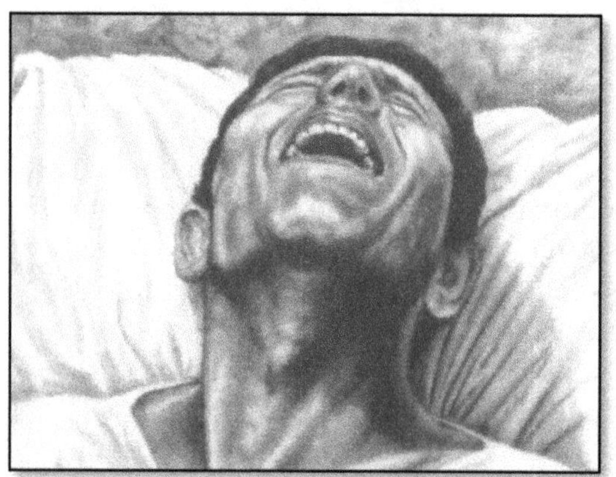

She prayed softly, spoke to him of Our Lady, and placed a Miraculous Medal around his neck. Then she told him the story of the Good Thief. He listened, and so that he could fully understand, she repeated the story to him.

The clock struck midnight, and the man kept asking Sarah to stay with him. At last, around the first hour of the morning, he said in an unforgettable tone that could not be misunderstood, "Now!"

Sarah looked intently at the man's tear-stained, suffering face, then immediately went to fetch a priest, who brought with him the Blessed Sacrament. When she and the priest arrived, the dying man was eagerly waiting for them. His time was very short. He confessed, then received Holy Communion and the Anointing of the Sick. He renounced everything connected to his wayward past, and it was a glorious moment when he was reconciled with the Church.

Sarah stayed with him until his blessed end. When she asked if she should notify anyone, he shook his head in the negative. He was a very lonely man.

In the morning, when the church bells rang for the first early Mass, the former Freemason gently breathed his last and returned home to his Heavenly Father, from whom he had been so bitterly distant only a few hours before.[338]

MARY AT GROUND ZERO
(FR. JOHN BURNS, UNITED STATES)

September 11, 2001, was a day that Americans will never forget, and Fr. John F. Burns, S.J., was at Ground Zero. After the World Trade Center had crumbled and the dust had settled, digging out and recovering dead bodies became part of the daily routine for police officers, firefighters, and many others.

Another priest working at Ground Zero offered Fr. John a bag of Miraculous Medals, tightly knotted into a ball. The idea of handing out more knickknacks to exhausted workers, who already had been inundated with donated items, seemed unfair and excessive to Fr. Burns; but their receptivity to faith and lack of cynicism gave him the nerve to give one worker the religious gift—and then another, and another.

The response from the emergency workers shocked him. The little Medal seemed to break open everyone's discouragement and isolation. Fr. Burns recalled, "I had never experienced the emotional response that occurred when the workers received the Miraculous Medals. Helmets and respirators came off, words ceased, and people prayed. Some cried openly, which even in the intense surroundings of Ground Zero, was rare."

The Medals had opened a floodgate. Before any were handed out, nearly no one had cried, no one had spoken of how they were truly feeling, no one had prayed openly or leaned on his brother or sister for comfort. Workers seemed lonely and depressed, performing their grim tasks as if in a state of personal shock.

The Miraculous Medals "served as a tool for many to talk about loss in honest, direct language," said Fr. John. They also evoked thankfulness for having faith during days that were smelly, tedious, and miserable: gratitude amidst horror. "Maybe that was the miracle."

Fr. Burns' first bag of about thirty Medals was depleted in one day. He located a supplier in Brooklyn who donated all the Medals he had in stock, but that supply was finished quickly. Then Fr. Burns' own father took up the charge, searching through religious stores and catalogs for more of the powerful sacramental. The demand for Medals never ceased because the Mother of God was there—at Ground Zero.[339]

IT IS TIME
(DR. PALTIEL, SWITZERLAND)

The Sotherbys had a Jewish family doctor, Dr. Paltiel, who treated their children for many years. The matriarch of the family, Lilly, had given the doctor a Miraculous Medal early in their acquaintance, unaware that he was Jewish. She often saw the Medal swinging on his watch chain, a convenient and popular means of telling time in the late 1800s. Dr. Paltiel and the Sotherbys became family friends. He was very fond, appropriately

so, of Mrs. Lilly Sotherby and one day asked her to come see him. She found him lying in bed with a fever. He had contracted an infection during an operation, and the doctor attending him considered the case quite alarming.

When Lilly entered the house, Dr. Paltiel said immediately, "I want to become a Catholic."

Startled, Lilly replied, "When you feel better, you will take lessons." His wife then told Lilly that he had read and studied much about religion and was well versed in everything. As Mrs. Sotherby was leaving their home, she promised to come back soon. But already in the afternoon, she received a telephone message that his fever had risen, and he had been hurriedly transported to the hospital for another operation.

The next day, Dr. Paltiel asked Lilly to send him a priest immediately. He wanted to be baptized "today."

His primary physician, however, said that since it was already six o'clock in the evening, a priest would not be available, except for urgent cases, and there was no acute danger. But Mrs. Sotherby thought the matter was urgent, and after a long search, was able to contact a clergyman. He, too, felt that going to the hospital so late would cause a stir and wanted to come the next day. But Lilly begged the priest to come right away, which he finally consented to do. Dr. Paltiel said upon her arrival with her husband, "I knew you would come to the hospital again today, for it is time."

Mr. Sotherby and the priest prepared a small altar, and the Rite of Baptism began. Then came the moment of professing the Catholic faith.[340] Dr. Paltiel held a lighted candle in his right hand and clearly repeated every word, while his left hand held onto Lilly's. His Jewish wife did not know what to do and wept continuously. Then he received Baptism, Holy Communion, and the Anointing of the Sick.

When the rites were over, the attending nurse said that Dr. Paltiel needed rest, and everyone should go. There was absolutely no danger to his life, at least not for the next few days. As the Sotherbys drove home, the husband said, "I'm glad it happened, but we shouldn't have been in such a hurry." But soon after they arrived home, and just as they were sitting down for dinner, the telephone rang: "Dr. Paltiel has just passed away." The graces of many years given to him through the Miraculous Medal on his watch chain had come to their full fruition in the last possible moment.

Two days later the doctor's funeral took place in the Catholic cemetery. Lilly recalled: "His entire Jewish family was very accommodating. Everyone shook my hand and thanked me for what I had done for them, which I didn't really understand from their point of view. His widow also became a Catholic. The ceremony took place in the Hietzing church, and I was edified by how devout the woman was. Their three children, however, remained Jewish. The mercy of God cannot be thanked enough. I often reflect with deep emotion that it really was the very last moment for conversion. An hour later, his soul would not have received the grace of Baptism."[341]

TOMORROW I WILL BE DEAD
(FREDERICK DE CASTILLON, FRANCE)

The following is condensed from a letter written on November 13, 1834, by Sr. C. Herault, a Mother Superior of the Daughters of Charity, who worked in a Catholic infirmary. She had already witnessed the efficacy of the Miraculous Medal in the conversion of several soldiers in their care who once obstinately resisted grace. But she was most profoundly affected by the change she witnessed in Frederick De Castillon, age thirty-five, Captain of the 21st Light Guards.

The Captain entered the infirmary on April 29, 1834. He was in the last state of consumption and attacked by paralysis on his left side. Regarding religion, he boasted of having none. The sisters nursed him a long time, but he got alarmingly worse. Sr. Herault tried several times to address his concerning spiritual state, but it was in vain. When she had the chance to speak to him privately, however, she asked if he was Catholic. "Yes, Sister," he replied, looking steadily at her. Surprised, she invited him to accept a Medal, to wear it and frequently invoke Mary Immaculate. She told him that if he did so with faith, this good Mother would obtain for him all the graces he needed to bear his sufferings patiently and meritoriously.

He received the Medal gratefully but did not put it on. The sisters noticed that he had placed the Medal on the side of his bed, but that wasn't the only Medal near him. The sister in charge of his hall had already slipped one in his pillowcase.

Captain Castillon's strength soon began to fade quickly, and Sr. Herault, hearing that he might not survive the day, called for a priest. The Father could get nothing from the Captain but the despairing words, "Leave me in peace. Tomorrow I will be dead, and all will be over!" Painfully, the priest and the sisters complied with his request. In sorrow, they redoubled their prayers to Mary.

The next day, the Captain asked the physician to tell him candidly if his case was hopeless, because he wanted to arrange his affairs. That very same evening, he said to the sister in charge of his hall, "Oh! How sorry I am to have treated the Superior so badly, and the good priest she brought me! Present my apologies to them, I beg you, and ask them to come again."

The sisters scrambled to see him. The next morning, he began his new chapter of a few last days of life, during which the priest chaplain visited him several times every day, remaining two hours at a time. Captain Frederick De Castillon received the Last Sacraments with a profound and grateful faith. He asked that his dying words be written down: "I die in the religion of my fathers. I love and revere it. I humbly beg God's pardon for not always having practiced it publicly." He departed this world in peace on October 23, 1834.[342]

A SOBERING STORY
(FR. ANTONIO RIBEIRO PINTO, BRAZIL)

In 1947, Fr. Antonio Ribeiro Pinto was assigned to live in the poor village of Urucania, in the state of Minas Gerai, Brazil. He was a zealous priest, fervent in spreading the faith and wholeheartedly devoted to the Mother of God. For twenty-seven years, he was a pastor in the remote interior of the vast country, where immorality, quarrelsomeness, and above all, religious indifference prevailed.

With unlimited trust, Fr. Antonio took refuge in the Blessed Virgin and invited people to partake of the sacraments. To the drunkards in the street, he offered a glass of water, in which he placed a Medal of the Immaculate that he had blessed beforehand. Handing them more Miraculous Medals, the priest recommended they do this for themselves as often as they felt inclined to drink alcohol.

Fr. Antonio Pinto's success was remarkable. After three years, no one in his small town indulged in the vice of drunkenness, and the majority went to church. "Have great confidence in Mary, Mother of Graces" he would say, handing everyone a Medal of the Immaculate. "And make a novena to her![343]

A NEW RIBBON OF HONOR

(CHARLES, FRANCE)

In 1834, the Daughters of Charity, Sisters Radier and Pourrat, wrote down and shared the following story of the last days of a soldier named Charles. Their care for him took place in Paris at the Royal Hotel des Invalides, in St. Vincent's ward, number 20, to be exact. "Sixty patients inhabited the ward," according to the sisters, "the majority of whom witnessed a part of these details."

Charles had been spitting up blood for about six months and was thought to soon die of consumption. Naturally polite and grateful for kind attention, Charles showed no signs of religious interest and had lived a life of serious sin for the last twenty years. It appeared, however, that faith was not entirely extinguished from his heart. When his neighbor in the ward was the point of death and refusing to see a priest, Charles entreated him to yield to the suggestion and was instrumental in bringing about the man's conversion. But when Charles was visibly wasting away and his own turn was near, he resisted the sacraments: "I am an honest man," he told the sisters. "I have never killed nor robbed."

"Even so," they answered, "we all stand in need of God's mercy. We are all sinners."

"Oh, sisters, just leave me in peace, I beg you."

Charles' body soon made him aware that he was dying, and one day, he said aloud in distress, "There is no hope for me!" On November 25, the disease took such a sudden turn for the worse that the sisters asked the priest at the Invalides, Fr. Ancelin, to come to his bedside. After the visit, the clergyman said to the sisters, "Your patient is very depressed, and I have not succeeded in getting him to do anything for his soul; and I did not urge him too much for fear he might say no and then would not revoke his word, like so many others after giving a decidedly negative answer."

Then a lady friend came to see Charles, and she urged him to make his peace with God. To sidestep her importunity, he answered, "I know the priest; he has already been to see me and will return this evening." Fr. Ancelin indeed returned, and the sick man jumped out of bed upon seeing him to prove that Confession wasn't a pressing matter. Being a good Samaritan, the priest offered Charles all the little services he could think of: helping him back to bed, and even offering to dress his bed sores. He then spoke to him about his soul, but to no avail. After an hour's conversation, Fr. Ancelin came to Sr. Radier and Sr. Pourrat and said, "I am deeply grieved, for I have done my utmost, but it has had no effect on him."

The sisters asked the priest if he should call on Charles during the night, in case he grew worse. "I think," said the Father, "that you had better not, unless he asks for me." A little later, one of the sisters reminded Charles again of the hospital chaplain, a different priest, who was passing by the ward, but Charles got enraged and began to swear, so that they had to drop the subject.

The death rattle was already in his throat, and it did not seem possible that he could survive the night. It was then that one of the younger sisters said to Sr. Radier, "Sister, perhaps our sins, as our holy St. Vincent says, have been the cause of this man's impenitence." After that, Sr. Radier expected nothing more from the patient. She turned all her hopes toward the Blessed Virgin. During night prayers, thoughts of the Medal came into her mind, and she said to herself: "If we put the Medal on him, perhaps the Blessed Virgin will obtain his conversion," and she decided to make a novena. After night prayers, she said to a companion, "Let us go see the sick man and put a Medal on him."

Sr. Radier went immediately to ward number 20 and found Charles awake and in a state of great agitation. He was about to leave the room.

All the other patients witnessed his behavior and said that it was with the intention of committing suicide. Sister Radier cautiously took away his knife and whatever else he might use, slipped the Medal unperceived between his two mattresses, and returned to the other sisters with a sad countenance, saying, "Let us fervently invoke the Blessed Virgin, because I very much fear this poor man will kill himself during the night."

The next day, immediately after rising, and even before seeing the sister who had kept watch, Sr. Radier hurried to visit the patient, with dire forebodings in her heart. But to her astonishment, Charles' mind was calm and he seemed better. On her inquiring how he felt, he said, "Very well, Sister. I had a good night. I slept well, which I have not done for a long time, and I am better as a result." As Sr. Radier got up to leave, he called to her, "Sister, I wish to make my confession. Send the priest to me!"

"You wish to confess?" replied the stunned sister. "Are you sure? Are you going to act as you did all day yesterday? Do you really want him?"

"Yes, sister, upon my honor."

"Well, since you want to see him, I will go for him. It will certainly be good for you to confess your sins, for it is said that your life has not always been edifying." Then, without the slightest care for human respect, Charles began to mention his sins aloud and with strong feelings of compunction. The sisters could scarcely get him to stop. Fr. Ancelin came, and the patient made his confession, which lasted an hour.

Afterward, Sr. Pourrat came to see the patient, and he was bursting with joyful news: "Oh, Sister! How happy I am. I have been to Confession, I have received absolution, and the priest is going to return this evening. Since my Frist Communion, this is the happiest day of my life!" Charles appeared deeply affected and sincere and expressed a strong desire to receive the good God.

"Do you know what we did?" Sr. Pourrat asked him.

"What was it, Sister?"

"We put between your mattresses a Miraculous Medal of the Blessed Virgin."

"Ah! That is why I passed such a comfortable night. Moreover, I felt as if there was something about me that caused a wonderful change, and I do not know why I didn't search my bed. I thought of doing so."

Sr. Pourrat then produced the Medal, which he kissed with respect and affection. "It is this," Charles exclaimed, "that gave me strength to brave human respect. I must place it on my chest."

"I will give you a ribbon to attach it to your decoration." (He wore the military cross of honor).

The first ribbon offered being a little faded, he said, "No, Sister, not that one, but this one," pointing to a brighter ribbon. "The Blessed Virgin must have a new ribbon." Sr. Pourrat, noticing his weak state, attached the

Medal so that it was somewhat concealed. "Oh! Do not hide it, Sister," he said. "Put it beside my cross. I am not embarrassed to show it."

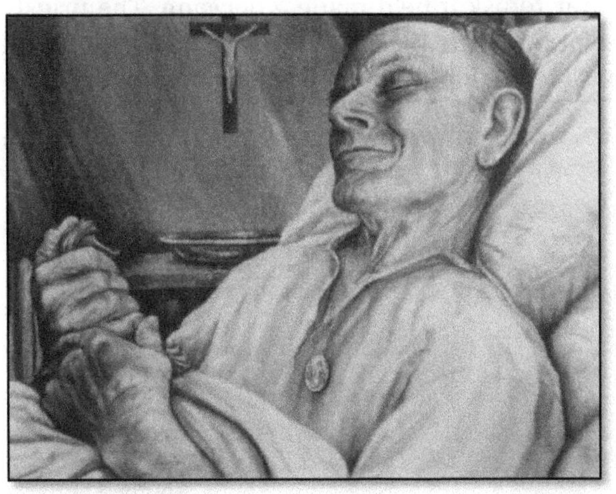

In the afternoon, Fr. Ancelin asked the sisters how the patient was doing, and he was no less edified by the news. Preparations were made to give Charles the last Sacraments. At the sight of the Host, he was so penetrated with emotion that he begged pardon aloud of God for all the sins of his life—in detail, and he could hardly be persuaded to lower his voice. Charles spent the next day in the same dispositions of faith, regret, and piety, and Monday morning, December 1, his soul went peacefully to God.[344]

LIVING IN SIN
(GAETAN, FRANCE)

Fr. Martin in Boulogne, France, learned of a young man in his parish area, named Gaetan. He was twenty-seven and cohabitating with a woman outside of marriage. Several years earlier, Gaetan had abandoned his mother and brother to live as he wished without restrictions. He was then struck by a serious pulmonary attack. Dr. Jean Pulioli, an excellent physician of the time, was unable to help him.

Gaetan, living in the home of his lover, was reduced to such exhaustion that he couldn't move from his bed. He told Dr. Pulioli that he would never need a priest, but the doctor thought it his duty to tell one about his condition. Fr. Martin got word of the dying man and asked a priest chaplain in his diocese to tend to him.

The priest paid him a visit immediately and earnestly entreated Gaetan to marry the woman he was with and end his sinful state of living, so his soul could heal and be restored in God. He refused. Then Fr. Martin decided that he, himself, should go see Gaetan and in conversation found that he had neither any intention of marrying the woman nor of separating from her. From the excuses that he gave, the priest perceived that his soul was enshrouded in an impenetrable indifference. Having exhausted his efforts to change Gaetan, Fr. Martin decided it would be better to let him spend time alone with the suggestion of serious reflection, and to return later to ask if he'd made a decision. The priest urged him to seek the mediation of the Blessed Virgin, refuge of sinners, and he slipped a Miraculous Medal under Gaetan's pillow before leaving.

There was no need for Fr. Martin to return to learn of Gaetan's decision. Gaetan asked for the priest through his mother, with whom he had become reconciled in the meantime. After informing Fr. Martin of the just reasons he had for not marrying his girlfriend, he asked the priest if he would request that she leave—a commission that he willingly accepted. She consented and immediately left the house.

The sick man's peace and joy over this development were indescribable. When the priest showed him the Medal, he kissed it fervently and impulsively, despite his state of exhaustion. Then, showing sincere repentance, he confessed, and expecting that at any moment he would breathe his last, received Holy Communion and Last Rites.

Interiorly, Gaetan shared that he felt unspeakable peace, a favor that he attributed to the Blessed Virgin. Then, entirely unexpectedly, he began to improve, and in only a few days, his health was completely returned to him. Fr. Martin maintained contact with Gaetan, who persevered in his good resolutions. With great affection toward the Blessed Mother, Gaetan continued to wear the Medal that Fr. Martin had snuck under his pillow, often kissing it with filial love.

Fr. Martin wrote the original of this account in a letter to Fr. Jean Marie Aladel, St. Catherine Labouré's spiritual director, and ended it with the assurance: "Monsieur, I was a witness of the above-mentioned report; I send it to you, not only with the permission of the newly converted and cured, but at his request, and I hope that the knowledge will redound to the honor and glory of the Omnipotent God, Who, through the intercession of the Blessed Virgin, has wrought this double miracle. I subjoin the certificate of the physician who attests the disease and its cure."[345]

WAITING IN A PILLOW
(FREEMASON, POLAND)

Medals were sent to a convalescent home in Poland, where a seventy-year-old nun, named Sr. Cecylia, lived. Freemasons occasionally came to live in the home, and the nun noticed who they were right away. She tucked the gift of the Medals away somewhere unseen, and several of the Masons converted to Catholicism. When the head of these Masons, who had also registered himself as a patient in the house, learned of this, he was enraged and wanted to prevent it. He immediately recognized that Sr. Cecylia was behind the conversions and told her that he forbade her from saying anything about God or the Catholic Church.

This Masonic leader, however, did not know that the Virgin Mary was waiting for him inside his pillow. Sr. Cecylia continued her mission and was verbally attacked by the man several times. Once, however, he came to her and said, "What is going on here? Every night a woman comes to me. She introduces herself to me as Our Lady, and in my body, I feel something like ants are on me. I have no peace here."

Sr. Cecylia answered him, "You have sacrificed your soul to Satan; therefore you find no rest." One day he was waiting for the sister to come by, and when he made sure there were no witnesses in the corridor, he fell to his knees and confessed very grave sins to her. Sr. Cecylia saw that the hour had now come for his conversion, and said only, "I am not a priest. You must tell that to the priest." She then invited a cleric to come to the convalescent home in civilian clothes so that the Masonic leader would not recoil at the last moment. Then she sent them both for a walk.

In the process of the walk, the Mason came to a complete conversion. Because his sins were very great, it was necessary for the priest to write to the bishop before giving him full entry into the Church. After a few weeks, the man died with a smiling, joyful face. Various banners from the Freemason sect were sent for the man's funeral. But they were sent back, because the body—and soul—had already been taken care of by the Church.[346]

AT THE LAST HOUR
(FR. J. ROTH, EUROPE)

It was a few months before the outbreak of war in Europe in 1939 when Fr. J. Roth was ordained priest. From his youth, he had venerated the Miraculous Medal and carried it with him always as a high school and then as a theology student. His first job after ordination was as a temporary second vicar in a border town between Germany and Poland.

On September 1st came the terrible news: Nazi Germany had invaded its neighbor. The day had hardly dawned when the first bombs began to fall. Those who could do so, fled, including the parish priest and another vicar. The new priest, however, remained at his post. Lamentation and terror everywhere!

Already in the morning, the hospital treatment hall was overcrowded with injured war victims, who had to be placed on emergency beds in the corridors. The nuns went to fetch the young priest. Today the sad event is still as vivid in Fr. Roth's mind as if it happened yesterday, and he recounts it as follows:

As quickly as possible, I made my way to the hospital. Indescribable distress, lamentation, and pain stared out at me. As always, I carried the Miraculous Medal with me. I put all my trust in the Immaculate Mother of God. I went to each soldier, consoled them, and asked how they were. The Catholics confessed, and I gave them the Sacrament of the Anointing of the Sick. There was only one consolation in this serious hour, that of the Good Shepherd and His most Holy Mother. How wonderfully reassuring those holy words were:

"Through this holy anointing, may the Lord help you in His abundant mercy. He is with thee in the power of the Holy Ghost. Amen."

But there was one who rejected everything, and he, of all people, was very close to death. I was deeply saddened when he rejected me, and then I knelt down over the last three who were lying there. Then I hurried into the house chapel and prayed fervently that Our Lady would work a miracle on the hard-hearted man: "Immaculate Mother's Heart, help him, for he is also your child." After half an hour I went back into the hall. I was so afraid for that man's soul! In order not to attract attention, I visited each one in turn, blessed, and prayed.

I came back to the hardened man, and again, I was turned away. I returned to the chapel, prayed, and pleaded for the sinner's salvation, for his hours were measured. The nurse told me the same. Then I remembered that I had the Miraculous Medal with me.

Again, after half an hour of hot entreaty, I entered the hall and bent over each of the poor men, in turn. My heart throbbed palpably when

I came to the hard-hearted one. I took the Medal in my hand and said, "Look, I want to give you something." To get rid of me, he nodded his head. I put the Medal under his pillow. Then I went into the chapel again. My plea became more fervent: "Mother of God, now you must help. It is high time."

For the fourth time, I visited the wounded, and the miracle happened. The poor sinner no longer refused me. The Immaculate had broken Satan's power. He confessed. Very humbly he received the Sacrament of the Anointing of the Sick. Then he lay still. I hurried back into the chapel and could only stammer, "Dear, dear Mother of God, thank you, thank you."

Only now did I remember that I had not eaten anything from 6 o'clock in the morning until then, 1:30 p.m. I returned home for a short time. Soon after eating, I made my way to the hospital again. When I arrived there, the nurse met me with the words: "He died first."

Oh, how I thanked the dearest, most powerful Mother for saving this soul! My confidence in the Miraculous Medal grew still greater."[347]

A DISTURBING CHANGE
(ADELE LAGIER, GERMANY)

Barbara Lagier of Lohmar, Germany, consecrated her two children to the Blessed Mother and gave them each the name Mary for a middle name. Barbara was convinced that in today's world she would not be enough protection for them to arrive safely in heaven. She was thankful that one of her children, sixteen-year-old Adele, would voluntarily accompany her to Mass and join her in the Fatima devotion of the Five First Saturdays.[348] But around the year 1993, Barbara noticed a change in her daughter.

In high school, Adele started listening to rock music, all the time. It was constantly playing—when she was relaxing, as she did her homework, at every moment she could find. It even blasted through the loudspeakers in her school between classes. In her course on religion, Adele was learning about Satanism, black masses, and occultism—lessons that were supposed to be enlightening. But this knowledge, coupled with the music and its accompanying lyrics, caused a disturbing change to come over her.

Adele grew reluctant to go to Mass. For two years, she rarely received Holy Communion and hardly, if ever, prayed. Barbara had never been coercive toward her daughter regarding religious matters, and when she did approach her, Adele's response was, "That's none of your business; that's my business."

In her distress, Barbara could not share her concerns with her husband or relatives, who had written her off as old-fashioned. On Fat Tuesday, the day before Ash Wednesday, Barbara's daughter surprised her. Without provocation, she approached her mother and asked for a Miraculous Medal. Barbara handed Adele a Medal on a chain, and she started to wear it. Clinging tightly to hope, Barbara decided to say a novena to the Mother of the Miraculous Medal for all of Lent.

Shortly after that, as a thank you to customers, Komm-Mit publishing house sent a short book addressed to Adele: *Wir wollen nur deine Seele*[349] *(We Only Want Your Soul)*. She had never heard of it—neither had her mom. The author, a rock fan for years, had compiled interesting background information about popular rock groups, presenting their demonic side.

On Good Friday, shortly before Barbara and her daughter left for a special liturgical service, Adele suddenly dissolved into tears. She cried to her mom, "I'm throwing away all the CDs and cassettes with the rock music. I don't want anything to do with it anymore!"

In the week spanning Easter and Divine Mercy Sunday, 1996, Barbara experienced the joy of watching her daughter change completely. Adele began going to Holy Mass voluntarily, even midweek, and started to pray the Rosary without anyone prompting her. Opening up to her mother, she said, "I no longer believed that God was present in the Holy Host. I only went to church because I thought I had to. I was not convinced. Now I know that I was sinning, that I was offending God."

What Barbara had feared was true. She wasn't enough protection for her daughter, but Mother Mary and her Medal were.[350]

RUNNING INTERFERENCE

(CLARA, GERMANY)

Clara left the Catholic faith of her upbringing and became part of a Transcendental Meditation (TM) New Age sect for many months. She soon entered so deeply into the practice that she began attending an expensive training course every other weekend to become a TM teacher. On one of those weekends, a young elementary school teacher came wearing a Miraculous Medal, which she had gotten from a church in Munich. Little did Clara and her TM counterparts know that the Medal would act against their meditation. No one was able to have a good experience in their transcendental practice, and nearly everyone concluded there was a bad spirit in the room. The young newcomer said spontaneously, "That would be me." But no one took the schoolteacher seriously.

On another weekend spent in a beautiful mountain setting outside of Munich, the TM teachers arrived at the site fresh from their own meditation time, feeling quite "enlightened." This time Clara, unknowingly, played interference. She arrived as part of a small group of three that practiced TM in her area, and around her neck she wore a Miraculous Medal pendant, which she had from her Catholic past. The completely "enlightened" TM teachers could not sleep the whole night. They got up in the dark early hours to look for the disturbance and discerned that it was in the exact corner where Clara was sleeping.

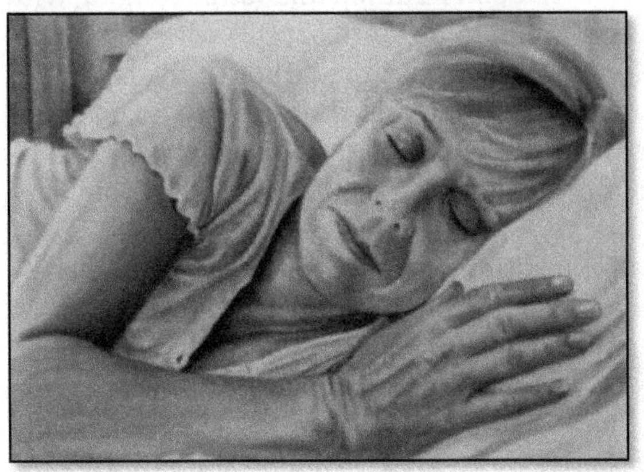

The next morning, however, the TM teachers couldn't decide which of the three students who had slept in that corner was the troublemaker. So they took all three to task, interrogating them and searching carefully through their notebooks. From that weekend on, Clara's group was never again allowed to spend the night on the mountain pasture; the trio had to go to a hotel in the valley to sleep.

Meanwhile, Clara's family never stopped praying for her, and after some months, she broke free from this sect, realizing that the Transcendental Meditation she had embraced was actually devil worship in disguise. She underwent great spiritual distress during this time of transition and cried often. Crippled with fear, she began to suffer from scruples, and her life seemed to collapse on top of her. The devil wasn't going to let her go easily.

Then Clara was introduced to the prayer, "O Mary, conceived without sin, pray for us who have recourse to thee." Praying it three times in a row left her feeling very calm. On the same day Clara was introduced to the Miraculous Medal prayer, she decided to go to a Catholic Church. Once there, she walked into a confessional—something she hadn't done for many years. A few days later, on August 9, 1999, Clara consecrated herself wholeheartedly to the Blessed Mother. That day, she took on a new life. Her existence was given new meaning, a purpose of love, and her worries and scruples fell away.[351]

VANQUISHED
(MELANIE, PRUSSIAN POLAND)

The following story was shared in a letter written by the Mother Superior of a hospital in Beuthen in Prussian Poland, in the year 1865.

Some years prior, a young Protestant woman named Melanie, who belonged to a troupe of actors, arrived in Beuthen and found lodging with a Catholic family. In little time, Melanie began to argue with the family over matters of religion. "Mademoiselle," said the father of the house, "It would be better for you to go see the Daughters of Charity about these things; the Blessed Virgin has caused wonders in their establishments. I am sure you would return fully enlightened on the subject you have brought up."

The girl laughed at such a proposition, but a few days later, impelled by curiosity, she went to knock on the front door of the Sisters of Charity.

The sister who opened the doors went for the Sister-Servant. "Invite her in," said the latter, who had already heard about the young actress. "No doubt, the Blessed Virgin has something in store for her here." After a few formalities of etiquette, Melanie introduced the subject of religion and attempted to enter into an argument. "Alas! Mademoiselle," replied the Sister, "the poor Daughters of Charity have neither the time nor learning necessary for a discussion of these subtle questions, but we have other arms with which to vanquish you."

Melanie bristled, and the sister, smiling, presented her with a little Medal of the Blessed Virgin. "Promise me you'll wear this little souvenir. It will be a constant reminder that we are praying for you." The young actress allowed the Sister-Servant to put the Medal on her neck, and then she left. From that day, the sisters lifted up the young actress in prayer and entrusted her to Mary conceived without sin.

A few weeks later, a priest said to the Sister-Servant, "Do you know, Sister, that Mademoiselle Melanie, who spent most of her time promenading with gentlemen and smoking cigarettes, is now coming to me for religious instruction? In a little while, she will make her profession of faith."

Indeed, it wasn't long before Melanie returned to the hospital. "Sister," she said, "I am going to Confession today, and tomorrow I will make my First Communion. On my first visit here, I was enraged at you. I could have continued fighting with you and was ready to cast to the winds this Medal that I now kiss. But from the very moment you put it around my neck, an unaccountable change happened in me."

The following day, the church was filled with Catholics, Protestants, and Jews, all anxious to witness a ceremony that had excited so much conversation. After Melanie's reception into the Church, the young convert paid another visit to the Sister-Servant. The Sister could see by her very countenance what great changes grace had caused in her soul. "Well," said the Sister-Servant, curious how she would respond, "here is a silver Medal to replace yours, which has become very black."

"Oh, no," Melanie replied, tenderly pressing her Medal to her chest. "I would not exchange it for any other in the world, for since I began to wear it, my soul has awakened to a new life."

Some years later, the Sister-Servant received a letter sent from Rome. It was from the young convert:

Sister,

Providence has led me to Rome, and it is no longer Mademoiselle Melanie you must address, but Sister Stelle of the Benedictine convent. Your desires have been accomplished. I now belong entirely to God, as I once did to the world. The Blessed Virgin vanquishes souls with other arms than those of controversy.

In narrating the details of this story, the Superior of the hospital at Beuthen added:

I could mention, for the greater glory of God and honor of the Immaculate Mary, countless incidents of this kind, but lack of time and my weak eyes prevent my giving the details. I will say, however, and without the slightest exaggeration, that not a week passes but the Blessed Virgin bestows upon our patients at the hospital some new proof of her maternal bounty. The Medal, so dear to us, is really miraculous, and the instrument by which we snatch from destruction souls that have cost Our Lord so much. Ah! How innumerable, in this unhappy land, the snares of the enemy of our salvation to entrap souls; but to vanquish him, I everywhere circulate the Miraculous Medal (you know what numbers of Medals we get), and my confidence in Mary is never deceived.[352]

FINALLY SAFE
(JITA, SOUTHERN CALIFORNIA, UNITED STATES)

Little Jita (pronounced "Jeeta"), a child of first-generation Hindu parents from India, was seven years old when she received a special visit. Lying on her bed in Fresno, California, she woke up from a night's sleep, and sitting on the side of her bed was a man. The sudden appearance of someone by her side would normally have startled her, but this man's presence gave her an immediate feeling of joy, even coziness. A warm light emanated from him, reaching out in soft beams that caressed and comforted her.

Though Jita had never met this man, she knew exactly who He was. He was Jesus Christ. Mesmerized, she sat up in bed to take a better look. Jesus had wavy, golden brown hair slightly past his shoulders, and His skin was a warm, dark tan color. His face was oval-shaped and unbearded, with a chiseled jaw and cheekbones, and a nose that was long but not large. He was dressed in a white robe, with a cord or belt around his waist, which she knew was there only because his robe was cinched in. What captured her gaze most were His soft, lighter brown, almost hazel eyes. They held her in a look of such profound tenderness that she melted in their gaze, feeling utterly safe.

"I love you," Jesus told her, "and I will always be here for you." His voice was strong, yet exuded great gentleness and trustworthiness. "Don't be afraid," He said to little Jita. "I want you to meet My Father."

"But I thought I'm not supposed to see the Father," Jita responded, her brow wrinkling with concern. "Am I going to be blinded?"

"No," Jesus reassured her.

Jita's parents had immigrated to the United States from the Fiji Islands. Her mother, who was Punjabi and a descendant of a high caste class, had come into contact with Christians who had treated her with kindness, and she had taken her five-year-old daughter to a Bible study in a Baptist church a number of times. Jita loved the experience and enjoyed learning stories about the Lord Jesus. But when her mother started to gain a support system through the church, Jita's father objected. He did not like his wife gaining that kind of freedom, nor did he want her to become Christian, so he insisted that she and Jita could no longer go. When they were pulled away, Jita felt like something beautiful had been stolen from her.

Now, the Source of the happiness that Jita had felt in the church was right in front of her, sitting on her bed. Embracing her with His eyes, Jesus reached out and took her tiny hand and motioned for her to get up out of bed. In one moment, they were standing side by side next to her bed. In the next, Jita found herself transported to heaven, walking alongside

Jesus, with her right hand holding His left. Nothing but white light surrounded them on all sides, and a golden walkway stretched forward beneath their feet, disappearing into the whiteness before them. Jita did not make out any details of the path because she was too occupied with staring up at Jesus. He was now smiling and playful, and the love that He exuded left her incapable of keeping her eyes off of Him. He said few words, but His every movement, every squeeze of the hand, every look, was a communication of love.

Jita knew when she was holding the strong hand of Christ that the moment was extraordinary and deeply significant. She was overcome with awe, feeling so special, and could not help but think, "He picked me to meet His Father! He picked me!" As a child who lived without a sense of love or safety from either parent, Jita felt like the one kid chosen among many to do what others could only dream of.

Reassured that she would not be blinded from seeing God the Father, Jita walked forward with anticipatory excitement, curious about what she would encounter. After walking but a few minutes, which somehow seemed eternal, they came to the end of the golden walkway. Suddenly, before them stood God the Father, wearing the same white robe as His Son. He appeared as a strong and loving father. Jita could not make out His eyes, due to an overwhelmingly powerful and vast Light of Love that was emanating from His Being in all directions. The Father looked and felt similar to Jesus, but for His white hair, beard, and slightly older appearance. His immense and brilliant glow overwhelmed Jita's senses. To remain in His luminous presence was difficult, for His Light was staggeringly beautiful, mighty, sublime, majestic, and astonishing. Jesus Christ was a man whom she could wrap her arms around, but the Father's presence was different. His all-encompassing, ecstatic Love passed through and around her, extending throughout eternity and beyond the far reaches of the universe. The encounter lasted seconds, but Jita knew she would remember it forever.

Then everything vanished, and Jita found herself back in her bed in Fresno, overjoyed and in awe, but also sad that the encounter had ended.

Because she was told to, Jita followed the Hindu practices of her father, as did her mother, who was forced to leave behind her Christian leanings. Then when Jita was fifteen in the tenth grade, she made friends with a group of Christian girls in high school, and because of their influence, Jita began to go with them to church. Her parents never knew. Her girlfriends would give her rides, and in that way, she escaped her father's hand.

During the course of the ensuing years, Jita would oscillate between prayer and attendance at non-denominational Protestant churches and falling back into the ways of the world. Because her parents were verbally, physically, and emotionally abusive, even disdainful toward her, Jita left home for good when she was eighteen. She went on to work three jobs and put herself through college. Jita became very successful in her field of medical sales, becoming a leader in a very male-dominated profession. Suffering from past abuse, she chose to be intimate with narcissistic men, and fell into sexual immorality. In her twenties, she married a man just as dangerous as her father, and because he was abusive toward their two children, a boy and a girl, she had to leave him for their protection.

After enduring a contentious divorce that cost her $150,000 in attorney bills, Jita eventually gained custody of her children and was ready to start a new life. Since she needed to leave her hometown of Fresno in search of safety in another location, away from her ex-husband, she was relieved to find a home to rent in a town called Templeton—an area where housing was scarce. In September of 2016, she moved into a nice house and a welcoming community, where Jita's ten-year-old son and twelve-year-old daughter began to thrive. The landlord promised Jita the place for at least two and half years, and she could finally take a breath. Then two months later, still exhausted from the divorce, her stressful career, the move, and getting the kids safely settled, Jita received an email from the owner of the house. The message: she would have to move out by July.

Jita's mind short-circuited. This news and the abuse she had again entered into without realizing it, was more than she felt she could handle mentally, emotionally, or physically. She raged and railed in utter despondency, and Jesus was her target: "How could You allow this?" Her children had finally settled into a place of safety, for the first time in their lives, and now they would be ripped away from it, again. To disassociate from the experience, she poured herself a glass of wine. It was the very first time that she turned to alcohol to cope.

Three months after receiving the fateful email from her landlord, a beautiful home opened up for rent just seven houses down on her same block, and Jita was able to move into it with her children. But it was too late. Her resentment toward the Lord had already taken root. In time, Jita not only turned her back on Jesus, Who she felt had utterly disappointed her, but also became less devoted to her children. Searching for additional sources of comfort, she dabbled in different New Age spiritualties and practices, deciding that there was One true God, but different manifestations of him, Jesus being only one of many. She also increased her drinking, starting an ongoing relationship with alcohol to the point of addiction.

Since the fateful day when Jita decided to blame and resent Jesus, she had felt a continuous low-grade nervousness, though she had never suffered from anxiety previously. She was able to eventually stop drinking, but her fears grew so extreme that she lived in an increasingly anxious state for several years on end.

Jita was watching her life decline. She knew that if she told a doctor about her mental health issues, they would think she was crazy. In desperation, she started to verbally rebuke the bad spirits she sensed within and around her in Jesus's Name, but didn't feel confident in her words. He still felt so distant, and she was shackled with shame, haunted by her sins and childhood traumas. She felt as though she were buried at the bottom of the ocean, physically restrained and bound over her entire body by chains from hell.

At age forty-seven, Jita's anxiety became debilitating. She and her children were plagued by menacing spirits and Jita suspected that evil had entered her home. In a quest to rid her family of the menacing spirits that followed them to their new dwelling, Jita tried burning sage. But it had no effect. She called in a female shaman to clear out the demons. But it had the opposite effect: not only did the demonic spirits stay and manifest, but they multiplied and became more aggressive. That is when Jita realized she was trying to cast out the devil with the devil.

At times, Jita was visited by demons during the night. She would wake up in the morning with bruises and imprints from fingers that were not hers, in places all over her legs that her own hands could not reach. Other times, she and her children heard noises in the house—running footsteps, cabinets slamming in the kitchen—when no one was there. Once, she saw the outline of a translucent black serpent, slithering rapidly, back and forth, about six feet in the air above the kitchen floor. Her daughter often saw dark spirits, and her son heard them. All of them were afraid. To make matters worse, a lingering spirit of suicide would tell

Jita to hang herself and put visions in her head of various ways to take her life.

One day in February 2022, when Jita was driving to her aunt's funeral in Sacramento, California, she grew nervous and felt spiritually attacked to the point of no longer being able to function. She had loved her aunt and desired to see her cousins, but she would also encounter her estranged parents and sister—and couldn't cope with the thought.

Spontaneously, she pulled over to the side of the road, stepped out of her car, and walked into a Catholic Church. Trembling within and finding it hard to breathe, she sat down in a pew during an afternoon Mass. Because the Catholic Church was an ancient institution, far older than any Protestant church, she thought to herself, "If there's anywhere that is safe and a place that can help me, it is going to be a Catholic church." She somehow understood, because of a friend's influence and a sense of knowing—a subtle internal voice guiding her—that the Catholic Church was more equipped to handle the demonic realm, having battled it for centuries.

When Jita was in college, she had gone with friends to a few Masses and a couple of Catholic funerals, but she hadn't known what to do or say during the service. On this pivotal day, she slid into a pew and began following along as best she could. Then she looked up at the large crucifix above the altar and stared at Jesus on the Cross. In that instant, she felt a very familiar and profound sense of safety and comfort come over her. By the time the Mass ended, her feelings of anxiety and frozen inability to function had vanished.

Jita walked outside, collected and calm. "In there was protection from evil spirits!" she realized. It was a moment of profound awakening. Her heart knew Who had been there, inside that Catholic Church. She had experienced that same warm feeling of love and safety long ago. That day, Jita began to reconnect with Jesus Christ in prayer, with the One True God she had left behind. Feeling at peace, Jita hopped in her car and drove to her aunt's funeral.

Humbly, Jita realized that she had displaced her anger onto Jesus for her life's difficulties, which were actually Satan's doing. She had blamed the Lord for not keeping her and her children safe, when in fact, He had been their source of protection all along. Tears flowed. In the days to come, Jita would drive to a Catholic Church to seek out Jesus in the afternoon hour, relieved that she could visit him in the middle of any weekday, and not just on Sundays, when she would also attend a local Catholic Mass.

Looking around at the church's interior, however, one concern gave her pause: "Why do they have a statue and pictures of Mary? Why is she everywhere?" God the Father and God the Son, she understood. She had even met them. "But who is this Mary person? And why are they worshipping her?" Our Lady's image was disturbing to her and made her question if she was in the right place. After all, non-denominational Protestant churches were a familiar part of her past, and Jesus had been there, too.

Jita had a close Catholic friend, Jennifer Tadlock, who had been working as a movie director and producer for thirty years. At the same time Jita was asking questions about the Blessed Mother, Jennifer was getting closer to Mary through the Rosary and a pilgrimage she had taken to Medjugorje.

When Jennifer returned from Medjugorje, she felt called to teach Jita more about Mary. She gave Jita a prayer card from the pilgrimage site and shared with her the miracles she was experiencing due to Mary's intercession: her daughter's inexplicable healings during cancer treatments; her Rosary turning gold in Medjugorje directly in front of her eyes and in the sight of five witnesses; and the deepening of her faith and conviction that she was called to defend and magnify the Mother of God. Jita listened, but was skeptical. Even when Jennifer and others told her that Catholics don't worship Mary—they honor her—she didn't believe them.

In October 2022, Jita attended a Marian conference at Holy Spirit Parish in Fresno, California, because her friend's mother had bought her a ticket. On the last day of the conference, one of the speakers stepped on the stage, frazzled, and shared that the Blessed Mother had just switched the subject she had planned for her talk. Jita remembered her saying: "I had my entire presentation ready. I knew what I was going to talk about, when all of a sudden, I had to switch things. The Blessed Mother, it seems, had other plans. I wasn't ready, but I need to be obedient. We don't always get to choose how things are going to work. I feel like I'm being told to talk about my husband's experience and his journey to the Blessed Mother, which began with his trip to Medjugorje."

Jita found the speaker's frazzled honesty indicative of the Holy Spirit, Who "blows where it wills" (cf. John 3:8). Intrigued, she began listening intently.

During the speaker's presentation, her eyes locked with Jita's as she shared how her husband had a hard time accepting the Blessed Mother because of his distant relationship with his own mother. Afterward, Jita approached the speaker, who said to her, "My eyes kept being drawn to you. At times, I felt like I was speaking only to you." Jita had felt like the speaker was addressing her personally the entire time.

That day, Jita walked away conscious of something that had been hidden from her awareness. As soon as she got home from the conference, she called Jennifer: "The reason I am refusing to accept the Blessed

Mother, Jen, is because I haven't forgiven my own." Jita had always felt unwanted and unloved by her mother, as far back as she could remember. She felt that in her mother's eyes, she was a worthless rag, something to discard in the trash. "How can I honor a Mother in heaven?" she asked herself, "if I refuse to in any way honor my mother on earth?"

From that October until the next Marian conference the following February, Jita started a process of healing by diving deeper into the resentment and anger that she had been harboring toward her mother. Eventually, she forgave her and released much of the pain from her past. At the same time, she was learning more about Mary and began utilizing tools of the Catholic Church that help to ward off demons: particularly, the St. Michael Prayer and the Hail Mary. When scared or bothered by an evil spirit, Jita would simply say three Hail Mary's, and peace would return to her. Yet she still wasn't sure if she trusted the Catholic Church to understand Mary's role and was leaning toward getting more involved in a non-denominational church—one that she was familiar with, one that taught that the Catholic Church was involved in idolatry toward the Virgin Mary.

Then Jita's friend, Jennifer Tadlock, invited her to another Catholic conference: a Women's Christian Fellowship Retreat in February 2023, at the Crown Plaza in Costa Mesa, California. Jen had just returned from France, where she visited the Chapel of Our Lady of the Miraculous Medal on Rue du Bac in Paris. There she purchased several gold- and silver-colored, inch-tall Miraculous Medals for her relatives and had them blessed by a priest at the French chapel.

On Saturday night of the conference, the Holy Spirit asked Jennifer to give Jita one of the Miraculous Medals and spoke aloud what the Holy Spirit was prompting her to do. Jennifer then learned that she had accidentally given two Medals to her son's girlfriend, Emily, who was present and had both on her necklace—thinking she was supposed to wear two. She was happy to relinquish one. Jen took the extra Miraculous Medal and put it on Jita's necklace, next to her cross. Jita felt very honored to receive it.

The following day was the closing Mass of the conference. Before the priest celebrant said the Eucharistic prayer of consecration, Jita was on her knees in prayer. Her elbows rested on the back of the folding chair in front of her, and her forearms enclosed her bowed head—blocking out the light in the room from her sight. The priest began to say the specific prayer of consecration over the bread and wine on the altar—the Epiclesis: "Make holy, therefore, these gifts, we pray, by sending down your Spirit upon them like the dewfall, so that they may become for us the Body and Blood of our Lord Jesus Christ."

Suddenly, while Jita was staring down into the darkness, she saw the bottom third of the Miraculous Medal on her chest light up brilliantly, like a small sun. A heartbeat later, the light went away. Then it came back just as quickly. "What is happening?" she wondered as she watched her Medal "turn on" and "turn off" to the beating of her heart. Turning to Jen, she whispered, "Is there some kind of battery in the Medal that makes it light up?"

Taken aback, Jennifer chuckled and brushed her off. "What are you talking about? No!" she answered, and returned to her focus on the sacred moment of the consecration.

"Well, if this isn't some kind of souvenir, what is it?" Jita wondered. Grabbing onto logic, she figured that a sunbeam must be streaming onto the Medal from a window, passing through a crack between her arms and head, so she moved her upper body trying to pinpoint the light's external origin. But the source was not outside the room. The rhythmic pace of the illumination continued, and Jita continued to stare at it, mesmerized. Then, suddenly, after about fifteen more blinks, half of her Medal lit up. And a few beats later, her entire Medal was glowing with bright pulsating rays radiating an inch in every direction, emitting light onto her dark-colored shirt.

That is when Jita understood she was experiencing a miracle—one that she knew was coming from heaven through the Heart of the Blessed Mother. Overcome with awe, she broke into sobs. When she looked up, Jen was already standing next to her. It was their row's turn to walk forward for Communion or a blessing.

The Miraculous Medal given to Jita that glowed

"Oh, my gosh," Jita gasped in a loud whisper, crying and hyperventilating. "You're not going to believe what just happened to me. My Medal—it was glowing, pulsating on and off—about forty times..."

Jennifer knew instantly that the Blessed Mother was trying to tell Jita that she was being called to become Catholic so she could receive her Son in the Eucharist—something that Jen and others had been trying to communicate to Jita for many months. Looking Jita square in the eye, she said, "If you don't believe that was a clear sign, I don't know what else would convince you."

In September 2023, Jita entered the Rite of Christian Initiation of Adults. She began the process of becoming Catholic so that she could receive the Body of Christ in the Eucharist, the same Body that had sat down on the side of her bed when she was seven years old, and told her He loved her.[353]

THE SENDING

"The harvest is abundant, but the laborers are few" (Matthew 9:37-38). If you traveled this far into a book about the Miraculous Medal, perhaps you have felt the gentle hand of Our Lady upon you. Through the multifaceted testimonies in this book, you have learned a bit about different organizations that spread the Miraculous Medal. Perhaps you feel called to participate in St. Paul Street Evangelization at www.streetevangelization.com; or you may wish to join a local chapter of the Legion of Mary www.legionofmary.ie, (See www.legionofmary tidewater.com/usa, or do an Internet search under "Legion of Mary" and your city or town.) On the contrary, you might tend to avoid groups and desire anonymity, but enjoy the spiritual connection of joining the Militia Immaculata online: www.militiaoftheimmaculata.com/why-and-how-to-enroll-in-the-mi. Perhaps you would like to fly solo, distributing Medals at your leisure in your own unique way.

Your desire may be to say one of the novenas that follow in the Appendix of this book. Or you may be inspired to bring the Perpetual Novena in Honor of Our Lady of the Miraculous Medal to your parish after reading below of its astounding effects. Maybe you are looking for a priest or deacon to say the investiture prayer for your personal Medal (see Appendix II)—or for you, just a blessing will do. Perhaps you are a spiritual warrior and ready for fasting and other mortifications, calling down from heaven waterfalls of grace with your use of the Medal.

Our Lady of the Miraculous Medal knows your personality, what attracts and what repels you; whatever she may be asking of you will tailor fit your life. Medals can be ordered in bulk through St. Paul Street evangelization. (See www.evangelizationschool.com/store.) If you would like Medals in bulk that are already threaded with a satin nylon cord, ready to be worn, and/or an attractive explanatory flyer of where the Medal came from and what it can do, Queen of Peace Media provides these at cost. If you are shy, the flyer does the speaking for you. Or if you are an extrovert, the flyer can back up your words and give your Medal recipient a reference to explore. (See www.QueenofPeaceMedia.com.)

You may recall the boldness of St. Maximilian Kolbe, who made it his mission to gather the world under the banner of Our Lady. To us, he says:

Away with indifference, then! Let us all make every effort to ensure that each of us, according to the intelligence and abilities that God has deigned to grant, win over to the Immaculata as many souls as possible. But how? 1. Distributing wherever possible, the Miraculous Medal among the good and the bad, Catholics and non-Catholics, inasmuch as if a person manifests this small tribute to the Immaculata, that is, carries her Medal, she will never abandon that person and will lead him to faith and repentance. Spread the Miraculous Medal, therefore, and pray fervently to the Immaculata for one's own conversion and that of others...

354

At minimum, consider keeping a stash of blessed Miraculous Medals with you, wherever you go, and distribute them freely, unabashedly, bringing joy to Our Lord and Our Lady and great graces to the world. Where they end up is not your worry. You need only give them away, and pray.

APPENDIX I

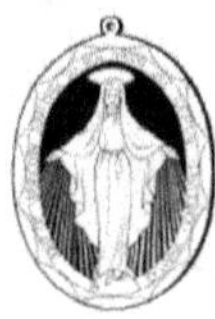

NOVENAS TO OUR LADY OF THE MIRACULOUS MEDAL

Several novenas to Our Lady of the Miraculous Medal are in existence. This Appendix contains an introduction to novenas in general; a brief history of the Miraculous Medal Perpetual Novena, which was introduced with great success to parishes at the time of the second World War; the Perpetual Novena itself; and three different versions of the Miraculous Medal Novena. They can be prayed from the 19th to the 27th of November, the feast day of the Miraculous Medal, or at any other time during the year.

WHAT IS A NOVENA?

A novena (from the Latin "novem"—nine), consists of praying nine consecutive days for a specific intention or grace. This traditional type of prayer, highly encouraged by the Church since the Middle Ages, generally has recourse of the intercession of the Virgin Mary or a saint.

WHY PRAY FOR NINE DAYS?

The nine days that make up a novena are associated with the nine days that separate the feast of Ascension from the feast of Pentecost. In the Bible, this period for the disciples and the Blessed Mother was a time of prayerful waiting, which culminated in the descent of the Holy Spirit upon them. "All these devoted themselves with one accord to prayer, together with some women, and Mary the mother of Jesus, and his brothers" (Acts 1:14). We, too, can use a novena as a period of waiting for a particular grace.

THE MIRACULOUS MEDAL PERPETUAL NOVENA FOR PARISHES (A BRIEF HISTORY)

Please share the following Perpetual Novena in Honor of Our Lady of the Miraculous Medal and its brief history with pastors, priests, and lay leaders, who may be inspired to bring the novena to their parishes.

The Miraculous Medal Perpetual Novena was initiated at The Miraculous Medal Shrine in Philadelphia, Pennsylvania, on Monday, December 8, 1930, by Fr. Joseph A. Skelly, CM, founder of the Central Association of the Miraculous Medal. To this day, the Perpetual Novena has continued without fail each Monday, when thousands of people around the world join the novena prayer, either at the Shrine, through the Internet, or in their parishes.

355

During World War II, the Miraculous Medal Perpetual Novena took on an ever-increasing importance in the religious life of Catholic families throughout the United States. When the country entered World War II, Catholic families placed their "boys" going to Europe or Asia under the protection of Our Lady of the Immaculate Conception. Four million copies of a prayer leaflet of the novena were distributed, assuring soldiers of prayers from back home.

In 1943, the Perpetual Novena was broadcast every week by 200 radio stations and held regularly in 700 military camps. After the war, a solemn thanksgiving novena was held in parishes throughout the United States. In this way, the "Perpetual Novena" was introduced to the Church in America and became an integral part of the life of North American Catholics, at that time.

Soon the novena was introduced in other countries—Ireland, England, Italy, France, Belgium, and Holland. In Dublin, Ireland, 4000 faithful took part in the first novena, inspiring many fallen-away Catholics to find their way back to the Church and the sacraments. On January 26 of the Marian Year, 1954, the novena entered the Chapel of the Miraculous Medal on Rue du Bac in Paris, which was filled to capacity, standing room only. From there it was held by more than 50 parishes in Paris, and in the cathedrals of Versailles, Chartres, Laval, Renne, Toulouse, Angers, Dax, Lucon, Perpignan, Toulon, and so on. Missionaries preached about and introduced the novena to more than 500 parishes, tirelessly continuing the fruitful apostolate.

Experience proved that the novena, along with zealous preaching, heartfelt intercessory prayers, and distribution of free Miraculous Medals to all who would attend, had a salutary influence on the ecclesial life of parishes. A few French priests gave their reflection on these "missions in miniature":

Fr. Badreau, Dean of Herbiers: "At the beginning of December 1961, my two chaplains and myself were surprised by the zeal and enthusiasm of our parishioners for the 'Perpetual Novena in honor of Our Lady of the Miraculous Medal.' We wanted to prepare our parishioners for the feast of the Immaculate Conception through a few discourses on the famous novena of the Rue du Bac, which had been brought to us by a missionary who had been recommended. Without propaganda, invited only by an announcement from the pulpit the previous Sunday, 800 people came to church nine evenings in a row, despite the very unfavorable weather. How can this fact be explained? Only heaven can give the answer. Our parish has experienced the blessing of the novena in the richest measure. We are very grateful for having begun it."

Fr. Culbin of Notre-Dame de Ferte-Bernard: "In the parish church of St. Anthony, almost all of the practicing parishioners participated in the novena. This was the first miracle. The second miracle was a source of great joy for the parish priest: spontaneously there was a real and true prayer, intimate and living contact with God, and fiery communal prayer for all the intentions recommended. There was no trace of the sluggishness or distraction that can otherwise be so easily disruptive. The grace of the 'Perpetual Novena' brought many people to the confessional and to the altar of the Lord. We wish the novena universal diffusion."

Fr. Mouilleau of Notre-Dame de Monts: "You ask what I think of the novena to Our Lady of the Miraculous Medal. Our parish was in need of this grace; it was in need of renewal. A missionary full of optimism proclaimed and explained the novena. He spoke about the meaning and value of the Miraculous Medal. He animated our prayer and our singing. His word resonated with everyone. We now wear the Medal with reverence and confidence. We no longer want to do without the novena in our parish."

Fr. Ferre of Rocke-sur-Jou: "Our Lady has once again worked a miracle. More than 3000 medals were distributed to my parishioners who listened with devotion to the message of Our Lady of the Miraculous Medal. They prayed with exemplary zeal. The hundreds of different intentions that were read revealed to us much hidden suffering and many crosses. The long litany was reminiscent of the procession at Lourdes, where an endless series of sufferings and illnesses pass before the eyes of the pilgrims. But what was even more reminiscent of the Grotto of Massabielle was the fiery supplication that went up from all hearts to the good, powerful and loving Queen of heaven and earth. The 'Perpetual Novena' has blossomed in my parish in a short time."[356]

PERPETUAL NOVENA IN HONOR OF OUR LADY OF THE MIRACULOUS MEDAL

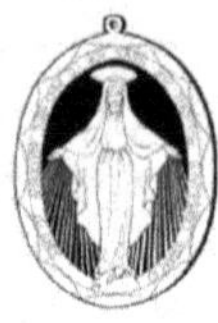

Opening Prayer

Priest: In the name of the Father, and of the Son, and of the Holy Spirit.

People: Amen.

Priest: Come, O Holy Spirit, fill the hearts of Your faithful, and kindle in them the fire of Your love. Send forth Your Spirit, and they shall be created.

People: And You shall renew the face of the earth.

Priest: Let us pray. Oh God, who did instruct the hearts of the faithful by the light of the Holy Spirit, grant us in the same Spirit to be truly wise and ever to rejoice in His consolation, through Jesus Christ, Our Lord.

People: Amen.

Priest: O Mary, conceived without sin.

People: Pray for us who have recourse to you (repeat 3 times)

Priest and People: O Lord, Jesus Christ, who have vouchsafed to glorify by numberless miracles the Blessed Virgin Mary, immaculate from the first moment of her conception, grant that all who devoutly implore her protection on earth, may eternally enjoy Your presence in heaven, who, with the Father and Holy Spirit, live and reign, God forever and ever. Amen.

O Lord, Jesus Christ, who for the accomplishment of Your greatest works, have chosen the weak things of the world, that no flesh may glory in Your sight; and who for a better and more widely diffused belief in the Immaculate Conception of Your Mother, have wished that the Miraculous Medal be manifested to Saint Catherine Labouré, grant we beseech You, that filled with like humility, we may glorify this mystery by word and work. Amen.

Memorare

Remember, O most compassionate Virgin Mary, that never was it known that anyone who fled to your protection, implored your assistance, or sought your intercession, was left unaided. Inspired with this confidence, we fly unto you, O Virgin of Virgins, our Mother; to you we come; before you we kneel, sinful and sorrowful. O Mother of the Word Incarnate, despise not our petitions, but, in your clemency, hear and answer them. Amen.

Novena Prayer

O Immaculate Virgin Mary, Mother of Our Lord Jesus and our Mother, penetrated with the most lively confidence in your all-powerful and never-failing intercession, manifested so often through the Miraculous Medal, we your loving and trustful children implore you to obtain for us the graces and favors we ask during this Novena, if they be beneficial to our immortal souls, and the souls for whom we pray.

(Here privately form your petitions.)

You know, O Mary, how often our souls have been the sanctuaries of your Son who hates iniquity. Obtain for us, then, a deep hatred of sin and that purity of heart which will attach us to God alone, so that our every thought, word and deed may tend to His greater glory. Obtain for us also a spirit of prayer and self-denial, that we may recover by penance what we have lost by sin and at length attain to that blessed abode where you are the Queen of angels and of men. Amen.

An Act of Consecration to Our Lady of the Miraculous Medal

O Virgin Mother of God, Mary Immaculate, we dedicate and consecrate ourselves to you under the title of Our Lady of the Miraculous Medal. May this Medal be for each one of us a sure sign of your affection for us and a constant reminder of our duties toward you. Ever while wearing it, may we be blessed by your loving protection and preserved in the grace of your Son. O most powerful Virgin, Mother of our Savior, keep us close to you every moment of our lives. Obtain for us, your children, the grace of a happy death; so that, in union with you, we may enjoy the bliss of heaven forever. Amen.

Repeat 3 times:

Priest: O Mary, conceived without sin.

People: Pray for us who have recourse to you.[357]

NOVENA TO OUR LADY OF THE MIRACULOUS MEDAL (VERSION 1: TRADITIONAL)

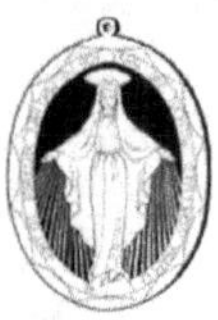

The following is prayed for nine consecutive days to Our Lady:

In the name of the Father, and of the Son, and of the Holy Spirit. Amen.

O Immaculate Virgin Mary, Mother of Our Lord Jesus and our Mother, penetrated with the most lively confidence in your all-powerful and never-failing intercession, manifested so often through the Miraculous Medal, we, your loving and trustful children, implore you to obtain for us the graces and favors we ask during this novena, if they be beneficial to our immortal souls and the souls for whom we pray.

(Mention your request here...)

You know, O Mary, how often our souls have been the sanctuaries of your Son who hates iniquity. Obtain for us then a deep hatred of sin and that purity of heart which will attach us to God alone so that our every thought, word, and deed may tend to His greater glory. Obtain for us also a spirit of prayer and self-denial that we may recover by penance what we have lost by sin, and at length attain to that blessed abode where you are the Queen of angels and of men. Amen.

O Mary, conceived without sin, pray for us. Who have recourse to thee, and for those who do not have recourse to thee, especially the enemies of the Church and those recommended to thee. Amen."

Say 1 Our Father...
Say 1 Hail Mary...
Say 1: Glory Be...

NOVENA TO OUR LADY OF THE MIRACULOUS MEDAL (VERSION 2)

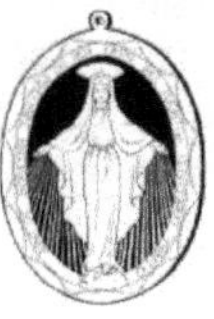

Sign of the Cross ...
Said three times:
O Mary, conceived without sin, pray for us who have recourse to thee (daily for nine days).

Day 1: First Appearance

Let us imagine the Immaculate Virgin as she appeared for the first time to St. Catherine Labouré. The pious novice was guided by her guardian angel and presented to the Virgin. Let us contemplate her inexpressible joy. We too will be happy like St. Catherine Labouré if we work diligently at our sanctification. We will enjoy the happiness of heaven if we renounce vain earthly pleasures.

Each meditation is followed by three Hail Marys, then: "O Mary, conceived without sin, pray for us who have recourse to thee" and the closing prayer (daily for nine days), as follows:

Said three times:
Hail Mary...
Said once:
O Mary, conceived without sin, pray for us who have recourse to thee.

Closing Prayer:
Most Holy Virgin, I believe in and confess your holy and immaculate conception. O most pure Virgin Mary, by your immaculate conception and glorious election to be the Mother of God, obtain for me from your Incarnate Son, true humility, pure love, faithful obedience, whole and undivided abandonment to God. Obtain for me the grace to recognize and also to fulfill the will of God in all situations of life, for only in this way can I honor God and praise His name. Please, my gracious Mother, obtain for me these divine graces for time and eternity. Amen.[358]

Day 2: The Tears of Mary

Let us contemplate Mary weeping due to the tribulations that will come upon the world because of the grave insults to the Heart of Jesus, her Son, and as a result of the contempt for the Cross and the persecution of her beloved children on earth. Let us trust in the compassionate Heart of Mary, and share in the fruit of her tears.

Day 3: Mary, Our Protection

Let us contemplate our Immaculate Mother as she spoke to Sr. Catherine in her second apparition: *"Have a Medal struck after this model. All who wear it will receive great graces; they should wear it around the neck. Great graces will be given to those who wear it with confidence."*
Through the Miraculous Medal, be also for me, O Immaculate Virgin, a shield and help in all of my needs.

Day 4: The Second Apparition

When Sr. Catherine was praying on November 27, 1830, the Virgin Mary appeared to her in radiant beauty, standing on the globe, crushing the head of the infernal serpent. In this apparition, one sees her desire to protect us at all times from the infernal enemy and adversary. Let us call upon the Immaculate Mother with trust and love.

Day 5: The Hands of Mary

Today, let us contemplate how luminous rays emanated from Mary's hands. She said: "*These rays symbolize the graces I shed upon those who ask for them. The gems from which rays do not fall are the graces for which souls forget to ask.*" Let us not overlook such great graces! Let us plead eagerly, humbly, and persistently, and Mary, the Immaculate Virgin, will ask for them on our behalf.

Day 6: The Third Apparition

Let us contemplate Mary as she appeared to Catherine in a radiant blaze of light, surrounded by twelve stars, and smiling with goodness. She gave the order to have a medal minted, and promised many graces to all those who wear it with love and devotion. Let us wear with confidence the Miraculous Medal, and the Blessed Virgin will be a shield of protection in all the dangers of our lives.

Day 7: Mary, Advocate and Refuge

O wonderful Virgin, exalted Queen, Mother without blemish, be my advocate, my refuge, my fortress, my stronghold on this earth, my protection in life and death! You are my heart's delight and my glory in heaven. Stand by me in trial and temptation, and bring me safely to your Divine Son Jesus.

Day 8: Mary, Mediatrix of All Graces

O Immaculate Virgin, make the luminous rays that emanate from your virgin hands illuminate my mind, so that I may better discern what is good. Protect my mind from the wiles of the serpent, that I may not be fooled in my thoughts or wayward in my decisions. May the rays of graceful light that you wish to extend to me enliven my heart in faith, hope, love and Truth.

Day 9: Mary Before the Cross of her Son

O Immaculate Virgin and Mother of God Mary, cause the cross to rise as a sign of victory in my life, uniting me intimately with you and your Divine Son. Give me the grace and strength to stand with you before the Cross of your Son and to persevere to the end, until my last task on earth is accomplished.[359]

NOVENA TO OUR LADY OF THE MIRACULOUS MEDAL (VERSION 3)

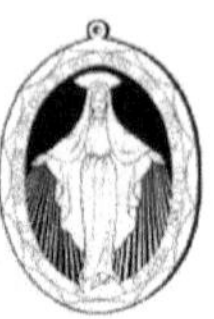

Opening Prayer

O Most Holy Virgin, O my Mother, ask your Son on my behalf for everything my soul and all mankind needs so that your Reign be established on earth. My most earnest request is that you may triumph in me and in all souls, and implant your reign on earth. *Amen*

FIRST DAY

The First Apparition

During the night of July 18-19, 1830, the Most Holy Virgin appeared for the first time to Saint Catherine Labouré, who had been awakened and led from the dormitory to the chapel by her guardian angel.
In the sanctuary, Saint Catherine later wrote:
"I heard something like the rustling of a silk dress, coming from the side of the tribune, close to Saint Joseph's picture. She alighted on the steps of the altar on the Gospel side, in an armchair like Saint Anne's… As I looked up at Our Lady, I flung myself close to her, falling on my knees on the altar steps, my hands resting on her knees. That was the sweetest moment of my life."

LET US PRAY

O Most Holy Virgin, O my Mother, look upon my soul with mercy, obtain for me a spirit of prayer that leads me always to have recourse to you. Obtain for me the graces that I implore of you, and above all, inspire me to pray for the graces that you most desire to grant me.

Our Father….
Hail Mary….
Glory Be….
O Mary, conceived without sin, pray for us who have recourse to thee!

SECOND DAY

Protection of Mary in times of trial

"The times are very evil, misfortunes are going to befall France, the throne will be overthrown, the whole world will be overwhelmed with misfortunes of every kind." The Holy Virgin looked very distressed as she said this. "But come to the foot of this altar. Here graces will be bestowed on anyone, great or small, who asks for them with confidence and fervor... A moment will come of such great danger that all will seem lost. But I shall be with you."

LET US PRAY

O Most Holy Virgin, O my Mother, amidst the great desolation in the world and the Church, obtain for me the graces I ask of you, and inspire me, above all, to request the graces that you most desire to grant me.

Our Father....
Hail Mary....
Glory Be....
O Mary, conceived without sin, pray for us who have recourse to thee!

THIRD DAY

The Cross will be despised

"The Cross will be despised and hurled to the ground, blood will run in the streets, the side of Our Lord will be opened again. The archbishop will be stripped of his garments." Here the Holy Virgin, her face filled with sadness, could no longer speak. "My child, the whole world will be plunged in sorrow," she said to me.

LET US PRAY

O Most Holy Virgin, O my Mother, obtain for me the grace to live in union with you, with your Divine Son and the Church at this crucial moment in history, as tragic as the Passion, when all humanity is about to choose sides for or against Christ! Obtain for me the graces I implore, especially the grace of requesting that which you most desire to grant me.

Our Father....
Hail Mary....
Glory Be....
O Mary, conceived without sin, pray for us who have recourse to thee!

FOURTH DAY

Mary crushes the head of the serpent

At 5:30 in the evening of November 27, 1830, as St. Catherine was praying in the chapel, the Holy Virgin appeared to her for the second time, standing as high as Saint Joseph's picture to the right of the main altar.
"Her face was so beautiful that it would be impossible for me to describe it. Her robe was white as the glow of dawn... Her head was covered with a white veil that extended to her feet which rested on a half sphere, with her heel crushing the head of a serpent."

LET US PRAY

O Most Holy Virgin, O my Mother, be my protection against the assaults of the infernal enemy. Obtain for me the graces I am asking of you, and above all, inspire me to request the graces that you most desire to grant me.

Our Father....
Hail Mary....
Glory Be....
O Mary, conceived without sin, pray for us who have recourse to thee!

FIFTH DAY

The Virgin of the globe

The Holy Virgin holds a globe in her hands representing the whole world and each person in particular, and offers it to God, imploring His mercy. She wears rings on her fingers, bearing precious stones that shed rays, one more beautiful than the next, symbolizing the graces that the Holy Virgin pours out upon those who ask for them.

LET US PRAY

O Most Holy Virgin, O my Mother, obtain for me the graces I am asking of you, and inspire me, above all, to request the graces that you most desire to grant me.

Our Father....
Hail Mary....
Glory Be....
O Mary, conceived without sin, pray for us who have recourse to thee!

SIXTH DAY

The invocation on the medal

During the second apparition, Our Blessed Mother explained, in the words of St. Catherine, "how pleased she is when people pray to her and how generous she is with them; how she gives special graces to those who ask; and what a great joy she takes in granting them."
At that point "a frame formed around Our Lady, like an oval, bearing the following words in gold letters: 'O Mary, conceived without sin, pray for us who have recourse to thee.'"

LET US PRAY

O Most Holy Virgin, O my Mother, obtain for me the graces I am asking of you, and inspire me, above all, to request the graces that you most desire to grant me.

Our Father....
Hail Mary....
Glory Be....
O Mary, conceived without sin, pray for us who have recourse to thee!

SEVENTH DAY

Revelation of the medal

Then a voice was heard, saying, *"Have a Medal struck after this model. All who wear it will receive great graces; they should wear it around the neck. The graces will be abundant for those who wear it with confidence."*

LET US PRAY

O Most Holy Virgin, O my Mother, obtain for me the graces that I ask of you, and inspire me, above all, to pray for the graces that you most wish to grant me.

Our Father....
Hail Mary....
Glory Be....
O Mary, conceived without sin, pray for us who have recourse to thee!

EIGHTH DAY

The hearts of Jesus and Mary

After contemplating the picture on the Medal, St. Catherine saw it turn to display the back.

There she saw an "M," the monogram of Mary, surmounted by a small cross, and below it, the hearts of Jesus and Mary—the first surrounded with thorns and the latter pierced with a sword. Encircling the hearts and the monogram were twelve stars.

LET US PRAY

O Immaculate Heart of Mary, make my heart like yours. Obtain for me the graces I am asking of you, and above all, inspire me to ask of you the graces you most wish to grant me.

Our Father....
Hail Mary....
Glory Be....
O Mary, conceived without sin, pray for us who have recourse to thee!

NINTH DAY

Mary will be proclaimed

St. Catherine Labouré, whom Our Lady entrusted with the making of the Miraculous Medal

Queen of the Universe Confirming the predictions of Saint Louis Grignion de Montfort, Saint Catherine says that the Most Holy Virgin will be proclaimed Queen of the Universe:

"Oh! How beautiful it will be to hear: Mary is the Queen of the Universe. The children and everyone will cry with joy and rapture. That will be a lasting era of peace and happiness. She will be displayed on standards and paraded all over the world."

LET US PRAY

O Most Holy Virgin, O my Mother, obtain for me the graces I am asking of you, and inspire me, above all, to pray for the graces that you most wish to grant me.

Our Father....
Hail Mary....
Glory Be....
O Mary, conceived without sin, pray for us who have recourse to thee![360]

APPENDIX II

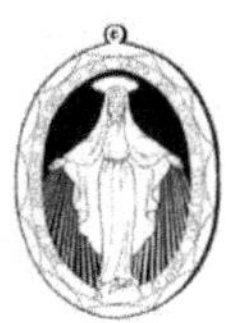

BLESSING AND INVESTITURE WITH MIRACULOUS MEDAL

Approved by the Congregation of Sacred Rites, April 19, 1895

(If you lose the Miraculous Medal used at your investiture, it does not matter. You are the one being invested. Any other Medal you may wear that receives a simple blessing from a priest or deacon will carry the same investiture blessing.)

Priest vests in surplice and white stole.
Priest: Our help is in the name of the Lord
People: Who made heaven and earth
Priest: The Lord be with you
People: And also with you
Priest: Let us pray.

Almighty and merciful God, Who by the many appearances on earth of the Immaculate Virgin Mary were pleased to work miracles again and again for the salvation of souls, kindly pour out Your blessing + on this medal, so that all who devoutly wear it and reverence it may experience the patronage of Mary Immaculate and obtain mercy from You, through Christ our Lord.

People: Amen.
Priest sprinkles Miraculous Medal(s) with Holy Water, then presents it (them) to the person(s) saying:

Take this holy medal; wear it with faith, and handle it with due devotion, so that the holy and Immaculate Queen of Heaven may protect and defend you. And as she is ever ready to renew her wondrous acts of kindness, may she obtain for you in her mercy whatever you humbly ask of God, so that both in life and in death you may rest happily in her motherly embrace.

People: Amen.
Priest:
Lord, have mercy.
Christ, have mercy.
Lord, have mercy.

Our Father... And lead us not into temptation
People: But deliver us from evil
Priest: Queen conceived without original sin
People: Pray for us
Priest: Lord, heed my prayer
People: And let my cry be heard by you
Priest: The Lord be with you
People: And with your spirit
Priest: Let us pray.

Lord Jesus Christ, Who willed that Your Mother, the Blessed Virgin Mary conceived without sin, should become illustrious through countless miracles; grant that we who ever seek her patronage may finally possess everlasting joys. We ask this of You, Who lives and reigns forever and ever.

People: Amen.[361]

NOTE TO THE READER

AMAZON REVIEWS:

If you were graced by this book, would you kindly post a short review of *The Door of Faith* on Amazon.com? Your support will make a difference in the lives of souls.

To leave a short review, go to Amazon.com and type in The Door of Faith. Click on the book and scroll down the page. Next to customer reviews, click on "Write a customer review." Thank you, in advance, for your kindness.

OTHER BOOKS

BY QUEEN OF PEACE MEDIA

GO TO:

www.QueenofPeaceMedia.com/catholic-bookstore

VIDEO BOOK TRAILERS:

www.QueenofPeaceMedia.com/great-catholic-books

ALL OTHER ITEMS:
SACRAMENTALS, BROCHURES, AND MORE

www.QueenofPeaceMedia.com/shop

Books are available through QueenofPeaceMedia.com and Amazon.com in Print, Ebook, and Audiobook formats

MIRACULOUS MEDALS

FREE AND BLESSED WITH SATIN NYLON CORD SOLD AT COST & EVANGELIZATION PACKETS

"The graces will be abundant for those who wear it with confidence."

—Our Lady of the Miraculous Medal to St. Catherine Labouré

Miraculous Medal Evangelization Packets at cost with FREE blessed Miraculous Medal

Unsure of what to say when you hand someone a Miraculous Medal? Let this evangelization packet do the talking for you!

Now, more than ever in history, we are being called to spread the graces of the miraculous medal to all.

Queen of Peace Media offers these Miraculous Medals free, blessed, and ready to wear, charging only for the cost of the cord and the evangelization flyer.

Please spread these Miraculous Medal Evangelization Packets far and wide in parishes, prayer groups, youth groups, first communions, R.C.I.A., confirmations, Bible studies, on the streets and to whomever you meet—everywhere! This was Our Lady's wish.

FREE Miraculous Medals in bulk

with cords sold at cost included are also available at

www.QueenofPeaceMedia.com.

THE DOOR OF FAITH

by Bishop and Doctor János Székely

"Compelling illumination of eternal truth."
—His Eminence Cardinal Péter Erdö,
Archbishop of Budapest who approved the FLAME OF LOVE

"A superb introduction to the Catholic Faith"
— Sister Deák Hedvig, Dominican Professor of Church History

"A masterful revelation of the meaning of life and the existence of God."
—Christine Watkins, author

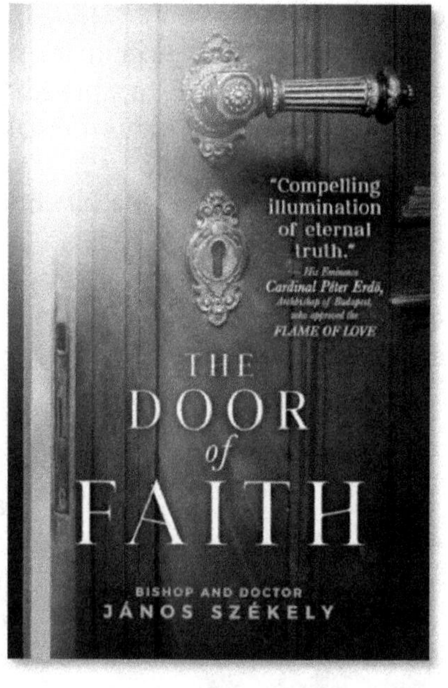

Bishop and Doctor János Székely has masterfully accomplished the near impossible. He has explored the essence of human life on planet earth through the lenses of science, history, philosophy, morality, and religion, and he has succeeded in revealing the meaning of life and the existence of God.

Are you seeking answers to the innate questions deep within yourself, which are common to all mankind, such as, Why am I here? What is life all about? Is this all there is? Then there is no time to delay. The questions in your heart need answers, if not for yourself, then for those to whom you could transmit your knowledge, if you but had a better understanding of your faith. The Door of Faith will not disappoint, no matter your personal starting point. It mixes in the beauty of poetry with the primacy of examined facts, speaking to the mind, while whispering to the heart. It is alive and breathing with the Spirit that animates the world, the same Spirit that animates you and me. You are invited to read and share this book—and open the door to faith.

THE WARNING

TESTIMONIES AND PROPHECIES OF THE ILLUMINATION OF CONSCIENCE

Revised and Expanded Second Edition

Endorsed by Archbishop-Emeritus Ramón C. Argüelles, Msgr. Ralph J. Chieffo, Fr. John Struzzo, and more...

The Warning has been an Amazon #1 best-seller, ever since its release. In the book are authentic accounts of saints and mystics of the Church who have spoken of a day when we will all see our souls in the light of truth, and fascinating stories of those who have already experienced it for themselves.

"With His divine love, He will open the doors of hearts and illuminate all consciences. Every person will see himself in the burning fire of divine truth. It will be like a judgment in miniature."

—Our Lady to Fr. Stefano Gobbi of the Marian Movement of Priests

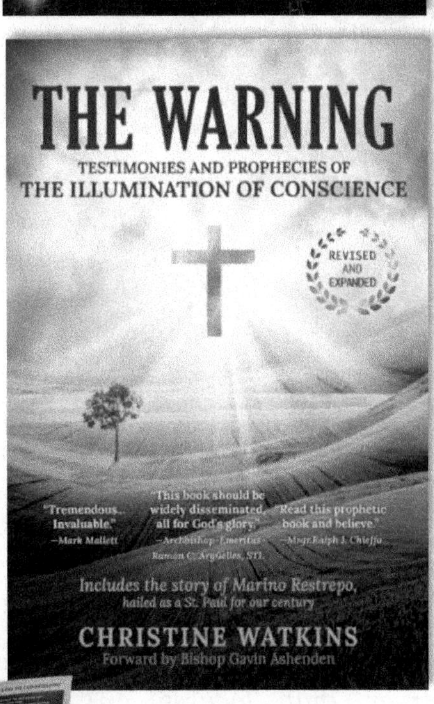

After the Warning brochures for mass distribution

FREE to download and available in bulk at www.QueenofPeaceMedia.com

MARY'S MANTLE CONSECRATION

A SPIRITUAL RETREAT FOR HEAVEN'S HELP

Endorsed by **Archbishop Salvatore Cordileone** and **Bishop Myron J. Cotta**

(See www.MarysMantleConsecration.com to see a video of amazing testimonies and to order)

CONSECRATION BOOK

"I am grateful to Christine Watkins for making this disarmingly simple practice, which first grew in the fertile soil of Mexican piety, available to the English-speaking world."

—Archbishop Salvatore Cordileone

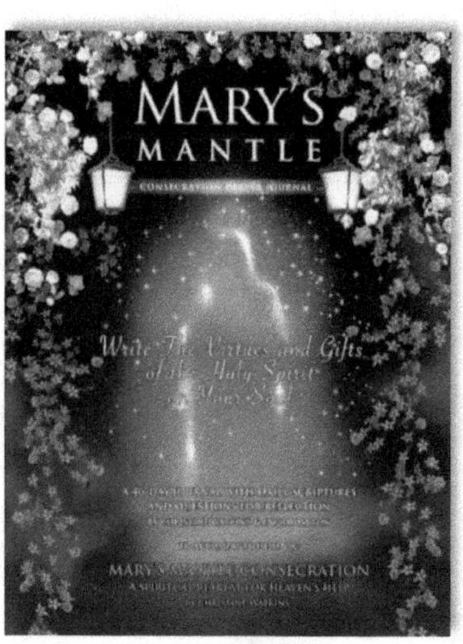

ACCOMPANYING PRAYER JOURNAL

"Now more than ever, we need a miracle. Christine Watkins leads us through a 46-day self-guided retreat that focuses on daily praying of the Rosary, a Little fasting, and meditating on various virtues and the seven gifts of the Holy Spirit, leading to a transformation in our lives and in the people on the journey with us!"

—Fr. Sean O. Sheridan, TOR

Former President, Franciscan University of Steubenville

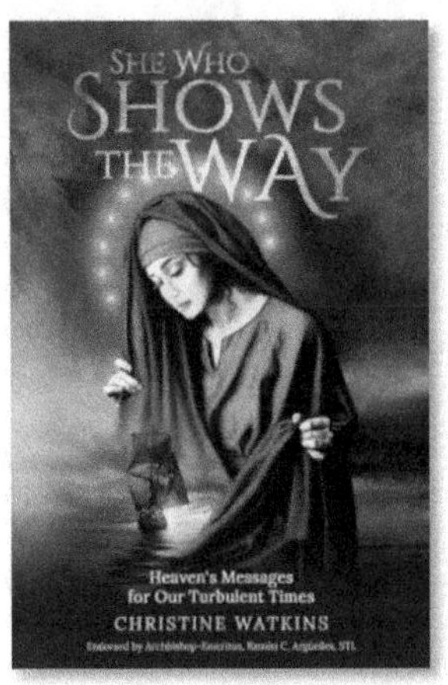

SHE WHO SHOWS THE WAY

HEAVEN'S MESSAGES
FOR OUR TURBULENT TIMES

Endorsed by Ramón C. Argüelles, STL, Archbishop-Emeritus

"A great turning point in the fate of your nation...will soon be upon you..."

— Mary's message of August 4, 1993

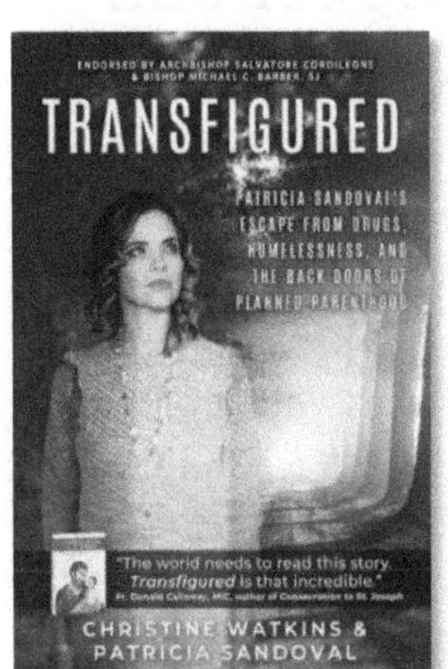

TRANSFIGURED

PATRICIA SANDOVAL'S ESCAPE FROM DRUGS, HOMELESSNESS, AND THE BACK DOORS OF PLANNED PARENTHOOD

Endorsed by
Archbishop Salvatore Cordileone & Bishop Michael C. Barber, SJ

"Are you ready to read one of the most powerful conversion stories ever written? I couldn't put this book down!"

—Fr. Donald Calloway, MIC

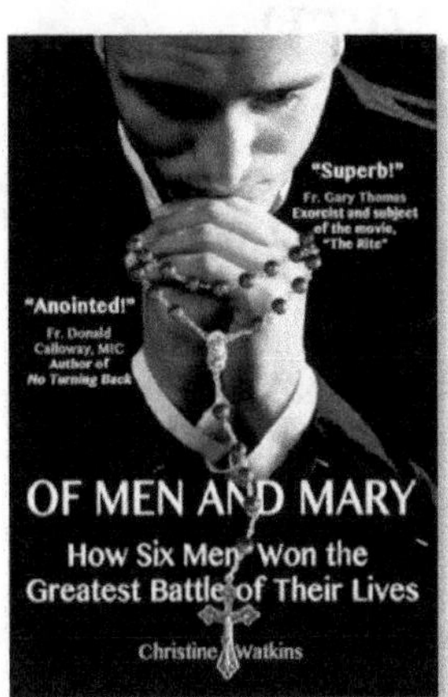

#1 AMAZON BEST-SELLER

OF MEN AND MARY

HOW SIX MEN WON THE
GREATEST BATTLE OF THEIR LIVES

"ANOINTED!"
—Fr. Donald Calloway, MIC

"Of Men and Mary is superb...miraculous, heroic, and truly inspiring."

—Fr. Gary Thomas
Exorcist and subject of the movie, "The Rite."

SERVANT OF GOD FRANK DUFF

FOUNDER OF THE LEGION OF MARY

This layman from Dublin, Ireland, multiplied a group of thirteen women into three million people—the largest Catholic lay apostolate in the world: The Legion of Mary. Discover the spiritual jewel of the story of Servant of God, Frank Duff.

FREE E-BOOK:

www.QueenofPeaceMedia.com/frank-duff

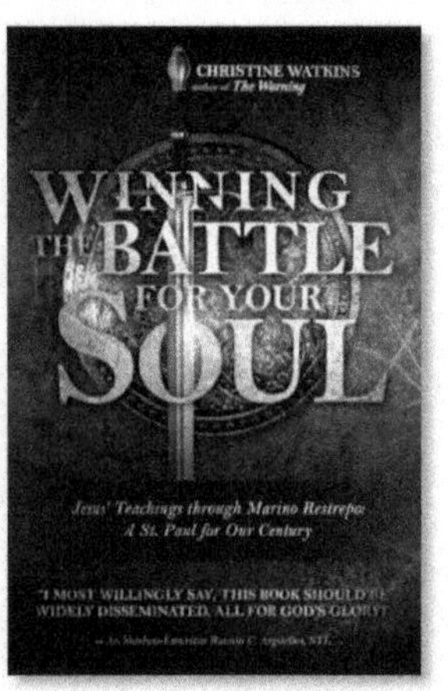

WINNING THE BATTLE FOR YOUR SOUL

JESUS' TEACHINGS THROUGH MARINO RESTREPO, A ST. PAUL FOR OUR CENTURY

This book contains some of the most extraordinary teachings that Jesus has given to the world through Marino Restrepo, teachings that will profoundly alter and inform the way you see your ancestry, your past, your purpose, and your future.

"This book is an authentic jewel of God."

— María Vallejo-Nájera
Internationally renowned author

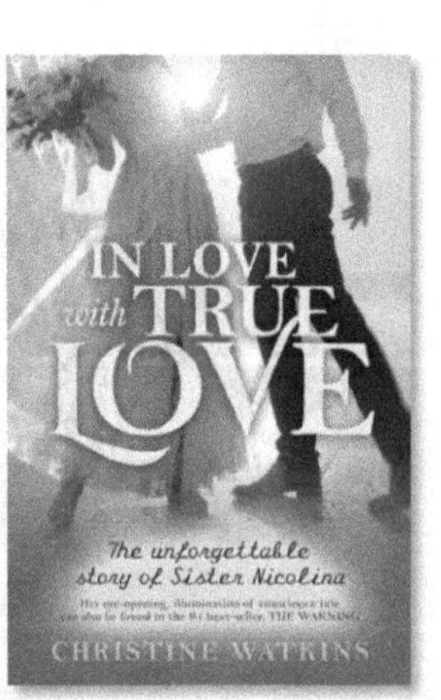

IN LOVE WITH TRUE LOVE

THE UNFORGETTABLE STORY OF SISTER NICOLINA

This book is a privileged view into not only a charming soul and an enthralling love story, but into the secrets of Love itself.

TO BE NOTIFIED OF NEW QUEEN OF PEACE MEDIA BOOKS, VIDEOS AND MORE...

SIGN UP FOR OUR OCCASIONAL NEWSLETTER:

www.QueenofPeaceMedia.com/newsletters

www.QueenofPeaceMedia.com/catholic-bookstore

EL AVISO

Testimonios y Profecías de la Iluminación de Conciencia

EL MANTO DE MARÍA

Una Consagración Mariana para Ayuda Celestial

EL MANTO DE MARÍA

Diario de Oración para la Consagración

TRANSFIGURADA

El Escape de las Drogas, de la Calle y de la Industria del Aborto, de Patricia Sandoval

HOMBRES JUNTO A MARÍA

Así Vencieron Seis Hombres la Más Ardua Batalla de Sus Vidas

PURPLE SCAPULAR

OF BLESSING AND PROTECTION FOR THE END TIMES

Jesus and Mary have given this scapular to the world for our times!

Go to **www.QueenofPeaceMedia.com/product/purple-scapular-of-blessing-and-protection** to read about all of the incredible promises given to those who wear it and use it in faith.

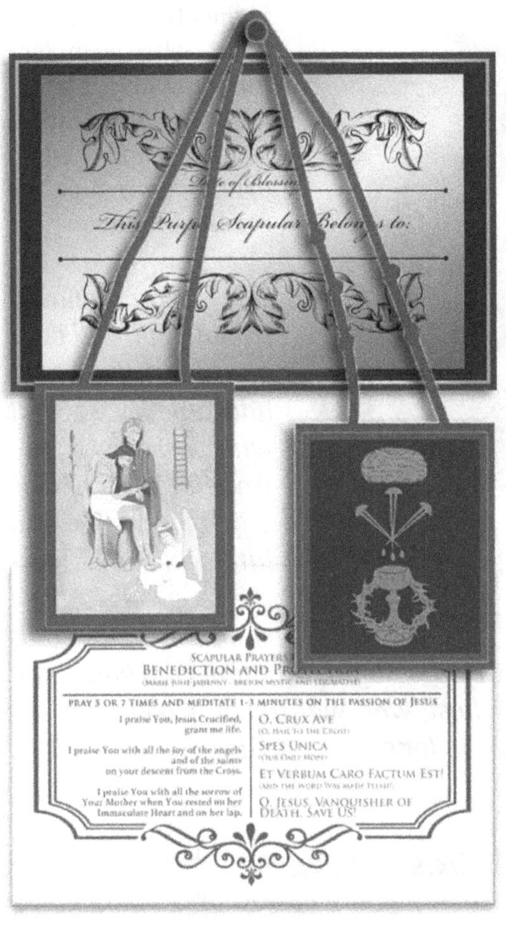

Our Lady's words to the mystic, stigmatist, and victim soul, Marie-Julie Jahenny: "My children, all souls, all people who possesses this scapular will see their family protected. Their home will also be protected, **foremost from fires**. . . for a long time my Son and I have had the desire to make known this scapular of benediction...

This first apparition of this scapular will be a new protection for the times of the chastisements, of the calamities, and the famines. All those who are clothed (with it) shall pass under the storms, the tempests, and the darkness. They will have light as if it were plain day. Such is the power of this unknown scapular. . ."

THE CROSS OF FORGIVENESS

FOR THE END TIMES

On July 20, 1882, Our Lord introduced THE CROSS OF FORGIVENESS to the world through the French mystic, Marie-Julie Jahenny. He indicated that He would like it made and worn by the faithful during the time of the chastisements. It is a cross signifying pardon, salvation, protection, and the calming of plagues

FOR MEN & WOMEN:

This bronze cross (1¾ inches tall and 1 inch wide—slightly bigger for the male) is a gift for our age and a future time when priests may not be readily available:

"My little beloved friends, you will bear on yourselves My adorable cross that will preserve you from all sorts of evil, big or small, and later I shall bless them... My little children, all souls that suffer, and those sifted out by the blight, all those who will kiss it will have My forgiveness—all those who will touch it will have My forgiveness." The expiation will be long, but one day Heaven will be theirs, Heaven will be opened."

Go to **www.QueenofPeaceMedia.com/shop** and click on "Cross of Forgiveness" to read about all of the graces and protection given to those who wear it in faith.

THE FLAME OF LOVE BOOK BUNDLE

THE SPIRITUAL DIARY OF ELIZABETH KINDELMANN

Go to www.QueenofPeaceMedia.com/shop to receive the Flame of Love book bundle at cost!

Extraordinary graces of literally blinding Satan, and reaching heaven quickly are attached to the spiritual practices and promises in this spiritual classic. On August 2, 1962, Our Lady said these remarkable words to mystic and victim soul, Elizabeth Kindelmann:

"Since the Word became Flesh, I have never given such a great movement as the Flame of Love that comes to you now. Until now, there has been nothing that so blinds Satan."

THE MOST POWERFUL SCAPULAR YOU CAN WEAR

FLAME OF LOVE SCAPULAR

COMES WITH THE UNITY PRAYER THAT **BLINDS SATAN** AND A FREE BLESSED MIRACULOUS MEDAL

Go to www.QueenofPeaceMedia.com/shop to order the Flame of Love Scapular for your protection.

Queen of Peace
MEDIA
.com

END NOTES

---

[1] Dirvin, Fr. Joseph, *Saint Catherine Labouré of the Miraculous Medal* (Tan Books and Publishers, Inc.; 1984), p. 9.
[2] Laurentin, René, *Catherine Labouré: Visionary of the Miraculous Medal* (Pauline Books and Media; 1983), p. 3.
[3] Laurentin, p. 2.
[4] Laurentin, pp. 1-4.
[5] Dirvin, p. 6.
[6] Dirvin, pp. 15-16.
[7] Documentary dossier (1806-1980) in the archives of the Vincentians and the Sisters of Charity: No. 520a, p.338.
[8] Dirvin, p.8.
[9] Laurentin, p. 15.
[10] Laurentin, p. 15.
[11] Laurentin, pp. 16-17, Dirvin, p. 36.
[12] Laurentin, p. 13.
[13] Laurentin, p. 21.
[14] Dirvin, pp. 60-62.
[15] Dirvin, pp. 59- 66.
[16] Laurentin, p. 35.
[17] Laurentin, p. 37-39.
[18] Laurentin, p. 40-41.
[19] In the decades that followed, pilgrims sat in this chair and touched it with piety and tears. Over time, the chair was left visible only for display, and eventually, after the turn of the 21st century, it was whisked out of sight for its protection—yet visitors say the grace of Our Lady's presence remains.
[20] Laurentin, p. 41-42.
[21] Dirvin, p. 84.
[22] Laurentin, p. 42.
[23] Laurentin, pp. 40-45.
[24] This was done by Pius IX in 1864 (Dirvin, p. 208).
[25] Laurentin, pp. 44.
[26] Laurentin, p. 46.
[27] "That Catherine transmitted the details of the serpent and the stars to her director, at least by word of mouth, is morally certain, for she approved the Medal, which bore both details from the first. Besides, in 1836, when the artist LeCerf was painting canvases of the apparitions, she described the serpent to her director as 'green with yellow spots'—a rather fearsome serpent, and one, certainly to offend the sensibilities of an artist!" (Dirvin, p. 97)
[28] Laurentin, p. 48.
[29] Dirvin, p. 219.
[30] Laurentin, p. 47.
[31] Dirvin, p. 93.

[32] The traditional position of Mary's arms and hands outstretched in the Miraculous Medal was decided by St. Catherine Labouré's confessor, Fr. Jean Marie Aladel. In St. Catherine's manuscripts, it is clear that Our Lady's desire in 1830 was to be represented with a globe in her hands with the attitude of offering it to God. And it was from the rings on her fingers that the graces to mankind poured forth onto the globe beneath her feet. Shortly before St. Catherine's death in 1876, Sr. Labouré's Mother Superior, Sr. Jean Dufès, worried that the Medal as it was might need to be changed because of this discrepancy, but Sr. Catherine said, "Oh, there is no need to touch the Miraculous Medal!" (Laurentin, p. 169)
[33] Laurentin, p. 48-49.
[34] Laurentin, p. 47.
[35] Dirvin, p. 105.
[36] The most distinctive feature of the Sisters of Charity, the cornette, was worn from the 15th to the 17th centuries by the common women of the area. This originally helped the sisters to blend in with others, though over the years, the cornette grew in size and distinction. St. Vincent de Paul approved of this headwear in order to shield the sisters from the cold and heat in their service to the poor. The cornette became a standardized part of the order's attire in 1685, and the Daughters of Charity set it aside for a simpler, more modern blue veil in 1964. See https://www.wikiwand.com/en/Daughters_of_Charity_of_Saint_Vincent_de_Paul and https://docarchivesblog.org/2013/06/05/818, accessed February 14, 2023.
[37] Laurentin, pp. 51-52.
[38] Dirvin, p. 101.
[39] Dirvin, pp. 72-73.
[40] The dogma of the Immaculate Conception of Mary was officially pronounced by the Catholic Church twenty-four years later in in 1854.
[41] Delineating this role, Pope Leo XIII would later write in his encyclical of September 8, 1894: "The recourse we have to Mary in prayer follows upon the office she continuously fills by the side of the throne of God as Mediatrix of Divine grace."
[42] Laurentin, p. 58.
[43] Alexandre dos Santos, Armando, *A Helping Hand from Heaven: The Story of the Miraculous Medal*, America Needs Fatima (Pennsylvania; 2017) p. 20-23.
[44] Alexandre dos Santos, p. 33.
[45] Alexandre dos Santos, pp. 31-32.
[46] Alexandre dos Santos, p. 33.
[47] Cooper O'Boyle, Donna-Marie, *The Miraculous Medal: Stories, Prayers, and Devotions*, Servant (Cincinnati; 2013), p. 40.
[48] See the next Chapter.
[49] Dirvin, p. 104.
[50] Dirvin, p. 190.
[51] Laurentin, p. 152.
[52] Dirvin, pp. 192-193.
[53] Alexandre dos Santos, p. 42.
[54] Dirvin, pp. 206-207.
[55] Laurentin, pp. 168-169.
[56] Laurentin, pp. 186-190.
[57] *The Miraculous Medal* (Kolbe Publications: 2016), p. 23.
[58] Dirvin, p. 209.
[59] Mares, Courtney, "The Miraculous Medal: St. Maximilian Kolbe's Weapon for Evangelization," CNA: Catholic News Agency, August 9, 2020, https://www.catholicnewsagency.com/news/42022/the-miraculous-medal-st-maximilian-kolbes-weapon-for-evangelization, accessed July 24, 2023
[60] Kolbe Publications, pp. 24.

[61] A Paris thoroughfare famous for its nightlife.
[62] De Bussières, Théodore, *The Conversion of Marie-Alphone Ratisbonne* (Catholic Publishing House: 1842), p 87.
[63] Kolbe Publications, pp. 24.
[64] De Bussières, *The Conversion of Marie-Alphone Ratisbonne,* pp. 88-91.
[65] Kolbe Publications, p. 91 / Aladel, p. 193.
[66] De Bussières, Théodore, *The Conversion of Marie-Alphone Ratisbonne* (Catholic Publishing House: 1842), p 22.
[67] De Bussières, p. 87.
[68] "Alphonse Ratisbonne," H.M. Magazine
[69] Dos Santos, p. 33.
[70] Kolbe Publications, pp. 24-25 / Aladel, p. 193.
[71] De Bussières, pp. 97-98.
[72] Kolbe Publications, p. 26.
[73] De Bussières, Théodore, *The Conversion of Marie-Alphonse Ratisbonne* (Catholic Publishing House: 1842), pp. 97-98.
[74] De Santos, p. 34.
[75] "Alphonse Ratisbonne," H.M. Magazine
[76] De Bussières, pp. 24-25.
[77] Aladel, p. 195.
[78] Aladel, p. 197-197.
[79] Kolbe Publications, pp. 26-27.
[80] Aladel, p. 197; De Bussières, pp. 26-27.
[81] Aladel, p. 197; De Bussières, p. 28.
[82] Aladel, pp. 199-201.
[83] "Alphonse Ratisbonne," H.M. Magazine
[84] Kolbe Publications, p. 28
[85] Kolbe Publications, p. 28
[86] Massatt, Joshua, "'After What Have Seen, I Obey': The Miraculous Conversion of Ratisbonne," Missio Magazine, https://missiomagazine.com/conversion-ratisbonne/mJanuary 20, 2015, accessed March 25, 2023
[87] Kolbe Publications, pp. 28-29.
[88] Aladel, p. 202 / De Bussières, p. 35.
[89] De Bussières, p. 116.
[90] Kolbe Publications, p. 30.
[91] Aladel, pp. 204-205.
[92] De Bussières, p. 120.
[93] De Bussières, pp. 40-41.
[94] Aladel, p. 206.
[95] De Bussières, p. 37.
[96] De Bussières, pp. 117-119.
[97] Kolbe Publications, p. 30.
[98] De Bussières, p. 38.
[99] De Bussières, p. 38-40.
[100] De Bussières, p. 43.
[101] De Bussières, p. 122.
[102] Aladel, pp. 214-215.
[103] De Bussières, pp. 69-70.
[104] Dirvin, Fr. Joseph, *Saint Catherine Labouré of the Miraculous Medal* (Tan Books and Publishers, Inc.; 1984), p. 170.
[105] Aladel, pp. 224-225.
[106] Dirvin, *Saint Catherine Labouré,* p. 170.

107 Aladel, pp. 224-226.
108 Aladel, p. 226.
109 De Bussières, p. 89.
110 Massatt, Joshua, "'After What Have Seen, I Obey': The Miraculous Conversion of Ratisbonne"
111 Dirvin, *Saint Catherine Labouré*, p. 170.
112 Sisters of Sion and the Fathers of Sion have since chosen to abandon the spirit of the Ratisbonne priest brothers, who desired the salvation of their Jewish kinspeople in Christ. Today, they do not seek the conversion of the Jewish people, but rather focus on Jewish-Christian learning, communication, and understanding.
113 Kolbe Publications, p. 33.
114 Notre Dame de Sion-Ein Kerem "History" Archived, July 12, 2012. Wayback Machine, https://web.archive.org/web/20120712182346/http:/sion-ein-karem.org/history/, accessed September 18, 2023.
115 "Convent of the Sisters of Zion," https://en.wikipedia.org/wiki/Convent_of_the_Sisters_of_Zion
116 Elio Passeto, "Ratisbonne: au Coeur de Jerusalem et au Coeur de l'Eglise," Cahiers Ratisbonne 1 (1996), p.7.
117 "Congregation of Our Lady of Sion," https://en.wikipedia.org/wiki/Congregation_of_Our_Lady_of_Sion
118 Notre Dame de Sion-Ein Kerem "History" Archived, July 12, 2012. Wayback Machine, https://web.archive.org/web/20120712182346/http:/sion-ein-karem.org/history/, accessed September 18, 2023.
119 Dos Santos, p. 39.
120 Massatt, Joshua, "'After What Have Seen, I Obey': The Miraculous Conversion of Ratisbonne"
121 St. Maximilian Kolbe's first doctorate was in philosophy from the Pontifical Gregorian University in 1915.
122 Freemasonry has been repeatedly denounced by the Catholic Church since Pope Clement XII's official condemnation in 1738. See https://www.vatican.va/roman_curia/congregations/cfaith/documents/rc_con_cfaith_doc_19831126_declaration-masonic_en.html, accessed November 16, 2022.
123 Giorgano Bruno (1548-1600) was tried for heresy by the Roman Inquisition on charges of occultism and denial of several core Catholic doctrines, including eternal damnation, the Trinity, the divinity of Christ, the virginity of Mary, and transubstantiation. He was burned at the stake in the plaza of Campo de' Fiori, where his statue was erected, made by sculptor, Ettore Ferrari. Ferrari would later become the Grand master of the Grande Oriente d'Italia, the Masonic jurisdiction of Italy. As a heretic, Bruno was "persona non grata" in Rome for centuries; his books had been banned and burned, and very few people had heard of him. Then in 1884, the Freemasons of Italy, furious at the Pope for denouncing Freemasonry in a papal bull, held him up as their mascot.
124 St. Maximilian Kolbe also gave an overarching review of Freemasonry in an account published in 1939:

> "Centers of this secret society have been established in every region [Masonic lodges]. Nevertheless, in various ways they more or less openly promote one and the same thing. In their plan, they use many and various kinds of societies which, under their leadership, promote neglect of divine things and the breakdown of morality. This is because the Freemasons follow this principle above all: Catholicism can be overcome not by logical argument but by corrupted morals.
>
> And so they overwhelm the souls of men with the kind of literature and arts that will most easily destroy a sense of chaste morals, and they foster sordid lifestyles

in all phases of human life. As a result, the once-strong characters of men are weakened, families are broken up by guilt-laden hearts, and an unhealthy sorrowfulness continues to grow. When such persons are unable to shake off the miserable yoke they carry, they avoid the Church and even rise up against her." —From: Madden, Fr. Charles OFM Conv., *Freemasonry - Mankind's Hidden Enemy* (Tan books: 1995).

[125] Kolbe, St. Maximilian Maria, *The Writings of St. Maximilian M. Kolbe: Volume II - Various Writings,* https://militiaoftheimmaculata.com/video-mi-history, accessed December 26, 2022.

[126] LeMay, William, *The Life of St. Maximilian Kolbe: Apostle of Mass Communications,* (2019) p. 15.

[127] Frossard, Andre *Forget Not Love: The Passion of Maximilian Kolbe,* trans. Cendrine Fontan (Ignatius Press; 1991), p. 23.

[128] Craig, Mary, "St. Maximilian Kolbe, Priest Hero of a Death Camp, https://www.ewtn.com/catholicism/library/st-maximilian-kolbe-priest-hero-of-a-death-camp-5602.

[129] "St. Maximilian Kolbe, Priest and Martyr (Memorial)", Living Space, Commentaries on the daily readings, https://livingspace.sacredspace.ie/f0814s/, accessed December 26, 2022.

[130] Craig, Mary, "St. Maximilian Kolbe, Priest Hero of a Death Camp, https://www.ewtn.com/catholicism/library/st-maximilian-kolbe-priest-hero-of-a-death-camp-5602

Raymond Kolbe's parents made an uncommon, but not unheard of, choice to give their lives to God separately, after having a family, although their love for each other remained. Patricia Treece writes, in her book, *A Man for Others*, p. 5: "One accepted progression in Hinduism is for an individual to be a householder for a period and then—at a new stage of development, having fulfilled obligations to society and family—to set that aside and become a full-time spiritual seeker. This progression is not common in Catholic families, but it is by no means unknown. To the deeply religious Kolbes, it seemed the proper course. In a document dated July 9, 1908, Julius Kolbe renounced his marital rights and gave his wife, who had longed to be a nun as a girl, permission to consecrate herself exclusively to the service of God. He pronounced his own readiness to take vows of chastity and went to a Franciscan monastery."

[131] Joseph Emeka, Did You Know {2}...*That Father Maximilian Kolbe Was An Exceptional Franciscan Friar?*" Modern Ghana, https://www.modernghana.com/news/667294/did-you-know-2.html

[132] "St. Maximilian Kolbe, Priest and Martyr (Memorial)", Living Space, Commentaries on the daily readings, https://livingspace.sacredspace.ie/f0814s/, accessed December 26, 2022

[133] "St. Maximilian Mary Kolbe", EWTN Global Catholic Network, https://www.ewtn.com/catholicism/saints/maximilian-mary-kolbe-699, December 26, 2022.

[134] Kolbe, St. Maximilian Maria, *The Writings of St. Maximilian M. Kolbe: Volume II - Various Writings,* (KW 1278), https://militiaoftheimmaculata.com/video-mi-history/

[135] Kolbe, St. Maximilian Maria, *The Writings of St. Maximilian Maria Kolbe,* (Nerbini International; 2022) Kindle Edition (KW 1278)

[136] Journal entry in Rome on Tuesday April 9, 1918. Kolbe, St. Maximilian Maria, *The Writings of St. Maximilian Maria Kolbe - Volume II - Various Writings,* (Nerbini International; 2022) Kindle Edition, p. 159.

[137] Kolbe, St. Maximilian Maria, *The Writings of St. Maximilian Maria Kolbe - Volume II - Various Writings,* (Nerbini International; 2022) Kindle Edition, pp. 182-183.
[138] Clark, John, "The Amazing Story of Maximilian Kolbe (And Why It Matters Now, More Than Ever)" Magis Center, https://www.magiscenter.com/blog/maximilian-kolbe-story, accessed December 26, 2022.
[139] Pontifical Council for the Laity, http://www.laici.va/content/laici/en/sezioni/associazioni/repertorio/milizia-dell_immacolata.html, accessed December 26, 2022. See https://militiaoftheimmaculata.com.
[140] Letter to Fr. Petru Iosif Pal, Halaucesti, Romania J.M.J.Fr. Krakow, January 8, 1920. Kolbe, St. Maximilian Maria, *The Writings of St. Maximilian Maria Kolbe - Volume I - Letters,* (Nerbini International; 2022) Kindle Edition, pp. 520-521, #35.
[141] Letter to Fr. Florian Koziura, Niepokalanów Maria! Mugenzai no Sono, May 30, 1931. Kolbe, St. Maximilian Maria, *The Writings of St. Maximilian Maria Kolbe - Volume I - Letters,* (Nerbini International; 2022) Kindle Edition, pp. 1065-1067, #341.
[142] Dirvin, Fr. Joseph, C.M., *Saint Catherine Labouré of the Miraculous Medal,* (Tan Books and Publishers; 1984) p. 208.
[143] "How the Militia of the Immaculate Started" Kolbe, St. Maximilian Maria, *The Writings of St. Maximilian M. Kolbe: Volume II - Various Writings,* (Nerbini International; 2022), entry 1011. https://militiaoftheimmaculata.com/video-mi-history/
[144] "Member of the Militia of the Immaculata?" Rycerz Niepokalanej, March 1925, pp. 49–50. Kolbe, St. Maximilian Maria, *The Writings of St. Maximilian Maria Kolbe - Volume II - Various Writings,* (Nerbini International; 2022) Kindle Edition, pp. 563-564.
[145] Kolbe, St. Maximilian Maria, *The Writings of St. Maximilian Maria Kolbe - Volume I - Letters,* (Nerbini International; 2022) Kindle Edition, pp. 1263-1264.
[146] Kolbe, St. Maximilian Maria, *The Writings of St. Maximilian Maria Kolbe - Volume II - Various Writings,* (Nerbini International; 2022) Kindle Edition, pp. 321-322.
[147] Mares, Courtney, "The Miraculous Medal: St Maximilian Kolbe's weapon for evangelization", August 9, 2020, Catholic News Agency, https://www.catholicnewsagency.com/news/42022/the-miraculous-medal-st-maximilian-kolbes-weapon-for-evangelization, accessed December 26, 2022.
[148] Letter to a reader, September 12, 1924.
[149] Letter to Fr. Florian Koziura, Niepokalanów Mugenzai no Sono, December 2, 19311. Kolbe, St. Maximilian Maria, *The Writings of St. Maximilian Maria Kolbe - Volume I - Letters,* (Nerbini International; 2022) Kindle Edition, pp. 1171-1172, #382.
[150] Dirvin, Fr. Joseph, C.M., *Saint Catherine Labouré of the Miraculous Medal* (Tan Books and Publishers, Inc.; 1984), p. 208.
[151] "When Will This Happen?" Article in St. Maximilian Kolbe's newsletter: "Rycerz Niepokalanej" ("Knight of the Immaculata"), May 1926, pp. 130–131. Kolbe, St. Maximilian Maria, *The Writings of St. Maximilian Maria Kolbe - Volume II - Various Writings,* (Nerbini International; 2022) Kindle Edition, pp. 639-641, #1122.
[152] Notes written in "Rome, April–June 1918" and from "March Thurs. 6th—Marseilles." Kolbe, St. Maximilian Maria, *The Writings of St. Maximilian Maria Kolbe - Volume II - Various Writings,* (Nerbini International; 2022) Kindle Edition, p. 255.
[153] Letter to Fr. Petru Iosif Pal, Halaucesti, Romania J.M.J.Fr. Krakow, January 8, 1920. Kolbe, St. Maximilian Maria, *The Writings of St. Maximilian Maria Kolbe - Volume I - Letters,* (Nerbini International; 2022) Kindle Edition, pp. 520-521, # 35
[154] Kolbe, St. Maximilian Maria, *The Writings of St. Maximilian Maria Kolbe - Volume II - Various Writings,* (Nerbini International; 2022) Kindle Edition, p. 258.

[155] Clark, John, "The Amazing Story of Maximilian Kolbe (And Why It Matters Now, More Than Ever)" Magis Center, https://www.magiscenter.com/blog/maximilian-kolbe-story, https://www.magiscenter.com/blog/maximilian-kolbe-story, accessed December 26, 2022.
[156] CNA staff, "Magazine Launched by St. Maximilian Kolbe Is Still Thriving 100 Years Later," January 10, 2022, National Catholic Register, https://www.ncregister.com/cna/magazine-launched-by-st-maximilian-kolbe-is-still-thriving-100-years-later, accessed September 19, 2023.
[157] "The Knight of the Immaculata" magazine is available here: www.militia-immaculatae.org/english/magazine-knight-of-the-immaculata and here: https://m-i.info/en/knight-of-the-immaculata-magazine/, accessed September 19, 2023.
[158] www.seibonokishi-sha.or.jp, accessed September 19, 2023
[159] To Fr. Florian Koziura, Niepokalanów Maria! Mugenzai no Sono, May 30, 1931. Kolbe, St. Maximilian Maria, *The Writings of St. Maximilian Maria Kolbe - Volume I - Letters,* (Nerbini International; 2022) Kindle Edition, pp. 1063-1064. #341.
[160] Kolbe, St. Maximilian Maria, *The Writings of St. Maximilian Maria Kolbe - Volume I - Letters,* (Nerbini International; 2022) Kindle Edition, pp. 1224-1225, #402.
[161] Letter to Fr. Florian Koziura, Niepokalanów Maria! Mugenzai no Sono, May 30, 1931. Kolbe, St. Maximilian Maria, *The Writings of St. Maximilian Maria Kolbe - Volume I - Letters,* (Nerbini International; 2022) Kindle Edition, pp. 1064-1065, #341.
[162] Ko Din, Jean, "Maximilian Kolbe accepted Our Lady's call to purity, martyrdom", The Catholic Register, August 17, 2016, https://www.catholicregister.org/item/22896-maximilian-kolbe-accepted-our-lady-s-call-to-purity-martyrdom, accessed November 18, 2022.
[163] "St. Maximilian M. Kolbe, priest of the order of the friars minor conventual and martyr", Vatican News, https://www.vaticannews.va/en/saints/08/14/st--maximilian-m--kolbe---priest-of-the-order--of-the-friars-min.html.

Treece, Patricia, *A Man for Others*: *Maximilian Kolbe Saint of Auschwitz in the Words of Those Who Knew Him* (Harper & Row Publishers; 1982).
[164] Treece, Patricia, *A Man for Others*: Maximilian Kolbe the "Saint of Auschwitz", (Marytown Press; 1993) and Foster, Claude R., *Mary's Knight: The Mission and Martyrdom of Saint Maksymilian Maria Kolbe*
[165] The account of Fr. Maximilian Kolbe's last years is gathered from:

Treece, Patricia, *A Man for Others*: *Maximilian Kolbe Saint of Auschwitz in the Words of Those Who Knew Him* (Harper & Row Publishers; 1982). "Name that Saint: Saint Maximilian Kolbe", The Miraculous Medal Shrine, https://miraculousmedal.org/inspire/name-that-saint-saint-maximilian-kolbe, accessed November 16, 2022.
[166]www.militia-immaculatae.org/english
[167] St. Gemma Galgani died on April 11, 1903
[168] "Without 'Clearer Evidence'" Rycerz Niepokalanej, January 1924, pp. 3–4 in Maria Maximilian Kolbe. The Writings of St. Maximilian Maria Kolbe - Volume II - Various Writings (pp. 469-471). Nerbini International. Kindle Edition. #1047
[169] Maximilian Maria Kolbe. *The Writings of St. Maximilian Maria Kolbe - Volume I – Letters,* pp. 505-507). Nerbini International. Kindle Edition. #29
[170] Maximilian Maria Kolbe. The Writings of St. Maximilian Maria Kolbe - Volume I - Letters (pp. 569-573). Nerbini International. Kindle Edition. (# 55) * Original text in Italian.
[171] www.militia-immaculatae.org/english
[172] Maria Maximilian Kolbe. The Writings of St. Maximilian Maria Kolbe - Volume II - Various Writings (pp. 511-513). Nerbini International. Kindle Edition. #1066

---

[173] Maximilian Maria Kolbe. The Writings of St. Maximilian Maria Kolbe - Volume I - Letters (pp. 652-654). Nerbini International. Kindle Edition. #97
[174] Maasburg, Leo, *Mother Teresa of Calcutta: A Personal Portrait* (Ignatius Press, San Francisco), pp. 62.
"St. Teresa of Calcutta and Her Medal of Charity", Miraculous Medal Shrine, https://miraculousmedal.org/inspire/st-teresa-of-calcutta-and-her-medal-of-charity/, accessed November 27, 2022
[175] McCurry, Fr. James, OFM Conv., "Mother Teresa and the Miraculous Medal," Militia of the Immaculata, https://militiaoftheimmaculata.com/mother-teresa-and-the-miraculous-medal/, accessed November 27, 2022.
[176] Maasburg, pp. 151.
McCurry, Fr. James, OFMConv., "Mother Teresa and the Miraculous Medal," Militia of the Immaculata, https://militiaoftheimmaculata.com/mother-teresa-and-the-miraculous-medal/, accessed November 27, 2022.
[177] Franciscan Friars, "Sep 05 - Homily: Bl. Mother Theresa and the Miraculous Medal", YouTube: https://www.youtube.com/watch?v=j9WnDGqdfPc&t=112s, accessed November 27, 2022.
[178] Maasburg, pp. 19-23.
[179] Mother Teresa and Kolodiejchuk, Brian, *Mother Teresa: Come Be My Light: The Private Writings of the Saint of Calcutta* (Image: 2009).
[180] Maasburg, p. 112.
[181] Mother Teresa and Kolodiejchuk, Brian, *Mother Teresa: Come Be My Light: The Private Writings of the Saint of Calcutta* (Image: 2009).
[182] Magliano, Tony, "When I Met Mother Teresa", National Catholic Reporter, August 30, 2016, https://www.ncronline.org/blogs/making-difference/when-i-met-mother-teresa, accessed November 27, 2022.
[183] Maasburg, pp. 66.
[184] Caulfield, Brian, "My Mother Teresa Story", Fathers for Good, http://www.fathersforgood.org/ffg/en/big_four/my-mother-teresa-story.html, accessed November 24, 2022.
[185] McCurry, OFMConv, Fr. James, "Mother Teresa and the Miraculous Medal," Militia of the Immaculata, https://militiaoftheimmaculata.com/mother-teresa-and-the-miraculous-medal, accessed November 18, 2022
[186] The Power of the Miraculous Medal by Saint Teresa of Calcutta," YouTube: 99 Catholics, https://www.youtube.com/watch?v=DUtTs44ZnxY, accessed November 27, 2022.
[187] Maasburg, pp. 60-61.
[188] Zengarini, Lisa, Nicaragua. Government Orders Missionaries of Charity to Shut Down," July 1, 2022, Vatican News, https://www.vaticannews.va/en/church/news/2022-07/nicaragua-government-orders-missionaries-of-charity-to-shut-down.html, accessed September 20, 2023.
[189] Maasburg, pp. 12-13.
[190] San Martín, Inés, "Ortega regime expels Missionaries of Charity from Nicaragua," Crux, June 30, 2022, https://cruxnow.com/church-in-the-americas/2022/06/ortega-regime-expels-missionaries-of-charity-from-nicaragua, accessed November 27, 2022.
[191] de Córdoba, Josém, "Nicaragua Convicts Seven of President Ortega's Opponents in Mass Trial," Wall Street Journal, February 23, 2022, https://www.wsj.com/articles/nicaragua-convicts-seven-of-president-ortegas-opponents-in-mass-trial-11645675796, accessed February 25, 2023.

[192] As of the year 2022, President Ortega and his wife, Vice President Rosario Murillo, have been ruling Nicaragua as autocrats, no different from the Somoza family that Ortega and the Sandinistas fought four decades earlier. In 2022 alone, the Ortega-Murillo government arrested several priests, expelled missionaries, closed the doors of a Catholic university, shut down seven Catholic radio stations and two Catholic television stations, and banned a Catholic procession and pilgrimage in the capital city of Managua at the Metropolitan Cathedral of the Immaculate Conception of Mary.
Lopez, Ismael, "Nicaragua police ban Catholic procession in Church crackdown", Reuters, August 12, 2022, https://www.reuters.com/world/americas/nicaragua-police-ban-catholic-procession-church-crackdown-2022-08-12/, accessed November 27, 2022.
[193] Allegri, Renzo, "Mother Teresa's secret agent," Messenger of St. Anthony, May 18, 2003
https://www.messengersaintanthony.com/content/mother-teresas-secret-agent, accessed December 4, 2022.
[194] Maasburg, pp. 111-120.
[195] Maasburg, pp. 125-126.
[196] Maasburg, pp. 163-164.
[197] "St. Teresa of Calcutta and Her Medal of Charity," The Miraculous Medal Shrine, https://miraculousmedal.org/inspire/st-teresa-of-calcutta-and-her-medal-of-charity, accessed December 4, 2022.
[198] Dossantos, Juliann, "St. Teresa and the Miraculous Medal," Catholic New York, August 31, 2016, https://www.cny.org/stories/st-teresa-and-the-miraculous-medal,14380, accessed December 3, 2022.
[199] Sr. Michaeline died in 1946, but Sr. Benna Henken lived until 2009. In retirement at the Convent of the Holy Spirit in Northfield, Illinois, she spoke about Claude Newman and her ministry at Warren County Jail many times, according to the nuns who knew her there.
[200] The legion of Mary: New York Regional Senatus, "What is the Legion of Mary?" https://www.legion-of-mary-ny.org/what-is-the-legion-of-mary, accessed August 19, 2023.
Micallef, Joe, "Legion of Mary is 90," Times Malta, September 3, 2011
https://timesofmalta.com/articles/view/Legion-of-Mary-is-90.383384, accessed August 19, 2023.
[201] See the website, Concilium Legionis Mariae: The Legion of Mary, www.legionofmary.ie, accessed August 19, 2023.
[202] Bradshaw, Fr. Robert, *Frank Duff: Founder of the Legion of Mary*, (Montfort Publications: 1984), p. 133.
[203] Bradshaw, p. 30
[204] Bradshaw, p. 33
[205] Bradshaw, pp. 27, 34
[206] Bradshaw, p. 211
[207] Bradshaw, p.57
[208] Bradshaw, p. 136
[209] Bradshaw, pp. 67-68
[210] Bradshaw, pp. 67-68
[211]Bradshaw, p. 212
[212] YouTube: https://www.youtube.com/watch?v=lxz9qEHhHD4, "Frank Duff," posted by Sm Parish, June 12, 2015, accessed July 28, 2023.
[213] Duff, Frank, "Monks of the West," Catholic Arena, September 7, 2021, www.catholicarena.com/latest/2021/9/6/g0bmhbs415xt2p7rkkp73b4raent1q, accessed May 12, 2023.

---

[214] Duff, Frank, *Miracles on Tap*, (Montfort Publications; 1961), p. 140.
[215] Bradshaw, pp. 71-72
[216] Bradshaw, p. 87
[217] All active and auxiliary members of the Legion of Mary say the Catena every day. "Catena" is Latin for chain. The Catena is the chain that binds members to the Legion and to one another, strengthening their spiritual connection and perseverance in the Legion. The main part of the Catena is the Magnificat, a Biblical prayer recited by Mary.
[218] The Vexillum Legionis is an adaptation of the standard of the Roman Legion. The dove, the signifying the Holy Spirit, surmounts the standard, replacing the eagle. Beneath the dove a cross-bar bears the inscription "Legio Mariae" (Legion of Mary). Below this, an image of the Miraculous Medal bearing a representation of the Immaculate Conception replaces a rose and a lily. The staff beneath the image is set in a globe which, for use on a table, stands on a square base. The design as a whole conveys the idea that the world is to be conquered by the Holy Spirit acting through Mary and her children.
[219] The Association of the Miraculous Medal, found on the Internet at www.amm.org. National Shrine of Our Lady of the Miraculous Medal, 1811 West Saint Joseph Street, Perryville, Missouri, 63775, 1-800-264-MARY (6279)
[220] Duff, Frank, *Legio Mariae: The Official Handbook of the Legion of Mary*, Appendix 6 (Concilium Legionis Mariae; 2014), pp. 350-351, https://www.legionofmary.ie/images/uploads/files/Official_Handbook_of_the_Legion_of_Mary_2014_-_as_updated_January_2022.pdf, accessed August 18, 2023. (With North American spelling added).
[221]Bradshaw, p. 140
[222] To the legionaries of France, July 13, 1960 (Bradshaw, p. 187)
[223] Bradshaw, pp. 197-199
[224] Moss, Msgr. C., *Frank Duff-a living Autobiography*, pp. 10-11.
[225] Duff, Frank, *The Woman of Genesis*, p. 517.
[226] Bradshaw, p. 236
[227] Bradshaw, pp. 236-237.
[228] YouTube: https://www.youtube.com/watch?v=lxz9qEHhHD4, "Frank Duff," posted by Sm Parish, June 12, 2015, accessed July 28, 2023
[229] Frank Duff is the one who threw the Medal into the wilderness area. Perhaps out of humility, he left out that fact.
[230] Duff, Frank, "Monks of the West," Catholic Arena, September 7, 2021, www.catholicarena.com/latest/2021/9/6/g0bmhbs415xt2p7rkkp73b4raent1q, accessed May 12, 2023.
[231] Marian Catechist Apostolate, https://mariancatechist.com, accessed September 21, 2023
[232] *Likoudis, Paul,* Fr. Hardon, a 'One Man Army of God', Catholic Culture, https://www.catholicculture.org/culture/library/view.cfm?recnum=3321, accessed September 21, 2023
[233] Hardon, S.J., Fr. John, *A Spiritual Autobiography*, 1,3.
[234] *A Spiritual Autobiography*, 37.
[235] *A Spiritual Autobiography*, 10.
[236] The Rite for Investing in the Miraculous Medal, Association of the Miraculous Medal (AMM), https://www.amm.org/MemberServices/investinginmm.aspx, accessed May 15, 2023.
[237] Milita Immaculatae Traditional Observance, *The Miraculous Medal*, (Kolbe Publications; 2016) pp. 45-46.
[238] Dawson, Steve, *Catholic Street Evangelization: Stories of Conversion and Witness*, (San Francisco: 2016), pp. 17-28.

[239] Rev. Ronan Murphy has served as Parochial Vicar in St. Mary's, Gloucester City and St. Peter's, Merchantville. He also served at All Saints, Perth City in Australia for two years. He was chaplain to a Carmelite Monastery in New York, a priest for the Camden diocese in New Jersey, and has given missions and conferences in many countries.
[240] To this day, her image has never faded or decayed, though out in the open air for 116 years around tens of thousands of candles and exposed to humid and salty air. It appears indestructible. In 1785, a worker accidentally spilled a 50% nitric acid solvent onto a large part of the image. It should have been instantly destroyed but reportedly self-restored over the ensuing thirty days, apart from small stains on the parts surrounding Our Lady's image—which mark the incident. Then in 1921, an anti-clerical radical hid a bomb with twenty-nine sticks of dynamite in a pot of roses just beneath the tilma. The blast destroyed almost everything nearby—a marble rail, twisted a metal crucifix, and even windows 150 meters away in the old basilica. But the image of Our Lady was untouched. ("4 Facts about Our Lady of Guadalupe," December 14, 2021, The Splendor of the Church, https://thesplendorofthechurch.com/2021/12/14/facts-about-our-lady-of-guadalupe-original-image/, accessed May 15, 2023.)
[241] Samaha, S.M., Brother John M., "Saint Juan Diego's Tilma: A Scientific Note About St. Juan Diego's Tilma," quote from Msgr. Virgilio Elizondo, University of Dayton, https://udayton.edu/imri/mary/s/saint-juan-diegos-tilma.php, accessed May 15, 2023.
[242] It is desirable, but not necessary, that a person be invested in the Medal by a priest or deacon using the approved rite, otherwise a simple blessing over the Medal is sufficient.
[243] The blue chair is no longer on public display in the Chapel of Rue du Bac.
[244] Today, the chair is no longer on public display.
[245] Spirit Halloween sold a "Bloody Mary Magic Mirror." When activated, a man would be heard saying "Bloody Mary." On the third time he said this, what appeared to be a possessed woman appeared inside the mirror with the words, "Bloody Mary" above her. A YouTube video called "Scary Mary Mirror—Bloody Mary Appears in Mirror!" (www.youtube.com/watch?v=G96VoAs1PJI) shows a mirror with a scary face that appears in it, sold by FrightProps (www.frightprops.com/scary-mary-mirror.html). This is a reenactment of the Bloody Mary "game."
[246] Zachary King notes: "Bloody Mary is not a game, it's a spell. To make a spell work, you need repetition, intention, and a demonic presence. If you're seeing the demonic face in the mirror, the mirror isn't some other place or world. The demon is not in the mirror. He's standing next to you. I was seeing his reflection in the mirror."
[247] "I asked my Baptist preacher," Zachary shared, 'Is magick real? Is that something you can really do?' He said, 'No. It's stuff that is only in the movies. It can't happen in real life.' So, I asked my parents. My parents said the same thing. But there are thirty-three verses in the Bible that tell you not to do magical things. Why would God tell you not to do something, if it was impossible for you to do? If you couldn't lie, for instance, 'Thou shalt not lie' wouldn't be in Scripture. If you couldn't kill somebody, 'Thou shalt not kill' wouldn't be in there. In the Old Testament, if you did magick, you were stoned to death. In the New Testament, you don't inherit the Kingdom of God. Why would God have laid out those mandates, if it was impossible to do? But, no one told me of that..."
[248] Zachary would later learn that "coven" meant a group, either or women or of both sexes, who follow Satan—knowingly or not.
[249] Details of Zachary's ritual of initiation: Dressed in a white robe signifying the loss of innocence, he was given a full-submersion "baptism" into a vat of human blood, pig's blood, and human urine. After emerging, he entered another room, took a shower, and came out donning a black robe, signifying his baptism into a world of darkness. Then he was told to sit in a chair and was handed a wheel, about a foot in diameter, with a crucifix in its center. While members read aloud parts of the document he had signed the

night before, Zachary lifted up his sliced thumb as proof that the signature was in his blood. Then he turned the crucifix upside down, symbolizing human sacrifice. The final act was to denounce Christ: he placed his hands on Jesus's arms and broke them downward.

[250] A councilman desired to get an ordinance passed. After trying every legal avenue without success, he contacted Ordo Templi Orientis for assistance. He told Zachary's coven what he wanted to have happen and paid a handsome fee for it. To bring such a request to life, death was required. First, the coven selected a nineteen-year-old "breeder": a woman who has as many abortions for the coven sacrifices as her body will allow. She was impregnated at a coven sex party, assisted by all the male members between twelve and fifteen years old. Eight months later, the coven gathered at night in a large farmhouse on a member's ranch.

At such events, a strong spell called a hex is cast, asking for the payer's wishes—in this case, the councilman's—and an abortion is performed. The acts done after the abortion are too disturbing to mention.[250] (Should you want to know more, Zachary King expresses the horrors of the satanic ritual in his book, *Abortion is a Satanic Sacrifice: The CD Transcript* (MCP Books, 2018), and in this interview on YouTube, "Rescued from Hell, The Testimony of Zachary King," Dr. Christine Bacon, https://www.youtube.com/watch?v=L5ydrLFZxWI&ab_channel=Dr.ChristineBacon.

The abortion brings power and efficacy to the hex, also called a "blood-tie curse." Satan, being pleased with the sacrifice and desiring to encourage more abortions, commands his legions to make the magick happen through the direct action of evil and through the weaknesses and sins of those under his influence.

The event involved the unthinkable from beginning to end. Chants and incantations rang through the air to please the devil. Naked women sat on the floor with their eyes rolled back, repeating, "Our bodies, ourselves," to keep away Christians and the cops. A statue of Baphomet stood amidst its adorers, and an abortion doctor stood next to Zachary. The particularly heinous techniques of a third trimester, otherwise called a partial-birth abortion were performed. When all was done, the councilman's wish was granted.

[251] Do not read the following, if you would prefer not to know what a third-trimester, or partial-birth abortion entails. The most common procedure used involves the baby removed from the woman's body, except for the head. Guided by ultrasound, the abortionist grabs the baby's leg with forceps and pulls out the baby's entire body, except for the head. The abortionist then takes a pair of sharp scissors and jams them into the base of the skull of the baby. He opens the scissors to widen the hole and then places a vacuum tube in the baby's head and sucks out his or her brains. The skull collapses, and the body is thrown into the garbage or sold for parts. On page 56 of the book, Partial-birth Abortion: The Truth: Hearing Before the Senate Committee on the Judiciary, outlines the procedure. (See https://play.google.com/books/reader?id=LZtWTRD96t8C&pg=GBS.RA1-PA56&hl=en, accessed July 19, 2023.

Perhaps the greater horror is that these abortions happen every day around the world. They are provided, desired, and protected under the sanitized and positive names of "freedom," "healthcare," and "choice."

Most of the actual details of what happens in a third-trimester or partial-birth abortion have been scrubbed from the Internet, leaving only clinical summaries for persons to read. No pictures of what actually happens are allowed to be seen. One resource that can still be found, which describes the actual procedure, is the senate hearing document, Partial-birth Abortion: The Truth: Hearing Before the Senate *Committee on the Judiciary...One Hundred Fifth Congress.* See p. 56 of the document. (https://books.google.com/books?id=LZtWTRD96t8C&printsec=frontcover&source=gbs_ge_summary_r&cad=0#v=onepage&q&f=false)

252 For a visual of the look of the tuxedo, top hat, corpse makeup and wand, Zachary King says that in the YouTube video "Like a Pill" by the pop singer Pink, a satanic high wizard appears and does the motions of casting a spell.
253 Zachary King was featured on Fr. Chris Alar's EWTN show, Living Divine Mercy. Fr. Alar shared that a high wizard is chosen by virtue of his ability to detect consecrated Hosts from unconsecrated ones. While Zachary says that any high wizard has this spiritual capability by virtue of being repulsed by holiness, he notes with charity that Fr. Chris Alar must have misunderstood him, since differentiating hosts is not the condition for being chosen to be a high wizard. (See https://www.thedivinemercy.org/videos/living-divine-mercy-tv-show-episode-8-halloween)
254 The Satanic Temple, for instance, operates under the motto, "Thyself is Thy Master." They have succeeded in being recognized as a federally recognized religion, even though they do not believe in Satan or the supernatural.
255 The Bohemian Club was ahead of its time in openly promoting homosexuality. President Richard Nixon, in one of his White House tapes, was recorded as calling the Grove "the most faggy g_d_m_d thing you could ever imagine."[255] (This he said in private, but in his book, *The Memoirs of Richard Nixon*, he admits his secret speech at the Bohemian Grove in 1967 marked the beginning of his path to the presidency.[255])
256 For Zachary King's fourth year of attendance at Bohemian Grove, he was surprised to see the Illuminati state quite plainly on their invitational postcard, which any postal worker could see: "Come to a mock sacrifice at the Bohemian Grove."
257 Another staple at the event was the Lolita Boys. Reader discretion advised: Zachary described the Lolita Boys as twelve and thirteen-year-olds hired to worked as messengers and to be raped on command or give oral sex—free for members, for hire by non-members. The boys were dressed in either a Native American costume with moccasins, a loincloth, an open vest over a bare chest, warpaint, and a headdress with one feather; or they wore black tuxedo pants, shiny shoes, bowties, a black open bare-chest vest, and short, clean haircuts. Both costumes left their butts completely bare. They delivered, from one man at the Cremation of Care event to another, handwritten memos under the lids of the covered food trays they carried; or they climbed in and out of men's trailers or tents.

When Zachary happened to be standing near one of the boys, he recognized his rear-end as female. Zachary asked the boy to meet him in his trailer, did some non-sexual investigating and learned that *he* was a nineteen-year-old *she*, recruited to work this job and others, and that all the Lolita Boys were girls who had received surgery or shots that stunted their puberty. In the last seven months, she had made 800,000 dollars and said she would continue as long as the money flowed. Zachary was actually relieved and happy that she was not a boy, for there was one evil that even he as a high wizard would not do, nor did he approve of, and that was the forced rape of children. He realized that this was how the Club got away with making the Lolita boys' service legal.
258 In 1998, Zachary King would learn what adrenochrome was. He did not know until then that other branches of The World Church of Satan, as well as members of other covens and the Illuminati, were participating in this tragedy. The torture of children was not his branch of evil-doing, which concentrated on intense study of spells and hexes that required ritual abortion.

Adrenochrome is esteemed by the elite and used by many Hollywood stars, as it keeps them looking younger and living longer. This terrible crime is currently being concealed from the public through media and online censorship and lies. In a mention of the movie, The Sound of Freedom, actor Jim Caviezel of the movie, The Passion of Christ, exposes this travesty inflicted on trafficked children. See him interviewed here in tears regarding the subject; www.rumble.com/v1014g3-jim-caviezel-reawaken-america-tour-tulsa.html.

Interview with Jim Caviezel, the Actor—told he can't say the word, "adrenochrome." The War Room with Stephen K. Bannon Episode 2742 PART 1, www.americasvoice.news/video/PyM46GTYYnJ7u7p/, accessed May 25, 2023.

Hamilton, Heather, '*Sound of Freedom* film highlights child trafficking crisis: 'God's children are not for sale'", May 12, 2023, www.washingtonexaminer.com/news/sound-of-freedom-film-highlights-child-trafficking-crisis, accessed May,13, 2023.

Ex-CIA agent, Robert David Steele, also sought to expose this growing crime. This video of Mr. Steele was taken down from YouTube, but reposted on Rumble: https://rumble.com/v2fchwy-chief-councel-robert-david-steele-at-the-international-tribunal-for-natural.html. The long version of this video was removed from YouTube: www.robertdavidsteele.com/steele-on-child-trafficking-adrenochrome-for-camelot-tv/. This site exposing the use of adrenochrome: www.ourgreatawakening.org/adrenochrome/, accessed May 13, 2023, was taken down shortly after that day.

259 Bitchute: ice.age.farmer, Concerning the intentional destruction of our food systems and "tools in order to shed light on the myriad risks to our food system and how they must inspire us to grow our own food." www.bitchute.com/iceagefarmer, accessed May 9, 2023.

260 Some of Zachary King's claims are shocking and controversial, so the author did investigative research to see if there were sources to back up his words. If you would like to see all of the resources found, go to www.queenofpeacemedia.com/resources.

YouTube: "Lockdowns, mandates, the rainbow agenda and the silence of church leaders w/Mar Mari Emmanuel," posted by Veraces Media, March 25, 2023, https://youtu.be/C1NhZGnIkOM, accessed April 29, 2023.

'Final Days' Worldwide Premiere, posted by SPN Exclusive Live, www.rumble.com/v2r0atk-final-days-worldwide-premiere.html, accessed June 3, 2023.

Plandemic Series of Documentaries: www.plandemicseries.com, PLANDEMIC, PLANDEMIC 2: INDOCTORNATION, and PLANDEMIC 3: THE GREAT AWAKENING, accessed May 25, 2023.

Rumble video: Following the Science?" posted by Something Is Not Right Series, http://rumble.com/vitcgn-following-the-science.html, accessed April 29, 2023.

261 Some of Zachary King's claims are shocking and controversial, so the author did investigative research to see if there were sources to back up his words. If you would like to see all of the resources found, go to www.queenofpeacemedia.com/resources.

Rumble video: "Pfizer Documents Prove 'Mass Murder,' Says Naomi Wolf," Posted by The New American, rumble.com/v27387c-pfizer-documents-prove-mass-murder-says-naomi-wolf.html, accessed April 8, 2023.

Rumble: Dr. Reiner Fuellmich - 1000 lawyers have evidence that pandemic is crime against humanity, www.rumble.com/vhsphv-dr.-reiner-fuellmich-1000-lawyers-have-evidence-that-pandemic-is-crime-agai.html, accessed April 29, 2023.

Ellefson, Meg, "Covid Shot Irreversible and Potentially Permanently Damaging to Children," WSAW 550 A.M, Dec. 16, 2021, www.wsau.com/2021/12/16/leading-researcherinventor-of-the-mrna-vaccine-dont-vaccinate-your-children/, accessed April 8, 2023.

Rumble: video: "W.H.O.-Dr. Tedros slips up and admits some countries using booster shots to kill children," posted by nonvaxer420, www.rumble.com/vr8g4m-w.h.o.-dr.-tedros-slips-up-and-admits-some-countries-using-booster-shots-to.html, accessed May 20, 2023.

Trozzi, Fr. Mark, "New American & Dr Trozzi | What is in the covid injections?" DrTrozzi.org, October 13, 2022, www.drtrozzi.org/2022/10/13/new-american-dr-trozzi-what-is-in-the-covid-injections/, accessed May 1, 2023.

Rumble video: "Infertility: A Diabolical Agenda (2022 Wakefield-Kennedy-CHD Documentary)," posted by Sunfellow On Covid-19, www.rumble.com/v184bw8-infertility-a-diabolical-agenda-2022-wakefield-kennedy-chd-documentary.html, accessed April 8, 2023.

262 Maria Zeee, "A Nation Under Threat by their Government – Australia's Quarantine Camps," January 13, 2022, Zee Media, www.zeeemedia.com/a-nation-under-threat-by-their-government-australias-quarantine-camps/

YouTube: "Inside Australia's Covid internment camp," posted by Unherd, www.youtube.com/watch?v=mGFdWcJU7-0&t=348s, accessed May 1, 2023.

Bitchute: MISTAKES WERE NOT MADE: AN ANTHEM FOR JUSTICE, posted by Let's Talk About It, March 27, 2023, www.bitchute.com/video/dimqwavayepp/, accessed May 1, 2023.

Rumble: "No Groceries, No Freedom. That's Your Business," https://rumble.com/vpw6g0-no-groceries-no-freedom.-thats-your-business..html, accessed April 29, 2023.

Rumble: "Dr. Julie Ponesse on the immorality of vaccine mandates," www.rumble.com/vm90du-dr.-julie-ponesse-on-the-immorality-of-vaccine-mandates.html, accessed April 29, 2023.

Rumble: "Former nurse describes COVID-19 protocols as 'medical murder'," posted by AlphaNewsMN, www.rumble.com/v2itqk5-former-nurse-describes-covid-19-protocols-as-medical-murder.html, accessed April 29, 2023.

263 "New York Times finally admits masks were totally useless at stopping the spread of COVID Feb 23, 2023," New York Times, www.lifesitenews.com/blogs/new-york-times-finally-admits-masks-were-totally-useless-at-stopping-the-spread-of-covid/, accessed April 29, 2023.

Mikovits, Judy and Heckenlively, Kent, *Truth About Masks: Exploring Theories Against Wearing Them* (Skyhorse:2021).

Rumble: "Wait a Minute - To Mask or Not to Mask," posted by Something is Not Right Series, www.rumble.com/v1vj9mu-wait-a-minute-to-mask-or-not-to-mask.html, accessed April 29, 2023.

264 Dodsworth, Laura, *A State of Fear: How the UK government weaponised fear during the Covid-19 pandemic*, (Pinter & Martin: 2021)

Bergman, Frank," Full List of WEF's Most Disturbing Plans for Humanity", Slay, March 27, 2023, www.slaynews.com/news/full-list-wef-most-disturbing-plans-humanity/?utm_source=mailpoet&utm_medium=email&utm_campaign=daily-newsletter, accessed April 8, 2023

"YouTube: You will OWN NOTHING, and you will be HAPPY" | Douglas Kruger," posted by Centre for Risk Analysis, accessed April 29, 2023, www.youtube.com/watch?v=60MzTlrOCXQ, accessed May 1, 2023.

265 Some of Zachary King's claims are shocking and controversial, so the author did investigative research to see if there were sources to back up his words. If you would like to see all of the resources found, go to www.queenofpeacemedia.com/resources.

Wood, Patrick, *The Evil Twins of Technocracy and Transhumanism*, (Coherent Publishing, LLC: 2022)

Rumble: "Dr. Carrie Madej - Nanobots, Transhumanism, Never-Ending Vaccines, HIV, Shedding, & Detox,", posted by Mariazeee, www.rumble.com/vvb4o4-dr.-carrie-madej-nanobots-transhumanism-never-ending-vaccines-hiv-shedding-.html, accessed May 9, 2023.

YouTube: "We Can Hack Humans | Dr. Yuval Noah Harari and Klaus Schwab," posted by Political Incorrectness, www.youtube.com/watch?v=3vrkTl9Sv6Y, accessed April 29, 2023

Allen, Joe, "Federal Research On Manipulating Brains And Rewriting DNA Should Worry Us All," September 29, 2022, The Federalist, www.thefederalist.com/2022/09/29/federal-research-on-manipulating-brains-and-rewriting-dna-should-worry-us-all/, accessed May 1, 2023

Rumble: How technology can be used to change DNA and people's minds. CRISPR, technique used to make the Covid Vaccines—YouTube: "Dr. Charles Morgan on Neurobiology and war," posted by Truth Search on December 6, 2020, www.youtube.com/watch?v=yxBjgUG9Pgg, accessed May 1, 2023.

The original uncut video can be found here: "Dr. Charles Morgan on Psycho-Neurobiology and War," posted June 14, 2018 by Modern War Institute, accessed May 1, 2023, www.youtube.com/watch?v=cTtIPBPSv0U, accessed May 1, 2023.

YouTube: Leaked Briefing in the Pentagon: weaponized mind control, "The Answer to Religious Extremism," posted by MinisterofYHWH, Jun 5, 2011, www.youtube.com/watch?v=WAyLiFSazgo, accessed May 1, 2023.

Also posted here on YouTube: "Pentagon Video Leaked Briefing on FUN-VAC _ 2005 Make Viral (mirror).mp4," posted by tntimberwright on Jun 12, 2011, www.youtube.com/watch?v=W_Zo1-5B30o, accessed May 2, 2023.

266 One might think that Zachary fabricated this story after the fact, based on the pandemic that later ensued, except for the evidence that Zachary told others of what happened at that 1991 Bilderberg meeting years before the pandemic hit.

Fr. Edward Murphy invited Zachary to speak in March 19, 2016, at the Basilica of the Immaculate Conception in Jacksonville, Florida. That day, he heard Zachary speak of the elites' plans for a future pandemic, vaccines that would harm and sterilize, global depopulation, a mandatory mark or chip, etc.

Karen Japzon, founder of John Leaps Evangelization, reports that in 2016 and 2017, Zachary shared with her that he had attended Bilderberg meetings whose agenda was to take control of the world. Ms. Japzon remembers him telling her that one way they planned to do this was through a manmade pandemic causing fear and alarm, and a vaccine that would be presented to the world as a solution, but kill in order to reduce the world's population. Their ultimate goal? Ultimate power. Karen also recalls him saying that Mr. G was a ring-leader whom Zachary challenged and who had presented everyone with a foul-smelling drink that he later learned was adrenochrome.

Other witnesses to Zachary's foreknowledge are Patrick and Joy Campbell, the founders of Cross of St. Benedict Society & Joyful Hope Missionaries, Zachary spoke on a large screen (via the Internet) at an in-person "Victory in Spiritual Warfare Conference" in August of 2022, where he mentioned many of the scenarios above. Patrick Campbell, the conference leader, interjected at this point, because it would have been easy for the audience to think, now that the pandemic had already happened, that Zachary had fabricated this portion of his story; Patrick assured the audience that he, himself, had heard Zachary say the same things before the pandemic hit, when Zachary spoke on December 2 and 3, 2017, at the Catholic Everything Expo at the Meadowlands Exposition Center in New Jersey.

267 Rumble: "Something Is Not Right" series: www.queenofpeacemedia.com/banned-videos, and www.rumble.com/c/SomethingisNotRight

"Are the Covid-19 Vaccines Safe? Something Is Not Right - Part 1," www.rumble.com/vcf0i5-are-the-covid-19-vaccines-safe-something-is-not-right-part-1.html, accessed April 29, 2023

"Censorship, Deception, and Lies: Something is Not Right - Part 2," www.rumble.com/vcoozf-censorship-deception-and-lies-something-is-not-right-part-2.html, accessed April 29, 2023

"Vaccine Venom & Covid-19 Cures: Something Is Not Right - Part 3," www.rumble.com/vdpo7t-vaccine-venom-and-covid-19-cures-something-is-not-right-part-3.html, accessed April 29, 2023

"God and the Great Reset: Something is Not Right - Part 4a," www.rumble.com/vg69vx-god-and-the-great-reset-something-is-not-right-part-4a.html, accessed April 29, 2023

"The Mark of the Beast: Something is Not Right: Part 4b (longer version)," www.rumble.com/vgpusl-the-mark-of-the-beast-something-is-not-right-part-4b-longer-version.html, accessed April 29, 2023.

268 Some of Zachary King's claims are shocking and controversial, so the author did investigative research to see if there were sources to back up his words. If you would like to see all of the resources found, go to www.queenofpeacemedia.com/resources.

Rumble: "CBDCS | 'What Is CBDC Going to Look Like? It Will Be Implanted UNDER YOUR SKIN. '- Professor Richard Werner + 'Gosh This Looks Like the MARK OF THE BEAST '- Glenn Beck" Posted by Thrivetime Show: The ReAwakening versus The Great Reset, www.rumble.com/v203rzi-cbdcs-what-is-cbdc-going-to-look-like.html, accessed April 8, 2023.

Bitchute: CANADA "DIGITAL CURRENCY" BETTER START WAKING UP CANADIANS-THIS IS NOT FOR YOUR HEALTH #CONTROLE, posted by nonvaxer420, www.rumble.com/vs9ebb-january-9-2022.html, accessed May 1, 2023.

Study Finds, "3D-printed microneedle patch could make painless 'on-demand' vaccines a reality," Study Finds, April 24, 2023, www.studyfinds.org/3d-printed-microneedle-vaccines/, accessed May 1, 2023.

"Covid-19: In Sweden, a vaccine passport on a microchip implant • FRANCE 24 English," FRANCE 24 English, December 21, 2021, www.youtube.com/watch?v=vnuJgvQB7kU&ab_channel=FRANCE24English, accessed May 1, 2023.

Rumble: "Naomi Wolf Sounds The Alarm On Vaccine Passports And A Social Credit System In America," posted by The Eric Metaxas Radio Show, www.rumble.com/vfearr-naomi-wolf-sounds-the-alarm-on-vaccine-passports-and-a-social-credit-system.html, accessed May 1, 2023.

Rumble: "Covid Vaccines Appear to Install a "MAC Address" Inside the Vaxxed," posted by laltuna, www.rumble.com/vu05fm-covid-vaccines-appear-to-install-a-mac-address-inside-the-vaxxed.html, accessed May 1, 2023.

269 Some of Zachary King's claims are shocking and controversial, so the author did investigative research to see if there were sources to back up his words. If you would like to see all of the resources found, go to www.queenofpeacemedia.com/resources.

Rumble: Fr. Altier gives an overview of what is happening in our world and what the Catholic response should be. "What's Going On in the World, the Country, and the Church? What is Our Response as Catholics?" Feb 7, 2023, Posted by Catholic Parents Online, www.rumble.com/v29em2k-whats-going-on-in-the-world-the-country-and-the-church-what-is-our-response.html, accessed April 8, 2023

Rumble: "Gates Microchips, 5G, 15-Minute Cities, & the W.H.O. Treaty... It ALL Makes Sense Now — Todd Callender," streamed March 7, 2023, posted by Man in America, www.rumble.com/v2c3qaw-gates-microchips-5g-15-minute-cities-and-the-w.h.o.-treaty-it-all-makes-sen.html, April 30, 2023.

Harris, Niamh, "RFK Jr. Reveals Globalist Plan To Use Health Crises To Impose New World Order Tyranny," April 12, 2023, www.thepeoplesvoice.tv/rfk-jr-reveals-globalist-plan-to-use-health-crises-to-impose-new-world-order-tyranny/, accessed April 30, 2023.

Jones, Alex, *The Great Reset: And the War for the World* (Skyhorse: 2022).

Klaus Schwab, the head of the World Economic Forum, in his own words:

Schwab, Klaus and Malleret, Thierry, *The Great Narrative: For a Better Future*, (Forum Publishing: 2022)

Schwab, Schwab and Malleret, Thierry, *Covid-19: The Great Reset*, (Forum Publishing: 2020)

Schwab, Klaus, *The Fourth Industrial Revolution* (Penguin Random House UK: 2016)

[270] Zachary King highly recommends that anyone who has been affected by abortion—male or female, parent or grandparent—attend a Rachel's Vineyard retreat. (See www.rachelsvineyard.org.)

[271] Zachary King can supply letters of recommendation and a letter of good standing upon request.

National Shrine of The Divine Mercy

2 Prospect Hill • Stockbridge, Massachusetts 01262
Tel. (413) 298-3931 • Fax (413) 298-3910 • E-mail shrine@marian.org

OFFICE OF THE SHRINE RECTOR

To whom it may concern,

I have known Zachary King for about eight years now. I first met him when he wanted to enter into the Catholic Church in 2008. Zachary entered the Catholic Church, receiving the sacraments of confession, Holy Communion, and confirmation, through an RCIA program within his local parish. Zachary has ever remained faithful to all the teachings of the Catholic Church and remains a devout Catholic to this day.

Zachary's conversion story has brought numerous conversions and reversions into the Catholic Church. He has enlightened many of the faithful with his first-hand knowledge of Satanism, the occult, and magic. Zachary has also been a source of great assistance to several exorcists in their ministry of deliverance. God is using Zachary's conversion for a great ministry of Mercy.

Therefore, I highly recommend Zachary King to be a speaker at any conference, retreat, parish, talk or any speaking engagement. His conversion story will inspire numerous faithful and sinners to trust in the infinite Mercy of God and draw them into the arms of holy Mother Church.

Sincerely Yours in Christ,

Rev. Anthony Gramlich, MIC

Rev. Anthony Gramlich, MIC
Rector
National Shrine of the Divine Mercy

Marian Priests and Brothers Serving Christ and the Church since 1673

[272] Guttmacher Institute: UNINTENDED PREGNANCY AND ABORTION WORLDWIDE Global and Regional Estimates of Unintended Pregnancy and Abortion, www.guttmacher.org/fact-sheet/induced-abortion-worldwide, accessed July 18, 2023.

[273] To help Zachary end abortion, go to www.allsaintsministry.org.
LIFE FUNDER: www.lifefunder.com/amp/zachary
PAYPAL: @allsaintscatholicmin
VENMO: 802-578-6554 OR @Zachary-King-50

[274] Catholic News Service, "Philippine weightlifter credits her Olympic success to her faith," July 27, 2021, Northwest Catholic, www.nwcatholic.org/news/catholic-news-service-c0d707ec-a664-47ba-8f59-2c063ded0999/philippine-weightlifter-credits-her-olympic-success-to-her-faith, accessed May 31, 2023.
Burkepile, Jacqueline, "Olympian Lifts Up Our Lady's Miraculous Medal After Winning Gold Medal for the Philippines," July 26, 2021, Church Pop, www.churchpop.com/olympian-lifts-up-our-ladys-miraculous-medal-after-winning-gold-medal-for-the-philippines/, accessed May 31, 2023.
[275] Celebrity Faith database, Jim Carrey, www.beliefnet.com/celebrity-faith-database/c/jim-carrey.aspx, accessed May 16, 2023.
[276]YouTube, "Jim Carrey | Law Of Attraction | Neuroplasticity | How To Manifest |," posted by Codice Gene, Nov 12, 2022, accessed May 16, 2023.
YouTube: "Jim Carrey Finds The Answer To His Prayers - The Graham Norton Show," posted by the Graham Norton Show, Dec 12, 2014, www.youtube.com/watch?v=yr-pwNDCM20, accessed May 16, 2023.
Jaromezuk, Andres, "Jim Carrey's Surprising Encounter with the Blessed Virgin Mary: His Amazing Story," Church Pop, www.churchpop.com/jim-carrys-suprising-encounter/, accessed May 16, 2023.
https://www.youtube.com/watch?v=5RsqdoUnTHo
[277] "Jim Carrey Finds The Answer To His Prayers - The Graham Norton Show," posted by The Graham Norton Show, Dec 12, 2014, www.youtube.com/watch?v=yr-pwNDCM20," accessed May 31, 2023.
[278] George Herman Ruth, "Guideposts Classics: Babe Ruth on the Foundation of Faith, Guideposts, https://guideposts.org/positive-living/guideposts-classics-babe-ruth-foundation-of-faith/, accessed November 29, 2023.
[279] Hanretty, John, "The Deathbed Confessional Letter of Babe Ruth," June 5, 2023, Relevant Radio, https://relevantradio.com/2023/06/the-deathbed-confessional-letter-of-babe-ruth/, accessed November 29, 2023.
[280] Fowler, Andrew, "The Return of the Prodigal Bambino," April 1, 2021, Knights of Columbus, https://www.kofc.org/en/news-room/articles/return-of-the-prodigal-bambino.html, accessed November 29, 2023.
[281] Adomites, Paul and Wisnia Saul, "Babe Ruth Battles Cancer, howstuffoworks, https://entertainment.howstuffworks.com/babe-ruth43.htm, accessed November 29, 2023.
[282] Te Deum laudamus, (Latin: "God, We Praise You") also called Te Deum, is a Latin hymn to God the Father and Christ the Son, traditionally sung on occasions of public rejoicing. According to legend, it was improvised antiphonally by St. Ambrose and St. Augustine at the latter's baptism.
[283] In the 1800s, blistering involved placing hot plasters onto the skin to raise blisters, which were then drained, which was believed to help with certain medical conditions. See "Medical Blistering in the Georgian Era" by Geri Walton, April 17, 2015, www.geriwalton.com/medical-blistering-in-georgian-era, accessed April 11, 2023.
[284] M. Aladel, C.M., *The Miraculous Medal: Its Origin, History, Circulation, Results,* translated from the French by P.S., (H.L. Kilner & Co.; Philadelphia: 1850), pp. 184-186.
[285] Weight loss and the so-called 'wasting away' associated with tuberculosis led to the popular 19th century name of consumption, as the disease was seen to be consuming the individual.
[286] M. Aladel, C.M., *The Miraculous Medal: Its Origin, History, Circulation, Results,* translated from the French by P.S., (H.L. Kilner & Co.; Philadelphia: 1850), pp. 111-118.
[287] Adapted from *Erlebnisse mit der Wunderbaren Medaille Heute, Booklet 18,* (Miriam-Verlag: 2000), pp. 15-16.

---

[288] Aladel, Fr. Jean Marie, *The Miraculous Medal: Its Origin, History, Circulation, Results,* (H.L.Kilner & Co.: 1880), pp. 139-141.
[289] Aladel, Fr. Jean Marie, *The Miraculous Medal: Its Origin, History, Circulation, Results,* (H.L.Kilner & Co.: 1880), pp. 151-153.
[290] Aladel, Fr. Jean Marie, *The Miraculous Medal: Its Origin, History, Circulation, Results,* (H.L.Kilner & Co.: 1880), pp. 163-164.
[291] M. Aladel, C.M., *The Miraculous Medal: Its Origin, History, Circulation, Results,* translated from the French by P.S., (H.L. Kilner & Co.; Philadelphia: 1850), pp. 254-255.
[292] Adapted from *Erlebnisse mit der Wunderbaren Medaille Heute, Booklet 10,* (2007), pp. 14-15.
[293] In the Catholic Church Extreme Unction and the Last Rites are now called the Sacrament of the Anointing of the Sick.
[294] Aladel, Fr. Jean Marie, *The Miraculous Medal: Its Origin, History, Circulation, Results,* (H.L.Kilner & Co.: 1880), pp. 162-163.
[295] Adapted from *Erlebnisse mit der Wunderbaren Medaille Heute, Booklet 2,* (2010), pp. 6-8.
[296] Adapted from *Erlebnisse mit der Wunderbaren Medaille Heute, Booklet 5,* (2010), pp. 5-12.
[297] M. Aladel, C.M., *The Miraculous Medal: Its Origin, History, Circulation, Results,* translated from the French by P.S., (H.L. Kilner & Co.; Philadelphia: 1850), pp. 234-235.
[298] Adapted from *Booklet 5,* (2007), pp. 21-22.
[299] Aladel, Fr. Jean Marie, *The Miraculous Medal: Its Origin, History, Circulation, Results,* (H.L.Kilner & Co.: 1880), pp. 189-191.
[300] Vatican News Services, "John Gabriel Perboyre (1802-1840)" https://Www.Vatican.Va/News_Services/Liturgy/Saints/Ns_Lit_Doc_19960602_Perboyre_En.Html, accessed November 24, 2023.
"Lives of the Vincentian Saints–St. John Gabriel Perboyre, C.M. (1802-1840)" September 11, 2022, Congregation of the Mission: The Vincentians Western Province, https://Www.Vincentian.Org/Lives-Of-The-Vincentian-Saints-St-John-Gabriel-Perboyre-C-M-1802-1840/, accessed November 24, 2023.
[301] Aladel, Fr. Jean Marie, *The Miraculous Medal: Its Origin, History, Circulation, Results,* (H.L.Kilner & Co.: 1880), pp. 187-189.
[302] Adapted from *Erlebnisse mit der Wunderbaren Medaille Heute, Booklet 7,* (2010), pp. 29-30.
[303] Adapted from *Booklet 8,* (1994), pp. 12-13.
[304] M. Aladel, C.M., *The Miraculous Medal: Its Origin, History, Circulation, Results,* translated from the French by P.S., (H.L. Kilner & Co.; Philadelphia: 1850), pp. 257-258.
[305] *Erlebnisse mit der Wunderbaren Medaille Heute,* Booklet 15, (Miriam-Verlag: 1996), pp. 17-21.
[306] Adapted from *Booklet 8,* (1994), p. 17.
[307] This armchair is no longer on display in the Rue du Bac Chapel in Paris, France.
[308] Adapted from *Booklet 16,* (1996), pp. 28-30, from an abridged version taken from "Feu et Lumiere," Lucia Fuego.
[309][309] Pipman, Kate, "Miraculous Medal Saved Woman from Fatal Bullet," Baltimore Catholic Review. See www.catholicgists.com/2022/04/miraculous-medal-saved-woman-from-fatal.html, accessed May 13, 2023
[310] Adapted from *Booklet 5,* 12th Ed. (2007), p. 13.
[311] Adapted from *Booklet 5,* 12th Ed. (2007), p. 12.
[312] Adapted from *Booklet 9,* (2010), pp. 7-8.
[313] Adapted from *Booklet 2,* (2010), p. 3.
[314] Adapted from *Booklet 1,* 17th Ed. (1999), pp. 6-7.

[315] Adapted from *Booklet 2*, (2010), p. 23.
[316] Reed, Betsy, "Paris falls to the Germans," The Guardian US, www.theguardian.com/world/1940/jun/15/secondworldwar.france#:~:text=The%20French%2C%20having%20decided%20not,justified%20the%20sacrifice%20of%20Paris accessed April 8, 2023.
[317] "Dietrich von Choltitz - Trümmerfeldbefehl" *choltitz.de*, http://www.choltitz.de/bilderseiten/redentexte/truemmerfeldbefehl.htm, accessed April 8, 2023.
[318] "Détruire Paris, les plans secrets d'Hitler": Paris fut bien à deux doigts de brûler". *Le Monde.fr* (in French). 2019-01-06. www.lemonde.fr/televisions-radio/article/2019/01/06/detruire-paris-les-plans-secrets-d-hitler-paris-fut-bien-a-deux-doigts-de-bruler_5405721_1655027.html, accessed April 8, 2023.
[319] History.com Editors, "Paris is liberated after four years of Nazi occupation," A&E Television Networks, History, April 7, 2023. Original Published Date: August 25, 2020, www.history.com/this-day-in-history/paris-liberated, accessed April 8, 2023
[320] Adapted from *Booklet 12*, (2002), pp. 26-27.
[321] Story from author interview with Thomas Greerty, April 9, 2023
[322] Joanne Harnette of Alameda California traveled to Medjugorje in 2006. She and Lyam struck up a conversation while standing outside of the home for rehabilitation of young men addicted to drugs, called Cenacolo, where pilgrims can take a tour and hear a couple of the myriads of personal testimonies of lives that pass through their program and are transformed.

Lyam, who spoke perfect English, seemed very keen on Joanne hearing his testimony and so she made a point of videotaping it and shared his story with the author on August 6, 2023.
[323] Adapted from *Booklet 6*, (1994), pp. 12-13.
[324] Adapted from *Booklet 7*, (2010), p. 28.
[325] "Calling All Czechs! The Prague Uprising of 1945," May 5, 2020, The National WWII Museum, www.nationalww2museum.org/war/articles/prague-uprising-1945#:~:text=In%20September%201938%2C%20the%20Munich,occupied%20the%20remainder%20of%20Czechoslovakia, accessed May 4, 2023.
[326] Adapted from *Booklet 6*, (1994), pp. 5-6.
[327] Adapted from *Booklet 1*, (1999), p. 11.
[328] Adapted from *Booklet 1*, 17th Ed. (1999), p. 7.
[329] Weight loss and the so-called 'wasting away' associated with tuberculosis led to the popular 19th century name of consumption, as the disease was seen to be consuming the individual.
[330] M. Aladel, C.M., *The Miraculous Medal: Its Origin, History, Circulation, Results*, translated from the French by P.S., (H.L. Kilner & Co.; Philadelphia: 1850), pp. 232-234.
[331] In a religious house, the person in charge of the sick quarters
[332] M. Aladel, C.M., *The Miraculous Medal: Its Origin, History, Circulation, Results*, translated from the French by P.S., (H.L. Kilner & Co.; Philadelphia: 1850), pp. 238-239.
[333] From the author's interview with Olga Avila, September 21, 2022
[334] From the author's interview with Lucy Marquez, September 21, 2022
[335] At that time, Protestants were baptized when they entered the Catholic Church.
[336] M. Aladel, C.M., *The Miraculous Medal: Its Origin, History, Circulation, Results*, translated from the French by P.S., (H.L. Kilner & Co.; Philadelphia: 1850), pp. 240-241.
[337] Frumentius Renner, *Benedictus – Bote des Friedens: Papstworte zu den Benediktus-Jubiläen 1880-1980*, (Editions Sankt Ottilien: 1982)
[338] Adapted from *Booklet 4*, 10th Ed. (1994), pp. 5-7.
[339] Mross, Renate, *77 Stories of the Miraculous Medal*, (Prayerworks Publishing: 2016), pp. 176-178.

340 The original text says, "renouncing his Jewish faith."
341 Adapted from *Booklet 4*, 10th Ed. (1994) pp. 15-17.
342 Aladel, Fr. Jean Marie, *The Miraculous Medal: Its Origin, History, Circulation, Results*, (H.L.Kilner & Co.: 1880), pp. 109-111.
343 Baeteman, Père J., Le mois de la Médaille Miraculeuse, (Broché: 1954)
344 Sr. Radier removed the Medal from the corpse before burial, and the patient in the next bed begged to have it, convinced that it had been the instrument of such a moving conversion. The sisters concluded their telling of this story with the words, "This consoling return to God was followed by several others not less striking or less sincere, and in that very institution, by the same means—the Medal. Quite lately two have taken place, but the details are so very much like the above that for this reason alone, we refrain from giving them. All this has been confirmed by Fr. Ancelin, priest of the Invalides."
Aladel, Fr. Jean Marie, *The Miraculous Medal: Its Origin, History, Circulation, Results*, (H.L.Kilner & Co.: 1880), pp. 118-123.
345 Aladel, Fr. Jean Marie, *The Miraculous Medal: Its Origin, History, Circulation, Results*, (H.L. Kilner & Co.: 1880), pp. 157-158.
346 Adapted from *Booklet 7*, (2010), pp. 17-18.
347 Adapted from *Booklet 9*, (2010), pp. 5-7.
348 For the Five First Saturday devotion, see https://americaneedsfatima.org/prayers/the-five-first-saturdays-devotion
349 Hintergründe Wir wollen nur deine Seele Hardrock: Daten, Fakten (Author), *Wir wollen nur deine Seele*. Hardrock: Daten Fakten Hintergründe Paperback – (Verlag der Evangelischen Gesellschaft; o. A. edition: 1984).
350 Adapted from *Booklet 15*, pp. 29-31.
351 Adapted from *Booklet 18*, (2000), pp. 9-11.
352 M. Aladel, C.M., *The Miraculous Medal: Its Origin, History, Circulation, Results*, translated from the French by P.S., (H.L. Kilner & Co.; Philadelphia: 1850), pp. 236-238.
353 From an interview with the author on September 9, 2023
354 Kolbe, St. Maximilian Maria, *The Writings of St. Maximilian Maria Kolbe* (Kindle)
355 The Basilica Shrine of Our Lady of the Miraculous Medal, accessed October 25, 2023, https://miraculousmedal.org/worship-and-prayer/miraculous-medal-novena-prayers/#:~:text=The%20Miraculous%20Medal%20Perpetual%20Novena&text=It%20was%20started%20at%20The,at%20The%20Miraculous%20Medal%20Shrine.
356 Adapted from *Booklet 5*, (2007), pp. 23-27.
357 The Miraculous Medal Perpetual Novena at the Miraculous Medal Shrine in Philadelphia, Pennsylvania, www.miraculousmedal.org/worship-and-prayer/miraculous-medal-novena-prayers/, accessed May 31, 2023.
358 Adapted from *Booklet 5*, 12th Ed. (2007), pp. 23-27.
359 Adapted from *Booklet 5*, 12th Ed. (2007), pp. 29-32.
360 Novena to Our Lady of the Miraculous Medal, America Needs Fatima, www.americaneedsfatima.org/prayers/novena-to-our-lady-of-the-miraculous-medal, accessed May 31, 2023.
361 From the Roman Ritual Booklet, www.static1.squarespace.com/static/53112767e4b06a95ceb2951a/t/55c0d707e4b0665eb3e7d9d2/1438701319210/Roman_Ritual_Booklet_2015.pdf, accessed June 2, 2023.
Catholic Online, www.catholic.org/prayers/prayer.php?p=360, accessed June 2, 2023.